The Broadcast News Process

7th Edition

Morton Publishing Company

925 W. Kenyon Ave., Unit 12
Englewood, CO 80110
http://www.morton-pub.com

Book Team

Publisher	Douglas Morton
Project Manager	Dona Mendoza
Typography	Ash Street Typecrafters, Inc.
Copy Editor	Carolyn Acheson
Cover & Design	Bob Schram, Bookends

Copyright © 1979, 1982, 1987, 1992, 1996, 2001, 2005 by Morton Publishing Company

ISBN: 0-89582-679-8

10 9 8 7 6 5 4 3 2 1

Printed in the United States of America

Preface

Even though this edition is new, the premise hasn't changed: Strong writing, powerful reporting, and compelling storytelling are necessary to become successful and — more important — worthwhile journalists.

Whether you work in radio, television, the Internet, or another form of packaging news and information within the context of video/audio technology, these abilities will be crucial. As infinite amounts of information become available to the public at lightning speed, and as the audience becomes more and more technologically savvy, journalists must help the public separate the important information from the trivial. The journalist who understands the significance of information and can present it to a fast-moving public in a comprehensive, yet interesting manner will rise to the top.

After more than 80 years of radio news and a half-century of television news, the broadcast journalism style continues to evolve, often as a product of technology. Chapter 1 provides an overview of the basic organizational structure to help you understand the world of electronic news media. Chapter 2 provides the stylistic characteristics of news writing, emphasizing the importance of word usage and grammar. In Chapter 3 you will learn how to write the script, whether for radio, television, or the Internet. Chapter 4 develops the foundation for writing the news story by examining the elements of news, different types of news leads, and story organization. In Chapter 5 we discuss the value judgments necessary for news selection.

Chapter 6 emphasizes features, a popular form of news reporting. Chapter 7 provides helpful hints on preparing for and conducting solid interviews, as well as producing good soundbites. In Chapter 8, we discuss the importance of editing and rewriting news scripts for the electronic media, including information on video news releases and turning broadcast news scripts into stories printed on a Web site. Chapter 9 offers the basics of producing a news story in the electronic media and presents an introduction to video editing.

Chapter 10 focuses on the principles necessary for effective live reporting, and Chapter 11 considers the entire process of producing a newscast. That chapter also includes information about writing and producing news in a converged media environment where journalism in print, broadcast and on the Internet intersects.

The final three chapters consider theoretical issues crucial to the electronic media industry. Chapter 12 covers the topics of ratings, research, and promotion in broadcast news. Chapter 13 addresses contemporary legal considerations in the electronic media environment. Finally, Chapter 14 presents a discussion of ethical issues within the industry.

The chapters in this book reflect:

- a new discussion on the trend in journalism toward news media convergence, giving examples of how it is being done in our newsrooms.

- additional interviews with industry leaders

- brief interviews with scholars and broadcast news journalists available for classroom use, on the Morton Publishing Web site.

- writing assignments that reflect current issues

- new critical thinking questions at the end of each chapter

- new Web sites for electronic journalists, Internet e-mail address finders, and multi-engine search tools.

- a completely updated and revised chapter (Chapter 13) on legal concerns within the electronic news world, including the latest case law and policies regarding obscenity/indecency, copyright, and political advertising; access to public information in a post-9/11 environment; and legal trends in cyber law, such as online music piracy, libel on the Internet, and attempts to regulate indecency on the Web.

- step-by-step instructions for digital video editing (Appendix C)

- the new Code of Ethics for the Radio Television News Directors Association (Appendix D)

- updated photographs representing an ever-changing industry

As you read, you may notice that numbers one through eleven in the text of this book are spelled out in words while 12–999 are in number form. We point out this stylistic element here because the style is different for broadcast than the typical style for printed material. For example, the number 11 is easily misread in a newscast as a Roman numeral II on a TelePrompTer. Also, single-digit numbers can get lost in the scrolling copy.

In script writing, we advocate writing large numbers as combinations of numerals and words because they're easier to read on a scrolling TelePrompTer, which usually displays only a half-dozen words on a line.

ACKNOWLEDGMENTS

We are grateful for the help of many people and organizations whose cooperation was instrumental to this and earlier editions. Though we cannot possibly list everyone who shared in this project over the years, we are especially grateful for the contributions of WIS-TV in Columbia, SC, KMOV-TV in St. Louis, WSB-TV in Atlanta, KCNC-TV, KUSA-TV, KMGH-TV, and KHOW-AM in Denver; WHBQ-TV, WPTY-TV, and WUMR-FM in Memphis; NBC news correspondent John Larson; Nick Walker of the Weather Channel; Randy Covington and August Grant of the Newsplex Center in Columbia, SC; and Denver radio and television news professionals Don Kinney, Roger Ogden, and Bob Palmer.

THE AUTHORS

James Redmond, Ph.D., is chair of the Department of Journalism at the University of Memphis. His undergraduate degree is in English Literature. He holds a master's degree in journalism from the University of Colorado, where he also completed his doctorate. Dr. Redmond worked for 20 years in television news as a reporter, producer, anchor, and managing editor. He has received numerous national and regional awards as a broadcast journalist. He also worked as a congressional press aide in Washington, DC, and is a retired Air Force Reserve Public Affairs Officer.

Fred Shook established the broadcast journalism program at Colorado State University. His professional experience encompasses television reporting, writing, production, television news photography, video editing, and production. He teaches and works nationally and internationally as a television writer, producer, and consultant, and as a director and editor for commercial television organizations, corporations and government agencies, including work in Germany, Canada, New Zealand, Fiji, Sweden, Finland, Denmark, Norway, Sri Lanka, and Africa.

Dan Lattimore, Ph.D. is Vice Provost for Extended Programs for the University of Memphis, as well as dean of University College and professor of Journalism. His undergraduate degree in journalism and economics is from Texas Christian University. He holds master's degrees from TCU in economics and Southwestern Baptist Seminary in education administration, and his doctorate in mass communication is from the University of Wisconsin. Among his professional work, for 10 years he was communication director for several international projects, where he produced numerous films and videos for distribution throughout the world. Dr. Lattimore represents the Public Relations Society of America for the Accrediting Council for Journalism and Mass Communication.

Laurie Lattimore–Volkmann, Ph.D., is a visiting professor at Georgia State University. Her master's and doctoral degrees are from the University of Alabama. She earned the bachelor's degree in journalism and history from Iowa State University. Dr. Lattimore–Volkmann served as reporter and editor for several weekly newspapers and magazines before pursuing graduate work in mass media law. Prior to joining the Georgia State faculty in 2004, she was a journalism professor at Mercer University, where she also advised the student newspaper and conducted a community broadcast news project with local high school students.

Contents

1 Working in the Electronic News Media 1

The Organizational Structure   2
- The Story Assignment Meeting   2
- Adapting to Changing News   2
- Newsgathering   2
- News Delivery   2
- New Technology   2
- News Departments   5
- Differences Between Small and Large Operations   6
- News Services   7

Jobs in Electronic Media   7
- News Directory (or News Manager)   7
- Executive Producer   8
- Web News Producer   8
- News Producer   8
- Newscaster   8
- Assignment Editor   9
- Reporter   9
- Photographer   10
- Writer   10
- ENG Coordinator   11
- Video Editor   11
- Related Jobs   11

Exercise 1A: Newsroom Organization and Jobs   13
Critical Thinking Questions   15
Self-Review Questions   17

2 Writing for Visual Media   21

Differences Between Print
    and Electronic Journalism   21
How the Ear Works   22
Treating Numbers   23
Writing to an Audience   23
Target Audience   24
Accuracy   25
- Attribution   25
- Quoting the Source   27
- Other Attribution Words   27

Names, Ages, and Titles   27
Using Verbs   31
- Verb Tense   31
- Active Versus Passive Voice   31

Phonetic Pronunciation   32
- Vowels   32
- Consonants   32

Time References   32
Journalistic Preferences in Word Usage   33
Grammar   34
Conclusion   35
Exercise 2A: Grammar   37
Exercise 2B: Style   39
Exercise 2C: Word Usage   41
Exercise 2D: Grammar   45
Exercise 2E: Pronunciation   47
Critical Thinking Questions   49
Self-Review Questions   51

3 Writing the Script   53

Formatting the Script   54
Writing to the Picture   56
- Preview the Video (VTR)   56
- Write Loose   57
- Avoid the Obvious   57
- Reference Words to Pictures   57

Script Formats   57
Story Samples   59
Story Sample 1: Typical Reader Format   60
Story Sample 2: On-Camera Reader
    with Graphic Format   60
Story Sample 3: On-Camera
    Reader Format (multiple changes)   60
Story Sample 4: VO-SOT-VO Format   60
Story Sample 5: VO-SOT-VO
    with Anchor Tag Format   64
Story Sample 6: Live-Shot Format   64
Endnotes   64
Exercise 3A: Writing a News Script   69
Critical Thinking Questions   81
Self-Review Questions   83

4 Writing the News Story   85

Elements of News   85
- Timeliness   85
- Proximity   85
- Significance   86
- Conflict   86
- Prominence   87
- Human Interest   87
- Visual Aspect   87

Writing Leads   88
   Summary Lead   88
   Other Types of Leads   89
Story Organization   90
   Inverted Pyramid   90
   Conversational Story Structure (Pyramid)   90
Freshening the Story   91
Updating Stories   91
Localizing   91
Communicating Effectively   91
Exercise 4A: Leads   95
Exercise 4B: Writing for the Electronic Media   97
Exercise 4C: Writing Exercises   99
Critical Thinking Questions   101
Self-Review Questions   103

5 News Selection   105
News Judgment   105
   Influences on Judgment   106
   Desires of the Audience   107
   Separateness   107
   Jargon   108
   Getting the News   108
Hard Versus Soft News   108
   Lead Stories   109
   Line-up   109
Content of Newscasts   110
   Spot News   110
Reference Sources   111
Exercise 5A: Selecting the News   113
Exercise 5B: Prioritizing the News   117
Assignment 5A: Analyzing a Local Newscast   123
Critical Thinking Questions   125
Self-Review Questions   127

6 Features   129
Features Versus Straight News Stories   129
A Conversation With Dateline NBC
   Correspondent John Larson   130
Telling the Feature Story   136
Feature Writing Hints   136
Endnotes   136
Assignment 6A: Writing Feature Stories   137
Assignment 6B: Kicker   139
Assignment 6C: Feature Writing   141
Critical Thinking Questions   147
Self-Review Questions   149

7 Interviews and Soundbites   151
Soundbites   151
   Sources and Purposes of Soundbites   151
   Using Soundbites   151
Interviews   152
   The Interviewer   153
   Basics of Good Interviews   153
   Tough Questioning   153
   Techniques to Put the Interviewee at Ease   153
Telephone Interviews   155
   Telephone Rundowns   155
   Telephone Courtesy   155
Lead-Ins and Tags   156
Editing the Soundbite   157
Writing Soundbites in the News Script   158
Assignment 7A: Writing Soundbits and Lead-ins   161
Assignment 7B: Interviewing   163
Assignment 7C: Writing Lead-ins and Tags   165
Critical Thinking Questions   167
Self-Review Questions   169

8 Editing and Rewriting the News   171
News Services   172
   Editing Wire Copy   172
   Rewriting Wire Copy   173
   Localizing Wire Copy   173
Using Public Relations Practitioners Effectively   173
Video News Releases   174
Internet Writing   175
Endnotes   176
Exercise 8A: Wire Copy Editing   177
Assignment 8A: News Releases   179
Critical Thinking Questions   181
Self-Review Questions   183

**9 TV Newscast Story
   Production and Editing   185**
Newscast Story Production   185
   Duties and Responsibilities   185
   News Story Format   186
   Some General Guidelines   187
   Editing the News Package   187
Video Editing   190
Steps in Editing a News Package   191
   Determine the Presence of the Control Track   191
   Use Color Bar and Countdown Leaders   192
   Record the Narration Script   192
   Edit the Various Elements into a Finished Story   193

Lay Down the Primary Audio and Video 193
Fill in Cover Video 193
Add Graphics to the Package 194
Pad Scenes to Avoid "Going to Black" 194
Deliver the Master Cassette 194
Editing Tips 194
Exercise 9A: Newscast Story Selection 197
Critical Thinking Questions 199
Self-Review Questions 201

10 Live Field Reporting
and Storytelling 203
Breakthroughs in Electronic Journalism 203
Electronic News Gathering (ENG) 204
Satellite Newsgathering 204
Audio and Video Streaming on the Internet 205
Bad and Good Live Reports 205
Live Interviews and Interviewers 206
Typical Problems 206
Challenges to the Live Interview 207
On-Camera Appearance 209
Personalizing the Story 209
Exercise 10A: Covering Stories 211
Exercise 10B: Wire Copy Editing 213
Assignment 10A: Field Reporting 215
Critical Thinking Questions 217
Self-Review Questions 219

11 Producing Across
Electronic Technologies 221
Format and Presentation 221
The Radio Newscast 222
Preparing the Radio Newscast 223
Putting It On the Air 223
Radio Delivery 225
The Television Newscast 225
The Script 225
The Visuals 225
Producing the Half-Hour TV Newscast 227
Internet News Production 237
Interview with Terry McElhatton 238
Media Convergence 241
What Is Media Convergence? 241
How Convergence is Being Practiced Now 242
Current State of Convergence 243
Endnotes 245
Assignment 11A: Formatting a TV Newscast 247
Assignment 11B: Writing
and Delivering a TV Newscast 255

Assignment 11C: Evaluating Local TV News 259
Assignment 11D: Determining the News Hole 271
Assignment 11E: Calculate News Time 273
Assignment 11F: Back-Timing Your Newscast 275
Critical Thinking Questions 277
Self-Review Questions 279

12 Research, Ratings, and Promotion 281
The News Product 281
Ratings 281
Household Meters/Diaries 282
People Meters 282
Online Databases 284
Tracking Surveys 284
Focus Group Research 284
Telephone Surveys 284
In-House Research 284
Rating and Share Defined 284
How Ratings Translate into Profit 285
Demographics 285
Consultants 285
Using News Anchors to Attract Audiences 287
Promotion 288
Community Involvement 288
Promoting Strengths, Not Weaknesses 288
Quality Reporting 288
Promotion Off-Screen 288
Sweeps 289
Image Advertising Versus Product Promotion 289
Topical Promotion 290
Proof-of-Performance Advertising 290
Other Promotional Devices 290
Content: The New Battlefield 290
Targeted Broadcasting 291
Psychographics 292
Market Research Problems and Traps 292
Problems with Focus Groups 292
Problems with Telephone Surveys 292
News as a Perishable Commodity 294
Reasons for Watching the News 295
What Lies Ahead? 295
Endnotes 295
Exercise 12A: Television News Research 297
Critical Thinking Questions 299
Self-Review Questions 301

13 Legal Considerations 303
Historical Background 303
The Radio Acts 303
The Telecommunications Act 304

The Scarcity Doctrine   304
Deregulation   304
The Entrance of Cable TV   304
The Fairness Doctrine   305
Political Candidates and Equal Opportunity   306
Political Candidates and Access   307
Staged News   308
Libel   309
New York Times v. Sullivan   309
Libel Defenses   310
Privacy   311
Contracting with a Source   313
Contempt of Court   313
Free Press Versus Fair Trial   313
Shield Laws   315
Access   315
Copyright   316
Federal Regulation   317
Obscenity and Indecency   317
Regulation of Violence   319
Regulation of Cable / Satellite / Telecom   319
The Internet   320
The 'Net and Libel   320
The 'Net and Obscenity   321
The 'Net and Copyright   322
Endnotes   323
Exercise 13A: How Would You Respond?   325
Critical Thinking Questions   329

14 Ethics and Professionalism   333
Ethical Foundations   333
The Marketplace of Ideas   334
News Versus Entertainment   334
Privacy   335
Fairness   336
Electronic Newsgathering (ENG)   337
Live Coverage   337
Media Competition   338
Camera Position   339
Benefit of Perspective   339
Instant News Policy   341
Specific News Coverage   341
Crime Coverage   341
Reporting on Government   342
Economic Pressure   342
Professional Codes   342
Media Organization Policies   342
Professional Behavior   343
Personal Ethics   343

Endnotes   344
Exercise 14A: Writing Stories
Involving Ethical Dilemmas   345
Exercise 14B: Ethical Decisions in Broadcast News   347
Critical Thinking Questions   351
Self-Review Questions   353

A Web Sites for Electronic Journalists   355

B The Linear Editing Process   359
Video Player and Recorder   359
Editing Control Unit   359
Player Controls   359
Recorder Controls   360
Editing Controls   360
Making an Insert Edit   362
Making an Assemble Edit   363

C Digital Editing   365
Getting Started   365
Set-Up   365
Digitizing   366
Capture   367
Entering Audio/Video and Editing   367
Importing   367
Rendering   367
Transitions, Filters, and Effects   367
Exporting Your Movie   368
End Note   368

D Code of Ethics and Professional
Conduct of the Radio Television
News Directors Association   369
Preamble   369
Public Trust   369
Truth   369
Fairness   369
Integrity   370
Independence   370
Accountability   370

E Society of Professional
Journalists Code of Ethics   373

Glossary   375

Index   381

## CHAPTER ONE

Working in the Electronic News Media

The cornerstone of journalism is the gathering of information. Journalists sift through the information to determine the most important pieces, decide how best to relay the facts and still maintain the human element, and help the audience interpret complicated issues.

Broadcast journalists have the particularly difficult task of reporting important information in a short time while also utilizing sound and visual components to strengthen the report. Crucial to this effort are good writing and solid reporting. Even the most brilliant writer cannot cover up a report with an information deficiency.

The principal task of the news department is to find and report information. Electronic journalists have the primary goal of creating a news report from that information. The actual news program is the culmination of efforts by journalists at the station and around the world.

This first chapter provides an overview of the basic organizational structure to help you understand the world of electronic news media. Who writes the news the anchor delivers on different newscasts? Who decides what stories to cover? Who decides what stories to use and in what order they will appear? Who decides whether a story will be a feature package or a 30-second wrap-up? When is a "live" report important? These are simple organizational questions that can help you understand where you fit into electronic media journalism and how the process works.

Broadcast news the audience watches on television is a culmination of work from journalists, editors, videographers, producers, and the production crew.

THE ORGANIZATIONAL STRUCTURE

To understand how contemporary electronic media organizations are set up, we will first discuss the organizational structure that was typically used in the second half of the 20th century. Start-up news organizations and evolving technologies in the 21st century have been adopting this general form of how to organize various media components, including many of the conventions in news values, basic job categories, and structure of other journalism efforts.

The manner of decision making and coordinating complicated information gathering seems to have stood the test of time. Although technology has changed the way in which news and information are delivered to consumers, the daily challenges of deciding what to cover, how to cover it, and then how to transform that information into coherent newscasts are basically the same.

The Story Assignment Meeting

Every news station begins its day with a story assignment meeting. Reporters, videographers, producers and assignment editors meet to determine what the news of the day is likely to be and how it should be covered. Though

Reporters look over the day's top news stories to be investigated in time for the first evening newscast.

the newscast often looks different at the end of the day than it began, a general blueprint results in a more cohesive final product and a less frazzled newsroom. It is easy to adapt to breaking news when everyone is clear about the original plan.

During the assignment meeting, reporters discuss stories they anticipate developing, or tips they received while out in the field. Assignment editors add stories they have been tracking through calls and reports to the newsroom. Once a list of potential stories is generated, the news director or assignment editor will determine which reporters and videographers will cover which stories and how they should be covered. If only video is needed for a short read, videographers are sent alone. Other times, a reporter is sent in the "live" truck to do a live report.

Adapting to Changing News

Most of these decisions are mapped out early and are changed as news develops. When a gas main explodes at 3 p.m. near one of the local schools, the newsroom recognizes the importance of the story and jumps on it. This kind of breaking news story suddenly becomes the lead for the 5 p.m. newscast with a live report while other stories may go from two-minute package stories to 30-second reports with video alone, or possibly could be postponed for a different newscast or the next day. The ability to adapt is an essential quality among broadcast journalists because no day is the same from one to the next and all typically veer from the original plan.

Newsgathering

The morning and afternoon are reserved for most of the newsgathering as reporters find out information on the phone or through the Internet, schedule and conduct interviews, and get video footage for the story. If they are lucky, they have saved an hour for writing the story and another hour for producers to edit the story in time for the first newscast. Typically, reporters do two or three versions of a story for the different newscasts.

News Delivery

Anchors come to the station several hours prior to a newscast to review the stories, write and edit copy, and prepare for the different newscasts. When a show comes together effectively, it is the work of a lot of people — reporters, videographers, producers, engineers, anchors, and others — to make sure it goes off smoothly.

New Technology

Figure 1.1 shows a typical television news broadcast organization. This model is still dominant in the electronic

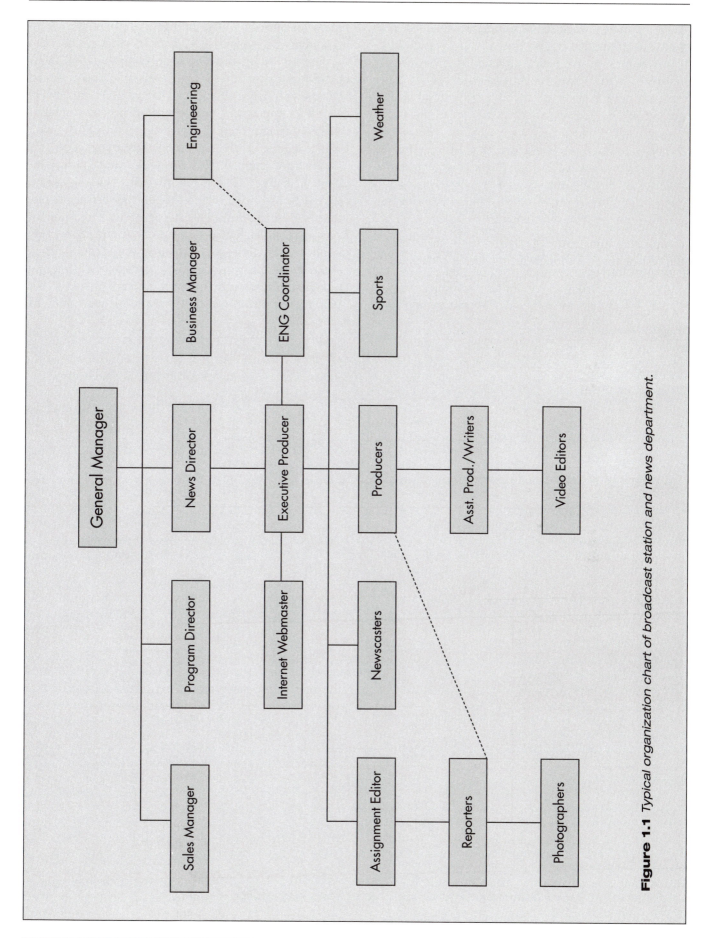

Figure 1.1 *Typical organization chart of broadcast station and news department.*

media industry, though many stations have added web-masters for their Web sites. Typically, the station web-master reports to the news director or the executive producer. In that case, the Internet side of the news organization is considered to be merely an additional promotional vehicle, or another way to republish the existing news product. It is a kind of side business for the news organization. Therefore, in existing industries trying to adopt new technology, the basic organizational design often remains the same. The new technology is simply added to the organizational mix without a fundamental organizational redesign.

Consider the difference between the organization chart in Figure 1.1 and the example in Figure 1.2, representing an Internet news organization that was created completely apart from a television station, a radio station, or an existing broadcast network. This organization chart

represents one of the first innovators of Internet streaming audio/video newscasting, techtvnews. Originated in the late 1990s by Ziff–Davis publishing, as ZDTV, it evolved quickly and eventually was sold and renamed techtvnews in late 2000. Thus, the figure should be considered as a model of how new information organizations approach their organizational structure with balance among the three types of news presentation.

We have retained the terms "TV" and "radio" for clarity in Figure 1.2. On the Internet, "TV" usually is referred to as "video," even though that can mean pictures only, including still photographs. This kind of news product is television-type programming of moving or still pictures with sound streamed to Internet users.

From the consumer's point of view, it's TV news through the computer monitor, though the user has much more control over which stories people watch by

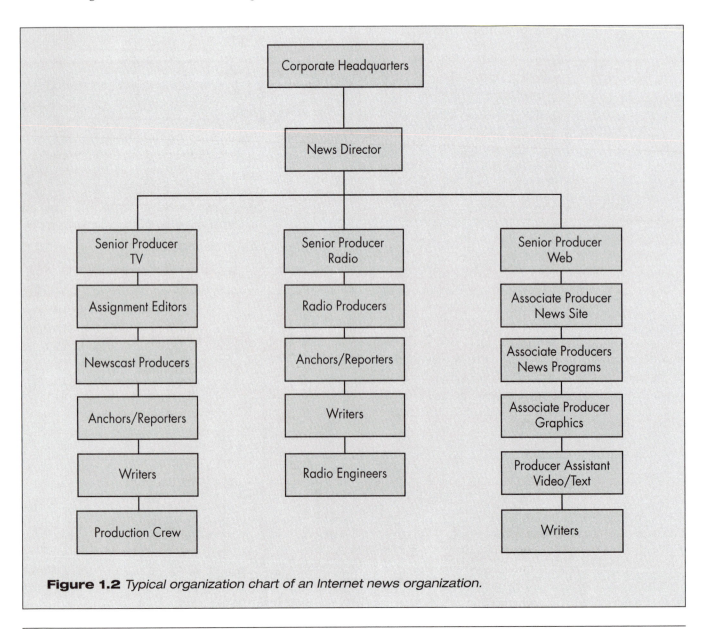

Figure 1.2 *Typical organization chart of an Internet news organization.*

clicking hot links to streamed video/audio stories. Even though the Internet often refers to "radio" as merely "audio," existing radio stations are moving rapidly into Internet audio streaming. That translates to many Internet consumers simply using their World Wide Web connections as glorified radios, albeit with access to radio stations from around the world.

The Internet news sites give news consumers something they don't have with a traditional news broadcast — the ability to look up the information they most care about. During a breaking story about a hurricane spreading across the Southeast, consumers watching a traditional news broadcast are forced to stay with the station's coverage as it unfolds. But consumers checking out the story on the Web can watch a traditional news story, or link to a map of the hurricane's path, or look at a timeline of recent hurricanes to hit the United States and the level of damage caused, or read a list of precautions if caught in a hurricane, or go back and forth between all of these. (For more on news organization and the Internet, see Chapter 11.)

When cable rose to prominence, critics pointed out that it was just the same old thing, only on more channels. That same argument applies to much Internet content. But with the Internet consumer totally in control by simply clicking a mouse, the days are quickly passing when a news organization can be cavalier in deciding what "most" people want and, in doing so, ignore the wide diversity of the audience.

Consumers don't care whether they get their news by radio, television, or computer. What matters is that the information makes sense and is relevant to the consumer. In a very real sense, new technology in the form of the Internet simply repackages former media forms that were separate (newspaper, radio, television) into a merged form that includes on-screen text with reinforcement of audio and video. In addition, new technology provides more flexibility for media consumers to click on "jumps" and go directly to items or audio/video elements that are the most interesting to them.

News Departments

Regardless of its technological form, news is a business, and as a business, media operations are organized into departments. Most have programming, operations, sales, and news departments. Some larger organizations also have their own promotional, research, and legal departments. Media organization size, target audience size, financial support, and the commitment of owners to the organization's perceived community all play major roles in how top management organizes and operates its various media properties, whether they be newspapers,

---

SPOTLIGHT

Doing the News

College students report that they get most of their news from television, so although you are beginners when it comes to reporting, writing and producing news in the electronic media, you are probably much more aware of the style than you realize. To prove this, form groups of three students each and pretend you are the anchors for the local evening news — one to handle local news, another for national news and the third student for sports.

Each anchor should write a short news story to deliver as if on camera. (Using a contemporary news story will help you in writing a hypothetical situation.) Be creative and have fun with the writing, trying to copy how the news sounds to you when you watch it. Deliver your "newscast" to the rest of the class and see how often you are able to pick up on the style, format, language and characterizations typical to a television news broadcast.

---

television stations, radio stations, or Internet news streaming companies.

In a small town on the East Coast near Washington, DC, where radio stations are plentiful and signal reception is good, you might find a radio station owned and operated by a husband and wife. They may be on the air only eight hours a day, from sunrise to sunset. The programming department staff meetings might take place over eggs and toast in the morning before they leave for the station. The operations department, which is responsible for equipment, production facilities, and engineering, might be run entirely on the advice of a consulting engineer.

This station might sell advertising time for as little as $20 a spot, with special discounts for long-term contracts, which bring down the price of an ad to as little as $15 or so. Local churches might get free airtime on alternating Sundays and Saturdays. The news department might employ a local high school or junior college student who is paid by the story plus minimum wage for working an on-air shift.

The news department never misses city council or school board meetings and tries to be on the scene when local emergencies arise. The station also might have a small Internet Service Provider (ISP) organization that runs Web pages for the station and community and

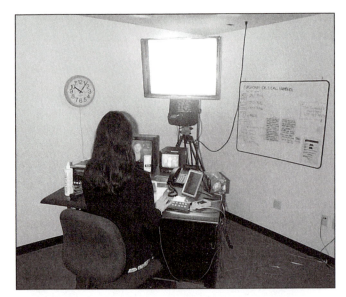

Contemporary video technology and computer software allow individuals to set up an automated video camera and use their computer screens for teleprompters to self-produce a news show on the Internet.

Wide Web sites for information and calendars of events that require coverage. Some media organizations have specially equipped mobile vans to help them transmit live from a news event. In larger markets the organization equipment inventory might include a helicopter or a small, fixed-wing airplane from which a reporter can broadcast live "over the scene" of a traffic jam or accident.

Whether the station is a mom-and-pop operation or is owned by a giant corporation, each department exists to improve the business profile. Department staffs work for their department and also for the media organization's overall profit picture.

Local-market radio, television, and Internet news operations in the United States vary in the extreme from one-person news departments to sophisticated operations with annual budgets of $30 million or more. Likewise, Internet news media organizations can have anywhere from a handful of people to worldwide staffs of thousands. As print and broadcast news media alike become more versed in supplying content online, all journalists will have to become multi-skilled and often must be proficient at multi-tasking, doing both reporting and producing.

provides dial-up access for local residents. The owners know that success, to a great extent, depends on their dedication to serving the community.

Differences Between Small and Large Operations

Larger media organizations in big cities and those that are focused nationally or internationally have similar organizational responsibilities, but they are operated quite differently. The programming department makes decisions about program content, placement, and length, to determine the general perception and market niche of the organization. Its staff meetings might include doughnuts and coffee, but the meetings are conducted in a more formal environment.

As organizations get bigger, regardless of the type of business, they tend to become more formal and structured. The news department might be staffed with many full-time reporters, news anchors, and a news management team with a news director, executive producer, and a number of news producers. The station might have a news service for national and regional news with regular audio/video feeds.

The organization probably will have a range of technologies for monitoring locations, such as the police, where information about news events tend to originate. That technology can range from radio frequency scanners and tipsters to daily checking of key World

An assignment editor for an electronic media organization must check the wire reports regularly and have police and fire scanners nearby for constant monitoring.

News Services

Almost all electronic news media organizations of any size subscribe to at least one news service, and sometimes numerous services for their national and international story-gathering activities. They then concentrate their local employees on local issues or areas of interest, or they use producers and anchors to create newscasts from syndicated material they have collected elsewhere. Some contemporary news organizations do little initial fact-gathering.

These organizations are, in effect, retailers of material generated by other news organizations. You see this in newspapers when the bylines read "Associated Press." And you see it on local TV newscasts when they include reports from their affiliated network. On the Internet, actual news sources can range from wire services, to local TV and radio stations, to news photography services, and even individual Internet users who send in video/audio files they've recorded themselves.

If the media organization uses only one news service, it often is a tip or stringer service. A tip hotline may invite listeners to call in story tips for special recognition or a small payment. Stringers report stories and may act as photographers, even though they're not full-time employees of the news organization. Stringers are paid for each story they're asked to generate, or, in the case of stories produced on speculation, receive payment only if the story is used.

JOBS IN ELECTRONIC MEDIA

Although the range of jobs varies greatly from one news organization to another, the most frequently encountered positions in electronic media journalism are somewhat similar in medium- to large-market operations. Typical positions in the electronic media include the news director (or news manager), the executive producer, the Web news producer, news producer, newscaster, assignment editor, reporter, photographer, writer, ENG coordinator, and video editor.

News Director (or News Manager)

Although all media organization departments tend to affect each other to varying degrees, in this book we are concerned primarily with the news department, usually headed by a news director. His or her responsibilities vary, depending on whether the operation is unionized, how large it is, size of the market being served, and how much commitment the organization has to interface with its community or perceived market. Basically, the news director is responsible for maintaining existing market penetration, for generating new audiences to expand the

media organization's market share, and for the overall journalistic quality of the news program.

In most local electronic media operations, the position of news director is the highest. The news director is a department head and should not be confused with the technician, who actually directs newscasts on-air. The news director usually has extensive news experience, administrative ability, and supervisory experience. He or she — in most cases responsible to the news organization's senior manager (typically a general manager or a station manager) — is in charge of the entire news operation.

In the smaller markets the news director may be called on occasionally as an "on-air" personality. Most traditional news operations, however, discourage on-air performances because the responsibilities call more for personnel management and policy decisions than news reporting and presentation otherwise might allow. This position demands public relations ability, as the news director frequently represents the station at-large, attending public functions, answering complaints about news coverage, and simply being a "personality" within the community. The news director also must have the basic management skills of dealing with personnel and budget issues within the news department of the media organization.

Besides overseeing the news department, the news director must work with other organization departments to assure that the proper equipment is available to gather and produce news stories, whether those stories

Ultimately responsible for the final product of a news station, the news director often addresses the staff regarding coverage, public opinion, and overall quality of the broadcasts.

are radio, television, Internet, or a combination. The news director's job is varied and, in the course of a week, probably will involve every other department at the station.

Executive Producer

The executive producer is usually the number-two person in an electronic media news organization. The "EP," as this person often is called, normally is in charge of the on-air "look" of the newscasts, with supervisory responsibilities over individual newscast producers, of which one usually is assigned to the station's various newscasts. The EP typically has substantial experience as a newscast producer and specializes in visualizing the day's events. This person must be highly skilled in writing, graphic technology, video presentation, and television story conceptualization, as well as blocking and executing complicated newscast programming.

The executive news producer — and, for that matter, individual newscast producers — must know which stories will have the greatest impact on the community and what information is available on the wire. A quick check of the program log will tell the producer at what times and how long the newscasts will be, and which commercials will be aired during the newscast. Knowing the advertisers and the order of the spots is important, as it might affect the order of the stories on either side of the commercials. For example, placing a hail-damage story just before or after an insurance commercial, or on the same Web page as a banner advertisement for an insurance company's hail policy, would be in poor professional taste.

For a newscast to look smooth and professional, producers are in charge of placing and precisely timing all program elements.

Web News Producer

The Web news producer is viewed increasingly as an experienced journalist with additional skills in Internet Web page design. Typically, this individual works directly under the executive producer and is responsible for all Internet Web site content.

This is a growing career field in electronic media organizations, requiring the Web news producer to understand video and audio story creation and presentation, as well as streaming technology and audience connectivity to the World Wide Web. To be effective in this growing area of responsibility, the individual has to embrace both new technology and new thinking about news coverage, presentation, and the individual audience member's control over what is used. In older forms of so-called mass media, news professionals basically packaged newscasts with limited space or time. Thus, they served as gatekeepers, sifting news and information beforehand and making only a limited amount of information available to audiences.

The Internet is turning this concept upside down. Internet news consumers now go wherever they wish and set an individual consumption preference that varies from one person to the next. It is arguable that there is no longer a "newscast" but, rather, news items of an infinite scope and variety that individuals are now empowered to use or not use at their discretion.

News Producer

The news producer is responsible for the total look of a newscast, from content to number of items, story line-up, commercial breaks, timing, and the most effective forms of story presentation. The job requires expert knowledge of electronic media news and production techniques, as well as working with the newscasters, reporters, writers, camera operators, editors, and directors.

Newscaster

The newscaster is the on-air personality who presents news to the audience. Some newscasters are little more than announcers who read prepared news scripts, although in many newsrooms the newscaster is a working journalist who helps write and prepare the newscast. The newscaster, also called "talent" or "anchor person," often edits news copy and writes and rewrites stories. The way in which newscasters are used in the newsroom is highly variable. Some are permitted little editorial voice, and others are central to the coverage and presentation decisions of the news operation throughout the day. Some are merely readers whose sole function is as a presenter. Others are truly anchors —

Newscasters, or anchors, are the on-air personalities who deliver the news during regular newscasts, breaking news reports, and hourly updates during primetime.

The assignment editor gives stories to reporters and videographers during the daily assignment meeting and remains in touch with journalists in the field throughout the day for breaking news or changes in the news schedule.

solid journalists who also are excellent on-air personalities. The job varies greatly from one station to the next but usually is among the highest paid.

As technology has evolved, some organizations with all remote-controlled equipment, such as emerging Internet news organizations, also use anchors to roll and switch to prerecorded newscasts. This is possible because of newer robot cameras, computerized teleprompting, and digital audio/video stored on mainframe computers. Although this saves considerable personnel expense (by eliminating former technician jobs in newscast production), it also can degrade the quality of anchoring because the newscaster can't concentrate on delivering the news but also must switch its technical components.

Assignment Editor

The assignment editor covers everything that happens. In touch with reporters and videographers in the field by two-way radio or cell phones, the assignment editor orchestrates coverage of the day's news. Known at some operations as the electronic news coordinator, this person assigns stories to reporters and photographers, lines up some interviews, and handles news calls. Telephones ring, monitors blare with exchanges between local police and fire and sheriff's officials, and fax, email, and wire service copy pours into the newsroom. In addition, the editor must study newspapers, monitor the competition, deal with public relations people who have story ideas, create a news file, and read the mail — all to find a new story or a different story angle.

In the midst of chaos, the assignment editor makes snap decisions about which stories of the day will be covered and by whom. Throughout the day, the assignment editor keeps tabs on which stories have been covered, which are yet to be assigned, and which are in the process of being covered. Obviously, the job demands expert knowledge of news and logistics.

Reporter

The reporter covers and writes stories that the news director, executive producer, and assignment editor have decided to include in upcoming newscasts. A reporter might be sent out to cover a meeting, interview a city official, or talk with merchants about how a recently passed piece of legislation will affect business. Reporters are the "foot soldiers" of the news department. Most words in a newscast are theirs. The interviews are theirs. The sweat, frustration, and anxiety of meeting deadlines are theirs. They attend the city council meetings that last past midnight, and they interview the belligerent union official who "doesn't listen to your station anyway," and they wait in a blizzard for four hours to get the fire chief's confirmation that the fire was possibly started by an arsonist.

After all that effort and time, the reporter may turn over his or her story to the newscaster to be read on the air. A thorough understanding of electronic media news is essential for this position. Much of the time, the reporter

Reporters are the workhorses behind the newscast. Some days they may cover two to three stories in a five-hour span before heading into the newsroom to begin writing and editing.

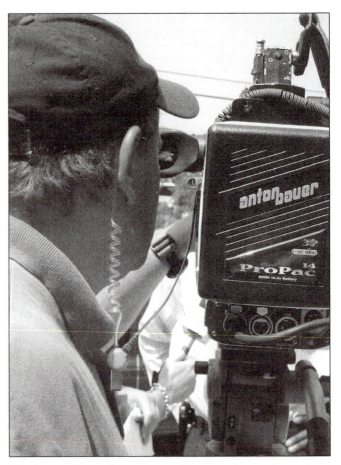

Photographers, known as videographers at most stations, must have a keen sense for visual effects and understand good storytelling, shot composition, framing, and sequencing.

gathers and reports news from the field to be delivered live from the field or recorded for later use.

Some organizations employ special assignment reporters who specialize primarily in one area of the news — such as science, government, or medicine — and others rely primarily on general assignment reporters, who are assigned to cover the news, whatever it may be, where it happens, and whenever it happens. The beat reporter follows a fixed routine each week, covering police headquarters, district court, the sheriff's office, city council, and the planning and zoning commission.

Photographer

The news photographer shoots video and may operate live ENG equipment (discussed later in this section). At small stations, this person writes and reports news as well but generally is restricted from such activity in union markets.

The position requires extensive knowledge of electronic and video equipment, sound recording, lighting techniques, news values, and creative editing. Some news photographers like to be called "photojournalists," "video journalists," or "videographers."

Regardless of the title, this person captures the visual images used in television news. The essential skills of photography, in terms of shot composition, framing, and sequencing, are the same regardless of the medium used to store those images.

Writer

Although reporters and newscasters do much of the writing for newscasts, few large operations can do without behind-the-scenes writers to help prepare the show. The news writer, also frequently called an "associate producer," is involved with everything from headlines to scripts, from wire copy to original feature material. At other organizations, newscast producers commonly write much of the newscast, including story teasers, headlines, hand-offs, and lead-ins to prerecorded video news packages — not to mention many of the news stories in a typical news production.

The writer also assembles finished reports from many sources: wire copy, telephone interviews, still pictures, and VTR. In radio, the biggest demand for writers comes from stations that offer news 24 hours a day. In television, writers are most in demand at stations that originate from one hour to one-and-a-half or more of news each day. Good writers tend to make good reporters and, assuming they understand the complexities of electronic media news production, may struggle through the ranks to become reporters and newscasters.

ENG Coordinator

The ENG (electronic news gathering) coordinator has evolved since the development of portable television equipment, enabling "live" electronic media newscasting from the scene of news events. Remote trucks or vans and small microwave or other technology links must be established and then coordinated. This is a complicated and sometimes time-consuming task that requires considerable knowledge of and skill involved in television engineering, as well as an appreciation for news coverage demands.

Sometimes the ENG coordinator is a former assignment editor or photographer, and other times an engineering or production person who has discovered a career in the newsroom. The ENG coordinator works with the assignment editor and newscast producer to get the proper equipment positioned at the proper place at the proper time. Larger newsrooms usually have this specialist on staff to relieve the assignment editor and newscast producer from yet another set of complicated problems to resolve, along with their regular news-coverage responsibilities. In small operations, this job often is layered on top of the other responsibilities. ENG is the topic of Chapter 9.

ENG coordinators must organize feeds coming in via live remote from the field plus national and international satellite feeds.

Video editing is constantly evolving as computer software becomes more sophisticated and also more user-friendly.

Video Editor

Because television, by its nature, is visual, it eats up large quantities of video stories, all of which must be edited. The video or VTR editor occupies a key position, as stories brought in from the field must be edited into polished, professional presentations. The job requires specialized knowledge of picture and sound editing.

Related Jobs

Other positions related to production of the daily newscast include the following.

- **Newsroom secretary:** handles incoming calls, general correspondence, and clerical duties
- **Graphic artist:** prepares graphics and other visuals to be used in the newscast
- **Sound person:** records and monitors sound during in-field recording
- **Lighting person:** is responsible for lighting news subjects and news events in the field
- **Engineer for live, in-field production:** ensures integrity of electronic media newscast transmission signals during live broadcasts of news events, or direct transmission of signals back to the station for recording and later playback
- **Field producer:** accompanies tape crews and reporters to oversee production of in-field news coverage

- **Researcher:** is responsible for researching files, old photographs, film morgues, and the like, during generation of news stories, special reports, and documentaries

Additional jobs that are related to newscast production but may not require specific knowledge of journalism include:

- Studio floor director
- Technical director

- Audio and video control
- Stage manager (also known as floor director)
- Set carpenter
- Electrician
- Studio camera operator

EXERCISE 1A: Newsroom Organization and Jobs

Name _____ Date _____

1. Interview an electronic journalist who holds the type of job you are most interested in learning. Find out how that person became interested in electronic news as a career field and rose to the position he or she now holds. Share pertinent comments with others in class discussion, or record the interview for playback in class.

2. Check with your professor about arranging to visit a radio newsroom to observe newsroom organization, typical staff duties, and the delivery of an on-air newscast. During your visit, you may wish to question working journalists about their job responsibilities and seek advice about obtaining a job in radio news. Prepare a report to deliver to the rest of your class.

3. If you are interested in Internet journalism, check with your professor about arranging to visit a local news organization's webmaster to see how that person works with the rest of the newsroom to integrate other journalism products into the Internet version of each day's coverage.

Critical Thinking Questions

Directions: The following questions are provided to help you examine the deeper meanings and complexities of the various issues under discussion. Answer each question to the best of your ability after a thoughtful review of the subject at hand.

1. In your view, are traditional newscasts likely to become more or less important to worldwide viewing audiences? Explain your reasoning.

2. Evidence suggests that news will soon be delivered to mass audiences in new ways ("paperless" newspapers and magazines, wireless media, 3-D holographic images, and the like). How will these delivery methods impact professional journalists, news organizations, and their audiences in the years ahead?

3. Assume you are the news director for a station in a medium-sized city (150,000 population). The day's top local stories include:

• Overflow of students at the local university is causing a housing problem as the fall semester begins.

• A popular downtown restaurant fails its second public health inspection.

• The football coach of the local high school could win his 100th game in tonight's home opener.

• The city's middle schools have a higher percentage than normal (10%) of non-certified teachers in the classroom because of a teacher shortage.

First, determine how long each story should be (from 30 seconds to 1:30) for a four-minute news hole. Second, determine which stories are most important and decide the order of the newscast. Third, decide what to do if a news story breaks about lightning striking a local elementary school just as kids were getting out of school. Where does it go among your lead stories? How long should it be? What other stories will have to wait or be shortened?

4. Structure your chosen career path on a timeline. Start by listing the job you hope to have by age 40, and its ideal geographic location. Work backward in five-year increments to the present. Identify all education, professional skills, and work experiences that will be necessary to achieve your career goals. As a final step, explain what additional preparation and professional abilities may be necessary if you decide to change careers after age 40.

Self-Review Questions

Directions: Each of the self-review questions below addresses information contained in this chapter. Answer each question to the best of your ability, then review the chapter as necessary to further strengthen your understanding of each concept or issue.

1. Create an organization chart for a typical electronic news organization.

2. Contrast the organization chart you created above with its counterpart for an Internet news organization.

3. What different news sources and technologies are used to produce an Internet newscast?

4. What are the roles and duties of a news "stringer?"

5. What are the roles and duties of a news director?

Self-Review Questions *(continued)*

6. How do the duties of an executive producer differ from those of a news producer?

7. What skills and knowledge must a Web news producer possess, beyond those required of a news producer?

8. What is the job of the assignment editor in a newsroom?

9. What careers in news are available both in front of the camera and behind it in electronic news media? List them.

10. What are the primary non-news career positions available at an electronic news organization?

2 Writing for Visual Media

Good writing is the foundation of all successful journalism. The major emphasis of this text, therefore, is on writing. You must learn to write, rewrite, and write again until your stories are polished and ready for transmission. It has been said, after all, that good writing is rewriting what you have rewritten.

The next several chapters cover the basics of writing for electronic media. Chapter 2 provides the stylistic characteristics of news writing, emphasizing the importance of word usage and grammar. In Chapter 3 you will learn how to write to the medium, whether for radio, television, or the Internet. Chapter 4 develops the foundation for writing the news story by examining the elements of news, different types of news leads, and story organization. In Chapter 5 we discuss the value judgments necessary for news selection. Chapter 6 emphasizes features, a popular form of news reporting. In that chapter, an interview with John Larson, an Emmy-winning network correspondent, gives tips on writing features.

We can't emphasize enough the importance of professional writing skills. If you want to be a successful journalist, you have to write well. The writer's challenge is to engage attention and motivate a half-interested person to become vitally interested in the news. Imagine encountering the following story leads:

- It was like a scene from Dante's Inferno.

- Everyone knows how dry it's been in recent months, but few residents knew how serious the drought has become until late this afternoon.

- Most of us would like to live to be 100, and today American scientists are saying it's possible.

If your audience is even a little interested in this sort of writing, these leads help spur even more interest. They can help you gather and hold an audience, although not all stories are suited to this treatment. Electronic journalism demands complex writing skills, because you must take a day's events, compress them into a few minutes, yet communicate the significant and interesting aspects of what has happened that day. You must learn how to communicate the essence of stories in little time in a way that is accurate, succinct, interesting, and full of imagery — and all this to an audience that will have only one chance to hear, understand, and retain what you have said. Few writers without well-developed skills are up to the task.

DIFFERENCES BETWEEN PRINT AND ELECTRONIC JOURNALISM

When you are writing for print media or a Web page, you are producing information that will be taken in through the eye. Print audiences don't hear what you are trying to say; they only see your words.

A simple experiment offers dramatic proof of the difference between writing for print and the spoken media: Find a copy of any newspaper and read one article into a cassette recorder. Now play back the recording. It probably sounds ponderous and artificial. That's because what you read into the recorder is the written word spoken aloud, not the way people talk. Newspaper writing as we know it is still evolving after 250 years, and it hasn't come close to meeting the demands for spoken copy that the electronic media make.

When you write for the ear, you are taught to write the way you talk — although obviously more

> *Sometimes all it takes is a phrase,*
> *two or three words, a small thing,*
> *something in the sound of it . . .*
> *and the substance,*
> *that helps make it memorable.*
> —EDWARD BLISS
> —Broadcast News Writer

formal and precise than in everyday conversation. Radio, television, and streaming audio on the Internet are good friends to most people. We often tune in to hear a friendly voice tell us what's happening in the world. If the voice talks like a newspaper, we probably won't listen long. Yet, writers sometimes overlook the maxim that speakers must read words intended to be heard — more formal, obviously, than most routine conversation between friends but much less formal and stilted than copy for print journalism.

Spoken stories, therefore, must be clear, concise, and economical. Listeners and viewers don't get a chance to replay a story if it is unclear. In a five-minute radio newscast, you must subtract a minute for the commercial and 30 seconds or more for the intro, weather report, and close, so you're left with only about three and one-half minutes in which to cram the news of the day. Even in a half-hour television newscast — after subtracting four commercial breaks of two minutes each, a show open and close, some "chat" time for the news anchors to toss to sports and weather, as well as the scripted sports and weather segments — only eleven to 13 minutes of actual news content time may remain.

HOW THE EAR WORKS

The ear has less patience than the eye. The ear gets upset when you drone on and on with a story or when you hurl fistfuls of detail at it. Newspapers are full of facts, numbers, and figures.

A federal survey shows that the number of meals served in public schools has dropped 18 percent in the last 18 months as more families send sack lunches to school with their children. The decline in number of full-price lunches has averaged nearly 12 percent, according to the survey, and the decline in number of reduced-fare lunches has averaged 27 percent. Officials attribute the fall-off in total number of lunches served to a 25 percent increase in the cost of full-price lunches, which have been raised from $2.60 to $3.00, and to a 140 percent increase in the cost of reduced-price lunches, which have jumped from $1.30 cents to $1.95 cents in the last 18 months. All increases are attributed to cutbacks in federal subsidies for school lunches.

Look closely at the story in the above example. What does it really say? Could you understand the story without studying it? Writing for electronic media has no room for such abstraction. Radio, television, and copy for audio streaming intentionally avoid this sort of detail, opting instead to deliver more generalized impressions. Compare the same story for media that do not

SPOTLIGHT

Writing for Electronic Media

A newspaper or online news story might report that public school teachers can earn an average annual salary of $50,000, while parochial teachers earn an average of $35,000 per year. The story also might report that the average yearly cost to educate a child in public schools is $8,000, while the same average annual cost in parochial schools is $3,000.

That same information presented for electronic news media might look like this:

The cost of education keeps climbing, but parochial schools seem to be holding the line. Figures released today show public school teachers in this area earn about 50 thousand dollars. That compares with parochial salaries around 35-thousand dollars a year. Officials say it costs about eight thousand dollars to educate a child in public schools this year . . . compared to about three-thousand dollars a year in parochial schools.

Notice that you have still used figures but you have not crammed them into two sentences. You also have given your audience reference points by saying that parochial salaries are about half the salaries in public schools, while the per-child cost of education is much higher in public schools.

Now try writing your own electronic news story with the following facts from a local newspaper story:

This year's average SAT score for graduating seniors at the local high school is 1080, which shows a steady climb over previous years and is above last year's average of 1050 but still lower than the national average of 1120. School officials also reported that the average SAT score for entering freshmen in the state's public universities is 1150. Local school officials believe new teaching methods and changes in the curriculum this year should help boost the school's average SAT score above the national average by next year.

provide the opportunity to reread the copy (radio and television):

> A federal survey shows that parents are fighting cutbacks in government lunch subsidies with the brown bag. Over the past year and a half, sack lunches have replaced nearly one hot school lunch in five. The cutbacks have hit low-income families the hardest. Nationally, reduced-price lunches average $1.95 cents. That's nearly 140 percent more than a year-and-a-half ago. Full-price lunches are about three dollars, or 25 percent more than a year and a half ago.

TREATING NUMBERS

The most effective rules for handling numbers in copy have been found to be the following:

1. Spell out numbers one to eleven.

2. Use numerals for numbers 12–999.

3. Use the words for thousands, millions, billions, and trillions.

4. Whenever possible, round off without distorting the meaning, unless the exact number is significant.

5. Spell out things like "dollars," "cents," and "percent," where the symbol normally used might be hard for the newscaster to read.

The larger the numbers become, the more abstract they loom to your audience. Some writers throw around the word "billions" almost as callously as some public servants do. Try to imagine a billion of anything. Imagine your audience trying to make sense of a story that talks about a $24 billion increase in defense spending. Your calculator will show that $24 billion is a yearly expenditure of close to $800 per second, $2,880,000 per hour, and nearly $70 million a day.

Somewhere within the story you can help the audience make sense of these figures by relating them with an eye toward understanding. Help your audience make similar sense of figures by telling them that the new supersonic transport is the length of two football fields, instead of 200 yards or 600 feet long. Radio and television media tend to be poor at abstraction, so vivid writing and imagery can be substituted. Your writing will be more interesting and easier to understand.

Similarly, as you write for radio, television, or Internet video and audio streaming media, you gain time and clarity for every unneeded word you lose. Every word you eliminate without losing essential meaning saves a second or two that you can give to some other story. Every unneeded word is one fewer element to muddle the meaning of your story. So write lean, be brief, and choose powerful words that telegraph your message without getting bogged down in rhetoric.

Anchors practice reading the news several times before the actual newscast, working on proper pronunciation, enunciation, and inflection so the spoken information is understandable to listeners.

WRITING TO AN AUDIENCE

Writing is both art and craft, but it is always an act of communication that requires not only a message but also someone to hear it. You must have something to say to someone else, and who that someone else happens to be (your audience) helps determine how you tell (your style) what you have to say (your message). To these considerations of audience, style, and message, you should add to your consciousness as a writer a fourth element: purpose. Purpose answers the questions of why you are writing the story, why it is important, to whom it is important, and how your story will affect those who hear it. Keeping in mind these four essentials — audience, style, message, and purpose — will immediately make you a more competent writer.

Who is your audience? If you work in radio, your audience at seven a.m. might be made up of sleepy-heads at the breakfast table or commuters fighting early-morning traffic. Your audience might be a grandfather just waking up to your newscast or a trucker driving down an interstate freeway. Whatever the hour of the day, your audience is not a faceless mass. Your audience is a single human being much like yourself. This is the single human being to whom you must write. Writing to the mass audience, the faceless crowd, requires little commitment to communicate what others need and want to hear. Much better is to imagine your audience as a single person who quite often is beset by distractions that lure her from your message, whether the distraction is a crying baby, a stoplight, the doorbell, or an article in the newspaper that just caught her eye.

When you are doing morning drive-time radio news, you are, in effect, a passenger in a vehicle on the way to work, having a chat with the driver about the day's events. It's a close, personal, one-on-one conversation. The same is true with television and streaming audio/video on the Internet. The newscast often is delivered to people sitting alone or in groups of two or three at the end of the day, or to people in bed watching the news before they go to sleep at night. Electronic news is not delivered to an audience in a stadium but, rather, individually situated people with whom you are having a one-way conversation of sorts. It's close and personal, not distant and aloof. You are not announcing to them. You are sitting there in the car, or in their home, or in the airport terminal, having a friendly chat.

TARGET AUDIENCE

Most media organizations have a **target audience** — a primary bloc of listeners or viewers with certain charac-

teristics of age, economics, or lifestyle that give it a somewhat common identity. The organization offers programming calculated specifically to attract that audience. The target audience of an easy-listening format FM radio station, on the one hand, might be affluent "oldsters" inclined toward travel, investment, and involvement in community cultural affairs. A heavy-metal station, on the other hand, might cater to a target audience of younger listeners between ages 18 and 30. Other organizations might program primarily to reach African American, Hispanic, Nordic, or other minority audiences, or a "middle-of-the-road" audience of the primary buyers in our society between the ages of 18 and 49. These audiences have different backgrounds, needs, and interests, and your writing can take these factors into account.

As a listener or a viewer, you sometimes can determine an organization's target audience by assessing the nature of its commercials. When one football personality had his own sportscast on a Kansas City, Missouri, station, he garnered a high percentage of women viewers. Station ratings reflected a "bulge" in the number of women viewers during the ten o'clock news when he began his sportscast. Subsequently, the nature and choice

A lot of the light-hearted talk between anchors during the newscast is to create an image of positive friendliness so viewers will more readily connect with the news team and invite them into their homes regularly to increase ratings.

of some stories within the sportscast were altered to reflect women's interests (more women's tennis, for example). The growing number of commercials for women's products indicated the increasing number of women in the audience. Conversely, in the radio medium, commercials for backpacks, bicycles, stereos, and similar products may indicate that the station is reaching an intended target audience of young adults.

With your audience defined, you can begin to write in a meaningful way to all those single human beings out there who are trying to listen. The story you write is your message. The way you tell it is your style. Some stories will be humorous; others will be deadly serious. Some will entertain; others will inform. The nature of the story, its essence, will determine your style and how you treat the story.

ACCURACY

An essential quality of fair reporting is accuracy. No organization can maintain journalistic integrity if its news reports are consistently inaccurate. Missed facts, mispronunciations, distortions of emphasis — all damage your credibility. Inadequacies, half-truths, and inconsistencies raise questions in listeners' and viewers' minds about the possibility of biased reporting. Journalism has come under attack for unfair reporting. Even when your accuracy and fairness are above reproach, some in your audience will castigate you for reporting what happened and others will chastise you for not reporting what happened.

Given the nature of journalism, this is to be expected. Anyone in the news, whether public official or labor union leader, wants to be shown in a favorable light. Accurate reporting demands that you show people as they are, whether good or bad, and "let the chips fall where they may." Your role as journalist is not to tell people what they would like to hear. Your job is to tell the story as accurately as you can, even when the facts are unpleasant.

Accuracy is demanded of you in many ways. In even the simplest stories, you will have to check and recheck the smallest details and verify that names, ages, and addresses are complete and accurate. You will have to determine whether streets and rivers run in the directions that news services and fellow writers claim. You will have to ascertain whether your use of statistics is fair or misleading. You will have to find out whether "yesterday" in Paris is still "today" in the United States. If you are diligent in your commitment to honest, accurate reporting, your audience will trust you and will seek out your station as a professional information source. On a more personal level, inaccuracy is one way to lose your

job or subject yourself and your organization to costly lawsuits.

Attribution

As a journalist, you should not take responsibility for predicting the future or vouch for the accuracy of statements you cannot substantiate. Statements don't have to be attributed unless you have a reason, and usually less frequently than in print journalism. Too much **attribution** in spoken copy interrupts continuity and makes the story more confusing. The following sample statements, however, must be attributed:

1. Sodium phenobarbital injections provide a more humane way than compression chambers to dispose of pets.
2. Abortion is a return to primitive, barbaric values.
3. Continued imports of foreign oil will drive America bankrupt.
4. Carlson will withdraw as the nominee for highway director.

Looking at the statements above, you can easily identify their controversial nature. As a journalist, why should you assume responsibility for reporting this type of information as fact? Statement 1 calls for attribution to an expert, someone with the qualifications to state as fact that sodium phenobarbital injections are more humane than other methods of pet disposal. Statement 2 is an emotion-laden value judgment, and you must either attribute the statement to a source or label your story as personal comment or an editorial. Statement 3 places you in the position of crystal-gazer unless you attribute. Who says foreign oil imports will drive America bankrupt? Tell your audience who made the statement, then let the audience judge for itself the accuracy of the statement and the integrity of the source. Statement 4 fails to include the source. Only Carlson could decide to withdraw his name from nomination, so the audience should know the source of the story.

In many cases, though, attribution is unnecessary, a situation that is most common when the source is obvious or obviously can be trusted:

Poor: According to Barbara Davidson, technical assistant for the Houston District Court, Judge Conrad Hill has deferred sentencing in the case until December 15th.

Better: Sentencing has been deferred until mid-December.

Equally futile is to attribute sources that can be summarized in fewer words:

Example: Marvin Atkins, acting assistant director of investigations for the St. Louis metropolitan strike force,

Attribution can be tricky with television news reports unless you have the source speaking directly on camera, in what is known as a soundbite.

said arresting officers took five suspected drug dealers into custody in the raid, including the 15-year-old daughter of a prominent St. Louis family.

Change to: Police say they arrested five suspected drug dealers, among them the 15-year-old daughter of a prominent St. Louis family.

While newspapers typically delay attribution until the end of the sentence, spoken stories usually sound more natural if you name the source at the beginning of the sentence:

Newspaper style attribution: The Fort Worth area can expect an unusually chilly month, according to the National Weather Service.

Radio or television attribution: The National Weather Service predicts an unusually chilly month in the Fort Worth area.

When you write the spoken word, sound, clarity, and brevity are all-important. "Says" is a helpful word. The examples of attribution above frequently use the word "say" or "says." "Says" is a clean, simple substitute for the more pontifical "stated" "asserted," and "according to" that appear often in newspaper writing. "Says" also is a clean way to reduce the sentence length,

as the following examples demonstrate. In each example, the word "says" substitutes nicely for the italicized words:

Example: Johnson further charged that the city will experience a decline in property tax revenue.

Change to: Johnson says the city can expect a decline in property tax revenue.

Example: He stated that new laws are needed to provide authority to close down pornography shops.

Change to: He says new laws are needed to close down pornography shops.

Or consider this problem and how it would sound in a newscast:

I'm proud I was able to sail the Atlantic by myself, but now I'm just glad the voyage has come to an end.

This wording might lead to confusion about who said what — the person in the news or the person reporting the news. An indirect quote here could ease you out of potentially confused reporting:

He says he's proud he managed to sail the Atlantic alone, but he's glad the voyage is over.

Quoting the Source

The problem with quotation marks in spoken copy is that no one can hear them. Unless the quote also appears on the Internet, no one in your audience will see your news copy. The challenge is to find acceptable ways of quoting news sources, whether directly or indirectly. Early broadcasters often tacked on the awkward "quote" just before reading the direct quote and finished with an equally awkward "unquote" after reading the direct quotation. More acceptable and natural sounding are phrases such as:

> Councilman Lee attacked the proposed power plant, calling it, in his words, "a public health nuisance and a waste of tax dollars."

Opting for the indirect quote in this example, you could say,

> Councilman Lee says the proposed power plant would be a public health nuisance and a waste of tax dollars.

Use the direct quote if it adds emphasis or additional impact to your story, but use it sparingly and with discretion. Most often, you can substitute attribution, naming the source at the beginning of the sentence that contains the quotation:

> The President says — and these are his words — "No person shall go hungry in America.
>
> General Electric calls the new capillary chips a "revolutionary discovery."
>
> German newspapers are asking for the execution of what they call "Israeli sympathizers."

Other Attribution Words

When you write any story that requires attribution, you may be tempted to try word substitutes for the familiar "said," as in the following example:

> Doctors said the new vaccine may cause cancer.

In this example, "said" is a neutral verb. It places no value of any kind upon the statement that follows. Equally neutral are the words "told" and "reported," which simply relate an act of communication without imposing any value on the statement communicated:

> Doctors told reporters the new vaccine may cause cancer.
>
> Doctors reported the new vaccine may cause cancer.

Beyond this point, attribution words begin to impose an editorial flavor to your writing because they tend to change the story's meaning. Words that change the meaning include, among others:

asserted	stated
added	declared
disclosed	vowed
warned	promised
pointed out	continued

The subtle changes in meaning become apparent when you substitute these words for the more neutral "said," "told," or "reported."

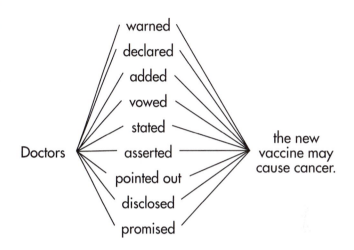

In this example, "asserted" sounds as if the writer is challenging the doctors' statement. "Warned" is an acceptable word for attribution, but "declared" sounds pompous. "Added" indicates that the possibility of cancer was given almost as an afterthought. "Vowed" is too strong; it implies a pomposity beyond the doctor's original intent. "Stated" is stiff and formal. "Pointed out" makes the statement sound as if it is secondary or peripheral. "Disclosed" makes the statement sound as if the doctors had exclusive information just now being made public. "Promised" sounds more dire than the doctors may have intended the statement to be. Each word imparts a slightly different meaning to the information.

NAMES, AGES, AND TITLES

Just as you treat attribution differently in spoken copy, so must you treat names, ages, and titles differently. The best advice in this regard is to write so your audience will have little chance of misunderstanding. As a general rule, names are delayed until you have prepared your listeners to be on the alert for the names. With some exceptions, titles and ages are placed before names, again so your stories will sound more natural and more conversational. Imagine how sticky and meaningless the following story would sound on the air:

> Surgeon General William H. Shearer announced today that Charles R. Mahaffey, 45, chairman of the U-S Pharmaceutical Corporation, had succeeded Donald P. Ingra-

ELECTRONIC MEDIA STYLE GUIDELINES

1. Use standard-size 8½ × 11 paper.

2. Double space.

3. Use only one side of the paper.

4. For radio copy, use 65-space line (set one-inch margins). When timing your copy, 16 lines will equal about one minute of air time.

5. Put slug in upper left corner of page: reporter's name, story identification, date, and page number.

6. Start story about four to six lines below the slug.

7. Indent five spaces to indicate a paragraph.

8. Make new paragraphs in the story every five to eight lines.*

9. Use plenty of commas and ellipses (. . .) in your copy to indicate phrasing and give it air. Many newscasters interpret commas as breath marks, and ellipses as slightly longer pauses. For electronic news readers, commas are not so much grammatical marks as phrasing indicators.

10. Use end mark (### or -30-) at the end of the story.

11. If a paragraph or sentence carries over to another page, try to break the copy at a comma or natural pause so the newscaster can change pages more easily while continuing with the story.

12. Start each new story on a fresh page; this will permit changing the story order if necessary.

13. Omit datelines.

14. For the person who will read the copy on air: Underline key words or those that may be difficult to pronounce. Writers: Call these words to the attention of the newscaster. Many newscasters prefer to mark their own copy to enhance their delivery and are taught to do so by announcing coaches. Writers may emphasize words by using all capitals or bold type, but all hand marks on newscaster copy should be left to the person who will read the copy on the air.

15. Include phonetic spelling for words with difficult pronunciation, with all capitals for the syllable to be emphasized, using a combination of common words or letters that will result in the correct pronunciation. Although wire services frequently provide pronouncers, you often will have to make up ones of your own, particularly with local names and stories. Put the pronouncer inside parentheses immediately following the correctly spelled word. For example: "Cairo (KAY-roh), Illinois."

16. Eliminate most abbreviations. Exceptions are Mr., Mrs., Dr.; commonly abbreviated groups such as YMCA and UN; and time designations.

17. Capitalize freely.

---

*The combination of #7 and #8 above makes it easier for newscasters to find their place as they glance up at the camera, or radio control room engineer, and back down at the copy. The indenting also helps reduce the "TelePrompTer eyes" effect for TV newscasters because it breaks up the regular caging of the eyeballs back and forth as the person reads the TelePrompTer.

18. Handle numbers in news copy as follows:

    ■ Spell out numbers one to eleven.

    ■ Use numerals for 12–999.

    ■ Use the words for thousands, millions, billions, and trillions.

    ■ Whenever possible, round off without distorting the meaning, unless the exact number is significant.

    ■ Spell out things like "dollars," "cents," and "percent," when the symbol normally used might be hard for the newscaster to read."

19. Use **st, rd, th,** and **nd** after dates, addresses, and numbers to be read as ordinal numbers (2nd, 16th Street).

20. In age references use a combination of the years and the words "year old"; for example, "21-year-old."

21. Avoid beginning sentences with the person's age and in general with any number.

22. Follow traditional punctuation, but use question marks only when needed for inflection.

23. Use direct quotes sparingly. Avoid the words "quote," "unquote," and "quotation." Set off a quote with phrases such as "in these words," "in his words," "as she put it," "his exact words were."

24. Do not begin a story with a name. Titles precede the name: "Senator Wayne Swanson says the U.S. must meet its social goals," never "The U.S. must meet its social goals, Wayne Swanson, senator, says."

25. Use complete name in the first reference, except the Pope and the President.

26. Omit obscure names and places if they are not meaningful to the story.

27. Strive to use present tense, but don't force it.

28. Avoid repetition of the time element "today."

The following editing changes may be made in radio or television copy. Other editing will require retyping the story. Many newsrooms use computerized script software, which eliminates hand-correcting scripts. Occasionally in live shots or late inserts, however, "hard copy" script editing may be necessary.

1. Eliminate material by completely blacking it out.

    Example: Officials said ~~said~~ school would open today.

2. Change entire words by blacking out the word(s) and inserting the new word(s) above.

    Example: Officials ~~said~~ _said_ school would open today

3. Add limited new material with a line indicating where it is to be inserted when read.

    Example: Officials _said school_ would open today.

ham, 64, president of the National Educational Media Association, to head the government's Anti-Smoking Campaign. The appointment is effective next month.

You can improve meaning dramatically by delaying names, ages, and titles until the ear is ready for them:

> The Surgeon General's office has appointed a replacement to head the government's Anti-Smoking Campaign.

In the lead, you have announced that someone has been appointed to fill a position. If audience members are interested in this story, they are alerted to hear the name you now can give them:

> He is 45-year-old Charles Mahaffey, chairman of U-S Pharmaceutical.

In this identification of the name, Mahaffey's age comes before his name. This treatment sounds more conversational than "Charles Mahaffey, 45, is Chairman of U-S Pharmaceutical Corporation."

An exception to the general rule of placing titles before the name is given in this example. You could write just as easily:

> The position will be filled by U-S Pharmaceutical Chairman Charles Mahaffey. The 45-year-old appointee will replace current chairman Donald Ingraham next month.

Now put the story together in two of its possible forms and compare it with the original version:

> The Surgeon General's office has appointed a new man to head its Anti-Smoking Campaign. He is 45-year-old Charles Mahaffey, Chairman of U-S Pharmaceutical. Mahaffey will take over from Donald Ingraham next month.

or

> The Surgeon General's office has named a major corporation executive to head its Anti-Smoking Campaign. Named to head the post is U-S Pharmaceutical Chairman Charles Mahaffey. He replaces Donald Ingraham next month.

These stories drop all reference to Surgeon General William H. Shearer and his middle initial. Attribution is not essential and only increases the story's complexity. The ages of the men involved are optional; they can be added or deleted at your discretion.

Consider another example in the treatment of names and ages:

> Mark J. Conley, 29, and Lester J. Callaway, 44, were injured in the crash. The two men, both of Plainsville, were reported in satisfactory condition at Pleasant Valley Memorial Hospital.

Reading this example aloud to an audience is dangerous because it dumps unknown names on listeners before they are prepared to hear them. A better approach to the story for electronic media is:

> Two Plainsville men were injured in the crash. They are identified as 29-year-old Mark Conley and 44-year-old Lester Callaway. Both men are hospitalized in satisfactory condition.

This approach alerts your listeners that two people from their community were injured. If listeners are interested in the names, they now are prepared to hear this information. The ear is prepared a second time for the identities by the "cushion" phrase, "They are identified as...." This treatment sets up the ear twice and makes names and ages easier to catch. Middle initials are unnecessary, so they are omitted.

Exceptions to the rule of delaying names in the news occur when the names are well known. No one is likely to miss or misunderstand the President's name or that of a widely known politician, athlete, or Hollywood celebrity. In these cases, beginning the story with the name is acceptable — and sometimes preferable — because the well-known name helps capture a listener's attention. When writing for the ear, titles usually go ahead of the name. The exception occurs when long or unusually cumbersome titles are involved. Imagine trying to say on the air:

> University of Wyoming Anthropology Department Chairman Doctor George Frison today announced the discovery of an ancient Indian burial ground long hidden from modern-day humanity. The burial ground is located ten miles north of Laramie, Wyoming, on a ranch.

Such a long title would confuse your audience. One of the following examples would be much better:

> Doctor George Frison, anthropology department chairman at the University of Wyoming. . .

or

> Doctor George Frison, the head of anthropology at the University of Wyoming. . .

You still would not start the story with Doctor Frison's name, though. He is not the news, nor is his announcement of the anthropological discovery. The real news is the discovery itself, and Doctor Frison's name is peripheral to the substance of the story. Granted, the implications of his expert title lend credibility to the story, but this expertise does not alter the substance or nature of the event. The final story might be:

> Scientists say they've discovered an ancient Indian burial ground about ten miles north of Laramie, Wyoming. The announcement was made by Doctor George Frison, the head of anthropology at the University of Wyoming.

An example of news attribution is given in Figure 2.1.

VIDEO	AUDIO
Midday report	
AB (*Anchor initials*)	(AB)
	Some local health officials think the federal government has exaggerated its warnings about smoking Mexican marijuana tainted with a deadly herbicide. But city health officials say they doubt even heavy use of the marijuana in question would pose a serious health hazard.
	Local toxicologist Dr. Daniel Rosenbaum calls the recent publicity . . . "An hysterical reaction to a relatively insignificant problem."

Figure 2.1 *Example of broadcast news attribution.*

Using Verbs

The main considerations in the use of verbs are the tense and the voice.

Verb Tense

Newspapers traditionally report the news in past tense, using words such as "said," "reported," "occurred," "burned," "announced," and "injured." Radio and television news, however, is "now." Your stories will sound old and out-of-date if you dwell too often in the past tense. News sounds more current and dynamic if you report in the present tense:

Police are questioning two suspects.

The White House tonight reports new developments in the controversial question of . . . .

Firemen are battling a two-alarm fire that broke out late tonight . . . .

> *There is no way of writing well and also of writing easily.*
> ANTHONY TROLLOPE
> English Novelist 1815–1882

Let's look at some other examples:

Present tense: Striking coal workers hope a settlement can be reached tonight.

Past perfect tense: Striking coal workers were reported hopeful that a settlement could be reached tonight. (Is there a chance they are still hopeful?)

Past tense: Striking coal workers hoped a settlement could be reached tonight.

The shift in tense changes the meaning of the story subtly and, as you shift from present to past tense, the immediacy of the story is lost. The sentence written in past tense sounds somewhat negative about hopes for a settlement. Present tense offers the writer an additional benefit: It helps keep sentences shorter. Sometimes, however, present tense sounds awkward and artificial. If it does, switch to past tense or past perfect tense.

Active Versus Passive Voice

Excessive use of the passive voice is often a sign of lazy thinking. Active voice, by contrast, results in more understandable copy, shorter sentences, and dynamic expression. If the subject of the verb receives the action, the verb is in the passive voice:

The burglar was shot three times by police.

If the subject of a verb is the doer of the action, the verb is in the active voice:

Police shot the burglar three times.

Although active voice generally is more lively, specific and concise, passive voice is useful to emphasize the object of the action. In the passive-voice example, emphasis is placed on the burglar (object of the action). In the active-voice example, emphasis is placed on the police (the doer of the action).

PHONETIC PRONUNCIATION

The news is loaded with "tongue-tanglers," those innocent and sometimes not-so-innocent-seeming words that reflect unusual or difficult pronunciations. Any newscaster who comes upon these difficult words without warning can easily hesitate, stumble, or massacre the word.

To avoid this, spell the word phonetically and put it in parentheses beside the offending word. Hyphenate between syllables, and use capital letters to indicate where the stress belongs:

Three traffic deaths are reported this Memorial Day weekend near Saguache (Suh-WATCH), New Mexico.

Flood control experts expect the next trouble spot along tributaries flowing into the Arkansas (Are-KAN-sus) River.

Audiences harbor strong feelings about correct pronunciation. Venerable newscasters have been the subject of national debate for pronouncing FEB-roo-air-ee (February) FEB-yoo-wary, Ill-ih-NOY (Illinois) Ill-ih-NOISE, ZOO-ology instead of ZOE-ology, and HIGH-ness instead of HAY-ness for "heinous." Other offenses have included saying NU-cue-lar instead of NU-clee-ar (nuclear), and calling Africa, Cuba, and Alaska, respectively, AF-ri-ker, CUE-ber, and a-LAS-ker.

Phonetic pronunciation helps the newscast flow smoothly and prevents the sudden loss of credibility when an anchor muffs a word with which audience members either are familiar or have heard pronounced correctly on competing stations. Almost all states have unusual spellings and pronunciations that confuse new employees, and foreign names crop up continually in the news, presenting new pronunciation problems. The news services provide a list of phonetic pronunciations each day for foreign names and places in the news, and most state media organizations provide regional pronunciation guides.

The following guide to phonetic spelling indicates correct pronunciations in broadcast news copy.

Vowels

A   Use AY for long A as in mate.
    Use A for short A as in cat.
    Use AI for nasal A as in air.
    Use AH for short A as in father.
    Use AW for broad A as in talk.

E   Use EE for long E as in meet.
    Use EH for short E as in get.
    Use UH for hollow E as in the or le (French prefix).
    Use AY for French long E with accent as in Pathe.
    Use IH for E as in pretty.
    Use EW for EW as in few.

I   Use EYE for long I as in time.
    Use EE for French long I as in machine.
    Use IH for short I as in pity.

O   Use OH for long O as in note, or ough as in though.
    Use AH for short O as in hot.
    Use AW for broad O as in fought.
    Use OO for O as in fool, or ough as in through.
    Use U for O as in foot.
    Use UH for OUGH as in trough.
    Use OW for O as in how, or ough as in plough.

U   Use EW for long U as in mule.
    Use OO for long U as in rule.
    Use U for middle U as in put.
    Use UH for short U as in shut or hurt.

Consonants

Use K for hard C as in cat.
Use S for soft C as in cease.
Use SH for soft CH as in machine.
Use CH for hard CH or TCH as in catch.
Use Z for hard S as in disease.
Use S for soft S as in sun.
Use G for hard G as in gang.
Use J for soft G as in general.

TIME REFERENCES

Unlike newspaper readers, radio and television audiences cannot reread your story or seek clarification if at first they do not understand a fact or figure. For this reason, broadcast writers use a slightly different style when referring to the time of day or week. The writer for print might say, "The meeting will begin Thursday at eight p.m." Knowing the audience will hear the information only once, the writer would strive for immediate clarity with a sentence to the effect, "The meeting will begin tomorrow evening at eight o'clock." References to days of the week are obscure and should be replaced whenever possible with phrases such as "the day after tomorrow" and "one week from tomorrow."

Time reference in newspaper copy: The next liftoff is scheduled for 5:33 a.m. (EDT), March 16.

The same time reference in electronic media copy: The next liftoff will be a week from tomorrow at 5:30 in the morning, Eastern Daylight Time.

Whenever the audio/visual writer must make reference to time or to days of the week, instant understanding is the immediate goal. The concern for audience understanding is the primary influence on writing style.

Copy written to be heard usually flows better and sounds smoother if time references in a sentence are placed near the main verb. Reading the following examples aloud, notice the effect that time-reference placement has on the sound and rhythm of your copy:

        (verb)   *(time reference)*
The body <u>was found</u> in a ravine near Pueblo <u>last month</u>.

          (verb)   *(time reference)*
The body <u>was found last month</u> in a ravine near Pueblo.

         (verb)   *(time reference)*
Another officer <u>was killed</u> in a similar accident <u>about a year ago</u>.

       (verb)   *(time reference)*
Another officer <u>was killed</u> <u>about a year ago</u> in a similar accident.

         (verb)   *(time reference)*
The fire <u>broke out</u> at eleventh and Central <u>late this afternoon</u>.

         (verb)   *(time reference)*
The fire <u>broke out</u> <u>late this afternoon</u> at eleventh and Central.

Achieving a polished sound in your copy sometimes requires that you ignore the rule and place time references elsewhere within some of the sentences you are writing. You seldom will go wrong if you listen to the sound of your copy.

JOURNALISTIC PREFERENCES IN WORD USAGE

Newswriters draw from a full, varied vocabulary, rich in specific words that convey exact meaning and connotation. The writers understand differences in words for specific situations. For example, the word "government" is more neutral than the word "regime." If a word has more than one meaning, it is used in the correct context to avoid confusion.

When examining word usage in the news story, the audience must be considered. Obviously, the New York NBC radio audience is different from that of the locally owned El Paso, Texas, station. The two audiences have different backgrounds and interests, and the language used in each location must be tailored to that audience. Generally, the simple word is preferable to the complex, the concrete to the abstract, and the active to the passive voice. Slang, foreign words, highly technical words or phrases, and clichés should be avoided.

The following list of words and phrases indicates word usage preferred by journalists.

1. ACCEPT, EXCEPT: ACCEPT means "to receive." EXCEPT as a verb means "to exclude," and as a preposition means "with the exception of."

2. AFFECT, EFFECT: AFFECT usually is the verb; EFFECT is the noun ("The drought will affect farmers. The effect will be higher food prices."). EFFECT may be a verb, however, when it means "to bring about." ("The change can be effected only by litigation.").

3. AFTERWARD, AFTERWARDS: Use AFTERWARD rather than AFTERWARDS. The same rule applies to TOWARD.

4. AGREE TO, AGREE WITH: You AGREE TO a proposed action, and you AGREE WITH someone.

5. AGGREGATE: Do not use when you mean "total." It means "a group of distinct things gathered together."

6. ALLUDE, ELUDE: You ALLUDE to a movie (mention indirectly), and you ELUDE a tackler (escape).

7. AMONG, BETWEEN: Use AMONG when referring to more than two. Use BETWEEN with reference to two only.

8. ANNUAL: The first time cannot be ANNUAL. A tradition must be established.

9. AVERSE, ADVERSE: AVERSE is the verb meaning "oppose" (you are AVERSE to it). ADVERSE is the adjective meaning "bad" (ADVERSE weather).

10. BESIDES, BESIDE: BESIDE means "at the side of." BESIDES means "in addition to."

11. BLOCK, BLOC: BLOC is a coalition or group with the same goal.

12. COMPOSE, COMPRISE: You COMPOSE things by putting them together. Once they are together, the object COMPRISES or includes various parts.

13. CONSENSUS: CONSENSUS means "general agreement." Therefore, to say "CONSENSUS of opinion" is redundant.

14. COUNCIL, COUNSEL: COUNCIL means "an assembly." COUNSEL means "to give advice."

15. COUPLE OF: The OF is necessary. Don't say "in a couple minutes."

16. DEMOLISH, DESTROY: Both words mean "to do away with completely." Therefore, "partially DESTROYED" and "totally DEMOLISHED" are incorrect.

17. DIE OF: One DIES OF an illness, not from it. Also, a person DIES after an operation, not from or as a result of, or following, an operation.

18. DIFFERENT FROM: Things are DIFFERENT FROM each other, not different than.

19. DROWN: "Someone was DROWNED" is incorrect unless the victim's head was held under water. Say, "John Jones DROWNED last night," not "John Jones was DROWNED."

20. DUE TO, OWING TO, BECAUSE OF: BECAUSE OF is preferable.

21. ECOLOGY, ENVIRONMENT: ECOLOGY is the study of the relationship between organisms and ENVIRONMENT.

22. EITHER: EITHER means one or the other, not both.

23. FARTHER, FURTHER: FARTHER applies to distance. FURTHER means "in addition to."

24. FIRST, FIRST EVER: The word FIRST is finite in definition. If something is the FIRST, it never has been before. FIRST EVER has come into common use, particularly among sports announcers attempting to make some new milestone sound greater than simply the FIRST time it was accomplished, but FIRST EVER is redundant.

25. FLOUT, FLAUNT: FLOUT means "to mock" or "to show disdain." FLAUNT means "to display showingly."

26. FUNERAL SERVICE. A funeral is a service. Leave out "service."

27. HEAD UP. Leave off "up." People HEAD committees; they do not HEAD UP committees. Likewise, people make rules; they don't make them up.

28. HEALTHFUL, HEALTHY: HEALTHFUL means "to cause health." HEALTHY means "possessing health."

29. IMPLY, INFER: The speaker IMPLIES. The hearer INFERS.

30. IN ADVANCE OF, PRIOR TO, BEFORE: Use BEFORE; it's more natural.

31. LEAVE, LET: LEAVE alone means "depart from" or "to isolate." LET means "to permit or allow."

32. LESS, FEWER: LESS applies to situations using the singular form. FEWER applies to the plural ("They have FEWER members now, and the chairman has LESS income.")

33. LIKE, AS: The formal writing style uses LIKE to compare pronouns and AS to compare phrases or clauses containing a verb. LIKE, however, is being used increasingly as a substitute for "as" or "as if" in informal usage. Thus, because audio/visual writing emphasizes the informal/conversational style, LIKE is generally preferred.

34. MEDIA, DATA, ALUMNI: These are plural forms of medium, datum, and alumnus, respectively.

35. OPINION, ESTIMATION: OPINION is a judgment. ESTIMATION is an evaluation or a guess.

36. ORAL, VERBAL: ORAL denotes use of the mouth. VERBAL can indicate writing, although it may apply to spoken words as well.

37. OVER, MORE THAN: OVER refers to the spatial relationships. MORE THAN indicates figures or numbers.

38. RELUCTANT, RETICENT. If a person doesn't want to act, he is RELUCTANT. If a person doesn't want to speak, she is RETICENT.

39. ROUT, ROUTE: ROUT (pronounced ROWT) means to "scoop up," or is what happens to an army when it is sent into full-blown retreat or what happens to a football team that loses 50–0. (The battle was a rout. The game turned into a rout.) ROUTE (pronounced ROOT) is "a road or direction"; also as a verb, "to direct or send something a certain way" (I'll be traveling on Route 95. Will you route this through Omaha?)

40. SINCE, BECAUSE: SINCE is time-related. BECAUSE is action-related.

41. THAT, WHICH: THAT restricts the reader's thought and directs it in the way you want it to go. WHICH gives subsidiary information. (The legislature that passed the speeding law must now rescind

it. The legislature, which passed the speeding bill, will take up a new bill now.)

42. UNIQUE: Something that is UNIQUE is one of its kind. It can't be very, quite, rather, or somewhat unique.

43. UP. Don't use UP as a verb. (The gambler upped the ante with his bet for $100,000.)

GRAMMAR

A working knowledge of the major grammatical principles is essential. The following list of ten basic grammatical rules provides a start toward a more detailed knowledge of grammar.

1. Verbs must agree with their subjects in number.

   Example: We are; you are; he is; a bloc of voters is; a group of women is.

2. Words intervening between the subject and the verb do not affect the number of the verb.

   Example: Improvements in security measures have increased travel costs.

3. When the subject is one of the following words, the verb must be singular: anybody, each, every, everybody, nobody, either. Neither and none almost always require a singular verb.

   Examples: Each of the news services has filed a story.

   Neither of the senators plans to attend.

   If "neither" is used to link plural nouns, however, a plural verb is used.

   Example: Neither astronauts nor cosmonauts have visited the orbiting space station in three years.

4. When the subject is a collective noun, the subject is considered singular or plural depending on the meaning you wish to convey. If the meaning of the subject is a collective body, use the singular; if you are thinking of individuals within the collective body, use the plural.

   Examples: The governor's staff is planning a victory celebration.

   The governor's staff are listed individually by position.

5. Verb tenses should indicate the correct sequence of action; therefore, a verb in a subordinate clause should be consistent with the verb tense in the main clause.

   Example: When Governor Johnson finished the speech, he realized he had overlooked his minority constituency.

6. Active voice is preferred for most verbs. Passive voice may be used to emphasize the receiver of an action (such as the person injured in a car accident) or to emphasize an indefinite statement.

   Examples: Write, "The plane hit the tower" rather than, "The tower was hit by the plane." To emphasize the receiver of the action, however, write, "The woman was injured in the auto crash."

7. Modifiers must be located closely enough to the word or phrases they modify for the reader to be able to distinguish clearly what they modify.

   Incorrect example: The President said after the news conference that he would return to Washington.

   Correct example: After the news conference the President announced he would return to Washington.

8. Pronouns must refer to their antecedents.

   Incorrect example: The senator told the investigator that his statement was incorrect (whose statement?).

   Correct example: The investigator's statement was incorrect, the senator told him.

9. The case of a pronoun must suit the function of the pronoun.

   (a) A pronoun used as an object of the preposition must take the objective case.

      Example: He came with me (not I).

   (b) A pronoun used as an appositive must agree with the word it explains.

      Example: Only two reporters, John and I, could go to the speech. ("I" refers to the subject; therefore, the pronoun must be in the subjective case.)

   (c) A pronoun modifying the gerund must take the possessive case.

      Example: The station management appreciates your exercising restraint in reporting sensational news.

10. The elements in a series must be grammatically parallel. Adjectives should be linked with other

adjectives, adverbs with adverbs, infinitives with infinitives, and so forth.

Incorrect example: The North Sea oil companies plan to install new drilling equipment, to hire additional employees, and computerize lab operations.

Correct example: North Sea oil companies plan to install new drilling equipment, to hire additional employees, and to computerize lab operations. (All three of the companies' plans were put in the infinitive form "to").

CONCLUSION

Writing is both art and craft, a discipline requiring many skills to master. Those who write constantly sharpen their skills most rapidly because good writing builds on practice. As you begin to sharpen your own writing skills, listen to radio and watch television. Decide for yourself what is good writing and what is not. Learn to discriminate, both in your own work and that of others. As your confidence builds and your skills increase, so will the quality of your writing.

EXERCISE 2A: Grammar

Name _____ Date _____

1 Using a pen or pencil, correct the following copy as it should appear on a radio-TV script.

Six women are reported missing a in an boating accident near Green River, Utah.

✻ ✻ ✻

thomas said it would bet he first time in three yeasr such an election hdas been called.

✻ ✻ ✻

Pilots soy they'll strike if further job cut are announced.

✻ ✻ ✻

At issue are recent tax cits for property owners outside city limits.

✻ ✻ ✻

Daylight Savings time has finally arrived — noon too soon for local schools.

✻ ✻ ✻

Banks currently pay 5125 per cent interest on passbook accounts.

2 Rewrite to eliminate passive voice and wordiness.

EXAMPLE: The car was struck by a falling tree.
             A falling tree struck the car.

Many retirees are affected by the new tax laws.

Thousands of migratory workers are hired by growers each year.

Restrictions on sex and violence in prime time television were thrown out by a federal judge.

Part of the reason for society's attitude toward alcoholism was verified last year by university scientists.

Unless voters come up with an answer, the schools will stay closed.

Air-conditioning for the public schools were turned down four times in a row by area voters.

Officials say most damage was caused by flooding along two minor tributaries.

More than 22 million cattle were believed ready for slaughter this month, according to information made public by the National Beef Association today.

Sidewalks, landscaping, five-foot bike lanes separated by a one and one-half foot raised median, parking and two lanes of traffic are recommended for Peterson Avenue improvements.

The flu is thought by officials at the Disease Control Center to be of the Type-A variety, and they believe up to ten million Americans could be struck this year by the disease.

EXERCISE 2B: Style

Name _____ Date _____

1 Rewrite the following story to make it conform to electronic media style:

Timothy Reynolds, 29, shot and killed his wife Joann, 24, while alone with her in their house today. Police arrested Reynolds on second degree murder charges.

2 Rewrite the following sentence in a way that will alert your audience to pay attention for the names. Include the men's ages, according to electronic media style, as part of the sentence.

The victims are identified as Simon Legget, 54, and Samuel Reed, both of Lenore City.

3 Rewrite the following story into a presentation suitable for radio or television. Pay attention to the need for attribution.

Quality of life in the town will be affected if developers are allowed to clear cut land. A group of concerned citizens, at a public hearing onland use, made that assertion last night at a Town Land Use Commission hearing.

4 Rewrite the following sentences in radio or television style to make them understandable for an electronic media audience.

Persons seeking information can call 491-6484 Monday through Saturday, eight a.m. to 10:30 p.m. and noon to 10:30 p.m. on Sunday.

Democratic Congress members formally challenged electoral votes from the state of Ohio in the 2004 election and sparked a two-hour debate yesterday. This was the second time since 1877 Congress challenged a presidential race.

A new state audit has discovered that the accounting firm hired by the Central Valley School District to oversee its financial affairs was hired without going through the required bidding process and is responsible for allowing a $1.5 million mistake to go unnoticed.

Several state colleges and universities are adopting a new scheme for increasing tuition so that students pay an increased percentage over four years rather than getting hit with large increases erratically throughout their college careers.

A Baptist preacher from Mississippi, 79, was charged yesterday with the murders in 1964 of three civil rights workers.

EXERCISE 2C: Word Usage

Name _____ Date _____

Underline the correct word usage in the capitalized words.

1 The new union proposals are UNIQUE/SOMEWHAT UNIQUE to past negotiations.

2 Mothers will GO UP/GO to Washington tomorrow in a parade to emphasize their new demands for gun control.

3 The new president today FLOUTED/FLAUNTED new weapons before the citizens in a display of power.

4 Correspondent Lamn witnessed George Sming's FUNERAL/FUNERAL SERVICE and files this report.

5 Randy Holstein volunteered to HEAD UP/HEAD the Democratic platform committee, after a chaotic meeting.

6 College graduates find jobs easier to land BECAUSE/SINCE they've attended school.

7 The finance committee is a committee THAT/WHICH legislators find challenging to work on during legislative meetings.

8 The court ordered police to LET/LEAVE African American demonstrators alone after three police-related killings.

9 The new Dell computer demonstrated LESS/FEWER problems than any other computer tested at the computer exposition.

10 Stock market trends look LIKE/AS IF the current bull market is over.

11 Pastor Simpson's prayer had a calming EFFECT/AFFECT on the audience.

12 All parties EXCEPT/ACCEPT the Cubans agreed to withdrawal from embattled Zinger.

13 AFTERWARD/AFTERWARDS the new Revised Standard Version Bible translation will be read to close the worship service.

14 A HEALTHY/HEALTHFUL vacation idea is a fun-filled week in beautiful Hawaii, where the sun shines daily.

15 Judge Tom O'Neal's speech IMPLIES/INFERS that he opposes abortions, his opponents claim.

16 Amtrak advises advance reservations PRIOR TO/BEFORE/IN ADVANCE OF departure time.

17 New employees are DIFFERENT FROM/DIFFERENT THAN their predecessors SINCE/BECAUSE they don't drink.

18 Sheriff's officers say the victim DROWNED/WAS DROWNED accidentally while alone in the municipal swimming pool.

19 BECAUSE OF/DUE TO/OWING TO the San Francisco earthquake, Senator Reed never did travel there.

20 In a COUPLE/COUPLE OF minutes we'll have a special report from Chicago.

21 Surgeon General William Leonard reports more Americans DIE FROM/DIE OF cancer caused by cigarettes than from all other illness combined.

22 "It is my OPINION/ESTIMATION that historians will be kinder to Harris than we were."

23 High school ORAL/VERBAL English scores indicate ignorance of basic English.

24 MORE THAN/OVER fifty percent of all Americans go on vacations each year.

EXERCISE 2C: Word Usage (continued)

Name _____ Date _____

25 Snowmobiles may TOTALLY DEMOLISH/DESTROY the ECOLOGICAL/ENVIRONMENTAL habitat of the wild zulu bird.

26 The new anti-obscenity law won't allow EITHER FILMS OR MAGAZINES/BOTH FILMS AND MAGAZINES.

27 The FIRST/FIRST ANNUAL energy meet took place in Willoughby Convention Center today.

28 Dorn National Bank plans to build BESIDE/BESIDES the Smith University campus.

29 Opponents claim the new administration will be COMPOSED/COMPRISED of many friends of President-elect Budynas.

30 The Oakland City Council has reached a CONSENSUS/CONSENSUS OF OPINION not to renew the Raiders football lease.

31 Reporters noted a RETICENCE/RELUCTANCE by President Clasquinn to speak during the news conference.

32 The AGGREGATE/TOTAL national debt today reached five-billion dollars, according to Treasury Secretary Sullivan.

33 Bank robbers ELUDED/ALLUDED police after they triggered the vault alarm.

34 Unemployment is highest AMONG/BETWEEN the 20 to 30 age group, the government reports.

35 New government DATA/DATUM show television to be the most-watched MEDIUM/ MEDIA.

EXERCISE 2D: Grammar

Name _____ Date _____

Edit the following sentences to conform with radio/TV style. Correct all errors.

1. These advantages, in addition to the clear presentation and simple style, makes this a stylebook you will want for your newsroom.

2. The finest cameras and most skilled videographers are used by this station.

3. When the letter you sent to the Business Office was not forwarded, there was naturally some confusion between their accounting division and I.

4. Neither of these possibilities were explained in your query to the station manager.

5. We were pleased to learn that the crowd at your tour were so enthusiastic about the new control room.

6 | If anyone else was on his beat, they would do the same thing.

7 | The videotape editor who had sent three orders and two requests for extra cassettes were visited by our representative.

8 | Beginning her report Monday, she found she would not be through until the following week.

9 | The reporter of the story and not the three accountants who supplied the facts and cost estimates believe the charge is necessary.

10 | This crusade was conducted to reduce the number of fatal highway accidents at the end of the year which was successful.

11 | Believing the man was innocent, the case was dismissed by the judge.

12 | Employing such communication media as newspapers, radio and television, the campaign platform of the party was presented.

EXERCISE 2E: Pronunciation

Name _____ Date _____

Write pronouncers in the right column for the words in the left column. Use phonetic pronunciation with the combination of words and letter combinations in upper and lower case letters. Upper case means more emphasis, lower case less emphasis. Try to make the pronouncer actually sound the way the word(s) should be pronounced with correct emphasis.

Example: Boston = BOSS-tun

Normally Typed Word	Pronouncer
1 Cairo (the Egyptian capitol)	_____
2 Cairo (the town in Illinois)	_____
3 Chicago	_____
4 Boise (capitol of Idaho)	_____
5 Arkansas	_____
6 Oregon	_____
7 Brussels (the city in Belgium)	_____
8 Junta (South American government)	_____
9 Tennessee	_____
10 Pueblo (American Indian dwelling)	_____

Critical Thinking Questions

 Directions: The following questions are provided to help you examine the deeper meanings and complexities of the various issues under discussion. Answer each question to the best of your ability after a thoughtful review of the subject at hand.

1. Some journalists contend that their only job is to provide information. To what extent, if any, is the journalist obligated to engage and motivate the audience as part of the reporting process?

2. Think of examples of how a numbers-laden story on rises in healthcare premium costs can best be told in an electronic news report.

3. Give at least one example for each of the following types of people on how you might write a story about the impact of terrorism in the local community so your words/language are relevant to the targeted audience:

- men over age 50
- mothers in their 30s/40s
- business-minded professionals age 25–40
- people over 65
- singles in their 20s

4. In television news, the "direct quote" from a source is in the form of a soundbite (person speaking on camera). Explain the importance of writing a good intro into and exit out of the soundbite so the comments make sense to viewers.

5. In 1869 the *New York Times* condemned journalists for "dramatizing the research process" by publishing direct quotations. Discuss the role and purpose of quoting sources directly, and how direct quotations sometimes harm the source.

6. Chapter 1 provides numerous guidelines to help writers produce conversational copy. Why is it important in electronic media to avoid "the written word spoken aloud?"

7. Audiences recognize and appreciate good writing. Why is mastery of the rhythms and patterns of language so important to the professional writer?

8. Discuss the changes in writing style and approach that any print writer must make when moving over to write the spoken word.

Self-Review Questions

Directions: Each of the self-review questions below addresses information contained in this chapter. Answer each question to the best of your ability, then review the chapter as necessary to further strengthen your understanding of each concept or issue.

1. Explain the major differences between writing for print and for electronic media.

2. Why is it important to write to a specific audience rather than to a faceless mass audience?

3. Explain how to treat numbers in copy when writing for the spoken media.

4. What are the differences between accuracy, fairness, and objectivity?

5. Explain how to quote sources (attribute) in spoken copy.

6. Explain how to properly use names, ages, and titles in spoken copy.

7. Explain the differences between active and passive voice. Provide examples of each.

8. Explain the role of phonetic pronunciation and provide an example or two.

9. Explain how to properly use time references in spoken copy.

10. Provide ten or more examples of proper word usage that you find most challenging in your own writing.

## CHAPTER THREE

Writing the Script

Electronic news media have dramatically expanded in recent years as a result of the rise of the Internet and digital recording forms. For most of the 20th century, there was only radio and then television, both using tape-recorded forms for field audio and video. At the turn of the 21st century, all that changed as digital media recording technology evolved. Still, many of the conventions used in the news industries that have historical roots in the old film, and then "tape," days have continued as part of the news culture.

Later in this chapter you will learn about terms such as **SOT**, often pronounced "saht." Although the acronym stands for "sound on tape," it has come to mean anything in an electronic media story that uses sound. That can mean a comment by a person, the natural sound of birds chirping, or the dominant storytelling audio source in a scene. SOTs are sometimes called nats, if the audio contains sounds from the natural environment, or **soundbite**, if the audio contains a person's comment or observation.

The foundation of each medium used to transmit news and information to an intended audience is the intended audience and the unique capability of the medium being used to transmit the information. For example, to fully engage with a newspaper and its text-filled columns, a person has to be able to read. Because audio is at the core of the medium of radio, the emphasis is on sound — whether from an event itself or from the sound of the reporter's voice. In television, pictures dominate everything

Although much emphasis is placed on video and visual effects in electronic media, sound effects are just as powerful — and sometimes more so — when putting together a package.

from the decisions within a newsroom operation of what to cover to how stories are structured to take advantage of the power of the available visuals.

The new context of the Internet blends the three dominant news technologies — text (from print), sound (formerly the province of radio), and video (from television). Thus, a Web page might have a few paragraphs of a story with separate jumps to streaming audio and/or video so a person can use the computer like a radio or like TV by clicking on the respective Web page navigation buttons.

In this text, the dominant form we address is television reporting and writing, as it is the form that most people in contemporary society use to get their news and information. Keep in mind, though, that the effective electronic media journalist must be able to convey information and tell stories effectively in all three forms — text, sound, and video.

FORMATTING THE SCRIPT

In contemporary news organizations, so much complicated information has to pass through so many hands to get a story constructed properly and transmitted to the intended audience that formatting of scripts is a key element. The focus of contemporary news organizations on immediacy and rapid transmission to audiences requires blending audio, video, graphic, and text elements, which usually involves many people in sometimes widely separated locations. Therefore, everyone connected with story production and transmission has to understand the same conventions of scripting, editing, and the linguistic shorthand of the industry. This often occurs in the context of a live update and requires that complicated operations be conducted quickly and correctly.

By its very nature, news is governed by minutes and seconds. The people in the control room during a live newscast have little time to figure out what a reporter or producer wants. The script has to be clear, concise, and correct so everything will be inserted at just the right time. Although journalists are accustomed to these requirements when collecting information and writing a story, they sometimes are not careful enough about the technical side of the script that is the road map of production technicians.

A television story is really three stories that come together on the air as one:

1. The story you write in words and the reporter or anchor reads.

2. The story of video and superimposed graphics to visualize what is going on.

3. Sound that helps tell the story.

When you bring the visual elements — constructed by photographers, editors, technical directors, audio engineers, character generator operators, and tape room technicians — together with the words of the journalist, you have the powerful combination known as a TV news story. Done well, the visuals and the written words reinforce one another and become more than either is separately. Done poorly, the story is deficient at best. At worst, it blows up on the air, disarming the viewer and embarrassing the news organization. We've all seen weird-looking things on television news. Most of them can be traced to a seemingly small error in script format that causes a major on-air disaster.

> *Print media can tell the story of the mail service, but visual media work best when they tell the story of a single letter.*
> JOHN GRIERSON
> Documentary Filmmaker

In radio, words-only carry the story. In television, pictures carry the story, with words serving to interpret and explain. So heavy is the visual impact of television that stations commonly rebate 75 percent of the airtime cost if the picture portion of a commercial is lost during broadcast. If only the sound is lost, the advertiser receives a 25 percent refund. Similarly, in television news, pictures carry great impact. In the best television news, words support visuals. Most half-hour television newscasts contain fewer words than appear on the front page of many newspapers. Visuals and graphics have to deliver a tremendous amount of information.

Watch any TV newscast with the volume turned down and observe how much information you can translate from visuals into words. If you were to write down every detail — height, weight, sex, age, facial features of every person in the news, descriptions of events and activities portrayed on television, and the information from graphics — your report would swell quickly.

In the developing world of Internet journalism, the television and radio elements are brought together within the context of a Web page using text blocks and menu buttons. Thus, concepts of writing for print — an inverted pyramid structure with the key elements of *who, what, when, where,* and *why* front-loaded within the first few paragraphs — are emphasized. Then menu buttons are provided for the media consumer to click into an audio or a video channel for more on the story in the sound and/or picture format.

Typically, an Internet site plugs in a television story with a few sentences of set-up text. That text introduction is similar to the way an anchor lead-in would be used to introduce the report in a regular newscast. Often, Internet sites boil down those leads to just a phrase that serves as a headline introduction with the story title as a hot link to click into the video, audio, or text full report. Taking a normal television script and converting it into an Internet site story (see more about this technique in Chapter 8) can be a simple matter, but if writers do it sloppily, the online version will be a waste of time.

The story samples in this chapter provide more information on how the narrative and video elements would be constructed. Also, you might go online and check out the following major Internet news sites for examples of how computer technology and Web site design bring together text, audio, and video technology. Of the hundreds of helpful news sites, these suggested sites are stable and unlikely to change their URLs in the near future:

CNN home page — http://cnn.com/

American Journalism Review home page (includes top news links) — http://ajr.newslink.org/menu.html

National Public Radio — http://www.npr.org

The New York Times online — http://www.nytimes.com

Regardless of what storytelling technique is used (print, sound, pictures), each has benefits and limitations. Print does not have the emotional power that is conveyed more effectively through pictures. Sound has a dimension of its own, as listeners create mental images based on what they hear. Television provides powerful

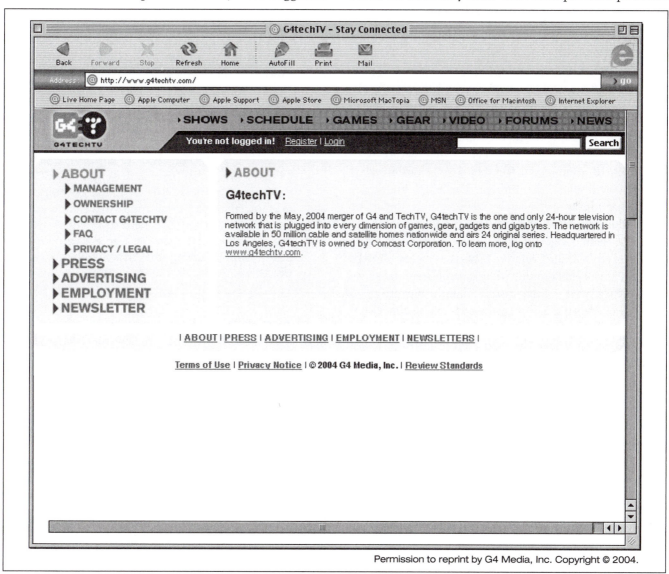

One of the pioneers of streaming audio/video news, techtvnews provided a high-tech-focused streaming audio and video product aimed at Internet users.

pictures that may be misunderstood because of what the camera does not show, or uses close-ups that distort reality.

Print without sound, sound without pictures, pictures without context — all limit storytelling ability to some extent. The details, such as names of people in the news, what direction streets run, how long police officers have been on the scene, or the complexities of a legal story, may not be clear when the story is told in one form. And, though the visual medium may show powerful pictures of something, viewers might not understood more abstract concepts that are not easily shown in video from the scene of an event. Because of these limitations, electronic journalists of the 21st century must understand how to bring words, sound, and pictures together and use each storytelling tool effectively.

WRITING TO THE PICTURE

Because television has come to dominate contemporary life, we receive a barrage of pictures. It is human nature to believe what we see, even when we know that pictures can lie just like anything else. Therefore, great care has to be taken to use appropriate pictures in a story, and to provide a narrative script that helps frame an accurate context for the media consumer.

When you write for electronic media, pictures will rule much of your script, for they are an omnipresent part of television and the Internet. The length and structure of the visual story determine how long the script can be, and sometimes the order in which your information is presented. The narrative copy must flow along with the visuals, and reference what is being shown. You will have to talk about what is being seen and show the audience what is being discussed in the narrative.

This **referencing** is a critical factor in effective visual storytelling. Without effective referencing and congruence between the narrative and pictures, a disjuncture occurs, creating misunderstanding and confusion as what a person hears and sees fight each other. What is heard or read in a narrative accompanying pictures must not fight the visuals being used.

Preview the Video (VTR)

The process of writing video copy begins with a preview of the video to be used before editing, if possible. The preview helps you in two ways:

1. The preview alerts you to possible treatments of the news based on the visuals you have to work with.

2. The preview lets you know which information you must put in words and which can be carried by the visuals alone.

SPOTLIGHT

Writing for Pictures

As one of the least intuitive pieces of writing for electronic media, you have to learn to use the pictures to help tell the story and not force the text to give viewers all the necessary information. The video should be supplemental and worthwhile, but it becomes wasted material if the text says exactly what viewers see on-screen. Two things can help new electronic media reporters and writers improve this craft.

1. Initially, in learning how to use video as well as audio you may want to take a front-page story from your local newspaper and create a broadcast news script, complete with details on possible video shots. Assume you have the time and resources necessary for any video footage you want, and be creative in using pictures to help tell your story. Remember, though, not t to let video serve as mere background material but actually help viewers better understand a situation.

2. A more sophisticated attempt to improve your audio/video writing skills is to record a newscast so you can review stories carefully. Choose one story (start with simple VO–SOTs before trying more difficult package stories) and turn the volume on mute. Try writing your own script to the video, and then watch how the reporter did it. Compare your attempts to use video in telling the story with the reporter's.

Almost always, you can glean ideas for the lead and body of your script as you preview the visuals. Linda Ellerbee, Emmy award-winning broadcaster and developer of Nick News on Nickelodeon, argues that changing the words to fit the video works best if you have good visuals. "Changing the words to fit the pictures makes more sense, because once the video is in the house, you cannot change it. . . . Don't misunderstand. This technique works only when the pictures do tell the story."[1]

Too often, when the process is ignored, the newscast has the look of a poorly produced slide show, with video serving mostly as visual fruit salad to support unrelated words. The same thing happens on a Web page. If the copy one reads is not the same message as the pictures presented, there will be a disconnect in viewer understanding.

Write Loose

If anything, the scriptwriter should underwrite scripts that accompany visuals. Few elements of the newscast are as distracting as the constant chatter of a newscaster's voice over powerful, dramatic visuals and compelling natural sounds. Pauses become an element of the script. If the copy has too much detail, the audience will not remember it anyway. Instead, the scriptwriter should deliver impressions and let the visuals tell as much of the story as possible.

Avoid the Obvious

Anyone who writes for visual media can profit from the advice of creative writers. The best writers deliver just enough detail to stimulate the imagination. They allow people to think, instead of telling them what to think. This approach allows the viewer to supply information from past experience and, hence, to participate more directly in the vicarious experiences of television news.

Edward R. Murrow became a legend because of his simple, precise reporting. One night during a World War II blackout in London, he remembered, "It was so dark I walked bang into a cow and she seemed glad to see me." Another time, after accompanying a bombing raid to Berlin, he reported, "The clouds formed castles and battlements in the sky." Murrow used few adjectives, yet his writing was descriptive and provided strong mental images for his listeners.

The same techniques can be used when writing to video. Written words should provide only the information the visuals cannot. The scriptwriter must ensure that the words do not create an image in the mind that conflicts with images on the television or computer screen. (Is the governor's wife really "vivacious?") If your tape shows tired people standing in long lines outside the unemployment office, the viewers do not need to hear how weary the waiting people are. The tape will show their fatigue.

Perhaps you have video of Miss America's arrival in your area on a windy day. When she steps from the plane and descends the steps, a gust of wind blows off her hat and frazzles her hair, and a piece of wind-blown paper wraps around her neck. As footage of these scenes is rolling that night on your newscast, you could say something to the effect, "High winds tore off Miss America's hat as she emerged from the plane, then wind-blown trash assaulted her again as she came down the steps." But consider how much more elegant your writing will be if you say, just before we see Miss America emerge from the plane, "The wind played tricks on Miss America from the moment she arrived," followed

by momentary narrator silence as the tape tells its own story and lets us see for ourselves what happened.

Reference Words to Pictures

When people or objects in the visual story must be identified, the words should be aligned to the pictures as closely as possible. This is what is known as referencing, mentioned earlier. The script must be exactly on cue, for example, when a close-up shot of a newsmaker appears on the screen. The person's name should be voiced on air just as the person's picture appears. Or a police officer might be holding up a murder weapon for display. The image will tell your audience that the murder weapon is a gun, but not what caliber it is or that it was stolen hours earlier from a pawn shop just down the street.

SCRIPT FORMATS

Script formats vary from one news operation to another, although almost all video scripts follow the split-page format that evolved in television news with director commands on the left and copy to be read by anchors/reporters on the right. The formats used in this text prepare you for the general approach to successful scripting. When you actually go to work in an electronic media newsroom, local preferences may differ from the script formats presented here.

The type of format depends on the technology. For example, radio scripts usually are not in the split-page form because they are less complicated and radio reporters often roll their own audio inserts, or **actualities,**

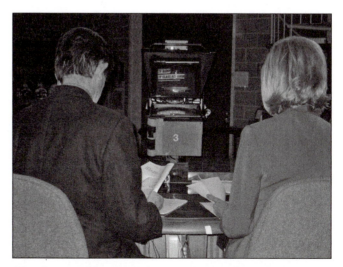

The format for television news scripts is done for a specific purpose. The left column gives directions for producers about what comes next in the report or newscast. The right column becomes the text for the teleprompter from which anchors read.

during newscasts. So usually there isn't a director. Depending on the size of the station, there may be an audio engineer, but even then, just a nod by the news anchor through the window to the radio control room will cue the engineer to roll an audio insert.

With Web sites, the actual story production of television type reports typically is done with the TV scripting formats included in this chapter. When the Internet service's Web site producers get the final report, they simply write headlines or short leads and insert click buttons to direct the Internet user to the location where the full report is stored for viewing.

The director's instructions for electronic media stories usually are written on the left side of the page, with major commands in ALL CAPS. Information the director needs, but is of lesser importance, is indented under the major commands and appears in upper and lower case. Generally speaking, anything that, if missed, will cause the story to blow up on the air is in ALL CAPS. In contrast, things such as superimposed titles of interviewees and indications of a geographical location are indented and in upper and lower case. That way, the director has immediate, visual clues regarding the relative importance of various elements. A lot is going on in the control room, and people have to glance away from scripts to monitors and at buttons to push. With easy-to-find visual clues, the director's job becomes easier.

News copy, on the right side of the page, usually is written largely with normal capitalization. Although some anchors prefer to use all caps for their scripts, research has shown that the normal type is easier for most people to read properly. Scripts for most short stories (20 to 30 seconds) can be written on a single page. Most scripts contain a short, on-camera lead that introduces the story and sets up the viewer for the tape that follows. If you consistently begin visuals and story narrative together, the show will look choppy and lack proper flow. This practice is acceptable from time to time, such

BASIC TERMINOLOGY

Actuality means a radio audio insert or sound cut played in a story. It is the same as a soundbite in television.

Soundbite means a piece of sound from the scene, or an interview of a person involved in a story. It is a bite of sound that helps bring a sense of immediacy and reality to the report.

CART is an old term used in radio for a taped actuality or report played on audiotape, often within a self-contained cartridge. New digital technology allows such storage in other forms, but the term is still used in many operations for anything inserted on recorded media. For that reason, the term is used in our sample script for a radio report.

VO means "voice-over" video. The pictures appear on the air with background sound, but the anchor keeps narrating story information while we're looking at scenes from where the video was shot.

SOT stands for "sound on tape," or video in which all the sound is from the scene, often an interview or a speech. Although SOT has become a common reference throughout the industry over the years to mean videotape with sound full, SOT is used also in operations that have converted to digital video and no longer use tape. The news anchor stops talking during SOTs.

TRT, which means "total running time" of the video element, refers to only the video's running time. It tells the director exactly how much video time exists before he or she has to get the anchor camera or other visual element on air before the picture goes to black.

Story time is recorded in the upper right corner of the first page of each story script. All stories have a story time, the time required for everything including the anchor on-camera lead, the video inserts, and any other elements that comprise the complete story. Story time is not the same as TRT. TRT is just the video element. Story time is the whole thing.

CG means character generator. It consists of computer type that will appear on the screen.

Outcue refers to the last three to five words in a soundbite.

Tag is the term indicating a brief wrap-up or ending to a story.

AT refers to the time when the sound on the video has to be raised while the person on tape talks, and lowered when the anchor resumes the narration.

Split-squeeze remote refers to placing one or more people in a frame along with a frame of the anchor all on screen at the same time.

as when you lead live with a related story, then cut directly to recorded video and begin reading the new but related copy. Otherwise, viewers will be most comfortable with the regular pattern of a brief, five- to ten-second lead-in before the video appears on screen.

Television news scripts are fairly simple if you keep a few technical things in mind. As mentioned, these are really two scripts stuck together. On the left is a script for the director of the show, which is a kind of road map for the technical crew to follow in switching among video sources, studio cameras, and other audio and video sources. The second script, on the right, is the one the anchors read. In a given story, part of the copy may be read on camera and part covered by field video.

Video is timed from its first frame. When video is inserted into a story, the video time is different from the story time. Story time is the whole thing, including the anchor lead-in. Video time — indicated in script formats as **TRT** — is just the video portion, not including the on-camera anchor copy.

All script pages have numbers. The preferred style is to use letters for segments of the newscast and numbers for stories within each segment. Thus, A-1, B-1, and C-1 are all the first stories in their respective segments. If a story has two or more pages, lower-case letters are added after the main page number (for example, A-1a, A-1b, A-1c).

STORY SAMPLES

The following pages present samples of various scripts. The first is of a typical radio newscast format including an **actuality** (or radio soundbite). That is followed by several different kinds of television scripts. Because television is a much more complicated medium than radio, different script forms are required for the variations of story types. The first TV format is a simple anchor on-camera read. The script samples then progress through more complicated stories including VOs, VO-SOT–VOs, reporter packages, and live remotes. Each script sample is in the proper format and includes the proper commands along with script copy explaining the details of the script. Scripting may seem complicated at first, but it really is quite simple — and logical. Please read through the sample scripts before continuing with the story samples.

You'll find actual news stories written in the proper script formatting beginning on page 61. The following story discussions refer to those scripts.

A reporting team interviews a news source for a broadcast news package. In the script, the source's comments, or soundbite, will carry the designation SOT, for Sound On Tape.

Story Sample 1: Typical Reader Format

Story Sample 1 (page 61) is about a plane crash in Nevada. It begins with the anchor on camera, so we have the anchor's initials, AB, at the left margin of the director's column (left column of the script format). Directly across from those initials, in the reader column, the anchor initials appear again, but this time within parentheses. Whenever you want to tell the anchor something that is not to be read, the information is within parentheses.

In this story, a **voice-over (VO)** video covers part of the anchor read. The VO instruction appears directly across from where we want the anchor narration to begin. The anchor column does not require instructions. Studio cameras have little red lights that indicate if they are turned on or off. When the anchor is reading along and the light goes out as the director takes the video insert, the anchor will know that the video has begun.

Just below the director's VO instruction is the **CG** indicator, indented. CG means "character generator," or computer type that will appear on the screen. The indentation indicates to the director that it isn't crucial and if something has to be dropped, eliminating CG won't cause the story to blow up.

Because the anchor takes about 22 seconds to read the portion of the script covered by video from the scene, the editor cuts 22 seconds plus a little pad. A little **pad** video always goes at the end of the tape to ensure that no "black" goes on the air. Otherwise the video might drop out before we get the buttons punched for the next visual element. Immediately across from the TRT (Total Running Time), in the anchor column, the end marks # # # are used to indicate that the story is finished after the last line of narration.

The on-camera anchor lead begins, "Just last week . . . ." Copy to be read on the air should be timed by reading it aloud. That way you will hear the sound of the copy and the times will be more accurate. This paragraph takes about six seconds to read. Therefore, the story time in the upper right corner will be :28 (the lead time of six seconds, plus the :22 for the video narration). The script contains no reference to individual video shots, their length or content.

Story Sample 2: On-Camera Reader with Graphic Format

In Story Sample 2 (page 62) we make a few adjustments to the format. First, following the anchor's initials in the director's column is a slash (/) and the notation "Box: Crash." That tells the director we want the anchor on

camera, but with a box graphic over one of the anchor's shoulder. Normally you don't indicate which shoulder, because that is a production format element the director determines ahead of time.

The anchor reads two short paragraphs, then stops for a soundbite of Sam Tucker. SOT, which appears in the director's column to tell the director to take the video insert with the sound full. SOT also appears in the anchor column, but enclosed in parentheses, which tells the anchor to stop reading. In this case, if the ( ) were not there, the anchor might take it as a cue to say "SOT" on the air. Parentheses are used in the anchor column to tell the anchor to do something, but the anchor is never to read it.

Sam Tucker's soundbite runs 26 seconds. We put the **outcue** — the last three to five words the person says in the soundbite — just above the **TRT** designation. That way the technical crew sees the outcue words and gets ready to make another switch when hearing them about 26 seconds into the tape.

After the soundbite ends, we have to come back to the anchor on camera for a **tag** to the story. So we put the anchor's initials in the director's column under the TRT, and in the anchor's column we put the anchor's initials inside parentheses, followed by the copy to be read. Finally, # # # indicates the end of the story.

Story Sample 3: On-Camera Reader Format (multiple changes)

Sometimes the anchor has to stay on camera, but the special graphics being used behind, or over the shoulder of, the anchor have to change. Story Sample 3 (page 63) is an example of how to do an on-camera anchor reader that has multiple changes in the over-the-shoulder box graphic commonly used in television news production. The anchor stays on camera all the time.

The director just has to know where to change the graphics in the shoulder box. Those indicators are placed directly across from the narration copy. The director can't read your mind, so if you put the box changes all in a short list together, some strange-looking things may go out on the air. Putting box changes across from the point in the narration where you want the change to occur gives the director a spatial sense of when they happen, along with the order of the changes.

Story Sample 4: VO-SOT-VO Format

Story Sample 4 (page 65) is an example of how to script a VO-SOT-VO format, starting with the anchor on camera, then covering some narration with video, then having a soundbite of a person, and concluding with

Story Sample 1: Typical Reader Format

Slug: Plane crash
Writer: Smith
Date:

Story Time: <u>**28**</u>

AB

(AB)

Just last week, two other planes crashed into the same mountain . . . earning it the new name, Nevada Triangle.

Any similarity to the Bermuda Triangle ends with the name. Mount Diablo is in desert country, a day's walk from civilization.

Search crews wandered the area for two days this week before they picked up signals from the plane's crash locator.

Two F-A-A officials suffered heat stroke and were evacuated after daytime temperatures reached 120 degrees.

Oldtimers call the area unfit for man and warn . . . enter at your own peril.

VO

CG: Mt. Diablo
        "Nevada Triangle"

TRT: 22+pad

# # #

Story Sample 2: On-Camera Reader with Graphic Format

Slug: Plane crash

Writer: Smith

Date:

AB/Box: Crash

SOT

    CG: Sam Tucker

        "Nevada Triangle" resident

    Outcue: ". . . it's just an old pile
        of rocks!"

TRT: 26+pad

AB

Story Time: :40

(AB)
Just last week, two other planes crashed into the same mountain . . . earning it the new name, Nevada Triangle.

Oldtimers say the mountain has claimed other lives in its time, but not because the peak has any mystical powers.

(SOT)

(AB)
The search resumes tomorrow for the three missing planes.

# # #

Story Sample 3: On-Camera Reader Format (multiple changes)

Slug: Faces & places
Writer: Smith
Date:

Story Time: __40__

AB/Box: Faces & Places

/Box: Madonna

/Box: Map

/Box: Kennedy

(AB)
In "Faces and Places" tonight . . . we'll start with the latest adventures of Madonna.

She peeked around a door at a New York restaurant today, while in town to take part in an international film festival honoring French actresses.

Speaking of faces, here's the political face of the United States showing the pattern of victory for recent Republican Senate candidates.

Republicans won throughout the West and Midwest. But Dixie belonged to the Democrats, and enough seats were retained in the Eastern states to retain a slim majority.

All of which is why Senator Ted Kennedy looked so relieved at his victory party in Boston. Kennedy won despite the most spirited campaign against him since he was first elected to office.

Obviously any margin of victory makes you smile, even a slim one.

# # #

more anchor narration covered with video. The big differences in this format are the AT times and a second voice-over tape element after the soundbite.

The AT times indicate when the sound on the tape has to be raised while the person on tape talks, and then lowered when the anchor is supposed to start narrating again. AT times indicate major changes in key elements for the technical crew to make while the video keeps going. In this case, the audio engineer will have to move the audio board slide up a bit — to increase the sound from the tape when the person talks — and then slide it back down again when the person is finished and the anchor narration resumes. The VO tells the director the anchor has to talk over the pictures. Again, the TRT is at the bottom of the story.

In this case, the on-camera lead is :07, a :15 voice-over lead into the soundbite, a soundbite of :34, and then another VO tag of :10. The story time is the TRT plus the on-camera lead-in, or about 1:06. You have two CG indicators, one for the locator over the first VO showing where this video was shot, and the second consisting of the name and second line title or description of who talks in the soundbite.

By the way, note that we do not use an abbreviation for the word "Mount" in the anchor column, but we do for the character generator (CG) in the director's column. Abbreviations should be avoided in the anchor column because they can be easily confused. The CG indicator, however, should be typed exactly as you want the information to appear on the screen. In many newsrooms the person who operates the character generator computer gets the information directly from the scripts. In this case, "Mt." would be best for the typed locator to be superimposed on the video.

Story Sample 5: VO-SOT-VO with Anchor Tag Format

Story Sample 5 (page 66) is not much different from what you've already seen. It is a VO-SOT-VO with the addition of an anchor on-camera tag finishing the story. Again, the major elements the director must see quickly are to the left margin of the director's column: the VO, the AT times for the SOT and second VO, the TRT when the tape runs out, and finally the anchor initials indicating when the anchor is to come back on camera again.

Story Sample 6: Live-Shot Format

The final example is Story Sample 6 (page 67), which shows how to do a **split-squeeze remote**. You've seen these before, when television operations put two people in little frames talking to each other or being interviewed by a reporter. This effect is commonly used for anchors to toss to and from live shots of reporters in the field or to interview people from remote locations.

In the director's column, you put the initials of the anchor who will do the talking first, followed by a slash (/) and the words "split-squeeze remote," followed by an indicator of what is to be in the second frame. In this case, we're putting Homer Jones there.

In the anchor column are the questions to be asked of Jones, following the anchor initials in regular script form. When Jones answers, we have an indicator inside parentheses for the anchor to wait for the answer.

As Jones answers, the director puts him full screen with his name in place of the left column anchor initials. Normally, when the person is shown full-screen for the first time, his or her name and title are placed after a CG. Or the name could be placed in the split-squeeze shot as long as the CG operator spaces the graphics correctly so the person's name appears under his or her picture. When the anchor asks another question, we go back to the split-squeeze remote of both of them on screen, then switch back to a full shot of Jones when he answers again.

Or both people can be up on the screen as they engage in the conversation, which is what our example does when the second question is asked, Jones answers, and the third question is asked. Then we go back to Jones full for the answer to the third question. We end the interview back on a split-squeeze remote. Usually the show director ad-libs these interchanges to some extent, as we don't really know what a person will say, and how long it will last, on a live interview.

ENDNOTES

1. Ellerbee, Linda. "And So It Goes: My Adventures in Television News," *Playboy*, April 1986, p. 198.

Story Sample 4: VO-SOT-VO Format

Slug: Plane crash
Writer: Smith
Date:

Story Time: __1:06__

AB/Box: Plane crash

VO

    CG: Mt. Diablo
        "Nevada Triangle"

(AB)
    Indian folklore credits Mount Diablo in western Nevada with mystical powers . . . and this week aviators are taking note.
    Since last weekend three planes have crashed on the mountain's western slope . . . earning it the new nickname, Nevada Triangle.
    Other pilots have reported close calls with the peak, among them Las Vegas charter pilot Ted Ferrell.
    He says he's not superstitious, but neither is he a fool.

AT: 15 SOT

    CG: Ted Ferrell
        Charter Pilot

    Outcue: ". . . a high, dangerous mountain I'd rather fly around."

(SOT)

AT: 49 VO

(AB)
    Ferrell says, if anything, he expects the legend surrounding Mount Diablo to grow bigger and more ominous with time.
    But it's a reputation for mystic power, the pilot says, of little real substance.

TRT: 59+pad

# # #

Story Sample 5: VO-SOT-VO with Anchor Tag Format

Slug: Food protest
Writer: Smith
Date:

Story Time: _58_

AB/Box: Protesters

(AB)
Mayor Davis walked straight into a
hornet's nest today . . . It was a
confrontation between truck drivers and
shoppers.

VO
    CG: Big Foods
        14th & Marshal
        North Little Rock

At issue is the price of food at two
local supermarkets . . . both with
contracts that guarantee annual wage
hikes for union truck drivers.

Today a group of citizens said
enough is enough. They demanded
Mayor Davis ask for the Governor's
support.

AT: 13 SOT
    CG: Elizabeth Windsor
        Grocery shopper

(SOT)

Outcue: ". . . on the state level,
           not the local one."

AT: 31 VO

(AB)
Local truckers argue they're already
underpaid and they'll shut down
deliveries if they don't get a raise. The
result would be a serious food crisis at
local supermarkets.

Just the talk about that possibility
has caused a run on groceries at Big
Foods and Wiggly Pig outlets in North
Little Rock.

TRT: 46+pad
AB

The truckers say a strike vote may be
taken as early as next week. No word
yet whether the Governor plans to get
involved in the dispute before then.

               ###

Story Sample 6: Live-Shot Format

Slug: Rescue interview   Story Time: _1:30_
Writer: Smith
Date:

AB/Split-squeeze remote

          (AB)
    Tonight we have Homer Jones, the man who rescued the little girl, live to talk about the ordeal.
    Thanks for being with us, Mr. Jones.
    What went through your mind when you jumped into the river after Amy Prescott?
          (Jones talks)

Remote
     CG: Homer Jones
          Rescued girl

AB/Split-squeeze remote

          (AB)
    Have you ever had any special training in rescuing people?
          (Jones talks)

          (AB)
    What did the little girl say to you after you got to her and were hanging onto that tree trunk, waiting for the firemen to get a line out to you?
          (Jones talks)

Remote

AB/Split-squeeze remote

          (AB)
    Thanks a lot for being with us tonight. You really are a hero, Mr. Jones, and what you did says a lot about the kind of people who live in South Railswitch, Utah.
          # # #

EXERCISE 3A: Writing a News Script

Name _____ Date _____

1 Use the following fact sheet to write a standard format news script, complete with director's instructions. (For your convenience, standard script blanks are provided at the end of this exercise.) Consult the scene breakdown so your script will match the visuals as edited. Commonly used abbreviations are:

Est. LS	= Establishing long shot	MS	= Medium shot
CU	= Close-up	MLS	= Medium long shot
MCU	= Medium close-up	LS	= Long shot

Story #1: Threshing Bee

Facts: This weekend (today) Platte County Fairgrounds Platte City, Mo. Twentieth Annual Old Fashioned Threshing Bee and Picnic. Dozen old time threshers McCormick Deering, John Deere International Harvester, Wilson's Thresher, showing how it used to be in the good old days 600 people attending the day film shot and aired machines (including dozens of old tractors . . . some with spoke wheels dating back to 1900) all makes and descriptions . . . most still running machines circling the block square fairground serving watermelons homemade ice cream barbecue beef many people brought tents and sleeping bags to stay overnight many old timers fairgrounds clogged with smoke old timers said the air still has a "clean smell" Photographer burned shirt as hot soot and sparks drifted through air no admission charge car races at night little boys impressed with the old machines and tractors some women wore sunbonnets. (Script should fill :47 total time.)

BREAKDOWN SHEET

Scenes		Scene Length	AT*
LS	— establishing shot fairgrounds with steam engine visible	04	04
MCU	— man taps throttle; series of rapid cuts shows machine speeding up, belt running, etc.	11	15
MS	— man feeds bundles oats from truck into thresher with pitchfork	08	23
Cutaway	— people (some "old timers" in straw hats) standing around watching	02	25
MS	— threshing machine and man operating it	06	31
LS	— smoke pours from thresher; man pitches oats into hopper (he's in a "T" shirt)	08	39
LS	— straw shoots onto pile	05	44
LS -	— fairground	03	47

*Accumulated Time

2. Write scripts from the following facts. No breakdown sheet is provided because the scenes are general and routine in nature. Video of the X-C 80 shows a routine take-off, flight, and landing on the California desert near Edwards Air Force Base. Tape of the packing plant shows general demolition scenes of the old tower (bulldozers, wrecking cranes, dump trucks, etc.). Use a blank script sheet, provided at the end of this section.

STORY #2: X-C 80

Maximum script length: 20 to 25 seconds

Facts: The U.S. Air Force today released footage of one of the two X-C 80 prototype planes built to test long-range bombers and their capability in modern warfare. The prototypes fly at speeds up to 2,000 miles per hour. The plane is made of a composite graphite skin invisible to radar, heat-seeking and laser devices — called by press releases a "revolutionary design concept" in airplane fabrication. Superior even to Stealth weapons technology. The planes were developed as bombers, but hold only the pilot. Each plane cost twelve billion dollars to design, test, and produce. The plane's guidance system was designed in your town.

Story #3: Packing Plant Demolished

Maximum script length: 35 seconds

Facts: Local packing plant is being razed today. It was shut down about two months ago when the company decided to relocate to the Midwest near Chicago, to be closer to major rail lines. The plant was built in 1898 and ran continuously until two months ago. It is located in the north part of the city, an area that will be converted into a new shopping center and low-cost apartment housing complex. The packing plant contributed four million dollars monthly to the local economy and employed 1,900 workers. Many of these workers have been relocated and transferred at company expense to Chicago, but approximately 800 are out of work, most of them with families. The building is an historic landmark and was designed by German architects who began work on the concept in 1895.

EXERCISE 3A: Writing a News Script (continued)

Name _____ Date _____

Story #4: Shooting

Facts: bodies gone when photographer arrived occurred 8505 E. 116th St. [your city] wife in process of getting divorce living with mother husband arrives about 5:30 barges into house has gun (.38 caliber revolver) shoots wife she dies at scene wife's sister in bedroom gets shotgun wounds man before he's wounded throws chair breaks out window flees with shotgun around back of house and into adjoining field police at scene investigating police helicopter called to join in search through woods suspect: John J. Jones, 31, 10001 S. Main St. killed: Jessica Jones, 29, no children, her sister, who wounded Jones, is Cheryl Smith, 22; she suffered head wounds when struck with gun in good condition at General Hospital suspect not located at newstime (ten p.m.) search continuing at that time, but helicopter had been called off search. Script should fill 1:07 total time.

SHOT LIST

Scenes		Scene Length	AT*
Est. LS	— of house shows broken front window	04	04
CU	— house address	02	06
MCU	— detective holding gun (murder weapon)	10	16
MS	— broken glass on floor; detectives in room	05	21
MCU	— blood-stained venetian blinds and other debris on floor	03	24
MS	— kitchen table still set for dinner — detective looking around room, in refrigerator	09	33
CU	— broken window	03	36
LS	— back of house; pan to show path suspect apparently followed; ends with people looking for second gun	06	42
MLS	— helicopter flying overhead	05	47
MLS	— police searching through woods	05	52
MS	— more police search	09	1:01
MLS	— helicopter cutaway	03	1:04
MCU	— police inspecting trail for signs of blood	03	1:07

*Accumulated Time

Script Format

Slug:

Writer:

Date:

Story Time: _____

Script Format

Slug: Story Time: _____
Writer:
Date:

Script Format

Slug:

Writer:

Date:

Story Time: _____

Script Format

Slug: Story Time: _____
Writer:
Date:

Critical Thinking Questions

Directions: The following questions are provided to help you examine the deeper meanings and complexities of the various issues under discussion. After a thoughtful review of the subject, answer each question to the best of your ability.

1. Explain the impact strong writing with great video can have in telling an important story. Likewise, explain when and how it can have a negative impact.

2. Discuss the benefits and limitations of print media, radio, television, and the Internet. As part of your answer, explain which one single medium you believe does the best job of communicating vital news, current events, and public affairs information. Why is this the case?

3. Assume you are teaching the art of writing for electronic media to a friend who has no experience. Explain to your friend all the ways in which a script makes possible the creation of radio and television newscasts. Couch your answer within the contexts of producer, reporter, news anchor, audio and video editor, technical editor, graphic arts department, news marketing and promotion, and audience member.

4. Discuss the importance of audio-video linkage, or referencing, as it contributes to the clear understanding of ideas in television news reporting. In your estimation, what is the likely impact of showing one thing while talking about another?

5. Although script formats vary from one news organization to the next, all audiovisual scripts have several features in common. Name these common features and discuss their contributions to the reporting process.

Self-Review Questions

Directions: Each of the self-review questions below addresses information contained in this chapter. Answer each question to the best of your ability, then review the chapter as necessary to further strengthen your understanding of each concept or issue.

1. What media fall under the heading of "electronic media?" List all of them, from the 1800s to the present.

2. What is the importance of script formatting, and what is its impact on the production process and audience understanding?

3. What is meant by the statement, "A television story is really two stories that come together on the air as one?"

4. What unique skills and abilities are required of the Internet journalist?

5. What is meant by "writing to the picture," and why does it matter?

6. Why is "writing loose" important when creating scripts for audiovisual media?

7. How does an actuality differ from a soundbite?

8. What is a VO-SOT-VO?

9. When writing to pictures, what essential guidelines govern scripting?

10. Define and describe the role of the story tag.

## CHAPTER FOUR

Writing the News Story

News sometimes is determined by information the audience wants to know. This is why some so-called "news" is little more than gossip, such as the latest development in a Hollywood celebrity's love life, or why some "news," such as the story of the attempt by a major tobacco company to help people quit smoking, is closer to public relations than news. Other news tells us of crime in our community or of a local school's effort to raise money for cancer research.

ELEMENTS OF NEWS

Regardless of the event, news contains one or more of the elements discussed next: timeliness, proximity, significance, conflict, prominence, and human interest.

Timeliness

What happens now, what happens in the present, or what will happen in the immediate future — **timeliness** — is news. Newspapers often tell you what happened yesterday. Electronic media are especially adept at fast reporting.

Often you will have little chance to include historical perspective in your writing. You will be unable to say why an event happened, simply because no one has had time to find out by the time you transmit your report. Then you must wait to report the important "why" of events in follow-up reports.

Proximity

What happens close to us, either emotionally or geographically — **proximity** — is another element of news. We tend to be interested in events that happen within our community because quite often they affect us in some way. Who can hear of a car–train

SPOTLIGHT

Applying the News Elements

An understanding of the elements of news will help you highlight what to search for in each story you write. You will be able to define treatment and style for any story because you know how to extract the essence of an event for emphasis in your lead.

Let's take an example: At six o'clock tomorrow morning, firefighters are going on strike for higher pay if wage negotiations aren't ironed out by that time. They want an average wage increase of 70 cents an hour, or a total additional cost for fire-protection services of about three million dollars. The property tax increase needed to cover the higher wages would amount to an average of 18 dollars per household in the community. City and fire union representatives are meeting late into the night.

This story contains all elements of news. The story is happening now. It is happening close to us. If the strike materializes, it has the potential to affect us financially, emotionally, and perhaps even physically by leaving the community without fire protection. Dramatic conflict is present in the form of person-versus-person — firefighters taking drastic action to force a response from the city. Prominent community leaders are helping resolve the problem.

As the reporter for your local news station, how would you cover this story so the "news" elements are highlighted in the most effective manner?

Constant updates and forecasts on the weather are one of the biggest audience draws for television news.

collision without wondering for a split-second whether the victim is someone we know? Who in a community is not affected by rising property values or increased taxes? Who is not interested about the drought or an approaching storm?

We also have tremendous affinity for reports of interesting events that happen far away from us. Sometimes, if the event is big enough, it overshadows the less important happenings in our own community. Stories about American troops fighting overseas, devastation from a hurricane along the East Coast or a tornado in the Midwest, new discoveries in space or in the depths of the ocean — all are of interest to us even if they did not happen close to home. Whether you are dealing with local, national, or world news, you will have to learn to "read" it as your audience would and determine what is most momentous, most interesting, or most significant about the story you are writing.

Significance

What has **significance** to the audience is news. Whatever the story, ask yourself who is affected by it or is interested in it. A metropolitan-area story about a teachers' strike, though important, might directly affect only about one in every 20 people in the audience. A story

about dramatic increases in food prices or a developing cold front could affect almost everyone. As you assess the potential significance of the story, always ask yourself how it affects your audience.

Conflict

Dramatic **conflict** is an another element of the news. Radio and television borrow heavily from traditional theater. These media formats thrive on dramatic conflict. Television prefers the visually dramatic, and both radio and television work best when the sounds and emotions of events are reported. In some respects the preference of electronic journalism for the dramatic is a strength, and in other respects it is a weakness.

Few people in the audience consciously recognize the essential differences that separate print from sound and pictures. Yet, the two are vastly different. Electronic media use sound, color, movement, and light to report. By contrast, print uses words and still pictures. Sound, color, movement, and light traditionally produce emotional responses, whereas print and still photographs tend to produce more literal, rational responses.

Dramatic conflict is whatever happens between two opposing forces. The conflict can be between one person and another, or one nation and another, or it can be between humans and an outside influence or force. Thus, dramatic conflict can be classified in four ways:

1. *Person versus person*: the struggle between individuals in a boxing match, a chess championship, or a senator's fight against organized labor; other examples include the test pilot who fights to keep his job after mandatory retirement age, clashes between pro- and anti-abortion forces, and an elderly woman on welfare struggling to avoid being evicted from her home.

2. *Person versus self*: the struggle of a person to kick a drug addiction; the triumph of athletic achievement in an individual sport (such as a runner seeking to improve her "best time"); the triumph of an individual over a physical handicap.

3. *Person versus fate*: the struggle of an individual to survive a plane crash in the wilderness until help arrives; a public figure's fight against cancer; shipwrecks; families made homeless by fires and disasters.

4. *Person versus nature*: significant weather events; consequences of air and water pollution; individuals who cross the sea alone, by balloon, or on a sailboat.

Prominence

News derives from **prominence**. What happens to prominent people, places, or things makes news. Nearly everyone is interested in prominent names from the U.S. President and his or her family to pop singers, movie stars, professional athletes, and eccentric personalities. Often, such newsmakers provide us with vicarious experiences in the activities and achievements in which we would participate in real life if only we were to have the opportunity, the courage, or the ability. Prominent names in the news capture and recapture listeners' and viewers' attention. Similarly, the famous places and things in our lives — from the Washington Monument to our favorite city landmark — pique our interest.

Human Interest

Ultimately, news is anything people are interested in, whether significant or trivial. These stories have **human interest**. If you think a story would interest most of your audience, it probably is newsworthy. We don't tire of stories about unusual bravery, triumph over incredible odds, success of the underdog, and courage amidst tragedy. The subjects of human interest stories tend to be more like us, and we like news that relates to our own lives.

ELEMENTS OF NEWS

1. *Timeliness*. News is what happens now, what happens in the immediate present, or what may happen.

2. *Proximity*. News is what happens close to us — whether within our own community or that affects us emotionally because we can identify with some aspect of the event.

3. *Significance*. News is what affects us in some way, whether financially (an increase in gasoline prices), physically (cancer-causing food additives), or in some other way that has a direct bearing on us.

4. *Conflict*. News is whatever happens between two opposing forces, whether between individuals, nations, or as the result of fateful occurrences.

5. *Prominence*. News is what happens to famous people, places, or things.

6. *Human Interest*. Ultimately, news is anything people are interested in. If you think a story would interest a majority of your audience, it is probably newsworthy.

Visual Aspect

In the electronic media, some stories become news because they have strong visual elements that we know will attract viewers. All stories have visual potential if the reporter's knowledge and vision are broad enough. How can you visualize abstractions such as inflation, political loyalty, subtle discrimination, or white-collar crime?

Perhaps a reporter stand-up might show what kind of house $350,000 buys today compared to what the same money would have bought a decade earlier, or maybe you can show how many groceries $50 might purchase at current prices in comparison to the amount of groceries the same $50 would buy if annual inflation were to reach 12 percent. Or a family's political loyalty might appear in the shot of a child on his father's shoulders wearing a cap with the candidate's name in bold letters, or political loyalty might be visualized in a meaningful way through a variety of devices ranging from file footage to graphics to legitimate reenactments and even occasional dramatizations, provided these are labeled clearly and presented within the context of a larger news story.

WRITING LEADS

One of the most important things a journalist does is to construct the **lead**, the beginning sentence or two of the story that provides the spark of interest for the audience. The lead is crucial because it must catch the interest of listeners/viewers, as well as hold them for the rest of the story.

Leads are the way stories are opened. In all of the several lead-writing techniques, the bottom line to creating an effective lead is simple: Whatever grabs the attention of the listener/viewer and makes that person want to know more is a good lead. Particularly in recent years, as available channels have increased substantially and fragmented the audience into ever smaller segments, electronic news organizations have emphasized retaining listener/viewer interest. That means providing interesting, compelling information in such a way that the person listening or watching doesn't have an urge to punch the remote for a different channel.

Few organizations encourage their writers to tell all of the essential elements of a story in the first few sentences in the style of a traditional summary lead, discussed next. Instead, even though you may use a summary technique to tell a key aspect of the story in the first sentence or two, facts commonly are salted throughout the story. The best stories are written in a powerful, crisp style with one strong and vital sentence flowing into the next. Each is a necessary and intriguing element to provide information to, and hold the attention of, the person to whom you are communicating.

Summary Lead

Based on knowledge of the audience, the writer has to choose the one or two essential facts for the lead that will telegraph the essence of the story to listeners and viewers. Through the technique of the **summary lead**, you can alert the listeners or viewers to what the story is about and indicate in the first sentence why they should be interested. Looking again at the essential facts of the story of the firefighter's strike, perhaps you decide that the significance of the protest is the potential loss of fire protection within the community if a strike materializes. Your lead then could summarize how the strike might affect your audience: Detroit might be without fire protection by six o'clock tomorrow morning.

In the story's lead you have said why the audience should know about the strike: The listener/viewer may be without fire protection by tomorrow morning. You've created personal interest in the story. Although the summary lead indicates what is to come, it doesn't give much specific information. For this reason, it is sometimes called the "throwaway lead." Certainly you can report just the facts of the story without concern for helping your audience understand the importance of the event,

Before this reporter can step in front of a camera with a coherent report, she must take some time to make the writing compelling so the audience is interested in becoming informed.

but a concern for understanding is the mark of a professional writer.

Other Types of Leads

The nature of news changes from story to story. Your choice of leads can help reflect the special emphasis that each story requires.

Hard News Lead. The **hard news lead** is used most often in breaking news or in updating an already established major news story, as in:

> At least 40 communities in western New Mexico are threatened by radioactivity that escaped late today from a nuclear generating plant near Albuquerque.

By contrast, the summary lead or throwaway lead to the same story would be far less specific, as in:

> Officials are keeping close watch on a potentially dangerous situation in western New Mexico this afternoon.

Another example of the hard news lead is:

> In Chicago, 15 firefighters were injured today and more than 200 persons left homeless in what the city calls its biggest fire in eight years.

In this example, a later hard news lead to update the story might be written:

> Three teenagers have been arrested in Chicago and charged with setting a fire that left 15 firefighters injured and more than 200 homeless.

The hard news lead strikes to the heart of the story. It is an intrinsic part of the story, unlike the summary lead, which can be eliminated without weakening the essential meaning of the story.

Soft News Lead. The **soft news lead** is used most often for feature stories or interpretive "think" pieces. These leads are appropriate whenever you wish to emphasize the lasting value of a story or to play upon the universal human interest inherent in a story. This treatment lifts the event you are reporting out of the category of hard news and gives it a perspective that otherwise might be lost or overlooked in hard news stories.

> Millions of today's Americans grew up in small towns, not knowing the stench of industrial smells or the hustle-bustle of big-city life. It's a memory that more and more Americans would like to go home to.

Within the category of soft news leads are several types of leads that can be used to spice up the newscast. These leads, although useful, are used less frequently than summary leads and hard news leads because of their obvious emphasis on the unusual.

1. A **suspended lead** delays the climax, or the essence of the news, until the very end of the story:

   > A Cheyenne rabbit grower couldn't figure it out last weekend when somebody broke into his garage and stole eight dishes and all his rabbit food. But it all became clear last night when the thief returned and stole all his rabbits.

2. The **question lead** is dangerous if the question lacks substance and fails to elicit audience interest. Again, use it sparingly and only with issues that may lead to debate:

   > Would you go to the moon for ten thousand dollars? A major airline is betting you would and may soon begin selling round-trip tickets to the moon . . . against the day when public space flight becomes practical. The airline says if you buy tickets now, at ten thousand dollars each, you'll be guaranteed passage on the airline's first flight to the moon . . . when and if such flights become practical.

3. The **freak event lead** is natural material for a lead that emphasizes the unusual nature of a story. The lead is constructed to give the unexpected event top billing:

   > A cemetery full of Canada Geese, from 50 to 60 thousand of them, seems to be Hinkley, Ohio's, biggest headache tonight. Conservation officials say the geese are far from their normal migratory routes and have settled on the one lake in the area — in the heart of Hinkley's cemetery.

4. The **well-known expressions lead** capitalizes on sayings that most members of the audience have heard before. But beware of using this type of lead very often. Generally, clichés should be avoided in news writing:

   > A ten-year-old Frankfort boy has proved again Ben Franklin's saying that "a penny saved is a penny earned." Today Jody Murray cashed in his life's savings . . . nearly 170-thousand pennies . . . for a total of nearly 17-hundred dollars. And what will he do with all that money? Why, save it, of course.

5. The **staccato lead** sets the tone of a story. It develops something of a one-two-three punch to get the story off the ground and into the consciousness of your audience. This lead is useful to help summarize a number of related events, such as actions at a city council meeting, or a collective impression of the day's weather.

   > Rain . . . then sleet, snow, and wind . . . that's how the day began along the upper Great Lakes.

6. The **metaphor lead** uses the figure of speech to the story's advantage. It invites comparisons with other aspects of life with which we may be familiar:

   > Mayor Stanford says San Diego is truly the windy city tonight . . . with more than 15-thousand politicians gathered here for the national mayors' conference.

7. The **literary allusion lead** features references to fictional or historical characters.

Edward R. Murrow made such a reference during a radio report from World War II London when he reported, "For a moment I thought I was back in the London of Mr. Pickwick's time."

Another lead of this type is:

Shakespeare would feel at home tonight in Ashland, Oregon . . . city of the famous Shakespearean festivals.

8. The **parody lead** is a take-off on events and sayings currently in vogue and of widespread public interest. Some television commercials, for instance, burn themselves into our consciousness and become part of our everyday national vocabulary. If not overdone, these events and sayings give life to some radio and television leads:

They say you go around only once in life, but Voyager crew members say they're going around the world twice this year . . . if favorable weather holds.

Many times you may not be conscious of the style or name of the lead you happen to use in a given story. More often, your judgment as a writer will dictate your approach to the story and your treatment of it. Still, knowledge of the various leads and their uses can help you form a starting point as you decide approaches to the various events that make up a normal day's news.

STORY ORGANIZATION

Organization of a story usually takes one of two basic forms: the inverted pyramid and the conversational story structure.

Inverted Pyramid

The **inverted pyramid** is also known as the newspaper structure because newspaper reporters have used the inverted pyramid style (see Figure 4.1) in news story organization since Civil War days, when dispatches were transmitted from battlefields via telegraph. The inverted pyramid style was used because the telegraph wires were subject to sabotage and other frequent interruptions in service. By putting all the essential facts at the beginning of the story, reporters had a better chance of transmitting at least some of the story in usable form.

The inverted pyramid style of lead summarizes as many as possible of the five W's (who, what, when, where, and why) and sometimes H (how). Although journalists no longer force all five W's and H into the lead paragraph, editors still insist on putting as many as

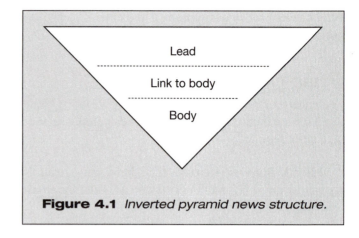

Figure 4.1 *Inverted pyramid news structure.*

possible in the first paragraph without being too wordy. The following pyramid organization contains the five W's.

Fifty [who] demonstrators were arrested [what] today [when] after they temporarily shut down a coal-fired electrical generating plant near Huntington, West Virginia, [where] to protest [why] what they called "unacceptable air quality standards" in the area.

Conversational Story Structure (Pyramid)

Conversational story structure resembles an ordinary pyramid (see Figure 4.2). The story begins with a concise lead that includes only the most important aspect of the story, emphasizing only one or two of the five W's. It then follows an informal style, with the rest of the information usually presented in decreasing order of importance. The story must be built around the lead, however, with the most important information coming at the beginning of the story, just as would be true in an inverted pyramid story. The difference is that sentences tend to be shorter and contain fewer facts. Often the story is told in chronological or narrative form. Today this is the typical style for the electronic news media as well.

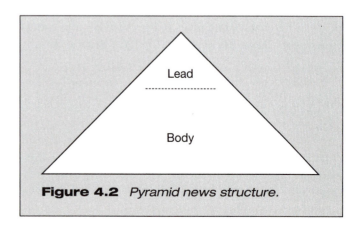

Figure 4.2 *Pyramid news structure.*

Because the inverted pyramid is too long for most spoken stories and would be difficult to follow if read aloud, the following is an example of a pyramid style:

Police in Huntington, West Virginia, today arrested 50 demonstrators for shutting down an electrical generating plant.

FRESHENING THE STORY

Because audiences expect to hear news that is happening now, you often can freshen and update old stories by delaying reference to when the event happened. Let's assume the morning edition of your local paper reports on the previous night's school board meeting:

The Board of Education last night recommended a no-smoking policy in the entire school district, even for teachers on break in the faculty lounge.

The early morning newscast might report the same story but with a different emphasis on the time reference. Although the story occurred the previous night, your radio newscast should move it into present tense:

The school board is taking a strong stand against smoking in public schools . . . and says regulations may be enforced even against teachers who smoke during coffee breaks. The board is recommending a districtwide no-smoking policy, approved last night at the board's regular meeting.

The reference to "last night" is buried near the end of the story. The lead and body of the story sound current and up-to-date. Consider how much brighter the story above sounds than if you were to start off by saying, as newspapers sometimes do, "The Board of Education last night recommended . . . ."

> *Your writing should be so conversational you could read it to your mother over the telephone and she won't know you are reading it.*
> MIKE LANDES
> Major Market News Anchor

UPDATING STORIES

Some news that you report will be in the nature of on-going, evolving stories and will have to be updated each time new developments occur. The best guide in knowing when to update a story is a generous application of common sense. In general, however, you should update a story every time new information arises. Even if new

information is unavailable, you should rewrite all copy at least every three radio newscasts. In television, early evening news stories are entirely rewritten for the late newscast.

The reasons for updating are obvious. No one in your audience wants to keep hearing the same story again and again throughout the day or evening. You are in the business of reporting news (new developments) and should pass along this new information to your audience at the earliest opportunity.

Imagine a downtown fire in which a business is destroyed and damage has reached an estimated $350,000. Your two a.m. story might be:

Firefighters are battling a two-alarm fire in the downtown business district.

By five a.m. when the fire is out, your lead might be:

Investigators are trying to learn what caused the fire that destroyed a downtown business during the night.

By eight a.m. your lead might be:

Damage is estimated at 350-thousand dollars in the aftermath of a fire that destroyed a downtown business early this morning.

Your lead at noon might be:

Arson is suspected in the two-alarm fire that destroyed a downtown business early today.

In a continuing, developing story, always lead with your most up-to-date information. Listeners will appreciate the freshness of your newscast.

Reporters often must make last-minute changes before breaking into normal programming with a special report.

LOCALIZING

A lead similar to the one below gives listeners in your region a reason to become interested in an otherwise national story. Whenever possible, you should search for local tie-ins to national stories.

> State Senator Richard Long is among those attending a national governors' conference today in Washington.

Other examples are:

> A Pittsburgh businessman is among 72 persons who escaped injury today in the crash landing of a passenger jet just outside Paris.

> Cold weather hangs over most of the western United States, but the weather service says Utah may escape the worst of it.

> Albuquerque seems to be doing more than its share in the national fight against muscular dystrophy.

Localizing is a crucial factor in any form of media writing. People in diverse media environments are highly selective in subjecting themselves to media. Armed with remote controls and continually expanding listening and viewing options, including the Internet, they have little patience for anything they don't quickly connect with.

Almost every day you see this effort by media outlets to achieve connectivity. When the local television station does a local angle on something that occurs far away, it is trying to relate the event to its viewers' world. Therefore, many stations do local angles on stories that really may not have much to do with their market.

For example, when a school shooting occurs, television news departments all across the country do "could it happen here?" stories. Likewise, when a major earthquake hits California, a spate of stories appears in other parts of the country about what would happen if a similar earthquake were to strike there. In the case of a notorious murder, or other crime that lends itself to market self-examination by media, local angles often are fashioned to help relate local viewers to the event in a personal way.

In other cases, stories that are local may not generate much listener/viewer interest unless the audience is told carefully in such a way that the story clearly has something specific to do with the individual. One of the best examples is the tax story. A school district asking voters to raise the mill levee makes a boring and distant story unless you tie it directly to people by pointing out how much their taxes will increase. Saying the tax levee will go up 25 mills doesn't mean much, but saying that taxes on the average $200,000 home will increase $92 a year helps the person listening or watching the story identify with what is being said and perceive the story in

meaningful ways for that person. A person may decide that's a small price to pay for better schools, or that the increase in taxes is too large. In either case, the audience can understand the story in concrete, personal terms instead of encountering it as abstract, impersonal information.

If you are going to put a story about car-jacking in the newscast because police in St. Louis just broke up a big ring of the thieves, you will need something to tie it to the place where you are producing the newscast. You could start with, "Police in St. Louis have a new way to prevent car-jackings." But that's far away and doesn't seem to have much to do with you or me (unless we live in St. Louis). The first thought that crosses our minds may well be, "Who cares?" Car-jackings are a concern in all major cities, so beginning the story by creating local interest could pull listeners/viewers into a story where they would learn some good prevention techniques. Consider this example of how to start.

> You're at a stoplight when the car-jacker strikes. What do you do? Some advice from a place where they have a lot of experience with that sort of thing, St. Louis . . . .

COMMUNICATING EFFECTIVELY

Good electronic news writing is not that complicated in many ways but is highly demanding in other ways. It is straightforward, is matter of fact, and provides a great deal of freedom that other forms of written expression do not. It is not burdened as much by traditional written conventions. But because it is heard only when the newscast is read and the audience cannot reread the copy several times to understand what it means, electronic media writing is one of the most demanding forms of writing. To be truly effective communication, five components must be present in all electronic media writing:

1. The writing must be *conversational*. Because writing for the ear is meant to be spoken aloud to an audience, it has to be written in normal conversational language. Generous use of contractions helps to achieve that and avoids traditional awkward written constructions. Although we don't want to end up being so informal that our newscasts sound like street jargon and, thus, alienate viewers with different perceptions of what sounds "right," we still need to sound like we're talking to the listeners/viewers rather than reading to them. Effective conversational tone is hard to achieve and takes considerable practice.

2. The writing must have *relatedness* to the listener/viewer. In our mass-mediated world, we are bom-

Relating to the audience means first covering stories that are local and relevant to viewers' lives. A good way for the news director to make sure the station is covering the news that matters is to research viewer interests and concerns, and to require aggressive coverage of social and political issues.

barded with so many sources of information that we have become adept at dumping from our minds the information to which we can't relate. We've all had the experience of watching television for an hour or two and minutes later having little recollection of what we saw and heard. We don't clutter our minds with unimportant information. In electronic media writing, then, we have to make stories tie in to the audience members' world. Like conversational writing, relatedness takes effort, experimentation, and practice. It helps to frame stories within the local context and use examples that enable most people to put the story in their terms.

Consider a lead with the intent of generating personal identification on the part of the viewer and, therefore, a greater desire to learn more:

> When your lights go out, you may wonder what's going on at the power company. Today, in Huntington, West Virginia, a lot of folks saw the lights blink as demonstrators temporarily shut down a coal-fired power plant. They were protesting what they called "unacceptable air quality standards."

The Huntington, West Virginia, power outage has nothing to do with our viewers, except that we've all experienced having the power go out and the inconvenience it causes. So that is a point of

relatedness we can use to create a tie between a distant event and the listener/viewer. It immediately means something to our audience in a personal way.

Sometimes techniques work. Other times you'll write something that sounds out of place. In cases when you can't make it work right, you can cut the copy.

When working at relatedness, a natural tendency is to overuse the word "you" and to slip into a predictable and boring pattern of phrases such as, "What would you do if . . ." or "You think you've got troubles . . . ."

As you work on making copy relate to individual audience members, you will have to work at being creative so you don't become predictable and dull. The fundamental question people have in the back of their mind as they engage with a newscast is, "What does this have to do with me?" If you can answer that question in the first few sentences of your story, you'll accomplish the goal of relating it to the viewer.

3. Writing must be *creative* to keep it and our newscasts interesting. The daily facts of life can get boring without creative phrasing, varying story flow, plays on words, and other devices at the writer's disposal to turn ordinary events into extraordinary stories. The late CBS reporter Charles Kuralt made a career of taking little stories about ordinary people in everyday life and turning them into creative art works through his storytelling genius. So can you, if you work at it. Try new things; experiment with different ways of approaching a lead, paragraph, or story. You have to let yourself go a little bit with creativity. Most creative writers do substantial rewriting. They start out with one thing and then decide it doesn't work and try another. To create a great piece of copy may take a half-dozen attempts.

4. Writing has to *make sense*. While we work at being conversational, relating the story to the listener/viewer, and being creative in the approach and phrasing, it all has to be tied together with logical flow. What we're all about is understanding. Sometimes, trying to be conversational, practicing relatedness, and generating creativity end up with something that is just confusing. Then we have to strip out the non-essential details and start over. The audience has to understand the who, what, where, when, why, and how of the journalistic effort.

5. Writing has to be *technically correct* so people reading the copy can understand it and deliver it

properly. As we've said before, writing for electronic media combines the oral form of human conversation and the written language our eighth-grade English teachers worked to help us learn. The newscaster has to be able to read properly constructed sentences with clauses that flow together. In addition, script formats in television and radio news must be precise because the technical crew depends on clear, concise script commands to execute the various elements such as audio/video inserts, special television graphics, and changes in anchors or remote locations. All of those things — from the conventional rules of language to the technical commands of the script — have to be applied correctly.

One of the best ways to test your copy is to read it aloud. When you do that, you hear it as the audience will. Often your ears will catch errors or awkwardness that your eyes don't when you proofread silently. When you try something and aren't sure if it works, you might ask a colleague to listen to it as you read it aloud, and then tell you what he or she thinks.

When radio or television writing incorporates excellence in all five areas — conversational tone, relatedness for audience members, creativity, making sense, and technical aspects — the result is excellence. When any one area breaks down, the result is, at best, diminished communication and, at worst, a story that fails.

EXERCISE 4A: Leads

Name _____ Date _____

Use the following information to write news story leads for electronic media. Use no more than three of the five W's found in many newspaper leads. Double-space all copy.

Example: It's raining again tonight in Chicago . . . after two straight days of serious flooding.
      What: raining
      When: tonight
      Where: Chicago

1 Another military aviation accident has occurred this afternoon. An Air Force F-16 fighter had mid-air contact with a P-38 jet trainer over Edwards Air Force Base, California. The P-38 crashed and one parachute was spotted coming from the plane. The P-38 is a two-seat plane, but it is not known how many people were on board the plane. The F-16 returned to base safely. The P-38 is sometimes used for training by NASA astronauts.

2 A 21-year-old man shot a 16-year-old girl this afternoon outside a classroom at John Glenn High School in Norwalk, California. The man shot the victim, then shot himself. Officials do not know of any relationship between the man and the victim. The girl died immediately and the man is in grave condition at a local hospital.

3 Washington, D.C. schools are having many building problems. Last month many schools reported leaks in their roofs. This month they face a different problem. Half of the schools in Washington, D.C. are having problems with their furnaces, leaving the schools without heat. The District Building Superintendent said 47 schools needed new boilers and their replacement could take months. At one school yesterday the school children had to be sent home because it got so cold. At some schools parents are bringing space heaters from home.

4 Last night at West Virginia University in Morgantown, West Virginia, a student was shot and then the attacker committed suicide. Officials said that a man drove 70 miles to the dormitory, where he shot his former girl-friend's new boyfriend as the former girlfriend watched. Then the man shot himself. The attacker died this morning and the victim remains in intensive care.

5 A man wanted in the murder of his uncle has locked himself into a room at Central Valley University. The man's girlfriend and her roommate have been taken out of the room. The man's uncle was found dead in Riverside County, California, last night, and the police say a vehicle missing from the murder scene was found outside the residence hall. At last report the SWAT team is at the dormitory and has made contact with the man.

6 In Los Angeles, California, gardeners are protesting a ban on gasoline-powered leaf blowers. The ordinance, which takes effect at the first of the month, bans the use of noisy gas-powered blowers within 500 feet of a home. The gardeners are protesting barefoot, saying officials are taking the shoes off their feet and the shirt off their back with the new ordinance.

7 In Easton, Maryland, today more than 24 students were injured after a tractor-trailer broadsided their school bus on a foggy highway. The bus was carrying 35 mostly middle school students. The bus driver was killed after the truck nearly severed the front of the bus. The driver of the truck was charged with failure to grant right-of-way.

8 The National Park Service is considering banning cars from Yosemite National Park because of the harm that car exhaust is causing to the environment of the park. In a plan to be released today, the National Park Service is expected to require visitors to park outside the park and take a bus inside. More than four million people drive to Yosemite National Park every year.

9 The Administration recently proposed eliminating 20 weather stations around the country. However, Central Valley appears to be winning the battle to keep its station. Both House and Senate Subcommittees on Weather Service Appropriations have favored continued funding for the 20 stations, members of the state's congressional delegation announced this morning.

10 A fourth grade school teacher in Kansas City has been acquitted of child abuse for spanking a ten-year old girl with a wooden paddle after the girl lied about having gum in her mouth. The Kansas City District Court jury returned a verdict of not guilty after deliberating three hours. Lynda Kristle had been charged with child abuse after her parents noted bruises on the child's buttocks.

EXERCISE 4B: Writing for the Electronic Media

Name _____ Date _____

1 Rewrite the following story for electronic media:

The State University Police have reported the injury of an 18-year-old freshman student, Thomas Schwanke. Schwanke was found at 7:40 a.m. this morning in the basement of a dormitory on campus. Police believe Schwanke fell anywhere from two to ten stories down a trash chute around 2 a.m. Witnesses who had seen Schwanke earlier that morning say Schwanke had been drinking. Mary Rouse, Dean of Students at State University said that the incident again raises concern about alcohol abuse on campus.

(WRITE YOUR STORY HERE)

2 Write an electronic media story from the following telephone conversation with a police detective in the metropolitan area.

"The suspects from the armored car robbery here last month were arrested this morning in Fort Lauderdale, Florida. We had been watching them for about a week at a hotel and arrested them without any problems. We got a tip soon after the robbery that they had been seen in Florida. The names of the two suspects we arrested are Bobby O'Neal, Jr. and Brandon Lutz. We are still not sure where the 2.7 million dollars they stole from the Loomis armored truck is."

(WRITE YOUR STORY HERE)

3 Write an electronic media story from the following telephone conversation with a police detective in a metropolitan area. Not all the information need be included.

"The white male came in the Sunset Bank at 2000 Main Street about one p.m. today and stuck a nickel-plated revolver in the face of a teller, Ms. Susie Smith. He shoved a paper bag at her and she put about $2,500 in it and he hurried out. Ralph Jones, another teller, followed the guy but lost him on the street. The robber was wearing a stocking cap, dark glasses, and was about five feet, three inches tall and weighed around 110 pounds. He fits the description of the same guy who robbed the place last September and got about $5,000. Nobody was hurt, but the employees were scared as hell."

(WRITE YOUR STORY HERE)

EXERCISE 4C: Writing Exercises

Name _____ Date _____

From each set of facts below, write a news story in proper style for electronic media.

1 A train and a tractor trailer collided early yesterday morning outside of Waldo, Arkansas. Two people were injured and 31 cars and two train engines derailed. The Union Pacific train was coming from Memphis, Tenn. en route to Long Beach, Calif. It was carrying 94 cars of mail for the United States Postal Service, food, appliances, and other non-hazardous items. Officials said the accident happened when the train hit the tractor-trailer carrying logging equipment. A railroad spokesman said the derailed cars may have to be cut apart into scraps to clear the area. The two injured persons were members of the train's crew.

2 A ring of thieves has been targeting high school computer labs in Fulton County, Georgia. In the past two months, the group has stolen 112 computers, estimated at between 500 and 2,000 dollars each. District officials are cooperating with local law enforcement to tighten security at all 43 schools in the county. The 112 computers have come from 14 different schools, including three elementary, five junior high, and six high schools. Fulton County police are installing security cameras in computer labs at each school.

3 An Air Force C-130 cargo plane had problems landing this morning in Wisconsin because its landing gear had jammed. Airport officials waited nervously as the plane was forced to stay in the air and circled Lake Michigan until the gear could be lowered and locked into place. Eventually, the gear was fixed by a passenger, Brigadier General Paul Cooper. The plane landed safely at the airport around two p.m. The plane had nine people on board and seven hours of fuel available.

4 The U.S. Department of Transportation reached a deal today between Amtrak and a railway maintenance workers union, which narrowly avoided a strike. The agreement raises pay in return for increased productivity. The union chairman expects the workers to ratify the contract within 30 days. A strike could have started as soon as this week, disrupting service to more than 100,000 rail passengers.

Critical Thinking Questions

Directions: The following questions are provided to help you examine the deeper meanings and complexities of the various issues under discussion. Answer each question to the best of your ability after a thoughtful review of the subject at hand.

1. What is your definition and philosophy of news? What is its role in helping keep the audience informed about (a) whatever may interest them, versus (b) whatever they need to solve problems and make important decisions?

2. View three news stories reported on your local news and three on a national news program. What news values are present in each story? How do the differences represent different targeted audiences? How do the similarities show common ground?

3. Compare the lead paragraph of a print story with the first three sentences of an electric news story on the same issue or event. How are they different? What factors contribute to this difference? What differences exist in the news values that are highlighted in each?

4. What major influences, both professional and personal, influence a journalist's judgment when determining what is news and what is not on any given day?

5. When is it preferable to tell a news story narratively — with a beginning, a middle, and an ending — in which the story's outcome is delayed until the end, as opposed to revealing the story's outcome in the lead?

6. To what extent should electronic media reports emphasize what is happening now? As part of your response, explain the tendency of some organizations to emphasize the "false present" (for example, "A mudslide closes a stretch of Interstate 80," when the slide has been cleared and the road reopened).

7. What is "relatedness?" Explain the need to address what all audience members have in common with a story. Is it up to you, the journalist, to find those common elements, or rather to just report the facts and let audience members decide what they have in common with your story?

Self-Review Questions

Directions: Each of the self-review questions below addresses information contained in this chapter. Answer each question to the best of your ability, then review the chapter as necessary to further strengthen your understanding of each concept or issue.

1. What are the primary elements of news? Define and explain them.

2. What is the role of story leads, and what are the main types of leads used when writing for electronic media?

3. What are the origination, role, and limitations of the inverted pyramid story structure?

4. How do you update a story? Provide examples of at least four updated story leads that could air over a six- to eight-hour period.

5. What is "localizing," and why is it important?

6. What qualities must be present in your writing to communicate effectively with an audience?

## CHAPTER FIVE

News Selection

"The news," journalists sometimes observe, "is what I say it is." Thousands of broadcast journalists around the country decide each day for millions of listeners and viewers what is and what is not news. The process of news selection involves countless judgments, including the news values discussed in Chapter 4.

But viewers are involved in the choice as well. People are involved every time they consume news. The stories the audience reads or doesn't read; the stories they watch or flip through to another channel; the stories they investigate further and the ones they surf past — all are indications to journalists what the audience cares about. But ultimately, journalists, as the news gatekeepers, must determine what is the "news" of the day.

NEWS JUDGMENT

The judgments involved in the news process are as individual as the people who make them. How do you decide what makes the biggest story of the hour? What stories should follow it? When is a story worthy of a live report? How long should a

News judgments are made constantly throughout the day in a television newsroom.

story be? Even the networks don't always agree on the lead story of the day. Experience is the best teacher in answering these questions, but you can follow guidelines of common sense as you select the stories you will air.

News judgment requires the same discipline as any other skill, and it must be developed over time. You can begin by studying newscasts of stations you respect. Study their news selection, talk with news personnel about what makes news, and then practice making news judgments in your everyday life. Learn to distinguish what is serious and significant, what events are essential to know about, what stories affect your life directly, which stories are nice to know about but have little impact in your life, which stories exist by themselves and which are "manufactured" (wouldn't exist if you didn't cover them).

Influences on Judgment

News judgment is affected by our background, our education, and our friends. All the things that make up one's own "culture" come into play in our fundamental values and the way we view the world. When covering the news, journalists must consider their personal perspective, particularly their context of daily life. A danger of "newsroom myopia," or nearsightedness, comes with working in the intense, deadline-driven world of news. This can exclude much of what most people consider normal activities. And journalists are intensely competitive, both for the status of being the best among their contemporaries and for advertising dollars that flow more abundantly to those with the highest ratings. Because of the paranoia of competition, in which journalists fear that another journalist will beat them to a

NEWS JUDGMENT

The news director at a Miami radio station sent his staff a memo of guidelines on news judgment. Here are some excerpts:

1. Lately a lot of material has been creeping into our news shows that does not belong there. Effective immediately, kill all but the most major developments in international news. Stay away from stories on obscure economic indicators. All we should be interested in are the Consumer Price Index and unemployment figures.

2. Emphasis should be placed on the following items:

a. Consumer	e. Transportation
b. Public education	f. Environment
c. Quality police matter	g. Aviation
d. Employment	h. Minorities

a. Consumer-oriented stories include items such as the clean meat-packaging ordinance, consumer frauds, dangerous items and substances, auto recalls, and price gouging.

b. Just about everyone has contact with public education in some way. The big ones here are busing, drugs in school, school money problems, and school taxes.

c. When I say "quality police matter," I don't want to hear about a robbery of under $1,000. In other police matters, I'm not interested unless they're dead. I don't want to hear about fires — unless the property loss is more than $25,000 (or there is injury or death).

d. Employment covers things such as the airline mergers, mass layoffs, companies moving large staffs here, or opening plants with mass local hiring.

e. Transportation covers new highway construction, continuing highway bottlenecks and unsafe conditions, development of rapid transit, and changes in fares. Also, coverage of the development of express bus lanes should be included.

f. The environment covers land-use management, water resources, water pollution, air pollution, resource recovery, land pollution, and endangered species.

g. Aviation-related businesses are the largest single category of employment in Dade County. When you hear a story from an airline, A.L.P.A. or the machinists union, I want your eyes to bug out.

h. Minority group coverage includes Cubans, Blacks, anti-war factions, abortion reform, etc.

major story, journalists maintain constant surveillance of the competition.

Many news directors have several television sets in their offices so they can monitor their primary market competition continuously. This can result in coverage dictated by what other news operations are doing rather than the conviction that "our audience needs to have this information." In "pack journalism," news organizations chase the same things because other media are pursuing them rather than considering the real merits of the story. The result, day after day across the country from the largest networks to the smallest stations, is almost identical stories in the same order of newscast. Rather than a variety of news voices, the news coverage, format of stories, and time allotted to them are alarmingly similar from station to station.

Several studies of the network evening news support this theory of limited news content despite seemingly unlimited news outlets. Rather than a marketplace of ideas, the highly competitive media in contemporary America seem to foster a marketplace of similarities because of their continuing effort to appeal to the largest audience possible.

Desires of the Audience

Journalists like to decide what the audience "needs" to know about, but market research reminds us to include audience "wants" in a newscast. You need to know what general areas concern your audience. But news is a combination of information "wants" and "needs," each of which has to be satisfied for the audience to be both attracted to and informed by a newscast.

People use news programming in several ways. Research has demonstrated that while the news is on, people ignore it, concentrate on it, argue about it, agree with each other about it, and use it to isolate themselves from others or to bring a family together in a mutual viewing group activity. In our culture, we maintain "surveillance" on the news. We read the paper each morning (actually, scan it quickly) and usually tune into a newscast or two on radio, television, or the Internet. We then have information to use in conversing about the concerns of the day and thus are part of the dynamic of contemporary life.

To many in the audience, news means a few minutes a day catching up on things to impress others positively, as well as for any other purpose. News is our common currency of the world and how we fit into it.

What's more, how people define "news" is highly variable. Some think of crimes of violence as news, and the daily process of politics more as boredom than as "news." We tend to be captivated by sensationalistic

events and disasters even though our long-term quality of life is affected more directly by the visually dull activity within the walls of state legislatures and congressional offices.

With overpowering pictures driving the visual media, television news often concentrates on what is titillating but not necessarily all that important in the course of life for most Americans. The combination of information about reality and entertainment values, often distorted in nature, has become known as "infotainment." Within that context, the journalist has to keep the audience's perspective in mind. It exists uniquely apart from the journalist's own world of shiftwork and obsessive consumption of current events. And journalists and the audience alike must recognize that the way a story is covered can misrepresent the reality.

Separateness

As a culture, news has a tendency toward **separateness**. Broadcast journalists often work around the clock and change jobs and city locations about every two years. This can result in a "sameness" of news values across very different markets and regions of the country where the journalists may be disconnected with local audience perceptions and preferences. Thus, you can have a journalist with "New York" news values making decisions

Television journalists have to remain connected to their community despite a broadcast news culture that may isolate them from everyday viewers.

about what to include in a newscast in Omaha, where the audience news values may be very different.

What would lead a newscast in Los Angeles might be of little or no interest to people in Casper, Wyoming. Broadcast journalists function in a kind of separate subculture among themselves, which can prevent journalists from experiencing the world the way their audience experiences it. This is partly because of the shift nature of news organizations, in which journalists work afternoons and evenings, making normal social relationships with non-journalists difficult. Journalists who are out of touch with the everyday lives of their audience run the risk of producing news content that is irrelevant and uninteresting. This kind of social isolation also can contribute to cynicism among reporters, preventing them from seeing the positive elements of a community the way their audience can.

Jargon

Another way journalists are distanced from the audience they are trying to serve is the tendency to be continuously around the same sources (police officers, politicians, government public relations people, and so on), in which jargon often becomes interwoven in the fabric of daily conversation. The language of the source

becomes the language of the journalist, who intrinsically understands its meaning. That meaning, however, sometimes is lost on an audience not used to interpreting the terminology.

What does the term JIC — pronounced in ordinary conversation as "JICK" —mean to you? To some federal employees JIC is understood immediately to mean the "Joint Information Center," which coordinates news releases and media queries during disaster and military operations. If that acronym sneaks into a reporter's script, however, the audience can be left wondering what the reporter is talking about.

Getting the News

The "news" of the day reaches the station through many sources. It is assembled locally by reporters, video crews, writers, stringers, editors, and producers. Information from all over the world is relayed to the newsroom. Syndications, news services, and networks send prerecorded stories, or **feeds,** down the line for recording and later broadcast. Two-way radios, telephones, and police monitors blare in the newsroom throughout the day, alerting the assignment editor to breaking news within the community.

This information would fill more than the day's broadcast schedule. Instead, it must be processed and distilled into compact reports that will illustrate the most important and interesting events of the day. When you put together a news broadcast, you are concerned with the total content of the show. You must organize the news, determine story order and length, the number of actualities or visuals and, as the day goes on, which stories must be added, shortened, and dropped.

HARD VERSUS SOFT NEWS

The two most classic news distinctions are between hard news and soft, or feature, news. **Hard news** is what people expect to see and hear. It is the news they need to know to get along in life from day to day, news that helps them decide which course of action to take or that affects them financially, physically, or in some other important way. Hard news tells about rate hikes in utilities, property tax increases, important Senate action, and major crime in the community.

Soft news is optional to most audiences. They might enjoy hearing soft news, but they can live without it right now. For example, soft news reports might feature a 100-year-old woman who still runs the school cafeteria, or a Rhode Island man who pushes a peanut up the sidewalk to pay off an election bet, or local school teachers who are exercising three times a week until the end of the semester. These stories might contribute to

---

SPOTLIGHT

Futures File

An indispensable part of the newsroom is the **futures file**, a simple filing system such as an accordion-style folder with pockets for each day of the month. Into these pockets are placed newspaper clippings about upcoming events, notes from telephone calls, public relations releases about political and business activities, dates of court hearings, and the like. The file contains ready references for events that should be covered in the days and weeks ahead, and consulted daily so you can prepare for "predictable" news events.

Based on what is happening in your community currently and what is going on around campus, make your own mental futures file and then compare it to your local television newscast this week. Are they covering what you considered newsworthy? Have they missed any stories you thought about? Perhaps you have a potential story from your campus that the local news should be covering.

our awareness of social or community trends or to our understanding of how events affect us. If they serve either of these functions, they are justified, but not if they replace stories we really need to know. The distinction between soft and feature news is important to recognize. Chapter 6 provides further discussion of feature news.

Lead Stories

The lead, or first story in the newscast, must be the biggest story of the hour — the event that merits special attention because it is the most important. The lead story may be obvious on some days and obscure on other days when several big stories are breaking. Usually you can solve the problem by asking which story affects or interests the most people in the audience. Sometimes the choices can be tricky.

Imagine that the state utility commission raises utility rates in your community, meaning that you will pay more to heat and operate your home. On the same day, police announce the fifth rape–murder to occur in your neighborhood within the last three months. Which story should be the lead? Only you can answer the question, based upon your knowledge of community interests and concerns. Ordinarily the rate hike might lead the newscast, but the unusual number of violent crimes may have created an issue of personal safety that would make the rape–murder story more important to your audience.

In the absence of such finely cut decisions, hard news generally takes precedence as the lead story at most stations. Whatever you decide to go with as the lead story, you always should lead with the most current developments.

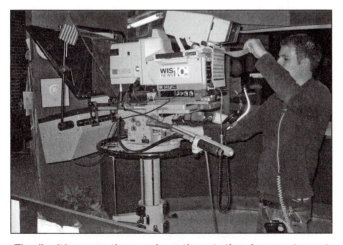

Finally, it's newstime, when the station hopes to put the day's most interesting and relevant content in front of the largest audience possible. Producers consider news values, audience desires, audience demographics at specific times and audience tendencies to switch channels.

Line-up

Local news usually is placed first in the newscast, unless it is obviously overshadowed by important regional, national, or international developments. The show builds from the lead story, with similar items grouped together. If you lead with a crime story, you don't jump immediately to a story about plans for a new shopping center in your area even if it is the second most important story in the newscast. Instead, a buffer will smooth the flow of the news — a story from district court, for example — followed by the shopping center story. Except in the shortest radio newscasts, you should avoid a line-up that groups stories from most to least important in 1-2-3 order. In doing that, the newscast would become progressively less interesting, and the audience progressively more bored.

Most television producers follow a concept called **thematic blocking**. In grouping similar items together, they use whatever logical thread seems to connect stories. That can mean grouping by subject, geography, or just about any other device that helps tie stories together. Suffice it to say, thematic blocking helps the audience digest the avalanche of news of the day by putting it into story groupings that flow into and out of one another easily. Thematic blocking also helps increase the story count in the newscast. Short copy can be slipped in among other stories to help make the transitions that bolster the feeling that a lot of news is included.

Some producers attempt to give each segment of a newscast the emotional flow of an entire newscast. By that, we mean they begin each segment with a strong lead story that lends importance and energy to the beginning of the segment. Then you move through a series of stories of lessening drama but still plenty of substance. The segment ends with a positive story or, at the least, the final story in the segment ends in a positive tone. It's similar to a newscast with a strong front end of dramatic news, lessening emotional power toward the middle, softer, more enjoyable material in the form of sports and weather, and a final "kicker" story to end positively.

The emotion of newscast blocking must be considered. If a newscast is full of depressing information — story after story of tragedy, violence, people dying — it becomes something to punch out of, not tune into. People will put up with only so much negativism in their lives, and then they seek positive reinforcement. That is not to say they should avoid putting in news that is important, just that they should be sensitive about its effect on the audience. This is particularly important since invention of the television remote control. When people had to get up and walk six feet or so to change channels, they did so only when they felt strongly about what they wanted to view. With the "clicker," though, flipping through the channels has become a sort of national recreation.

It's easy to lose a viewer, and in the ever more fragmented world of the mass media, that's the last thing you want to do. Therefore, newscasts are produced increasingly with an appreciation for the way viewers receive the information and react to it.

CONTENT OF NEWSCASTS

The time available in a newscast should be used for stories of substance. Stories to avoid include minor robberies and other minor crimes, fender-bender traffic accidents, suicides, minor court decisions, and small fires. Each of these examples may have special properties on a given day, however, that make it special enough to include in the news. A minor traffic accident becomes news if the driver lost control because he saw a nude sunbather.

Spot News

A **spot news** story is an event that breaks out, day or night, without warning. As you begin your career in broadcasting, you may find yourself covering a variety of spot news — the fires, hold-ups, car wrecks, plane crashes, drownings, and murders that occur from time to time in almost any community. Gradually you will learn that news doesn't change. Only the names change. The same stories return day after day, year after year. The stories often are accounts of violence, and they will leave some people in your audience cold. Still others in your audience will be interested in these events. Listeners

When news breaks, television stations cannot afford to waste time getting equipment together. Most stations have trucks and vans already equipped for remote broadcasts when spot news occurs.

or viewers in your audience who have witnessed a car–train collision will be eager to learn the details in the news. Others in the audience might be vitally interested in hearing about the third hold-up in as many days at the mom-and-pop grocery just down the street from where they live.

Some spot news is momentous: a million-dollar warehouse fire, a major drug raid, a train derailment, flash flooding, a grain elevator explosion. Other spot news barely qualifies as such and requires unusual angles to make it airworthy.

In general, as you make judgments about spot news, ask yourself what lifts the story out of the ordinary. Try not to waste precious airtime reporting minor-injury accidents, inconsequential fires, and $25 hold-ups. Many reporters are satisfied covering only the "what" of

---

EFFECTIVE SPOT NEWS COVERAGE

Many stations keep vehicles in the field to cover spot news. These remote vehicles can be cars, station wagons, or vans equipped with two-way radios and, in the case of television, videotape gear and live broadcast capability. In-car monitors and two-way contact with assignment editors back at the newsroom assure continual awareness of reports from fire, police, sheriff, highway patrol, and other government agencies in the community. Mobile news reporters often can reach the scene of spot news within minutes if they are in good field position to begin with.

Whether minor spot news is a legitimate component of your newscast is a value judgment. Many people in your audience will want and expect to hear it. Others will wonder why you bothered with it in the first place. Somewhere in most of us lies a source of morbid fascination with the disaster and mayhem that befall others. Often, when we disavow our interest in such events, we still secretly like to know about them and will listen in spite of ourselves. Almost always, pedestrians and motorists turn to watch as an ambulance goes by with sirens blaring and red lights flashing.

Spot news is only one component of broadcast journalism, and should not dominate the news line-up or upset the balance of an otherwise representative report of the day's events. Momentous events occur by the thousands each day all over the world. Is the car wreck at Fifth and Main one of them?

events. Others go beyond surface coverage whenever possible and ask why events occurred and what consequences are likely. These questions help the reporter probe for the cause of stories. This is not to imply that you should become a crusading journalist, only that you should go beyond the symptom of a problem (the grain elevator explosion) and get to the cause (lax safety standards that surround the handling of grain dust). When people are aware of problems, they can address the causes.

REFERENCE SOURCES

Tools of the broadcast writer include reference materials. Although all of these references can also be accessed on the Web, no newsroom should be without at least the minimum references.

- City directories help us locate people, their addresses, and telephone numbers. People not listed in telephone directories might be found in the city directory. This reference is especially useful in trying to contact someone near the scene of a fire or an accident for eyewitness information. Most city directories also provide cross-sections by name, address, and telephone number. This enables us to locate individuals even if we know only their addresses or telephone numbers and are unsure of their name.

- Computer databases provide quick answers to many questions. Information available on databases includes census data, articles from various publications, encyclopedias, and much more.

- Internet access provides the reporter the ability to research even the most detailed aspect of a story, adding a valuable dimension to the story.

- Lists of radio and television stations in the region are helpful when we need audiotape or videotape feeds from locations outside our immediate geographic area.

- Pronunciation guides are essential references for state and local pronunciations, as well as national places and names. If we have any doubt about a given word, we can look up the word in these references.

- Out-of-town telephone directories help us locate people and agencies outside our immediate area.

- Unlisted telephone numbers and frequently called numbers can be listed to speed the reporting process. Such a file of numbers contains many numbers that aren't listed in the phone book — a police dispatcher's private line and the home number of a competing station's news director, for instance —

GUIDELINES FOR NEWS CONTENT

Because all guidelines are meant to illustrate an "average" news day, and few news days are average, the following tips are set down only to help you develop a news sense.

- Use recordings from the field whenever possible, but keep them brief and concise, generally not more than 30 seconds in length.

- Write your news stories in present tense whenever possible.

- Stress local news of substance and interest, and cover it live whenever possible.

- For at least two stories in a five-minute radio newscast, provide as much detail and depth as a balanced newscast allows. Make all other stories more snappy and concise.

- End newscasts whenever possible with a bright, upbeat story (or kicker) that will leave your audience smiling or amused. Much of the news is sober, and few people want to leave newscasts feeling somber.

- Make most news stories at least two sentences long. One-sentence "headlines" are appropriate, however, if used in association with a series of other one- and two-sentence stories, as in a news-in-brief wrap-up.

- Try to use two or three short stories rather than one long one to make a five- minute radio newscast sound more comprehensive.

- Update and localize wire stories whenever possible. Look for a local tie-in with state and national stories, and lead these stories with local emphasis in the first sentence.

- Regardless of their source, check all stories for accuracy, especially when they involve crime, legal action, or political charges.

- Rewrite all stories that are used in subsequent newscasts. No listener wants to hear the same story again and again.

and may be unavailable from other sources on a moment's notice. (Of course, unlisted numbers are not to be given out to anyone except those who are authorized to use them.)

- Public officials and agencies comprise another reference source, listing political affiliation, position held, pertinent telephone numbers, political record of the official involved, function of agency, and the like. Most states have a "Blue Book" directory listing congressional representatives by name, party, terms, office address, and telephone number. These directories are helpful when we must quickly learn as much as possible about a public official. Most states now have all this information on their state government Web site, which can be found for every state. The following URL example is for the Georgia government site but any state can be found by replacing its abbreviation in the URL. For example: http://www.legis.state.ga.us.

- Dictionaries, of course, are indispensable to any writer. Besides an up-to-date dictionary, we use a dictionary of synonyms, a thesaurus, and even a book of famous quotations as a stimulus on days when we suffer from uninspired writing.

- Newspapers and news magazines help us keep abreast of local, regional, state, national, and international news. Most newsrooms subscribe to local and state newspapers and at least one or two news magazines.

- Newsroom radio monitors and television monitors help us keep tabs on the competition and as a check against our station's news coverage. Monitoring the competition keeps us alert to any stories we may have missed in the day's news coverage.

EXERCISE 5A: Selecting the News

Name _____ Date _____

Write a broadcast news story from each set of facts. Pick the most newsworthy elements. If the facts do not warrant a news story, say so, and explain why not.

1. Food poisoning today sent 39 West Allis students to the West Allis Memorial Hospital for treatment. Symptoms seemed to have started when ten students were sent there last night. A student cafeteria worker, Beverly Knocks, suggested that the cause of the poisoning may have been a chicken salad that students were given at lunch yesterday. President of West Allis, Dr. Robert R. Reid, said lab tests were being conducted today on samples of yesterday's food. Only two students are still in the hospital tonight.

2. Jennifer Rambler and Tommy Horton will receive the Illinois Press Association award for outstanding contributions to journalism in the state at the annual press association meeting next week. The two journalists uncovered a five-million-dollar a year daycare center fraud during an investigative reporting series last fall. The reporters also have been nominated for a Pulitzer Prize, the first nomination by a Central Valley newspaper in 35 years.

3 In a special meeting this morning, the city council passed next year's budget. The total budget will exceed $25 million for the first time. It will require a tax increase of approximately 30 cents per $100 of assessed property valuation. This means the owner of a $100,000 home will pay $300 more a year in taxes.

4 Central Valley University will receive a federal grant of $2.5 million to help develop specialized programs for the people with disabilities. It is the only school in the state to receive the federal grant that was awarded by the U.S. Department of Education for next year. Dr. Peter Tomlinson will direct the project for the university. He is a professor of higher education in the Leadership Department.

EXERCISE 5A: Selecting the News (continued)

Name _____ Date _____

5. Mrs. Jolene Smith was elected president of the Central Valley Chamber of Commerce last night. Mrs. Smith has been a member of the Chamber for 12 years. She is the first African American woman president in the 48-year history of the chamber. Mrs. Smith owns the Campus Book Shop. She and her husband, Stan, moved to Central Valley 15 years ago from Minneapolis. The 42-year-old Mrs. Smith has two children, both attending Central Valley University — Tom, a 19-year-old sophomore, and Ted, an 18-year-old freshman. She will be installed at the Chamber's annual banquet next Thursday at the Varsity Inn.

6. United Fund Executive Director Paul Simmons said today that Henry Brown will head this year's fund drive, which begins in October. Goals for the new year will be set by the executive committee at its next meeting. Brown is president of the Union National Bank and a former state senator.

7 | Two local college women were attacked by a knife-wielding assailant in separate incidents last night at St. Petersburg College for Women and Central Valley University. Both escaped serious injury, and both took place as the library for their respective schools was closing.

8 | The state highway budget was approved by the legislature yesterday. The $87 million budget contains funds for three new four-lane highways in the state. One of the highways will be a ten-mile stretch of U.S. 287 that runs through Central Valley. $18.6 million was appropriated for construction to begin on that section. Additional funds from next year's budget will be required to complete the project, according to Stan Cass, highway director. The governor is expected to sign the bill, an executive office spokesman said.

EXERCISE 5B: Prioritizing the News

Name _____ Date _____

Write news stories from the following facts. If, however, you think the facts are not newsworthy enough to write a story, tell why not. If you could choose five of the following ten stories for tonight's five-minute radio newscast, which five would you include?

1. Testimony resumed today in circuit court in a suit brought by Central Valley University to determine liability for $22,877 in illegal long-distance phone calls made from the city and county building last year.

2. A majority of the House Ways and Means Committee is tentatively supporting a proposed $25 billion income tax reduction. This is well below the $100 billion tax relief the President asked for. The committee's proposal contains a $40 billion rollback in social security taxes that the President's package does not include. The Democratic coalition has been pushing the compromise bill. Coalition members believe they have the necessary votes to get it out the committee, but "there isn't total unanimity among the Democrats," he said. He hopes the committee will approve the bill sometime the early part of next week.

3 Preliminary results from the Republican precinct caucuses in Collins County resulted in 382 delegates selected to the county assembly next Saturday. The assembly will be held at the high school auditorium. About two-thirds of the delegates chosen were uncommitted. The present lieutenant governor received only three delegates in support of his candidacy.

4 Gov. Ted Locke vetoed the state legislature's major air pollution bill today, terming it "unworkable," but saying the necessity for rejecting the measure was "tragic." He said he feared if the bill went into law, it might conflict with federal requirements and could lead to federal takeover of the state program. The Democratic governor failed to mention that in this election year, the measure was supported and passed by the Republican-controlled legislature.

EXERCISE 5B: Prioritizing the News (continued)

Name _____ Date _____

5 Robert R. Rankin, 63, chairman of the board at Union National Bank, died at Central Valley Memorial Hospital early today of heart disease. Private funeral services will be held at Goodwin Funeral Home Wednesday. Rankin stepped down as bank president three months ago but retained his position as chairman of the board. He had planned to retire from that position at the end of this year.

6 A garage fire in Central Valley this morning claimed the life of William Townes, a ten-year old elementary student at Crosswind Elementary School. The student was playing in the garage before school when a gas can exploded, witnesses say. The fire also caused $50,000 damage to the house. William is the son of Mr. and Mrs. Robert Townes, 2828 State St.

7 Two area women have been charged with three counts of vehicular homicide. The charges come from a car accident in which a man and two of his children were killed. Charged in the Collins County District Court were Melody S. Melanson and Tina Lou Lambert, both of 501 Maple St. They also are charged with leaving the scene of an accident. The accident occurred four miles south of Central Valley on U.S. 287 and Hatchell Road.

8 An autopsy report has determined that the two DiVece girls killed in last week's rape/murder case in Central Valley died as a result of severe head injuries. Both girls were sexually molested, the report showed. Investigators continue to search for a male suspect, approximately six feet tall with medium complexion, who was last seen with the girls a couple hours before their deaths. Ann DiVece and her sister Melinda had gone to the Spartan Hotel Lounge. Witnesses saw them leave with the suspect in a light brown sedan about two a.m. Their bodies were found early the next morning on a deserted road near the lake.

EXERCISE 5B: Prioritizing the News (continued)

Name _____ Date

9 | The FBI may bring charges in a ten-state prostitution ring uncovered first in Lexington, KY, according to the Kentucky state FBI director, Arthur Beel. About 70 prostitutes are thought to be involved, with 18 of the 70 suspected of managing the operation. Indictments are expected sometime tomorrow.

10 | The discovery of a 60–70 foot Sauropod dinosaur in New Mexico close to Las Vegas "will add to our knowledge about the geographic distribution" of dinosaurs. No dinosaur of this age had been discovered as far south as New Mexico, according to paleontologist Dr. Robert Kuner. It was discovered in an arroyo by a class of students from the University of New Mexico.

ASSIGNMENT 5A: Analyzing a Local Newscast

Name _____ Date

Choose a TV station you respect, and log all the stories broadcast in half-hour news broadcasts.

STATION YOU WATCHED: Channel _____

Call Letters _____

After completing the log of stories on the next page, determine the percentage and actual broadcast time of:

Hard news   (percent) _____ %

(length) _____ minutes

Soft news   (percent) _____ %

(length) _____ minutes

News you consider essential to know about:

(percent) _____ %

(length) _____ minutes

News that would affect the audience in some way, whether financially, physically, or emotionally:

(percent) _____ %

(length) _____ minutes

NEWSCAST LOG

Story #	Length	Hard News (check)	Soft News (check)	Essential? (check)	Affects Audience?
1.	_____	_____	_____	_____	_____
2.	_____	_____	_____	_____	_____
3.	_____	_____	_____	_____	_____
4.	_____	_____	_____	_____	_____
5.	_____	_____	_____	_____	_____
6.	_____	_____	_____	_____	_____
7.	_____	_____	_____	_____	_____
8.	_____	_____	_____	_____	_____
9.	_____	_____	_____	_____	_____
10.	_____	_____	_____	_____	_____

Story #	Length	Hard News (check)	Soft News (check)	Essential? (check)	Affects Audience?
11.	_____	_____	_____	_____	_____
12.	_____	_____	_____	_____	_____
13.	_____	_____	_____	_____	_____
14.	_____	_____	_____	_____	_____
15.	_____	_____	_____	_____	_____
16.	_____	_____	_____	_____	_____
17.	_____	_____	_____	_____	_____
18.	_____	_____	_____	_____	_____
19.	_____	_____	_____	_____	_____
20.	_____	_____	_____	_____	_____
21.	_____	_____	_____	_____	_____
22.	_____	_____	_____	_____	_____
23.	_____	_____	_____	_____	_____
24.	_____	_____	_____	_____	_____
25.	_____	_____	_____	_____	_____

Critical Thinking Questions

Directions: The following questions are provided to help you examine the deeper meanings and complexities of the various issues under discussion. After a thoughtful review of the subject, answer each question to the best of your ability.

1. What major influences, both professional and personal, influence a journalist's judgment when determining what is news and what isn't on any given day?

2. As a working journalist, what steps can you take to avoid social isolation from your audience and your community?

3. Explain how a reporter's views may differ from a news director's views on what is a good story for the broadcast. What are the major influences for each in their decision-making?

4. Assume you are a television news director in a medium-sized market. Write a brief, one-page statement, double-spaced, suitable for posting in the newsroom, that outlines your philosophy of news and "newsworthiness."

5. Local television news developed a reputation for having a "if it bleeds, it leads; if it's sex, it's next" philosophy of news coverage. Do you find this is still true? If you were to become news director of a station with that reputation, what would you do to overcome that?

6. Research on audiences continues to indicate that audiences want balance in their newscasts — neither all bad news nor all good — in a proportion that reflects life as they live it. What impact does this finding have on achieving balance in the nightly newscast line-up?

7. In your view, should the nature of news more nearly emphasize accounts of things gone wrong or "society's pursuit of winning?" Or does it have to be an either/or choice? Defend your answer and provide examples of stories and story treatment to back up your position.

8. The human organism hasn't changed much in the last 10,000 years, yet the ways in which we communicate have undergone hundreds of transformations. In your opinion, what factors have most influenced the nature of news content throughout human history, and what factors are most likely to influence it in the century ahead?

Self-Review Questions

Directions: Each of the self-review questions below addresses information contained in this chapter. Answer each question to the best of your ability, then review the chapter as necessary to further strengthen your understanding of each concept or issue.

1. What are the most important news sources available to electronic journalists? List them.

2. What influences can affect a journalist's news judgment? Address competitive influences as part of your answer.

3. How can the concept of "separateness" impact you as a professional journalist?

4. How can professional journalists fall victim to the use of jargon?

5. What are the differences between audience "wants" and "needs," and how might your perception of these concepts influence the nature of your reporting?

6. In general, how accurately is the society at large reflected in newscasts that consistently contain a high proportion of crime stories?

7. How do hard and soft news differ? Explain how the two can be reflected fairly in news line-ups.

8. What is thematic blocking within a newscast? Provide an example.

9. What is spot news? Provide an example of a legitimate spot news story.

10. What are the primary ways to reference news sources within an audiovisual story?

6 Features

People fascinate people. We imitate them, listen in on their conversations, secretly admire their accomplishments, and watch in awe at their goings-on. What is it about people that "tickles our fancy" so much? For one thing, we all share a sympathetic interest in what life does to us and for us. At news time, we watch it and listen to it not only for the big stories of the day. We want to hear the "little happenings," too — the scandal, the gossip, the humor in the lives of others. The news is full of stories every day about heroism, tragedy, greed, winning and losing — events that lead electronic journalists naturally to the feature story.

Feature stories are about people and things that interest people. They are stories your audience can feel something about and become involved in — stories that entertain and inform. They help keep life in perspective by showing us how other people cope with life, and sometimes they remind us that life isn't all bad news after all. The feature story is one means of imposing balance in newscasts that otherwise would be primarily about things gone wrong.

FEATURES VERSUS STRAIGHT NEWS STORIES

If you are alert to life, interested in people and the things they do, you will be able to identify dozens of potential features. Most important is your ability to bring a fresh perspective to events that seem common and ordinary to the average person. The mark of any creative writer is to see the unusual in the commonplace. It is a capability that comes from

Reporters must do a lot of background research on topics and sources before doing worthwhile feature stories.

learning all you can about everything in life, and from an intense interest in other people.

Feature stories have come to be defined as soft, "non-news" stories about subjects such as lace-making in Denmark or the man down the road who still plows with mules. The true sense of a legitimate feature story, however, incorporates the concept of hard news stories told through people and also what *New York Times* writer Bill Carter calls the serious journalistic treatment of highly emotional, personal stories.

Legitimate feature stories speak to topics of universal interest and concern, and they allow audiences a way to care more about "the facts" than they would about a traditional fact-based story crafted solely from the reporter's words. Consider the story of an elderly New York woman who takes in heroin-addicted babies and helps minister to their mothers. Such a report may say more about how a community addresses drug abuse and rehabilitation, and how ineffective government programs have become, than a facts-only story about the number of drug-addicted babies born each year in New York City.

The main difference between writing straight news and writing features is in the approach. The straight news story usually follows the "four W's" approach: who, what, when, and where. Although feature reporting also covers the four W's, it often deals with the "why" of the story and tries to speak to the consequences of events. Consider first the following straight news story:

> A flu vaccine shortage of nearly 50 million doses in the United States is forcing the federal government to scrounge for alternative sources overseas and prohibit healthy Americans from getting a flu shot this year. If up to five million doses from European countries do become available for use in the United States, officials say only priority populations will get the vaccine, including people over 65, children under five, and the chronically ill. But even for those groups, the availability is no guarantee.

Now compare the above treatment to that in the feature story below:

> Seventy-three-year-old Betty Morgan doesn't like standing outside in the rain. But if she wants a flu shot this year, she is going to have to brave the elements and beat the crowd. The Spring Hill Emergency Health Clinic opens at 7 a.m., and by 6:30 a.m., when Betty arrived, at least 100 people were lined up. The grandmother of 15 would rather take her chances with the cold and wet weather today than increase her chances of getting the flu this year. With only half the expected supply of the flu vaccine, the United States could be on the verge of a flu pandemic, so health officials are asking only the elderly, young children, and chronically ill to get a flu shot.

The basic difference in the two stories is one of approach. The first story has a standard news approach that tells about the flu vaccine shortage nationwide and its impact on certain groups. The second approach, the feature story, tries to evoke some human emotion as it focuses on one woman's frustration over trying to get one of the coveted flu shots.

A CONVERSATION WITH DATELINE NBC CORRESPONDENT JOHN LARSON[1]

John Larson looks for the little details that many other journalists miss in their reporting — just one trait among many that give his work its singular style. In 2001, Larson earned an award for his Dateline NBC investigation on the insurance industry, "Paper Chase." He has won the prestigious Alfred I. du Pont-Columbia Silver Baton, the George Foster Peabody, the George Polk, the IRE for Investigative Reporting, the Loeb

Award for Business Reporting, and the Edward R. Murrow Award, among others. Prior to joining Dateline NBC, Larson worked as a general assignment reporter for KOMO, Seattle, Washington.

He began his journalism career as a stringer for the Boston Globe in 1979. He graduated from Colgate University with a Bachelor of Arts degree in 1975.

Larson's reporting insights and philosophies provide a valuable foundation both for practicing and aspiring journalists.

Question. Some journalists drive by some of the stories you report without ever seeing them. What accounts for your ability to identify the often-overlooked story and pinpoint its larger meanings?

Larson. The first step, of course, is that I look for them — the stories, and their larger meanings. I discovered years ago how some reporters use detail to tell powerful stories. John McPhee of *New Yorker Magazine*, or John Hart, formerly of NBC News, would use small, carefully chosen details to craft extraordinary stories. They frequently collected these details from everyday people, interviews other journalists might not take time to do. The result — their stories came alive with fresh, meaningful detail.

Following their example, I began looking inside my stories for telling details. I think of them as "small truths" — the things people say, a daughter's nickname, the shape of a scar, the platoon's motto — anything that might reflect greater meaning.

I began reporting in Anchorage, Alaska — a wonderful city, rich with stories. It was a small market, and I was assigned a lot of small stories: city hearings, local political races, fund-raisers, etcetera. I learned that when I pay attention to detail, small stories tell me much about who we are — our beliefs, frustrations, ambitions, values. I learned that small stories often illustrate bigger stories. Once I began looking for details and small truths, everything changed. I looked at stories differently. I looked for stories other reporters weren't looking for. I asked different questions. I looked at videotape and listened to recorded sound differently. I accepted that talented photographers and videotape editors hold keys to powerful television.

Question. Many of your stories and the people in them linger in the mind long after your reports are aired. What practices do you follow to make your stories so memorable?

NBC News Correspondent John Larson uses carefully chosen details to make his feature reports powerful.

Larson. First, I try to take time to have regular "What if?" conversations with people I respect. For example, I'll be talking with a colleague about covering government stories, and one of us will wonder, "What if we did a story about one piece of legislation from the point of view of the piece of paper? Who touches it? Who gets copies? Who changes it? Why?" Or we'll be talking about covering crime and we'll wonder, "What if we did a story about crime, not about the most immediate victims, but about people who live next door to crime scenes? What would that tell us about our city?"

I've learned that memorable stories frequently begin at the moment of conception, before I ever make a phone call or shoot a frame. And they are frequently the product of "What if . . . ?" conversations with a friend, family member, editor, or photographer. Great ideas produce memorable stories. I look for stories that are most likely to produce memorable moments on videotape, moments that will surprise the viewer or reveal a truth. A friend calls these moments "wow's" or "ah-ha's." A spontaneous moment on tape can involve viewers more than a reporter's voice or narration. Memorable moments allow viewers to participate and experience the story for themselves.

I look for what I call "echoes": characters, details, small stories that suggest higher themes. For example, one child's confusion speaks to the greater fear shared by flood victims. The details of one man's nightmare show us a real effect of an arsonist. I like to think powerful stories bounce off the back wall of viewers' living rooms and echo in their mind.

Such echoes are seldom literal. They remind viewers of something special that they know to be true, a shared understanding. I look for universal themes such as aspiration, fear, pride, sorrow, arrogance, in even the most common assignments. We are all players in the one, great story of human existence. I try to remember the things we share, and look for them while I work.

I've found memorable stories are often the result of memorable effort. Good stories seem to happen when I try hard, or care a lot. I have my own values and sensibility — the things that make me who I am. When I bring them to work, my work gets better. When I get in touch with my own curiosity, outrage, insecurity, or joy, my work gets better. I do not mean biases. I mean passions, emotion, values.

Question. Some journalists and media observers dismiss the feature story as "soft" and anecdotal, even though it might provide serious journalistic treatment of a subject and address larger issues. What do you say to such critics?

Larson. Such media observers are not very observant. "Feature" is the way you tell a story, not the subject matter or topic. Feature does not mean soft. I've done investigative features, breaking features, general news features. Feature reporting is the process of applying basic storytelling techniques — character, setting, surprise, metaphor, plot — to daily news reports. For example, instead of reporting the effects of a flood by concentrating on statistics, a feature reporter will follow a family, moment by moment, as they return to their neighborhood, allowing detail to help viewers understand the extent of suffering.

Question. What is your definition of the legitimate feature story?

Larson. I think legitimate feature stories share common characteristics. They are almost always about people — strong, central characters. They usually offer a sense of place. They bring special light or added depth to a topic. A legitimate feature should strike a familiar chord, or "echo," with the viewer. A legitimate feature also has several levels. As NBC correspondent Bob Dotson has long said, good stories have a "story within a story." It may, at first glance, be a simple story, but as the story unfolds, it is really about something deeper. A story about a homeless man trying to tune his radio becomes a story about confusion, mental illness, and losing one's way. Features are not frivolous. If a story is poorly focused, or just plain silly, it doesn't matter what you call it. It's just a poor story.

Question. In your opinion, what is the role of the feature report in television news?

Larson. Feature reporting — or, as I would prefer to call it, storytelling — is essential to television news.

Storytelling puts human faces in the news, not generalizations and stereotypes but, rather, unique and unmistakably human faces. Headlines, by definition, must highlight and simplify the news. Storytelling delivers information and, in the process, reveals small truths about all of us. It offers pieces of life. News can be so dehumanizing! Feature reporting — storytelling — stuffs humanity back into the headlines. It helps us understand each other better. It builds bridges between people. Feature reporting reminds us who we are and who we want to be.

Question. What interview sources make the best television? The best journalism?

Larson. Good television and good journalism are not always the same thing. For the sake of clarification, let's say "good television" means good production technique and the elements of good storytelling: powerful pictures, rich sound, action, a dramatic story line, surprise, and strong delivery. Good production techniques can apply to a situation comedy, a movie of the week, or a news story. "Good journalism," on the other hand, is about truth. It is penetrating, elevating, moving. It helps us understand ourselves, our community, our world. I believe good journalism brings us together, building bridges of understanding. The best interview sources for television, just like the best television news stories, reflect both good journalism and good production technique. The best interviews are therefore surprising, informative, active, telling, and true.

I prefer that people I interview share their experience with the viewer rather than discuss or analyze it. People caught in the middle of a story unfolding before your eyes make terrific interviews: a flood victim piling sandbags on the river bank, a rancher rushing to secure his home in the path of a wildfire. The best interviews are immediate — allowing both the person being interviewed and the viewer to forget a television camera is present and tape is rolling.

Let me state here what should be obvious: Television reporters must first be good journalists. Whether they are good "producers" will determine how powerfully they tell their story. Spontaneity is key to good interviews, even in the most staged press conference. If you can't control which people you interview or where you interview them, make sure your questions are fresh, sharp, engaging.

Question. Even when under deadline, how do you manage to avoid formula reporting (VO, bite, VO, standup close, or a variation thereof)?

Larson. I consciously work to avoid formulas and predictable reporting. Unfortunately, this often means I have to work harder. People use formulas because they generally work. Formulas get the basic job done with an acceptable amount of effort. However, formulas kill one of the most powerful story-telling tools I have — surprise. Here are some ways I try to avoid formula reporting:

I look for different perspectives and different "voices." If other reporters are writing about what the city council said, I might write about what the person sitting in the back row of the city council heard. Jackie Shearer, who helped produce the memorable series on the American civil rights movement, "Eyes on the Prize," once told me she looks for the least powerful person in the room, and tells his or her story. I try to avoid always telling stories from the official point of view, that of the police chief, the politician, the bureaucrat, or the manager. The most powerful stories are frequently told from the perspective of the least powerful person, the least powerful voice.

I remember what surprised me, and then write my story to allow viewers to experience the same surprise. For example, I once walked into a factory that had just gone out of business. It was eerie. I was surprised how all the giant machines were silent and the people were gone. So I wrote to that surprise, "The first thing you notice about the Rayonier Pulp Mill is the silence. . . ." Then I was silent long enough for viewers to be struck by the silence, too. The silence probably surprised them, made them curious, and helped them understand something important has been lost, just like it had done to me.

Instead of always organizing my stories by the "facts," I sometimes organize them by pictures and sounds. Good pictures and sound can drive my writing decisions. A strong piece of videotape can focus and simplify my story immensely. This often helps me beat the most brutal deadline. The facts will still be there, but told a different way.

I try to take time, even under tight deadline, to ask for input. I ask photographers what they think the story is all about, or how they think the story should begin. I'll ask the subjects of my story what they think the real story is, and I'm often surprised by their answers. I try to remain open. I'll ask at the end of most interviews, "Is there anything I haven't asked you about, anything you just want to say?" Interviewees sometimes try to avoid the question, but I usually don't let them off the hook too easily.

Question. At what point in the reporting process do you begin to write your story?

STRONG FEATURE STORIES

The most memorable television feature reports reflect a skillful blend of both art and craft — that magical combination of words and pictures, sound, and content. Generally, reports that contain most of the following elements will produce the strongest feature stories.

- An attitude that the reporter is not the story.
- A lead that instantly telegraphs the story to come.
- A script free of information that viewers already would know.
- Strong, natural sound to lend added realism to the story.
- Historical perspective that defines the story's larger context.
- A point of view.
- A strong, central character or characters engaged in compelling action that is visual or picturesque.
- An element of the unexpected.
- Short soundbites (interviews or other shots of people talking on screen) that act to enhance and prove the story you are showing.
- No more than two or three main points in the story.
- A strong closing element that the story builds toward throughout its entirety

Larson. No surprise here. I start at the very beginning. I begin thinking of words, sentences, observations, or anything that might help lead the viewer to the story just as soon as I understand my assignment. I call these lines "handles" — ways the viewer can become interested in the story, and hang on. Handles are striking observations, details, ironies. I search for handles throughout the story, and they help determine what to write.

I begin writing as soon as I can, even if it's just an opening line or a section I know won't change during the day. I try not to set my writing goals too high at first. It just blocks me. I found that once I get a few ideas down on paper, new and better ideas often follow. I rewrite throughout the day — as I meet new people, see a great picture, or learn something. I've learned not to stop writing until I have to.

Some of my best writing is in the edit bays, right on deadline. I may have already written a script, but then I see how pictures and sounds are falling together, and I know I need to rewrite something right now!

Question. Your writing shows restraint and discipline. What tips can you share to avoid overwriting, especially when dealing with abstract or complex issues?

Larson. First, find an editor. You must have a strong person to edit your writing. No exceptions. Before he moved to work at KATU in Portland, Gary Walker edited me expertly for years. So did Janice Evans, who left for KUTV in Salt Lake City, Utah. Good editors bring out your best work. If you tend toward overwriting, you may be protecting your favorite lines and soundbites too much. Be ruthless. Drop anything that isn't absolutely necessary.

Remember, less is more. Good writing has a tendency to disappear, drawing attention to the story and not to itself. Avoid adjectives and adverbs when possible. Use nouns and verbs. And watch your verbs. Avoid the verb "to be" in any form. Search for stronger verbs. Tighten your story's focus by continually asking yourself, "What is this story really about?" "Who really are my strongest characters?" "How am I proving this story with sound and pictures?"

Answer these questions, and your writing will be clearer, stronger. Poor writing is often the result of unfocused thinking, not poor writing skills. Keep paring your words and story line down until they are as lean as they can be. Again, be ruthless.

Question. Often, you let the pictures, sound, silence, or even other people do the talking. What is your philosophy about when to use the various writing instruments in television — words, images, sounds, silences, actions, and behaviors?

Larson. Pictures and sound — the argument of a farmer, a cry from the back of the room, the sound of wood splitting — are the bricks I use to build stories. My words are mortar. Properly used, pictures and sounds offer the most compelling television. When I first began reporting, I inadvertently began organizing my stories by video. At the time, I assumed everyone did it this way. I'd draw a vertical column of eight or so boxes in my notebook at the end of each day. Then I'd write the name of a specific piece of good video or sound in each box: an airplane landing, the sound of the wheels hitting the pavement, a soundbite with a pilot, and so on. Next I'd arrange my video boxes, searching for the best order of pictures to surprise my viewer, and demonstrate points I wanted to make in my story.

I have since refined this practice somewhat, but I realize I was doing things backward — organizing my stories by video instead of by editorial content. Yet, this was giving me better stories than other reporters working the same story. I'd prioritize my video first, then decide how my facts could follow. I wouldn't omit facts, but I would let the video drive my decisions of how to tell my facts. Interview sound, natural sound, silence, and pictures all permit viewers to experience stories for themselves. I try to use words to guide viewers through their own experience of discovery.

In some ways, I think learning to write for television is about learning when to shut up. I try to be equally demanding of my words, sounds, soundbites, silences, and pictures. They all must support or advance a story, or be cut. I also use sound to punctuate sentences. Sound can be used as an exclamation point ("Look out!"), comma ("On your mark,"), or ellipses ("I've always wondered . . ."). Some words of caution: Sound is not noise. I try to use only sound that advances my story line or proves a point. Every story has a voice, a storyteller who takes the viewer by the hand. Usually it is the reporter/writer voice, but in "natural sound" stories, it is a main character's voice. Whoever it is, I'm careful not to confuse or lose that voice by mixing it with too much sound or too many voices. This makes the viewer work too hard to follow the story.

Question. What criteria help you determine when to stop writing words?

Larson. Practically speaking, I rarely put more than two sentences together without breaking the sentences for sound. I always try to stop talking long enough to allow the sounds and pictures to prove whatever I'm reporting. For example, if I'm writing about people waiting to buy tickets to a big game, I shut up and let them wait for a while. I also choose words to deliberately set up a rhythm, a cadence. I make sentences short when I want to build tension, immediacy. Just like a preacher, a reporter can use the rhythms of a sentence, of his or her own voice, of a soundbite, or the combination of all three to draw the viewer closer.

Question. Viewers often listen to television news rather than watch it. What do you do to help keep renewing the contract with viewers so they watch your reports rather than merely listen to them?

Larson. A reporter once told me, "I wish I could just say to the viewer, come here and look at this!" Well, why can't you? I sometimes "call" viewers to the television set and challenge them. For example, I've written, "If you've ever wondered how an 80-year-old man picks himself up after losing everything he owns, take a minute and listen . . . ," and then I let him talk. I believe you sometimes must strongly encourage viewers to give you their full attention: "She hoped she would never see what you are about to see now . . . " or, "If you've listened to what Clara Wells has been saying, you can guess what happened next." I'm careful not to overuse this kind of writing. If the sounds and pictures don't pay off with a memorable point, I've abused it. Viewers and news directors don't like that.

Question. When you arrive at a story, what is the first thing you do?

Larson. I search for a reason to care. I look for a character, a predicament, a quest, a telling detail that will help me and my viewers care. When I'm on the scene, I look for people who have strong stories to offer. I do not choose them because they are loud, colorful, or odd.

Once I find people who care, I try to be quiet and listen. I don't interrupt them. I listen for what they are trying to accomplish, or trying to understand. It may be a personal goal or quest of some sort. They may be trying to fix a water hose, or get a message to someone.

These small details can help me tell a good story. When I'm at a breaking news story — a fire, a shooting — I sometimes walk up to the front line, turn my back on the action, and look in the opposite direction. I often find my story in the people who are there helping, worrying, caught up in the action. Sometimes I'll close my eyes and concentrate on sounds. I've never found a great story in the flames or body bags.

Question. What story elements do you look for throughout the reporting process?

Larson. I look for plot. I call it "quest" — any search, goal, task, or ambition I can build into a story line. This can be something as simple as someone hoping to get to the head of the line at a rock concert. I look for universal truths, "echoes," or handles — details about the people in my stories that my viewers will recognize as true and will help them care. This can be something as serious as the saddest moment in a woman's life, or something as simple as watching a child take his first steps while waiting in an airport.

I look for spontaneous moments captured on tape. They are rarely what you set out to find, but they are exactly what happened and are often more interesting

than your original story idea. Then I try to make sense of the moments, putting them in an order that helps people understand the greater meaning of the story, and allows them a sense of participation. And last, but definitely not least, I look for a strong character. I give viewers a reason to care about the character. A good character is more than a loud soundbite.

Question. When you cover stories, how do you put people at ease?

Larson. In general, I try to treat people the way I would want my own family treated. I say hello. I wipe my feet on the mat outside. I try to listen closely. I do my best to forget my deadline and remember that I'm a guest. I try to talk to them before the cameras arrive and, when possible, after the cameras leave. All of this helps put people at ease.

Sometimes I try to let the photographer interview the people in my stories. People who are not accustomed to being interviewed tend to freeze when a reporter shows up, wearing the suit and tie. They tend to relax while chatting with a photographer. The photographer and I will discuss questions beforehand, and then the photographer can ask the questions while shooting pictures of the subject doing something. Sometimes I'll purposefully walk away, telling the subject to talk to the photographer while I do something else. It helps put people at ease.

I try to avoid sit-down interviews whenever possible. Sit-down interviews almost seem as though they were designed to make people uncomfortable. If I must do a sit-down interview, I try to be as casual as the situation allows, talking honestly with them, expecting honesty in return. Some people have asked me, "How do you get people to trust you?" The question itself makes me worry. I'm not sure I trust a reporter who thinks trust is a way to get things. The best way to get people to trust you — and I mean this — is to be trustworthy. If you are worthy of the trust you ask people to place in you, they tend to sense it and open up.

Are you willing to walk away from a story for the right reasons? If not, maybe you're not to be trusted. Are you willing to withhold something from your viewers to protect them [the interviewees] or their family from undeserved pain? If you are, your interview subjects will begin to trust you. Take your reporter hat off and put your human being hat on. Then burn the reporter hat.

Question. What interview settings do you most prefer?

Larson. I prefer interviews that take place while people are doing something — the victim of a fire searching the ashes of her home, a Little League pitcher warming up before entering the game. When people are doing something familiar, they are more likely to be relaxed. Don't wait for the big moment to start talking to people. Get a wireless mike on them as soon as you can. Often the best comments are made while everyone is getting ready for whatever is supposed to happen. Now that I'm working for "Dateline NBC," I'm doing a lot of sit-down interviews. In sit-downs, I most like unexpected exchanges, unexpected discussions about off-topics, and moments that allow the real face of the interviewee to be seen.

Question. Documentary filmmakers have said one of their responsibilities is "stockpiling history." What do you most hope to accomplish as a television journalist?

Larson. I'd like the body of my work to be filled with compelling human stories, stories that engage viewers' hearts and minds. I hope my work breaks stereotypes and puts uniquely human faces in the news. I hope my work helps people care. I want to help keep the light burning.

Question. How do you want your stories to be remembered?

Larson. In Alaska, there's an impossible-to-pronounce Eskimo word, "Qavlunaq," which, loosely translated, means "the movement of an unseen object." It describes what happens when a great fish swims just below the surface of the water, out of sight but very real. Eskimo fishermen can sense a great fish's presence by reading subtle changes in the surface tension of the water.

I'd like my stories to be remembered as efforts to accurately cover the news of the day, and something more — to report the movements of the unseen objects, the great fish that swim just below the surface of daily news. Daily news stories are often stories of greater truths: greed, ambition, hope, desperation, humor, and faith. We all share these truths on one level or another. I hope I have paid attention well, like the fisherman, and have noticed what is of value. I want viewers to remember the people in my stories — their heart, backbone, humor. I'd like to be remembered as someone who was grateful for the work, respected the people he met, and loved the stories they offered.

TELLING THE FEATURE STORY

It's been said "there are no dull subjects, only dull writers." Good feature writing presupposes that you have an overwhelming interest in people. This interest in people — and sometimes in places and things — allows you to write interesting stories about almost any subject.

By definition, feature writing is a more personal form of journalism than most reporting, more intimate in its expression, which in turn allows you more freedom to decide story treatment, emphasis, and tone.

> *Great visual storytelling attracts and holds a larger audience.*
> JOHN LANSING,
> Scripts Network Executive

FEATURE WRITING HINTS

Few rules govern the style or form of features, but you will usually need some kind of angle if you are reporting about subjects not well known to your audience. The angle can be as simple as an emphasis on the unusual in which you give your audience a little surprise:

> Jonathan David lives in Fargo, North Dakota. He's just starting third grade and says by Christmas he'll know how to read. Nothing unusual there, except that Jonathan is 81, and he says it's hard to run a business these days without some "book learning."

Besides your angle, you will need a treatment appropriate for the subject — a way to establish the tone of your story. As a feature writer, you are a storyteller, a "show-and-tell" expert who draws in the audience by revealing, tidbit by tidbit, the fascinating story you have to tell. As a storyteller, you can drop straight news style and concentrate on what some writers call the "anecdotal approach." In your story lead, you set up interest and make the audience hungry to learn more of what you have to tell. Like the master storyteller, you tease and delay (while still keeping your story simple and concise) until finally you drop the punch line.

When you avoid typical news style, your writing can become more conversational, more casual than usual. As your story unfolds, you reveal its various elements of human interest and emphasize them for maximum audience interest and understanding of the larger issue about which you are reporting.

ENDNOTES

1. Source: From "A Conversation with NBC Correspondent, John Larson." Used by permission. Copyright © 1995, 2000, 2004 by John Larson.

ASSIGNMENT 6A: Writing Feature Stories

Name _____ Date _____

1 Research and write a feature story on one of the following topics, or a similar subject of your choice. If you choose your own topic, secure permission from your instructor before developing the story.

Identify individuals who *build, strive, achieve, triumph, overcome,* or otherwise distinguish themselves through their accomplishments. Find strong, central characters who illuminate larger issues. Be certain your subjects are engaged in compelling, visual activities that help to illuminate the central message.

• How streets are named in your community

• In what ways people use laptop computers

• How email has affected mail and express delivery services

2 Identify and list ten potential feature stories in your community. Write a 90-second feature story for radio, television, or the Internet on at least two of the topics you have identified. Imagine you have your choice of visuals to work with.

Note: If you or other members of the class can shoot videotape and have access to equipment, arrange to shoot and edit a visual piece to accompany your script.

Arrange a day in class for presentation, discussion, and critique of your feature stories (and videotape).

3 Watch feature stories on television. Determine which subjects, visual elements, word combinations, and treatments make the best feature stories in your view. Discuss your findings in class.

To make this assignment more meaningful, invite a local reporter/photographer team to speak in class on story coverage, and discuss how the news team covers feature stories.

4 Get a county map of your area, select a location, go there, and dig out and write a story suitable for radio or television.

| 5 | Using the classified ads from your newspaper, identify at least three subjects who would be worthy of feature treatment. Using the classified ad as your starting point, write a feature story suitable for a television report.

Note: To fulfill this assignment, you will have to use in-field research, using the ad as your starting point.

| 6 | Compare the coverage of feature news on local stations with those on your favorite network news. Identify common types of stories found on network news versus a local newscast. Discuss your findings in class, along with a general discussion of the value of feature material in local newscasts.

ASSIGNMENT 6B: Kicker

Name _____ Date _____

Write a kicker (last story of the newscast that leaves the audience smiling) from the following facts:

An art contest was recently held in Pittsburgh, Penn., by Campbell's Soup to see who could come up with the best artwork based on its soup. The winner turned out to be 70-year-old Dino Sistilli of New Jersey who created a sheet of stamps with pictures of soup brands on them. Sistilli went to Pittsburgh yesterday to pick up his $10,000 reward. The judges said Sistilli's artwork was "mmm mmm good." John Warhol, brother of famous pop artist Andy Warhol, said the pop-artist would have been proud.

(WRITE YOUR STORY HERE IN ACCEPTABLE STYLE)

ASSIGNMENT 6C: Feature Writing

Name _____ Date _____

First write a straight news lead for each set of facts. Then write a feature lead. Finally, write a feature story for each set of facts.

1. Yesterday in Madrid, Spain, shepherds herded their sheep through the streets to encourage authorities to protect animals' natural migration routes. Some of Spain's 78,000 miles of animal paths are 800 years old. The sheep herding has been held each October for four years. Witnesses said the bleating of the 2,000 sheep drowned out car horns in the street.

2   Twenty teams competed in an annual brick-laying contest in Phoenix, Arizona, this morning. The winner of the contest will be given $1,000 and the chance to compete in the national championship in Charlotte, North Carolina. Participants in the contest are judged on the quantity of blocks laid, visual continuity of the mortar joints, vertical plumb, story height, and just keeping the whole thing level. Also, an award for fastest trowel in Arizona will be presented.

ASSIGNMENT 6C: Feature Writing (continued)

Name _____ Date _____

3 Christie's Auction House is about to hold its Hong Kong autumn auction. One the largest diamonds ever to be auctioned off is for sale. It is a 22-point, 13-carat almost flawless diamond. It is expected to bring more than ten million Hong Kong dollars. The sale will also feature artworks and a jade necklace expected to bring in more than thirty million Hong Kong dollars.

4 | Sewer crews in Cocoa Beach, Florida, found a seven-foot manatee stuck in a storm drain yesterday. They estimate it had been stuck in the sewer for over a week. It was discovered when a crew replacing the grate over a drain opened up the sewer. Officials believe the manatee entered the pipe through a canal leading from the Banana River. Sea World was called in to help get the manatee out. Rescuers were forced to climb in the black widow infested tunnel to pull the manatee to safety. The manatee was then put on a stretcher and lifted out of the sewer. It is now recovering in a medical pool at Sea World.

ASSIGNMENT 6C: Feature Writing (continued)

Name _____ Date _____

5 A new exhibit opened at the National Air Space Museum in Washington, DC, today about the movie, "Star Wars." The exhibit is to be open to the public for one year and is entitled, "Star Wars: The Magic of the Myth." The exhibit, which features more than 200 original costumes, characters, and other props from the movie, examines how the movie trilogy touched people through its use of classical mythology. The exhibit also commemorates the 25th anniversary of the debut of "Star Wars" in movie theaters.

Critical Thinking Questions

Directions: The following questions are provided to help you examine the deeper meanings and complexities of the various issues under discussion. After a thoughtful review of the subject, answer each question to the best of your ability.

1. Some journalists have proposed that, in the end, all stories are features. Make a case for this point of view, then build a case that purely factual stories (inflation or interest rates, storm damage, crime statistics, etc.) must fall outside the definition of feature stories.

2. When, if ever, is it appropriate for a journalist to convey an emotional outline in a news report?

3. What is the distinction between fairness, objectivity, and bias? As part of your answer, discuss "bias" as it may exist in the eye of the beholder (the audience). Assuming the role of a television news director, explain to a newly hired reporter your requirements for selecting feature stories — the selection process, content, treatment, and justification.

4. What essential qualities distinguish the hard news story from the feature story? As part of your response, convert a feature story to a hard news story, and a hard news story to a feature story.

5. What is your response to NBC Correspondent John Larson's comment, "Feature is the way you tell a story, not the subject matter or topic."

6. In reporting stories for electronic media, how important and ethical is it to find story subjects who make "good interviews" and "good television?" To what extent should these considerations matter? Why?

7. To an extent, people tend to remember what they see, not what they hear. How, if at all, should this idea influence the choice of interview settings?

8. If, as one adage holds, audiences will never care more about a story than the reporter does, what are some ways by which you can become interested in story content, regardless of subject?

Self-Review Questions

Directions: Each of the self-review questions below addresses information contained in this chapter. Answer each question to the best of your ability, then review the chapter as necessary to further strengthen your understanding of each concept or issue.

1. What is the nature of feature stories? How do they differ from straight news stories?

2. How can you make news stories, regardless of content, more interesting, memorable, and relevant?

3. What is your definition of a "legitimate feature story?"

4. What is the difference between interview sources that make for the best "television" versus the best journalism?

5. What approaches can you follow to avoid "overwriting" news stories that include video?

6. In a sense, the electronic journalist is always writing, even when the script contains no spoken words. How is this possible?

7. What does "quest" mean, and how does it contribute to the storytelling process?

8. To what extent do journalists have a responsibility to "stockpile history?"

9. What did John Larson mean when he said feature stories "stuff humanity back into the headlines?"

10. John Larson likes to use "natural sound" in his feature stories. Why does he believe this makes the story stronger?

## CHAPTER SEVEN

Interviews and Soundbites

A t their best, electronic media have tremendous power to involve, to sweep up their audiences in psychological and physiological ways, because they use sound and motion to dramatic effect. In a newscast, the sight of a starving child, the sound of a crying person, the roar of a fire out of control, the angry voice of a taxpayer — all are capable of altering your blood pressure, your heart, and breathing rates, and your point of view.

SOUNDBITES

A **soundbite** is the sound — and in television, the video — of a person speaking. Soundbites — or **actualities** as they sometimes are called — take the audience to the scene of an event. They allow the audience to vicariously experience news events and, hence, enable them to understand events more fully. Electronic media prefer the dramatic, however, and can pull the news out of context through unduly dramatic actualities. The isolating glare of microphones and cameras can make the sounds and sights of 100 angry protesters in an emotional frenzy seem to the audience like a mob of thousands unless the report maintains perspective.

Sources and Purposes of Soundbites

Soundbites constitute one form of writing for electronic media. They allow you to stop writing words for a moment or two and let a person in the news craft an observation, express an idea, or reveal a thought or feeling. Soundbites come from many sources: excerpts from a speech, news conferences, public statements, experts, interviews, and eyewitnesses. The list goes on, but you can count on obtaining bites from day to day from almost anyone who makes news or watches it happen. A soundbite can come from the mayor at a news conference, a bank teller who has just been robbed, an underwater rescue diver, an expert on solar energy, or the survivor of an airplane crash.

Some reporters think of soundbites as an essential part of the story, but the best soundbites are not self-contained reports. They help illustrate a story in somewhat the same way a newspaper picture might, and typically they add a dimension that the script could not.

Soundbites provide new information and credibility, help reveal the person, and add a sense of spontaneity. If you understand that, you are able to use soundbites in more varied ways. Skilled writers easily can rewrite what a person says in an interview into a more concise, clear description, but the soundbite adds an air of authority, first-person experience, and expert support for the points made. Therefore, you select the portion of what is said that provides the most impact. Soundbites are not there to tell the story but, instead, to enhance the report and help provide a sense of "being there."

Using Soundbites

The basic test of soundbites is whether they reflect reality accurately. If what you've done distorts the meaning the speaker intended, you must make adjustments so your work is ethical and furthers the pursuit of truth instead of creating a false illusion of reality.

You can use a soundbite in three ways:

1. To provide factual information.
2. To help prove a visual or add a dimension of realism from the news environment itself.
3. To reveal a person's inner self.

Often, soundbites function at all three levels. If a political candidate announces, "I choose not to run for another term," the bite contains the literal information of the announcement, and it also may carry a sense of the environment (reporter reaction, silence from a roomful of stunned supporters), as well as the speaker's emotion as conveyed through the speaker's voice, emphasis, pauses, and rate of delivery.

Frequently, bites can be used not only for information but also to help prove the visual. If you show store-owners sweeping mud from flooded stores in a mountain community, a bite to the effect, "We'll reopen for business by noon" may reinforce the video's message that flood damage is relatively light.

Just as commonly, bites help reveal the inner person. If, in an interview, you ask an elderly person, "Do you ever think about accepting charity?" the person may reveal a deeply held conviction in her reply, "I'd rather live on the streets than accept government handouts." If a soundbite doesn't say anything new, or doesn't add to what you have written or shown in the main story, it can be dropped.

Because soundbites serve to enhance stories rather than substitute for your own reporting, they should be kept fairly short, usually no longer than eight to 12 seconds. Occasionally a bite is so dramatic or full of information that it can run longer, but in most cases ten seconds should be the maximum.

The reason for keeping bites short is that longer bites can take on the speaker's pace, authority, and focus, and may even impose an unintended editorial point of view, particularly when institutional news sources are used in interviews. When electronic media stories average between 20 to 70 seconds, bites longer than about ten seconds begin to dominate editorial content. Print journalists sometimes speak contemptuously about the short length of bites in electronic stories, but almost never do quotes in the print media run more than a sentence or two — about ten seconds if they were to be spoken aloud.

Reporters who know little about a subject sometimes take the lazy way out by cutting a long bite of 30 to 45 seconds in which the interviewee explains something in detail beyond what the audience needs or wants to know. That makes for a boring, ineffective story. Better, the reporter would paraphrase concisely most of what an interviewee says and then drop in the strongest ten seconds or so of the interviewee's comment as the actual bite used in the piece. Soundbites are the electronic journalist's version of quotes, and they should be used the same way a good print reporter uses quotes — to provide support, first-person perspective, and drama — but always concisely and powerfully.

Outstanding reporters use parts of an interviewee's sentence, with the lead-in by the reporter (in a package report) or the anchor (in a story to be read in the studio) providing the rest of the sentence. For example, the anchor could say, "The governor went on to blast the legislature as . . . ." (now the governor's soundbite picks up angrily) . . . "a bunch of clowns who keep fiddling while Rome burns!" Or the most powerful part of a statement can be used to kick off the story, followed by the anchor's or reporter's narration of the rest of the sentence to weave the soundbite into a meaningful context.

To continue the example: The governor pops up on camera fuming, "That pack of wild dogs in the legislature wouldn't know a bone with meat on it if it was right in front of 'em." The reporter or anchor then adds, ". . . the governor angrily charged at today's news conference." It's entirely appropriate to use sentence fragments as soundbites, with the anchor or reporter completing the sentence, as long as the context of the comment is not distorted.

INTERVIEWS

Interviews provide raw material for soundbites, yet they are such an everyday part of reporting that we often take them for granted. Interviews spice up our reports and give it another dimension. The interview is a reliable way to enhance viewer and listener interest in the newscast, provided it is honest and conversational. As with most actualities, the best interviews are spontaneous, not stilted, rehearsed, or contrived.

> *A portion of the daily newspapers of New York are (sic) bringing the profession into contempt, so far as they can, by a kind of toadyism or flunkeyism, which they call "interviewing."*
> LONDON DAILY NEWS 1869

In the range from simple entertainment to serious discussions, the most frequently heard interviews are brief news or spot interviews. Some interviews, for example, provide a vehicle through which eyewitnesses can describe, in their own words and emotions, the drama of hard news events. Someone who has just witnessed a helicopter crash or escaped from a burning apartment house transmits a vitality of description that few reporters could ever match without becoming personally involved in the story.

Interviews may expose the sincerity or falseness of political figures as they speak their opinions about important social issues. Interviews can entertain and inform us with intimate glimpses of celebrities being themselves, children's first frightened confrontations with department-store Santa Clauses, and talks with experts on every subject from overpopulation to parapsychology. Interviews are powerful tools that contribute to news much of its immediacy, mood, essential detail, expert interpretation of important events, and the kinds of entertainment values that give zest to electronic media reports.

The Interviewer

Good interviewing takes practice — sometimes years of it. The Ted Koppels, Tim Russerts, and Katie Courics of the world work hard to develop and maintain their interview skills. To become a skilled interviewer — the person who asks the right question at the right time, who consistently asks insightful questions, a journalist who can probe for honest answers without offending — you will have to practice the art of interviewing. All prerequisites for successful interviews presuppose that you come to the occasion thoroughly prepared, that you know everything you can about the interviewee and the subject at hand. Few things kill an interview more quickly

Good interviewing takes practice. One of the keys to success is making the source feel comfortable in the interview so you can have a conversation that yields good information and articulate soundbites.

than an interviewer who obviously is not knowledgeable or interested in the subject at hand.

Basics of Good Interviews

When you conduct an interview, you are the mind and mouthpiece of your collective audience. You are responsible for asking questions your audience would ask if given the opportunity, seeking clarification if the interviewee wanders, making sure the interview is an exchange of information instead of a conveyor belt of information from special interests, and pacing the interview so it builds to a satisfying conclusion.

Interviewing is an art that builds upon another art — the art of listening. Many people, even so-called professional interviewers, are so intent upon formulating their next question that they fail to hear what the interviewee is saying. Honest responses to honest questions are the heart of spontaneous interviews. You can kill the life of any interview quickly by concentrating so intently on your next question that you fail to listen.

Electronic media journalists seldom have time or sufficient reason to write down every question they intend to ask. A better method is to list on a note pad the topics you'd like to cover in the interview. Some journalists write down a few key words or the four or five most important questions they intend to ask. They store other questions or subject areas in the back of their mind in case the interview falters or fails to develop as they anticipate. Questions cannot be prepared in detail or totality because interviews often develop spontaneously. The attentive interviewer capitalizes on the situation at hand by listening carefully to responses and guiding the interview so it develops naturally.

Tough Questioning

If the interviewee is especially reticent about responding to controversial subject matter, tough questions are sometimes warranted, but tough questions may offend the audience if they are asked without just cause. Tough questioning should be saved for interviewees who intentionally try to change the subject or who talk nonstop to avoid the subject. When warranted, the tough question works wonders: "Twice you've avoided answering the question, Mr. Mayor. Did you ever accept bribes from bail bondsmen?" If silence is the ensuing "answer," it can be more eloquent than words.

Techniques to Put the Interviewee at Ease

As the on-camera interviewer, you can help put the other person at ease by appearing relaxed yourself. Prepare the interviewee before you actually start, especially

SPOTLIGHT

Tips for Interviewing

No matter what the topic, the following tips constitute sound advice.

- Listen. Because the interview is a conversation, it demands that you be an active, courteous listener just as you would be in a normal conversation. To a great extent, the art of good interviewing is the art of conscientious listening. Reporters who half-listen to the interviewee while they think up more questions to ask can kill the interview quickly. Careful listening helps the reporter build the interview around what's just been said.

- Avoid "yes and no" and leading questions. Questions that require only a simple "yes" or "no" as the answer impart little real information to your audience. And leading questions that begin with, "Do you think...?" "Were you scared...?" "Are you against..." should be replaced with questions that begin with "Why?" or "What do you mean...?" Questions that require an articulate response from the interviewee almost always result in the strongest interviews. A related problem is demonstrated by the interviewer who asks and answers each and every question. For example:

  > Chief Walters, we know you've had a tough time maintaining discipline among your officers. We know all the steps you've taken to reinstitute good morale, but the feeling among most people in the community seems to be that your changes have come too late to do any good. Based on those facts, don't you think you should resign?"

  This litany tends to make the interviewee hostile, which in turn makes your audience hostile toward you and your newscast. Questions that require an articulate response from the interviewee result in the strongest interviews.

- Avoid saying "I see" or "uh-huh" after each response from the interviewee. These comments may be an honest attempt to show interviewees that you understand what they are saying, but too often they imply to your audience that you agree with the interviewee. The same advice applies to head-nodding during live broadcasts or via Internet video streaming.

- Avoid asking two-part questions. For example:

  > First, sir, is it true that Dotcom plans to double its workforce within the next four years, and second, is it true that profits have jumped from seven dollars a share to more than fifty dollars during the past year?"

  If your interviewee doesn't forget one or both parts of a double-barreled question, your audience almost certainly will.

- Avoid obvious questions.

  > Senator Kennedy, you're a member of the Democrat Party, are you not?"

- Avoid questions of bad taste. Sometimes journalists, without thinking, ask insensitive questions of accident and disaster victims who are still in shock. Examples are:

  > How did you feel after you learned your son had drowned?

  > Did you fear for your life when the high-voltage current passed through your body?

  Should questions such as these be asked? Do the responses add substantially to information contained in the accompanying report? Also, ask yourself if you would want to be on camera following such a tragedy. More than likely, good interviews are available from people who have witnessed the situation but are not directly affected. This gives you good material for a strong story and does not alienate you from an audience angry that you would put suffering individuals on camera during some of their most difficult moments.

if the person lacks interview experience. Preparation helps you set up everything right and avoids potential problems. Say something like:

> I don't know how many of these you've done. Just talk to me. Ignore the camera. It's only a window to our conversation. If you are using a stick microphone, say: "I have to point the mic at you to pick you up, but don't reach out and grab it or it'll make a 'clunk' noise and we'll have to cut that out."

Constant eye contact with the person will help minimize the intimidating effects of microphones and other electronic media gear. When you offer yourself as the reference point, the interviewee can concentrate on you as a person — not on the lights, camera, and action that's happening all around.

To help put interviewees at ease, the crew's conduct is especially important. For example, the person in charge of lighting shouldn't shine bright lights directly into the interviewee's eyes and, instead, should bounce lights indirectly off walls and ceilings or hand-held reflectors. Microphones — another intimidating aspect of television — should be as inconspicuous as possible. Sometimes a microphone mounted on the camera or a miniature microphone pinned to the speaker's lapel solves the problem.

Telephone interviews in electronic journalism are generally done for background information or to check facts and late-breaking news before going on-air.

TELEPHONE INTERVIEWS

Another source for soundbites is the statement or interview from a news source recorded off a telephone line into a sound recorder. The telephone is also used to run down breaking information.

By law, the people you speak with must be told that their voice is being recorded. Telephone interviews are commonly used when you are pressed for time and can't interview a news source in person, or when a reporter in the field must phone in a late-breaking story in time for an upcoming newscast.

Most telephone recording systems feature a normal telephone receiver with a hand switch that shuts off the telephone mouthpiece to exclude extraneous noise from the newsroom while the recording is being made. A simple press of the switch reactivates the mouthpiece so you can converse normally with the news source when you wish.

Telephone Rundowns

At most organizations, news personnel routinely make telephone rundowns a check just before major newscasts to determine whether important news is breaking. These checks are made with police, fire, sheriff, and other local agencies according to a master list of the most frequently called and important agencies. Some

stations have automatic dialing devices that make calls at the push of a button.

Often, as you make these rundowns, you will be greeted with a brusque "no news today" and a slam of the receiver on the other end even as you identify yourself. This happens because news sources have their own deadlines and are contacted daily by your station and by competing stations.

Telephone Courtesy

Whether you are recording a telephone interview or using the telephone for routine checks of fire, police, or sheriff's department happenings, telephone manners are important. When you call sources, give your name and the station call letters or channel number and tell them whether you plan to record and air their comments. When the conversation has ended, thank the source for taking time out from a busy schedule to talk with you.

Courtesy pays off two ways:

1. It helps you get the story.

2. It makes access to information easier next time you have to call the same source about a story.

LEAD-INS AND TAGS

When used alone, soundbites require lead-ins and tags — a way to introduce the bite to the audience and a way to get out of it and on to the next story, respectively. The common formula for handling actualities in short newscasts at many radio stations is: two lines in (the lead-in), 20 seconds for the actuality, and one line out (the tag). This formula is somewhat arbitrary and won't apply in every situation.

The lead-in can be both the story and an introduction to the actuality. Here is an example written and prepared for a radio newscast.

> The blizzard is moving north to Canada tonight...after dumping more than a foot of snow on the Dakotas and Minnesota. The blizzard was so intense it made driving impossible . . . and many drivers were forced to spend the night in their cars . . . or truck stops along the road.
>
> CT
>
> :14
>
> (Outcue" . . . all day trying to get out.")
>
> The storm left many rigs frozen solid. The forecast for wind and cold makes even worse driving conditions likely tomorrow.

The 15-second lead-in introduces the story and sets up the soundbite. In this case, the soundbite contains excerpts of interviews with stranded motorists telling of their experiences in the blizzard. The actuality is noted on the radio script as **CT**, meaning a prerecorded cartridge for radio. Increasingly, news operations are using SOUNDBITE or even **SOT** for sound-on-tape. We recommend the SOT designation because it is less confusing for people moving among different formats.

Following the CT or SOT is a number that indicates the length of the soundbite. The outcue, a standard in news scripts, gives the last five or six words of a soundbite and cues the engineers when to get the mic ready for the newscaster following the SOT.

The **tag** wraps up the story and brings it to a polished, professional ending. It most often refers to the bite even if only to re-identify the speaker in the SOT. The tag tells the audience that the story has ended and that you are ready to move to a new story. Lazy writers often eliminate story tags. Professionals almost never omit them.

Lead-ins should be kept to about 15 seconds, and tags no more than ten seconds. If you are writing the intro to a comprehensive stand-up report from an infield reporter, a one-sentence lead-in may suffice. Lead-ins usually sound best if they are self-contained and do not announce that a soundbite follows. With these lead-ins, also are called blind lead-ins, the story can stand alone, although it is admittedly more complete and interesting with the bite. Note the following improvement on a lead-in:

> *Original*: Johnson was asked how the wheat agreement will affect bread prices.
>
> *Rewrite*: Johnson says wheat subsidies will not cause higher bread prices in America.
>
> *Johnson (on tape)*: "We anticipate absolutely no economic effect in the supermarket from this measure . . . ."

The lead-in helps summarize the tone and substance of the soundbite with Johnson. The original example lacks impact and will leave your audience hanging in mid-air if the soundbite fails to play or if loose production causes a brief interruption or pause before the sound begins.

Here are some more examples of lead-ins edited for stronger impact and improved clarity. Notice that the rewrites avoid telling the audience what the question was but, instead, tell the answers. This is strong journalistic writing because it is direct and more informative:

> *Original*: We asked councilwoman Lopez if lower tax bills will result.
>
> *Rewrite*: Councilwoman Lopez says the council is not certain the measure will result in lower tax bills. Councilwoman Lopez (on tape): "I don't see one drop of relief for any property owner in town."
>
> *Original*: We asked foresters what caused the fire.
>
> *Rewrite*: State foresters say lightning probably caused the fire.
>
> *Forester (on VTR)*: "There were no people in the area, no campfires, but the area is extremely dry, and the lightning buildup last night was tremendous."
>
> *Original*: We talked with Senator Clark today, and she said . . . .
>
> *Rewrite*: Senator Clark says she's in favor of the bill.
>
> *Original*: We asked Russell how he thinks the council will decide.
>
> *Rewrite*: Russell says he thinks the council will vote against annexation.
>
> *Original*: Here's what Martinez thinks.
>
> *Rewrite*: Martinez says he thinks professional hockey in Boulder is years away.

When writing lead-ins, you should avoid an echo chamber or parrot effect. This is a lead-in that says in almost the same words what is on the start of the tape. **Parroting** in the lead the identical content of the actuality makes the newscast sound unprofessional. The problem arises most often when someone else has edited the soundbite and the writer has not taken time to check how it begins. Often, you can cut the first sentence of the soundbite you will use on air and use the information contained in that sentence as the substance of your lead-in. Then the lead-in will flow even more naturally into the piece you air. Or a quick rewrite of the lead-in is always a good option. For example:

Original (Newsperson): Brand retailers say independent stations are behind the gas war . . .

(Audiotape): Independent stations are behind the gas war.

Rewrite (Newsperson): Brand retailers maintain this fight will not jeopardize their relationship with independent stations.

Original (Newsperson): . . . but say it will be months before the stadium is completed.

(Video): Despite earlier predictions, the Bears say it will be months before the stadium is completed.

Rewrite (Newsperson): Fans eager to cheer from a new home are going to have wait a little longer.

Original (Newsperson): The President is in Japan, signing the final agreement that returns control of three American missile bases to the Japanese government.

(Video): The President is in Japan to sign the final agreement that returns control of three American air bases to the Japanese government.

Rewrite (Video): The Japanese have been requesting the American pull-out for months, and finally the Administration acquiesced.

EDITING THE SOUNDBITE

Almost no soundbite can be transmitted to an audience without some editing. News conferences, especially those called by special-interest groups, can drag on and on. Eyewitnesses often are emotional, confused, and wordy. Scientists sometimes are complex and obtuse. The aim is to pull out the gems or nuggets of what you have recorded and use just those sections to illustrate the essence of the event as succinctly as possible.

Signs are posted in many newsrooms warning personnel to reserve anything more than two minutes for World War III or the Second Coming. A minute often is too long for most taped inserts in radio, and in television reports and Internet stories, few soundbites are worth more than 20 seconds.

Rarely does an interview or soundbite open with the newsperson's question. This sounds clumsy in radio and takes over what the function of a lead-in should be. In television, nothing looks worse than a vacant-eyed interviewee's head on the screen while a 15-second voice-over opening question caresses the audience into mental oblivion.

Be judicious in your choice of what to run from a long-winded interview or press conference. Pre-screen what is important for your audience to hear. Don't leave

that job up to your listeners and viewers. Common practice calls for careful selection of the cut or cuts you will use, then demands that you tighten even what you have chosen. A few edits will eliminate a 15-second harangue of no importance or unnecessary pauses (unless they are needed for dramatic effect or as telltale signs of the speaker's hesitancy to answer a question).

Often, you will use more than one cut from the interview or news conference in separate soundbites, which requires writing a **bridge** or **audio link**, between the cuts you plan to use. Bridges, whether between tape cuts or delivering voice-over pictures between two or more cuts of SOT (sound-on-tape), help transfer the story smoothly from one related subject to another without wasting time.

The bridge can be something as simple as delivering a question on air: "Does Davis support public education?" Davis then answers this question on tape. The question just cited is five words long, much cleaner and quicker than a 15-second fumble question.In the unlikely event that an interview runs on the air unedited, some stations ask that you identify the reporter in the lead-in so the reporter's voice is recognizable as the interview progresses. Then you would say something to the effect: "Davis told KBNS reporter Mark Johnson that he's against any public support of parochial schools." This treatment prepares listeners for two voices. They now can identify the second voice as the newsperson.

Note how a bridge is used in the following radio script. Also pay attention to the lead-in and tag:

(LEAD-IN) Three police detectives were shot-gunned to death outside a Miami Beach apartment today while investigating a routine car theft. Eyewitnesses say the three officers had knocked on an apartment door and were waiting for it to open when the shots broke out.

SOT

:32

(OUT: ". . . the most awful thing I've ever seen.")

(BRIDGE) Miami Beach police have identified at least two suspects. Police Chief Martin Smith says eyewitnesses are helping create police sketches of the third suspect.

SOT

:15

(OUT: ". . . a stocky man, about six-feet-two inches, with dark, curly hair.")

(TAG) Chief Smith says all three slain officers had families. A benefit fund has been established through Miami Beach police headquarters.

KEYS TO SUCCESSFUL INTERVIEWING

- Except in special circumstances, begin the interview with a couple of questions that you have no intention of using on the air. Don't spend a lot of time doing this, just enough to "break the ice." Once people start talking, they settle down a little. Just two or three minutes spent getting them to talk about themselves makes all the difference in the quality of the interview you'll have when you get down to the real material you're interested in.

  You can ask things like, "What brought you to Seattle?" or, "Tell me a little about yourself. What do you do for fun?" or "Do you have a family?" What you are doing is setting a personal tone and relationship with the person in which the veneer of distance will disappear and the interviewee will come across as a person, not as a robot with well-rehearsed answers.

- Before the interview,

  - Jot down two or three key questions in a reporter's notebook or pad. Refer to it as necessary in the interview. In standard interview shots you won't be on-camera most of the time anyway, so looking at your notes will not be distracting.

  - Always keep in mind the purpose of the interview. It is not to get a lot of material that will go on the air exactly the way it was recorded. You will be able to rewrite it in a much tighter script that will be clearer for the audience. You're doing the interview to elicit a powerful, concise statement (emotional or factual) from a credible source, to enclose within your package.

- Listen to the answer. When reporters have a list of questions to ask and run through them without listening to what the person replies, they'll miss the follow-up opportunity that could lead to an Emmy-winning disclosure. The questions you think are important are only an interview guide. Often the richest material is found when those questions are used as a framework for exploring a subject and you ask follow-ups freely along the way.

- Know when to shut up. Some reporters, thinking they have to fill any pause, jump in with a question when the interviewee is pausing naturally and is about to continue. In addition, when a person finishes an answer, if you keep looking and pointing the microphone toward him or her, the interviewee will tend to say something more. Your body language tells the person to keep talking. When interviewees do continue talking, subconsciously thinking they need to fill in more detail to complete the answer, they often provide much richer material. The first answer to a question can be rather dull. The ensuing additional detail can be the stuff of exclusive revelations.

  Don't hesitate to ask a subject to explain a point again. What you are after is a short, concise, clear answer that just about anyone could understand. Particularly with specialists in highly technical areas, things get complicated fast. After a complex answer from a world-renowned physicist on the ramifications of Einstein's theory of relativity, you may need to say something like, "How would you explain that to a fifth-grade class?"

  Here are some other excellent ways to ask people to answer again, but in a different way:

  "Could you take me through that again but explain it in a different way?"

  "What does that mean to the average person?"

  "I'm not sure I understand what the key point is. Could you boil it down for me?"

  Often, when you ask to have something explained again, the interviewee will smile, relax a little, and give you a more conversational answer. Then you'll have a great soundbite.

WRITING SOUNDBITES IN THE NEWS SCRIPT

The TV script is fairly simple and straightforward, but the inclusion and placement of soundbites in a script are crucial. (For a general review on scripts, refer to Chapter 3). Notice, in the example of the sextuplets, that the commands in the left margin refer to directions for the engineers, usually with acronyms in front to cue the type of command.

For example, the first direction in the left column — AB/Box: Babies — indicates that the anchor (with initials AB) is speaking and there is a box graphic on screen about babies, because that is the subject of the first story.

Script Sample: Sextuplets

Slug: Six kids
Writer: Smith
Date:

AB/Box: Babies

SOT
  CG: Kristy Martin Reporting

  CG: Belleview Hospital
     New York City

  AT: 31 CG: Bill Williams
     Babies' father

  Outcue: ". . . Kristy Martin
     reporting for TV-9
     News."

TRT: 1:371pad

Story Time: 1:55

(AB)
For only the sixth time in the world since the turn of the century . . . a woman has given birth to six children at once.
    TV-9's Kristy Martin has more on the multiple birth from New York City.
(SOT)

(AB)
At news time, doctors report the remaining two children have little chance for survival.
    They say given another month, all six children might have survived.

# # #

The right column shows what words will be spoken on camera. If the anchor is speaking, his or her initials will appear in parentheses above the text.

When a soundbite is part of the story, SOT will appear in the left column, usually with CG indented underneath. **CG** (character generator) indicates that whatever words follow it should be superimposed onto the video during the soundbite. The CGs are indented because we want them to be inserted, but if the director misses them, the story will still air without viewers' recognizing the omission as a major error. In the example, the reporter is speaking on tape, so SOT appears in the left margin and CG is below it with the words: "Kristy Martin reporting" and "Belleview Hospital, New York City." Therefore, we know that when Kristy Martin is speaking on tape, her name will appear on-screen along with her location.

At 31 seconds into the report, when Bill Williams is on tape, his name will appear. We know the time because **AT** accumulated time for the entire story at that point) appears in the left column just before the CG. An AT time is included only for the CG for the babies' father, because that has to hit at the specific time when his interview pops up in the piece.

The director knows when the soundbite will end because the **outcue** in the left column indicates that the final phrase will be "Kristy Martin reporting for TV-9 News." Finally, because we're coming back to the anchor for a tag to the piece, that has to be indicated after the **TRT** (total running time). Note that the SOT and TRT designations in the director's column are at the left margin because they are crucial commands that, if missed, will cause major on-air errors.

ASSIGNMENT 7A: Writing Soundbites and Lead-ins

Name _____ Date _____

1. Record and edit a soundbite from a news conference, speech, or similar event in your community. Write the story (lead-in and tag) that will accompany your soundbite, using standard newscast script format.

2. Using a newspaper or magazine as a source for facts, choose six news stories and assume that the quotations are tape-recorded soundbites. Write blind lead-ins for each of the six stories. Include standard time and out-cue designations as part of your script for each story. In each case, identify the speaker who will be talking in the soundbite. Identify the speaker by name and title preceding the SOT to set up the speaker's identity for the audience. Otherwise it will seem like a different voice out of nowhere.

3 Listen to several radio and TV newscasts. Write down, verbatim, five blind lead-ins you hear. Rewrite to improve them.

4 Attend a city council meeting and tape-record the proceedings while you take handwritten notes. After the meeting, write the script and edit the tape into a one-minute presentation suitable for a newscast. Allow only one hour for this assignment!

ASSIGNMENT 7B: Interviewing

Name _____ Date _____

1. Conduct a minimum of three practice interviews with friends to help develop your ability to phrase ad-lib questions. In each instance, have a friend decide spontaneously on a topic about which the friend is knowledgeable. Then begin the interview. Pursue the subject seriously and extract from your friend as much information about the subject as possible. Some possible topics are: movie directors, how to grow indoor houseplants, tips for beginning cooks, the job market for college students, rock-climbing, hang-gliding, county politics, the future of newspapers.

2. Interview a prominent or interesting person in your community. Call the person in advance to arrange an appointment. Research the subject area and prepare meaningful questions. Arrive on time with a tape-recorder that works and with which you are familiar. In advance of the interview, make a short test recording to be certain that sound levels are set properly and that your audio is of electronic media quality.

3 Edit the tape you recorded #2 into a story suitable for electronic media. Write a lead-in and tag to accompany the edited interview. Play the tape and critique your interview in class.

4 Repeat Items #1 and #2 a minimum of three times. Practice makes perfect!

ASSIGNMENT 7C: Writing Lead-ins and Tags

Name _____ Date _____

Following is an interview between a television interviewer and Dr. Raymond Beardsley, supervising research engineer in a solar energy research laboratory at a major university. Write a self-contained or "blind" lead-in and tag, and mark in bold brackets which portion(s) of the interview you would air. Follow proper script format, and include a time and outcue as part of your script.

(WRITE YOUR LEAD-IN HERE.)

Interviewer: After more than twenty years of research, what are your findings about using solar energy to heat and cool homes?

Engineer: Solar energy has many possible uses, but the heating of buildings and water is the most advanced and the most competitive with fossil fuels.

Interviewer: How practical are these systems?

Engineer: Practical enough to supply about three-fourths the heat requirement in average homes . . . and about three-fourths the hot water an average family uses in a year's time.

Interviewer: But aren't you talking about areas where the sun shines most of the time? What about areas where there's not much sunshine?

Engineer: Of course, abundant winter sunshine, high heat requirements, and expensive fuel . . . all these things favor the use of solar energy, but most regions in the United States are suitable for solar heating.

To this point, the interview has developed along predictable lines, but now comes a departure from the original subject, and the interviewer follows up.

Engineer: As a matter of fact, we're seeing increased sales of solar heating equipment in the Northeast, areas that receive less sunshine than, say, people get in the far West states. Even then during cloudy stretches, a gas-fired furnace can take over, but we find it's not used more than about one-fourth the time. Sunlight provides heat the rest of the time.

Interviewer: Is solar heating competitive with natural gas at today's prices?

Engineer: Not if gas prices increase as expected. But it's cheaper than electric resistance heating in most parts of the country and will be on a par soon with propane and fuel oil in sunny climes. We're going to see savings continue to increase as energy prices go up and solar equipment prices hold steady or even decline.

(WRITE YOUR TAG HERE)

Critical Thinking Questions

Directions: The following questions are provided to help you examine the deeper meanings and complexities of the various issues under discussion. Answer each question to the best of your ability after a thoughtful review of the subject at hand.

1. The length of soundbites in news stories has diminished over the past 50 years from as long as a minute to as short as ten seconds or less. What is the purpose of the soundbite? Contrast its role of: (a) providing important information, (b) acting as a device to prove the image (a shot of rising floodwaters and a sheriff's deputy urging, "Move along folks, water's rising fast"), and (c) serving as an exclamation mark to the story's larger focus (a man who raises bobcats smiling and talking as they play on his lap).

2. In a 1:15 television story, a ten-second soundbite accounts for 13 percent of the story's editorial focus. In a 1:15 story, a 30-second soundbite accounts for 40 percent of the soundbite's editorial focus. From this perspective, define your philosophy of how long a soundbite should be as it relates to fair and reasonable editorial focus in the short-story format.

3. The perception of bias in news stories sometimes stems from the reporter's failure to address unanswered questions that are uppermost in the audience's mind. What methods can you as a journalist employ to avoid viewer charges of false, incomplete, or biased reporting during the interview process?

4. Is the interview more appropriately a series of questions and answers or a conversation? Provide a thoughtful response to this question, and explain any exceptions that come to mind.

5. What primary interview skills do you possess, and which skills require development? What steps can you take to become a fully competent interviewer before you enter the profession as a working journalist?

6. What is the impact of editing on soundbites, both positive and negative? What are the dangers of presenting bites out of order or out of context?

7. Interviews with key sources provide good info and potentially good soundbites. What is the danger of relying only on sources for info to a story? How can this reporting affect your story?

8. Soundbites that are too long tend to lose the audience's attention. What measures can you take — both in interviewing and in editing — to prevent this?

Self-Review Questions

 Directions: Each of the self-review questions below addresses information contained in this chapter. Answer each question to the best of your ability, then review the chapter as necessary to further strengthen your understanding of each concept or issue.

1. What differentiates an actuality from a soundbite?

2. What are the primary sources for soundbites?

3. How do soundbites help make news reports more credible and interesting?

4. What is the role of the soundbite in helping support or "prove" the visuals? The VO script? The storytelling process?

5. Explain the basics of the good interview.

6. What skills, knowledge, and personal attributes does the strong interviewer have?

7. What are the most important interview tips you would recommend to someone entering the profession as a reporter?

8. What techniques can help put an interviewee at ease?

9. Make a compelling argument for keeping soundbites short in 1:00 to 1:30 news packages.

10. What is the nature of lead-ins and tags, and what are the potential pitfalls in their use?

8 Editing and Rewriting the News

News comes from various sources. You might gather some news as a reporter, although most news your station broadcasts will come from other journalists. That news might be from other reporters, stringers, network news feeds, wire associations, feature services, Internet services, and public relations agencies or departments. No matter what the news source, editing is just as important for the electronic news media as it is for print.

Although the various media have some facets of editing in common, they differ in several ways. In electronic media, the news must be edited for the ear and, therefore, the writing style must be sound-oriented. Rhythm is important. Leads must be quite short for instance, and specific items may be repeated in certain stories. Writers also must be careful to produce clean copy.

Electronic media strive for uniqueness in the sound and style of their newscasts. News, after all, is integral to the image of any electronic media organization — how it is perceived by its listening or viewing community. Local news can help set the news operation apart from entertainment options on the networks, on cable, via satellite, or from the Internet. Although all have access to common sources of information, they rarely can set themselves apart if they use only those sources.

Local news organizations, for example, monitor area police, fire, and emergency channels. They cover the same news conferences, the same spot news events, and they subscribe to the same news services. Typically, they also receive the same public relations releases, video news releases, and similar weather reports. And they patronize similar audio and video syndication services, subscribe to the same newspapers, have access to the same Internet resources, and create virtually identical futures files.

To make themselves unique, the best news organizations insist on **reporter enterprise, story ownership,** and **story follow-up** on major stories. In these three areas, no competitor can cover daily news exactly the same. As a further benefit, the news is covered less from the perspective of treating important stories as one event after another and more as part of an ongoing process.

> *If you tell me, I will forget; if you show me, I may remember; but if you involve me, I will understand.*
> STEVE TELLO
> ABC News

"We rush from event to event simply because we are able," said Tom Brokaw, former anchor of the NBC Nightly News, "too seldom pausing to reflect on what we have just witnessed. As a result, too many developments are left unresolved or in a bewildering state. The place of contemplation is overrun."[1]

Reporters who generate unique story ideas and follow the stories as they develop over time infuse a station's newscasts with uniqueness and perspective available in no other way. These reporters realize that stories that matter take different twists and turns as they develop. Few news organizations provide as much follow-up as audiences would like, but reporters with a strong sense of story ownership follow stories as a matter of routine, relying less on the assignment editor to point them in the direction and treatment of news stories than upon their own news judgment and philosophy.

At too many stations, the job of determining what is news has shifted away from reporters. During site observations at the three network TV affiliates in

Memphis, Dr. Kathleen Wickham of the University of Mississippi found that "television reporters . . . initiated almost no story assignments on their own."[2] Assignment editors still play a key role in advance story planning and sometimes are the "first reporter" on stories, but ongoing communication must exist between reporter, producer, and assignment editor.

"Putting together a news story for TV must be a collaborative undertaking, much more so than in newspaper journalism," according to Stephen Hess of the Brookings Institution. "It is the nature of technology."[3]

This is also true in the developing area of **Internet journalism,** in which there is often collaboration across technologies. Newspapers, television, radio, and other media organizations merge fact-gathering and writing to then publish information in a variety of media platforms.

NEWS SERVICES

As another line of defense to preserve uniqueness in newscasts, most legitimate news organizations insist upon complete rewrites of material that likely will be duplicated elsewhere. When deadline pressure or a small staff prevents does not allow complete rewrites of copy, most news shops still insist that you edit the copy so it will sound different from the competition. Editing and rewriting have the additional advantage of tailoring the copy to special styles and rates of on-air delivery.

The major news services provide stations with news of non-local origin. Each wire service supplies multiple wires — a principal or "trunk" wire plus a broadcast wire, sports wire, financial wire, state wire, and other special services. Depending upon the number of wire services to which a station subscribes, it could receive as many as one to two million words per day.

A portion of stories that appear in a newscast are news service stories that station reporters have edited and localized.

One task of the newsperson is to select and edit wire copy for each newscast. The "rip and read" method is not professional. Even though wire services may do an excellent job of writing, the copy at the very least should be edited to your style and voice. Extra attention must be given to putting the story into electronic style. All wire copy has to be checked for misspellings, excessive modifiers, and too much attribution.

If you have a question about a story that cannot be answered locally, you should call the nearest bureau for clarification. Newsrooms commonly display the nearest bureau's telephone number near the wire service printer or in a special newsroom telephone directory of important numbers. Additional information is available in the wire service stylebook, which contains spaces for the phone numbers of regional, state, national, and international wire service news centers.

Editing Wire Copy

If the required changes are minor, you can edit wire copy both to improve flow and to make the copy conform more closely to a given style of delivery. This example shows how copy can be edited without changing the essential meaning:

~~098CCP~~

~~(Leavenworth) Prison officials in Leaven-~~ ~~worth say a~~ <u>A</u> 45-year-old inmate <u>who</u> escaped from the U.S. Penitentiary in Leavenworth remains at large today. The man apparently walked away from the prison's honor farm ~~earlier today~~ and escaped with ~~the~~ help ~~of~~ <u>from</u> accomplices ~~who waited nearby~~ <u>parked</u> in a car outside the prison walls. The suspect was ~~sentenced in Kentucky in September to~~ <u>serving</u> a five-year term for importing ~~narcotic~~ drugs from Mexico.

Although the changes made in this wire copy are relatively minor, they do reduce wordiness and improve flow. Even so, unless changes are made neatly, the copy is difficult to read on-air and should be retyped if time permits.

Rewriting Wire Copy

If wire copy requires major changes, the entire piece should be rewritten. Consider the following example:

083DDR

Stress-Women

(Cambridge) A British Endocrinologist warns that young career women who get too wrapped up in their activities may start to have such problems as hair on their faces and chests; and baldness of the head. According to Dr. Ivor Mills of Addenbrooke's Hospital in Cambridge, England, the problem is known as "stress disease," and involves hormonal changes. Dr. Miles says strain on the brain is blamed for increased male hormone production in women, resulting in aggression, ruthlessness, infertility, and insomnia.

(handwritten edits: doctor / that stress may / trigger hormone changes that can lead to / baldness and hair on the / of / calls / He / causes)

UPS 09-19A10:58 AMD

Although editing has tightened the story and made it flow more easily, this copy obviously is difficult to read. When changes of such magnitude are made, the copy will be almost impossible to read, a problem that can be eliminated through rewriting:

> A British doctor warns young career women that stress may trigger hormone changes that can lead to baldness and hair on the face and chest. Dr. Ivor Mills of Cambridge calls the problem "stress disease." He says strain results in male hormone production in females, resulting in aggression, infertility, and insomnia.

Localizing Wire Copy

Wire copy should be **localized** when appropriate. Many stories of national importance can be localized by an interview with a local authority. A story about the impact a slow economy had on national auto sales can be localized through an interview with a nearby auto dealer. An economics professor from a local college could be used to add noteworthy perspective to the story. Look at the following wire story:

> Auto prices fell in the first month of the fourth quarter thanks to a sluggish economy, lagging consumer confidence in oil prices, and a record-setting hurricane season, auto makers said today after releasing the numbers.
>
> But industry analysts are optimistic the overall annual sales will remain slightly above auto sales last year.

Then compare it with the localized story below:

> Local car dealers say recent hurricanes that damaged many dealerships here were the final straw in causing auto sales to dip lower last month than they have all year. The dealers also blame a slow economy and higher gas prices.
>
> Steve Roper, owner of the Central Florida Honda dealership, is hoping analysts are correct in predicting an upsurge in total auto sales for the year.

Finally, wire service or newspaper copy is often rather stiff. Electronic news should be written as if spoken to another person conversationally. When you are reading electronic copy on the air, you are chatting with individuals sitting quietly in their homes, or at work, or even riding along with them in a car (if it's for radio). So you have to incorporate some conversational tone and audience relatedness to that copy. A good test of your writing is to ask yourself, "Is this the way I'd explain it to a person over coffee?" If the answer is no, rewrite it. Although you have to be somewhat formal, you want to work to make the copy sound natural when it is spoken aloud.

Consider the following two rewrites of the previous examples on the British doctor's warning and the fourth-quarter drop in auto sales. These examples push the conversational tone and audience relatedness approach.

> If you're a working woman, stress may be making you bald and, at the same time, growing hair on your face and chest. Sounds crazy, but a British doctor, Ivory Mills of Cambridge, says stress among young career women can trigger hormone changes that will do just that. He says increased mental strain results in male hormone production in females, resulting in aggression, infertility, and insomnia.

> A local car dealer is not worried his sales last month were the lowest they have been all year. Honda dealer Steve Roper is surprised that sales were not worse because of a slow economy, rising gas prices, and four hurricanes that ravaged the state and leveled several dealerships.
>
> Industry analysts echo Roper's optimism. They blame last month's nationwide dip in auto sales on unusual circumstances and expect to see little impact on total auto sales for the year.

USING PUBLIC RELATIONS PRACTITIONERS EFFECTIVELY

Public relations practitioners often are called media relations officers, public information officers, or press aides.

They can be extremely useful to a news organization, providing substantial material, particularly stories that involve large companies, government agencies, well-funded candidates, and personalities who can afford the services of professional communicators. *Internet and Broadcast PR News* claims that 98 percent of TV stations in the United States use Broadcast PR productions every day in their newscasts, while 70 percent of U.S. radio news programs use Broadcast PR content.[4]

Regardless of the title, the job of PR practitioners is to make their employer look good and to generate positive news coverage. Although most public relations agencies understand the importance of preparing material for specific media, many public relations practitioners do not have experience and do not understand the differences among the forms of media. In evaluating publicity material, you must exercise sound news judgment for style and also because it may represent undue emphasis on special-interest points of view.

Because public relations practitioners have an agenda to communicate a specific point of view, the material has to be considered within that framework. They are not fact gatherers as much as fact providers, in ways that reinforce the positive image of their organization. No journalist should put public relations material in a newscast without checking it and, in controversial circumstances, double-checking opposing points of view.

Virtually every government agency has public relations officers, with titles ranging from "public information officer" to "media relations specialist." Their abilities vary considerably with their training and experience. Often they are the point of contact for data on government programs or official positions on controversies. A call to the public information officer of a U. S. Forest Service regional headquarters can generate a landslide of reports, charts, even video news releases on whatever subject you may be investigating involving that agency. You often will get much more information than you need.

When dealing with public relations practitioners, you will have to get to know them and, through trial and error, develop a sense of whom you can trust to provide what you need. Particularly in the case of television, PR people with no experience in the visual media don't understand the need for video. In some cases, public relations people are on only temporary assignment and have marginal, if any, experience in the medium for which they are supplying information.

VIDEO NEWS RELEASES

Public relations practitioners provide television operations with video news releases, or **VNRs**. With reduced budgets in many newsrooms, public relations professionals have seized the opportunity to provide video news packages that usually are transmitted via satellite to news organizations, along with a fax or email of the script. Although some VNRs are distributed by mail on videocassette, these distributions are limited because of their high cost.[5]

Digital delivery of a VNR file directly to the assignment editor's desktop will soon be the exclusive delivery method, but many stations still prefer either satellite feeds or hard copy tapes.[6] Usually the major video supplier is a company specializing in VNR distribution. The public relations agency or corporation pays that company to distribute the VNR for it. Each day, the major video companies send a **budget**, or list of stories, along with story scripts and time of day the video will be transmitted. The newsroom can record all, part, or none of the material as it chooses.

Normally the video material includes several packages of about 90 seconds each, along with additional B-roll (background video) material. **B-roll video** is useful if stations prefer to produce their own stories from the material or want anchors to voice the stories from the studio. In addition to the budget and story scripts, the printed material may include suggestions for ways to localize the story.

Research has shown that about 75 percent of all television station newsrooms regularly use VNRs.[7] The most popular topics for VNRs are health, business, politics, lifestyles, fashion, and sports. Key to their use by the news operation is the story's news value. Douglas Simon, president and CEO of DS Simon Productions, argued that it's more important than ever (since 2001) that your story bring value to the TV viewers. That's why health remains a favorite topic of VNRs.[8] Assuming that the VNR's core idea is strong, you often can improve it and further localize it by redoing the entire piece or by using only B-roll video and perhaps a soundbite from the VNR. Regardless of how they're used, VNRs provide a valuable addition to the sources for television news.

Other forms of public relations video contribute valuable material for electronic media. These include satellite news conferences and satellite interviews, also called **satellite media tours**. The news conference allows news personalities to participate in a question-and-answer session via satellite with a spokesperson from an organization. The person may be the chief executive officer, a key person within the organization or, infrequently, a public relations person. Often a press conference follows the presentation. Sometimes the journalist will be in a studio equipped with interactive uplink facilities or may watch the satellite feed and phone in questions.[9]

Satellite media tours offer individual interviews with an expert or a celebrity in a remote studio or a remote location such as the person's home or office. Each interview is exclusive and may even be carried live. The guest, however, may do 20 or 30 of these interviews a day for stations around the country.[10]

INTERNET WRITING

Today, electronic media journalists entering the profession absolutely must know how to write and produce for the Web. Initially, many print and broadcast news media organizations put stories from the newspaper or transcripts from a newscast directly on their Web sites. But as the Internet has evolved into a common and rather sophisticated delivery tool for news from print and broadcast media, journalists have realized that the audience is not interested in the same information from traditional media being regurgitated on the Internet.

Although basic writing principles apply to all news media, including the Internet — short, concise sentences, strong verbs, active voice, most important information first — there are some key points to keep in mind when putting news stories on the Web. A television or radio news station will have stories in print and broadcast form on their Web sites, but the majority of the information is in text format, so it is imperative that broadcast journalists know how to write well for cyberspace.

- Strong, interesting headlines are a key to conveying information on a Web site. News sites in particular are full of information on the home page, so viewers need a way to find the top news of the day.

- Likewise, subheads are the primary copy on a home page and help viewers find the specific topics they are looking for.

- Icons with strong, short subheads indicate audio and/or video reports that viewers can listen to or watch. For example, "Lives, homes shattered by Hurricane Charley. PLAY VIDEO" will appear in a list of related stories alerting viewers to a multimedia presentation of information.

SPOTLIGHT

Using VNR's in Television News

Many times the information in VNRs is newsworthy but may have to be reworked to meet the news department's requirements. Answers to the following questions offer a guideline.

1. Is the self-interest point of view unduly emphasized? If so, can it be eliminated?

2. Is the material localized? If not, can it be localized?

3. Is the lead well written to capture the most important aspect of the story? If not, can you rewrite the lead?

4. Does the news story have unnecessary material? Can you condense it? (Publicity material often is padded.)

5. Does the material correspond to your electronic style? If not, can it be edited to conform?

6. Do you have any questions about the story? If you do, call the contact person (whose name should appear on the release). If the source lives outside your area, call collect. The public relations practitioner should be happy to answer your questions.

DEALING WITH PR PEOPLE

Fax transmission and emails have become favorite vehicles of public relations practitioners to funnel information to newsrooms. Overuse of either can reflect negatively on the organization represented. The following hints can help you when working with public relations professionals:

- Know your PR contacts as well as you know your other sources. They can be extremely valuable, or worthless — or somewhere in between.

- Double-check the information provided, and always be aware that it is provided to advance a given point of view (which is the case with most sources of information). Often, you may have to seek out opposing views to balance your coverage properly.

- If you are going to have anyone send a fax to you, make sure that he or she sends a cover sheet with your name on it, as well as a short description of the material or a story slug.

- Email may provide a good alternative to faxes. If you screen the sources to whom you give your address, you may control unnecessarily heavy email traffic. Having the material in an electronic form, though, may save a great deal of time in editing.

- Story copy is still written in inverted pyramid form, the common format for print news, but is generally shorter overall and is presented as bulleted information more often than in paragraph format.

CONVERTING TV SCRIPTS TO THE WEB IN TEN MINUTES[11]

1. *Combine copy.* If you're converting a package script, combine the **toss,** lead-in, and tag on the same page. Delete any redundancies. Make sure the story starts with a strong sentence, not a **tease** line.

2. *Remove extraneous remarks.* Strip out computer coding, including director, editing, and graphics notation.

3. *Fix capitalization.* Convert the script from upper case to lower case, correctly capitalizing as you go along. Many newsroom computer systems let you drop an entire script to lower case with a single keystroke.

4. *Add quotes.* Change the soundbites to quotes, adding the correct attribution. To speed up the process, get in the habit of writing out the full text of each soundbite in package scripts.

5. *Form complete sentences.* Drop unnecessary punctuation such as ellipses and hyphens, and convert sentence fragments to complete sentences.

6. *Remove references to video.* The best TV stories are written to video, but not on the Web. Delete any language that makes a direct reference to video and audio, but add appropriate adjectives to bring a visual element to your copy.

7. *Beef up the story.* Add any important details that hit the cutting room floor. Web copy is shorter than newspaper copy but should deliver more information than 20-second TV stories (except with breaking news).

8. *Bring it all together.* Make sure the story reads well from beginning to end, with appropriate paragraph breaks. Usually, a little smoothing is in order.

9. *Add interactivity.* Finally, add links to any relevant reference materials. Tack on interactive elements, pictures, and multimedia — and run the spell checker. See, wasn't that easy?

Reprinted with permission by Cory Bergman, editor of Lost Remote, www.lostremote.com. Copyright © 2000-2002.

- Writers for the Web constantly look for key words in the copy that can become hot links for other information. This helps keep stories shorter and provides more interactivity for readers, to keep their interest. For example, in a story about the city's plan to build a new courthouse, one word could be a link to architectural drawings of the new building, another could link to a city locator map, and another could link to an informational graphic breaking down the budget plans for such a project.

- Consider the best ways to advertise other special reports related to the main story, especially video clips or slideshow presentations.

- Resist the temptation to overly complicate your site with graphics that are slow-loading. Include lists of key things in menus so it will be easy to jump past the home page to the desired content. Many consumers don't turn over their computers to the latest models for several years.

ENDNOTES

1. Brokaw, Tom, "The New News Technology: Master or Servant?" address presented at The Cost of Technology: Information Prosperity and Information Poverty, a national conference sponsored by Gannett Center for Media Studies, Nov. 10, 1986.
2. Wickham, Kathleen W., "The Presentation of Story Ideas: An Exploratory Study of Gatekeeping in Local Television News," unpublished master's thesis, University of Memphis, 1987.
3. Hess, Stephen, "Television Reporting: Self-fulfilling News," *IRE Journal*, 13, Fall 1989.
4. "Information for 21st Century Professionals," *Internet and Broadcast PR News*, May 20, 2000.
5. Lattimore, Dan, Otis Baskin, Suzette Heiman, Elizabeth Toth, and James VanLeuven, *Public Relations: The Profession and Practice.* New York: McGraw–Hill 2004, pp. 193–194.
6. Sweeney, Kate, "What's Next for VNRs?" *PR Tactics*, June 2003, p. 19.
7. *Medialink, The Video News Release Handbook* (New York: Video Broadcasting Corp., 1990), pp. 4–5.
8. Sweeney, p. 19.
9. Brody, E.W., and Dan Lattimore, *Public Relations Writing* (New York: Praeger Publishers, 1990), pp. 165–175.
10. Ibid, p. 1.
11. Bergman, Cory. "Converting TV Scripts to the Web in Ten Minutes." via http://www.lostremote.com.

EXERCISE 8A: Wire Copy Editing

Name _____ Date _____

Edit the following wire copy. Indicate which copy could have possibilities to localize and to add visuals or taped actualities. Try to include conversational tone, and see what you can do to make the story relate to the average viewer.

The Food and Drug Administration announced today that Olive Oil producers may add a label stating there is limited evidence the product could reduce the risk of heart disease. The FDA has approved similar labels for only two other products — walnuts and omega-3 fatty acids. Before last year, food producers could only make claims for which there was significant scientific agreement.

-30-

The Consumer Product Safety Commission is suing Black and Decker for not sufficiently notifying consumers about the recall of a toaster. Black and Decker recalled more than 200,000 of its Spacemaker Optima Horizontal Toasters. If food catches on fire in the toaster, flames can shoot out the door when it automatically opens. The toasters have been linked to 242 fires and two minor injuries.

-30-

Mir Aimal Kasi, a Pakistani man charged with killing two people and injuring three in a deadly shooting spree outside CIA headquarters, has entered a "not guilty" plea to all ten charges against him. Testimony in the case is expected to begin tomorrow after a jury is seated. Security is in the process of being tightened at the courthouse where Kasi is to be tried. Kasi was captured by the FBI in Pakistan in June when he returned there as a fugitive after the shooting spree.

-30-

Officials in Colorado are still cleaning up after a disastrous winter storm last week. The storm blew through the divide between Buck and Buffalo mountains, with winds topping speeds of 120 miles per hour. The high wind destroyed over 20,000 acres of timber including many old-growth forests and a protected wilderness. Forest officials in Steamboat Springs, Colo. said the storm was one of the worst they had ever seen.

-30-

ASSIGNMENT 8A: News Releases

Name _____ Date _____

1. Call or write to a public relations agency or department and ask for a copy of a news release sent to a radio or TV station. (If you cannot obtain one from your area, use the news release provided at the end of this assignment.) Analyze the release by answering the following questions:

   a. Is it written in electronic style? Does it require any changes? If so, what are they?

   b. Is the lead the best it could be? If not, rewrite the lead.

   c. Could you delete any copy? If so, delete it.

   d. Is the story important to your local community? Can it be localized? If so, localize it.

   e. Does the story have any gaps? Does it have any problems that you cannot find out about on your own? If so, call the public relations person and ask.

2. Edit or rewrite the news release on the following page for a radio broadcast.

NEWS RELEASE

LIFELINE BLOOD CENTER   Contact: Bonita Smythe
888 Fifty First Ave.   800-678-0000
Central Valley, MO.   800-678-0001 FAX

CENTRAL VALLEY, Mo.—Lifeline Blood Center announced an emergency blood drive today to get 15,000 pints of blood to restore the blood supplies to an acceptable level. The Center is operating at dangerous levels, according to the Thomas Reese, director.

The Center supplies 55 hospitals in the region. Reese said in the past when supplies have been this low, the response has been "quite impressive" by the community. The drive is being sponsored by the local Hospital Association in conjunction with the CBS-TV affiliate.

The state university ballroom will be set up for the next week to receive donors from 8 a.m. to 7 p.m. Monday through Saturday. Saturday the ballroom will close at 5 p.m., however.

Reese said that the Center is particularly in need of O-negative blood, but needs all kinds to replenish the supply. He said that the plane crash three weeks ago that caused three deaths and injured 145 contributed to the low blood supply.

For more information, call the toll free number 800-000-0000.

###

Critical Thinking Questions

Directions: The following questions are provided to help you examine the deeper meanings and complexities of the various issues under discussion. Answer each question to the best of your ability after a thoughtful review of the subject at hand.

1. Given that most news organizations have access to the same news sources and technology, what are some ways they can set themselves apart from competitors and build larger, more loyal audiences?

2. Assignment editors, producers, writers, reporters, and video editors all help to decide what audiences will see and hear in daily newscasts. What personal qualities and professional abilities must each of these individuals have to become "gatekeepers" of information?

3. This chapter recommends that journalists localize news and strive to make stories more relevant and appealing. Why does any of this matter? Why not just present the facts and let audiences determine their usefulness and significance?

4. Video News Releases (VNRs) represent special-interest points-of-view and sometimes even are intended to change audience attitudes and behavior. From the perspectives of (a) a professional journalist and (b) a general manager, how can news organizations justify the dissemination of news content largely outside the journalist's editorial control? What safeguards must news directors and producers use to ensure that VNRs represent accurate and balanced information?

5. Every public relations practitioner has an agenda. As a professional journalist, how do you fairly incorporate information with a specific point-of-view, yet retain fairness and balance in your reporting?

6. What audience demands must you keep in mind when writing news for the Internet versus writing for television?

7. Which single news medium (print, TV, Internet, radio) do you believe is most useful, accurate, and fair and will best serve audiences over time? Explain your answer.

8. To what extent does the Internet represent new technology versus an amalgamation of old technologies used in new ways?

Self-Review Questions

 Directions: Each of the self-review questions below addresses information contained in this chapter. Answer each question to the best of your ability, then review the chapter as necessary to further strengthen your understanding of each concept or issue.

1. What is the nature of reporter enterprise, story ownership, and story follow-up? How can these elements help to differentiate a news organization from its competitors?

2. What steps would you take in proofing and tailoring newswire copy for a local newscast?

3. Name five or more benefits that can result from editing and rewriting wire copy.

4. Define the Video News Release (VNR), and explain the pros and cons of its use in newscasts.

5. What major considerations must producers, writers, and reporters take into consideration when working with PR people?

6. When using information from public relations sources, how can you maintain fairness, balance, and accuracy in your reporting?

## CHAPTER NINE

TV Newscast Story Production and Editing

Television has the capacity to take the viewer to the scene of an event and is unique among news media in showing viewers the news as it happens. Within this context, the field crew's job is at once difficult and rewarding, a task that requires mastering a complex blend of creative and technical skills. The process of working in the field to gather news electronically, and then creating the finished story for use in a newscast, is complicated and requires teamwork and attention to detail. The gathering process has to be done properly by all involved, and then, once back at the newsroom, the video and audio elements have to be put together carefully in an electronic editing system so they can be transmitted to viewers.

Currently, two different kinds of editing systems are used in the electronic news industry.

1. **Linear editing:** Two video recorders are hooked together to play and record video images and sound.

2. **Digital** or **non-linear editing:** Video is fed into a computer system and then edited digitally on a computer hard drive. Stories may be played back in a newscast directly from a large computer server system, or they may be recorded back out of the computer system onto digital tape or videotape for newscast playback.

Increasingly, stations are updating their technology to be exclusively digital, but currently many stations — even in some major markets — are still using linear editing equipment. The basics of both systems are covered in this chapter, and more specific information for the two types appears in appendices at the end. We begin this chapter with how newscast story production begins, and then consider how the pieces of gathered material are finally put together for viewers to see.

NEWSCAST STORY PRODUCTION
Duties and Responsibilities

At most television operations, you will be part of a crew whose membership is determined by available staff and operating procedures, newsroom resources, and possible union regulations. Regardless of how many members it has, each crew is responsible for story research, contacts with news sources, scheduling times to shoot the story, conducting interviews, shooting the video, setting up lights, working the sound and video equipment, and editing or supervising the editing of the story into a product ready for use in a newscast.

Many small news operations have one-person reporting crews — typically called "one person bands" — that are responsible for all the duties just mentioned. Larger news organizations normally divide the responsibilities between producer, reporter, and news videographer. Specific duties of some of the possible positions are outlined in the following discussion.

Producer. The news producer identifies the story (or consults with the assignment editor about the story), works with the reporter to help decide upon story content and treatment, and coordinates story production with other members of the crew. This includes shooting and editing schedules, transportation logistics, and deadlines. In addition, the producer determines newscast line-up, writes news copy and news teases, and works with news anchors to produce compelling presentations that attract, hold, and build ever larger target audiences.

Reporter. The reporter presents all on-camera material, conducts the interviews, and

Strong visual impact is key to a good broadcast news story, so a videographer who understands film techniques as well as newsworthiness is invaluable for powerful stories.

scripts all material for the story. In the absence of a producer, the reporter assumes the producer's duties as well.

News Videographer. The videographer usually sets up lights, if necessary, and then shoots the scenes that are recorded or beamed live to the newsroom. The photographer should expect help from everyone else on the crew. Depending on any union regulations, different individuals may be involved in handling audio recording, carrying and setting up the lights, and stringing necessary power cords.

The videographer, or in some organizations a sound person, is also responsible for the sound quality of all story components and for monitoring battery levels in the field. Sources of sound for which this person is responsible include: (a) all sound recorded in the field (reporter's voice, interviews, natural background sound — also referred to as **nat sound**); (b) reporter narration, if the story is a package report and narration is recorded in the field; and at some stations (c) music or other sound selections used as part of the story.

During editing, the reporter and the videographer work closely with the producer in making editing decisions. In most operations the videographer and editor are the same person. In larger markets, full-time editors work in the station and videographers are kept on the street producing new field video throughout their shifts.

News Story Format

You will cover two basic types of stories in the field, the predictable and the unpredictable — those under your control and those not under your control. Whenever possible, story preparation and research should be done in advance. Unless the story breaks without warning, you often can make advance telephone calls to gather information, develop story angles, and set up schedules for any interviews you may want to video. In this way you will know as much about the story as possible before you go to the field. You'll have an idea of what questions to ask, what scenes to shoot, and which people to contact.

The producer or assignment editor often assigns the on-air format of the story, based on the day's budget of news. The story may be used as a VO — video that the anchor will voice over on the air. Or a story may be assigned as a **reporter package**, which means a self-contained story with reporter narration.

VO or VO-SOT-VO. Often the decision is to make a story a VO-SOT-VO, in which the anchor will narrate the story but it will include a soundbite (normally an interview of someone talking to a reporter or making a statement at a news conference). Natural sound from the scene, such as a woman crying out for her lost child, may be aired with audio up full as a soundbite. Frequently, package stories are edited as VO-SOT-VO stories for different broadcasts.

Reporter Packages. Stories are called packages if they meet one crucial test: By definition, a reporter package must stand alone as a complete report of the event, aside from the few seconds of copy (the lead-in) that the studio newscaster reads to introduce the report. Video packages are constructed something like the classic short story with a beginning (the open), the middle, and the end (the close).

The Open. The open may take any of several forms. Some examples are:

1. The voice-over: open with reporter's voice-over-video from the scene (sound under) throughout the opening segment of the package.

2. The reporter's voice heard over sound-under video of the news event for the first few seconds of the open, then the scene cutting to the reporter on-camera who delivers the balance of the open as a **standup.**

3. Open with reporter standup (15–20 seconds), in which the reporter speaks directly to the television camera in the field.

The Middle. The middle section of the package can be either an interview or scenes of the news event with the reporter's voice-over.

1. If the middle section is an interview, the video and sound will be of the person talking.

2. If the reporter reads voice-over narration during the middle section, video from the scene of whatever is being covered will be shown with natural background sound laid in the story at a lower level than the narration track. The natural sound of a brook babbling, or cars driving by on the freeway, adds realism to the scene as it is shown.

   Technically, the reporter's voice may be delivered (a) live from the studio or announce booth; (b) prerecorded as part of the video package; or (c) prerecorded on separate audio media, hard-drive disk, cassette, or reel-to-reel. Normally, reporter package narration is edited onto the same playback video source as everything else. Occasionally, however, it is easier to prefeed video to the station and cut it there while narrating live from the field during the actual newscast. That's what often occurs in live reports, particularly with breaking news events.

3. If the middle section of the package contains an interview, it normally does not begin with the reporter's question. Instead, to help keep the pace moving, the reporter should introduce the interviewee with a blind lead-in as part of the open, and then cut immediately to the interviewee's response.

The Close. The close of the package is similar to the open: The reporter's voice-over may be heard, or the reporter may deliver a standup close on camera. Sign off the close with something to the effect: "For KBNS News, I'm (Your Name) at the Federal Courthouse." A reporter on camera is not the news. Generally, you'll do best to show the news. For this reason, consistently showing the reporter in the open or close of the package should be avoided, if possible.

The reporter can be on-camera, occasionally, in what is called a standup bridge in the middle of the piece. The standup should have something to do with the story. The background should be selected carefully to help support the story. Standups that are shot against neutral backgrounds just to pop the reporter up on camera look silly. By showing the news instead, the audience will be grateful and you'll have done a more effective job of reporting.

Some General Guidelines

Some general guidelines in newscast story production are the following:

- *Avoid beginning the story with a soundbite*, unless the bite has some extraordinary quality such as

unusual emotion or exceptionally dramatic information. Otherwise, natural sound up full should be used whenever possible as a way to draw audiences into the story. Sound is as important as the picture in transferring meaning. We are creatures with senses of sight and sound, and much of what we draw from our world comes in mutual reinforcement of the two. Voice-over stories normally follow the form of: voice-over lead-in, soundbite(s), voice-over tag.

- *Avoid ending the story with a soundbite.* The strongest packages normally don't end on a soundbite but, rather, begin and end with scenes of the news event.

- *Reporter standups.* Here, the home audience typically sees some of the story before the reporter appears in a standup bridge or a standup close. During live reports, however, the reporter usually pops up at the beginning as the anchor tosses to the reporter on scene. And sometimes a reporter doing a live shot will have another prerecorded standup inside of the pre-recorded video portion of the live report.

- *Standup background.* Whenever a reporter is shown on camera more than once, whether as part of a live shot or a normal package report, the standup background should be different and help tell the story by adding visual information relative to the use of the standups. It looks bad to just have several standups of a reporter cut into a piece, all from the same location and position, without any reason other than giving the reporter "face time."

Better, the reporter delivers a standup in front of the supermarket where soft drink bottlers are picketing. Some protesters are visible behind the reporter. When the middle of the package begins, the screen might be filled with shots of protesters, followed by a shot of the reporter inside the supermarket interviewing a shopper. Because the shopper is in a setting entirely different from where the standup took place, there is no danger of a **jump cut** — the illusion that the interviewee magically pops on and off the screen. This jump cut would have occurred if the shopper had been interviewed outdoors in the same location where the reporter standup was photographed.

If you can't change backgrounds, you might begin with the reporter standup (a wide view), then cut to the shopper in a close-up (without the reporter appearing in the frame). This approach also can avoid a jump cut problem.

Editing the News Package

The news package is a standard feature in virtually all video newscasts, whether they are aired in normal

A video editor previews scenes in an editing bay before making a final edit.

television operations or used in Internet video streaming situations. Functioning as a self-contained report of an event, the package combines voice-over narration, visuals, natural sound (nat sound), and soundbites. Most news packages are able to tell a complete story in as little as one to one and one-half minutes, with an average length of around one minute, ten seconds.

Although packages should not be edited according to any formula, they often follow a standard format: a voice-over (VO) open, a soundbite (interview or statement), more voice-over, a standup, and a final VO to close. The only real difference between an anchor-delivered VO-SOT-VO and a reporter package is that, in the case of the package, the narration voice is that of the reporter.

Who Edits the News Package? The task of constructing news packages falls most often to the video editor working in association with the reporter or producer, or both. At some stations, photographers both shoot and edit the package. An advantage of this system is that the photographer is familiar with each shot from the field, and sometimes the photographer's recall of available shots can save time.

Conversely, the editor who has not shot the story may be more objective about scenes that come in from the field. The uninvolved editor, with less emotional attachment to the visuals, may be able to construct a more smoothly flowing visual narrative. Photographers have a habit of making sure their favorite shot gets in the package, even if it really isn't the best one for use on-air.

Time Constraints. The typical half-hour newscast may contain ten or more packages. Smoothly edited packages often appear deceptively simple to those who are not familiar with the editing process. A rough guideline for packages with soundbites and reasonable sophistication is one hour of editing time per finished minute of edited video. Or a simple two-minute package that requires no sophisticated editing may be cut in as little as 40 minutes.

At most stations, four to six video editors are required to edit the various packages that will be used in a half-hour newscast. News line-ups are subject to frequent change as stories are changed, added, or dropped, so each package normally is edited on a separate videocassette to allow for maximum flexibility in the final news line-up.

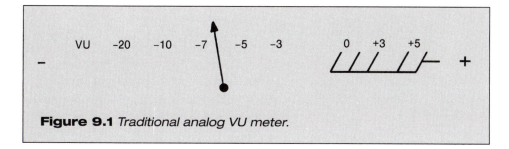

Figure 9.1 *Traditional analog VU meter.*

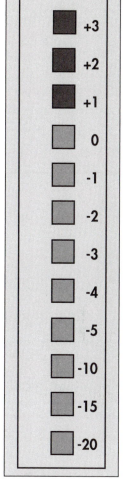

The Sound Track. The sound track is an essential part of the video package, and the editor should monitor sound quality and recording volume closely during the editing process. Sound transferred at low volume to the master cassette must be boosted in volume for playback. Boosting low signals amplifies buzz, hiss, and other objectionable background noise on the master videocassette. Proper sound levels can be determined only by consulting the VU (sound level) meters on the video recorder and playback units.

The VU Meter. The VU meter provides a visual check of sound levels in db's (decibels). Figures 9.1 and 9.2 show two kinds: the traditional analog VU meter with a needle, and the digital meter with a bar of lights. A safe level of audio is up to zero on both meters. When you go into the plus levels, usually red-colored in digital meters, you will get some audio distortion. A change of one db in level, up or down, is just enough to be perceptible to the human ear. To assure proper recording volume, the VU meter should register most of the time between 23 and 27 db for primary sound levels, with occasional swings into the red zone on the VU meter (between 0 and 15 during extremely loud passages).

Recordings made with the audio consistently in the red will be distorted and of poor sound quality. Secondary sound sources, such as background sound for video that accompanies reporter narration, should be kept at –10 to –7 db on the VU meter. These are general guidelines, and you will have to listen to the mixed sound and adjust the balance depending on the kind of sound being used (a brass band might be mixed in lower as background sound, a babbling brook higher).

Although the meter shown in Figure 9.1 is still used in all types of audio equipment, newer digital units typically use a graphic showing sliding bars or a series of lights to indicate audio levels, with sound that is distorting shown in red. Figure 9.2 is an example of such a digital audio metering interface. Depending on your specific equipment, digital audio meters may be vertical or horizontal bars.

The Control Panel. The control track gives beginning videotape editors more headaches than any other part of the editing process, although it's nothing more than the electronic equivalent of sprocket holes in film (see Figure 9.3). The control track consists of an electronic pulse applied to each frame of video. Because there are 30 frames of video per second, the videotape must have 30 separate pulses for each second of running time. Without these pulses (the control track), the tape will not record or play back at normal speed, and a bad picture will result.

To lay down the control track, you first must record

Figure 9.2
Digital VU meter.

black on the master cassette in a manner appropriate to the process established by your station. Once the control track is recorded, you can edit in the INSERT mode and insert or replace any combination of the VIDEO, AUDIO CH-1, or AUDIO CH-2 portions of the program.

A control track must be present on the master editing tape. If the existing control track has first been laid down and is suitable, the INSERT mode can be used. If the control track is absent or is unacceptable, the ASSEMBLE editing mode must be used.

Sound Overlaps. Sound overlaps help tie the video package together and make it flow smoothly. **Overlaps** are the extensions of a specific sound past the beginning of an incoming sound. Music may be faded out, for example, a couple of seconds after a soundbite begins, or natural sound of playing children may be faded out gradually just after voice-over narration begins.

THE CONTROL TRACK

The control track gives beginning videotape editors more headaches than any other part of the editing process, although it's nothing more than the electronic equivalent of sprocket holes in film. The control track consists of an electronic pulse applied to each frame of video. Because there are 30 frames of video per second, the videotape must have 30 separate pulses for each second of
running time. Without these pulses (the control track), the tape will not record or play back at normal speed and a bad picture will result.

To lay down the control track, you first must record black on the master cassette in a manner appropriate to the process established by your station. Once the control track is recorded, you can edit in the INSERT mode and insert or replace any combination of the VIDEO, AUDIO CH-1, or AUDIO CH-2 portions of the program.

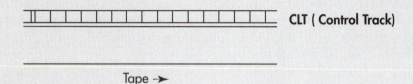

CLT (Control Track)

Tape →

To summarize: A control track must be present on the master editing tape. If the existing control track has first been laid down and is suitable, the INSERT mode can be used. If the control track is absent or is unacceptable, the ASSEMBLE editing mode must be used.

Figure 9.3 *The Control Track (CLT).*

Overlaps eliminate the abrupt, jarring nature of packages in which sound and picture end together at the end of a cut, to be replaced the next instant by completely new sound and pictures, known among editors as the "cold cut."

VIDEO EDITING

Video editing, both art and craft, is an essential part of television news. Without editing, raw visuals from the field could not be molded into compact, concise presentations of maximum effectiveness. Editing means selecting images and sounds, their timing and sequence. Editing — often ignored or misunderstood by the public — is the heartbeat of any visual presentation. Without editing, the news story could not exist.

Editing video is different from any editing process used in the history of filmmaking. Unlike film, video splices are accomplished electronically. No cement, no physical splices, no film reels or projectors are involved. Electronic videotape replaced film in television news in the mid-1970s.

Beginning in the mid-1990s, news organizations began converting to digital video equipment. As with any new technology, economics were prohibitive for most news organizations to switch to digital equipment

until their existing facilities had been fully depreciated, and early digital equipment was extremely expensive. As prices fell, however, more organizations began using digital equipment.

The basic concepts of picture organization are the same across technologies. In news film, shots were pulled off the processed film reel and hung in a box device. The editor noted what each shot contained and placed it in the order to be spliced for the final story. The scenes then were cemented together.

In *electronic media editing*, editors are not able to separate the shots, or glance at small frames of them to check them physically. The electronic media editor often keeps a sheet of paper handy while previewing the tape, noting the time into the tape of various key shots. That way, the editor knows where to find them on the tape when the editing begins.

With *linear editing*, you have a minimum of one playback deck and one record deck. The field tape is put in the playback deck and the editor selects the shots, recording them onto the playback deck with a switching device called an *editor*. When shots that have to go next to one another on the final record tape are far apart on the original tape, the editor has to fast-forward or fast-reverse the tape, whizzing through all the shots between.

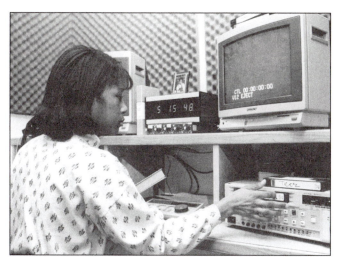

Linear editing requires two monitors with a video player and video recorder, to transfer raw video into an edited story.

Digital editing involves a computer monitor and hard drive onto which all video has been downloaded plus often a second monitor to view the final version.

This back-and-forth nature of editing videotape can be tedious if the photographer in the field has failed to shoot the story in a logical sequence.

In non-linear digital editing, the field video is fed into the computerized editing system through a playback deck. Once into the computer, the shots are displayed as icons on the screen. Each icon is the first frame of each shot. Thus, digital editing is a kind of return to the film-editing technique of a shot box. The computer monitor is filled with all the shots from the field as icons. The editor selects them and pulls them down into an editing strip at the bottom of the screen. Certain shots can be made to run in slow motion or

even to run backward. When the piece is assembled, the editor can play back the video to check it. Finally, the edited video is recorded onto another medium for playback or sent to a file server for use in the newscast.

Traditional filmmaking techniques of mixing wide, medium, and close-up shots, along with the theory of screen direction, apply across media. Since the days of Charlie Chaplin, one of cinema's earliest and foremost innovators, the concepts of telling a story with moving visual media have remained much the same. What is important is not the technology used to deliver moving pictures to the audience but, rather, the meaning conveyed in those pictures and whether they support the narration script, and vice versa. What we're doing, regardless of whether it is on film, videotape, or digital media, is telling a story.

STEPS IN EDITING A NEWS PACKAGE

The following is the basic procedure for linear editing, as that is the technology still used in many newsrooms. The same fundamentals apply to digital editing, in terms of multiple audio track manipulation and using varying sound levels to mix audio for maximum realism. For more detail on linear and digital editing techniques, see Appendices A and B to Chapter 9, at the end of this chapter. It will be helpful, though, to discuss some technique-related concepts here, so you will have an understanding of the general process.

Although editors often switch audio tracks for various reasons, we recommend keeping primary audio on audio channel 1, and background sound or special effects audio on channel 2. That works best when the story is played back on the air because the audio engineer can open both channels on the audio board and not cause errors by "chasing" the audio sources as they switch around.

Determine the Presence of the Control Track

Determining the presence of the control track is necessary only for linear, non-digital editing systems. At many television news operations that still use linear editing systems, master cassettes with prerecorded control tracks are provided to each video editor. Tapes with prerecorded control tracks save valuable time in the editing process. If no control track is present on the master tape, it must be recorded before editing can proceed.

All editing from this point proceeds in the INSERT mode. If the editor reverts to ASSEMBLE mode editing for any reason, the control track will be destroyed for approximately four seconds at the end of the assemble edit and the tape will not be usable for a newscast transmission. Each time the scene crosses a break in the control track, the video will roll. This occurs because the spinning video record head randomly disorients signals on the videotape at the end of each assemble edit.

A basic technique is to **black** your record cassette with a control track and no picture. In television stations the edit suites have "black burst" fed into them through a special routing switcher. You can create the same kind of source by jacking a video camera into the recorder input, turning on the camera while leaving on the lens cap, then recording the signal on the tape.

If you black an entire tape, you won't have to worry about where the break in the control track might be. When you lay down only four or five minutes of control track for an individual piece, you'll always have a breakup or "video roll" between pieces if you want to play back all of them for some reason.

Use Color Bar and Countdown Leaders

Regardless of whether the news operation uses the old linear systems or new digital editing equipment, there still have to be ways to check the playback setup equipment and to ensure that stories are cued properly for the newscast. Although some operations use only color bar video when engineers are checking equipment, virtually all of them use countdowns at the front of each story to help cue pieces to air in the newscast. The viewer at home sees neither of these.

A color bar typically consists of a rectangle containing various colors of the rainbow in vertical-bar patterns, plus a contrast scale ranging from pure white to no exposure at all. The color bars and contrast scale allow engineers to set optimum video levels before the tape is aired and are available as standard resources in all editing rooms.

The countdown leader allows the story to be easily cued for playback. The countdown begins with the number 10 and continues through 9, 8, 7, 6, 5, 4, 3 to the number 2. Two seconds of black follow the last number (2), at which point the first picture of video begins in the news package. During playback, the package is cued to allow enough roll time for the tape to reach stable playback speed. Editors normally begin sound two seconds after the first picture in the package. This helps avoid **clipping**, the annoying loss of the first word or so when the package is sent to home audiences.

Record the Narration Script

As the next step in editing, the voice-over script of reporter narration is written and recorded before the visuals are edited. Most frequently, the reporter records sound through a microphone directly onto a videotape cassette, a digital media, or directly through an input to the digital editor. You end up with a narration track, which on a videotape fills only part of the actual tape, as shown in Figure 9.4.

Highly efficient reporters often record the narration in the field at the end of the field cassette. That's the smartest thing to do for three reasons:

1. Writing the story immediately after you've finished gathering the facts and done the interviews is easiest because everything is fresh in your mind.

2. When you record narration at the scene, you have a "normal" background sound presence in your narration track, and it won't sound different from your standup, which will be the case if you use an expensive sound booth at the station to record tracks.

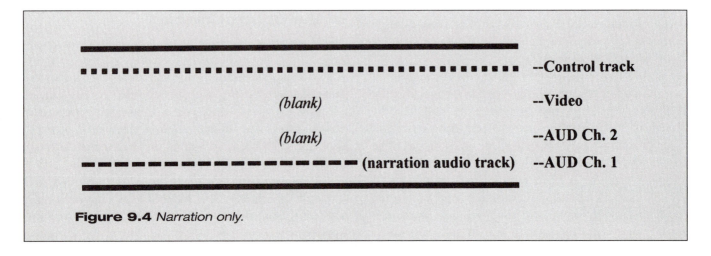

Figure 9.4 *Narration only.*

3. You don't wind up at the end of the day trying to fight other reporters to get into the sound booth, which would slow the editing procedure to the point that you possibly might not make your slot in the newscast. When you record narration in the field, you can sit back and read the paper or drink coffee late in the afternoon while everyone else is scurrying around.

At this point in the editing process, the narration is only one resource to be used, along with the video of the story and interviews shot in the field. It may contain several takes of a given sentence or paragraph — each take an effort on the reporter's part to achieve perfect delivery of his or her lines. In the industry, a reporter routinely puts an audio label at the beginning of each take of narration. That is accomplished by saying, "Take one" (or "Take two," "Take three," etc.), followed by "three . . . two . . . one" and the beginning of the sentence to be used.

Noting which take to use is helpful to the editor — something penned onto the script, such as "use third take." When an editor lays down a piece of narration only to hear a retake later and have to redo it, valuable minutes are lost and sometimes stories get dropped from the newscast because they aren't ready when they're supposed to be.

Edit the Various Elements into a Finished Story

Once you have a record cassette that has been blacked with a control track, a cassette with the reporter narration, and a field cassette with the video, soundbites, and reporter standups, you're ready to put the piece together.

Lay Down the Primary Audio and Video

Here you want to put together the primary audio portion of the story with video appearing only when it is a soundbite portion or a standup. First, you make sure you have whatever countdown is appropriate. Be certain that the edit controller is in INSERT mode, and that you will be recording onto a tape with a control track. Edit in the countdown leader. Now you are ready to begin building the actual story.

Edit-in the first thing in the story. If it is a soundbite, edit it with audio on channel 1 and "video" selected. If it is a reporter narration track, edit it with no video inserted. You're going to add visuals to cover that audio track later. Lay down only the good takes of the voice track, in order, on audio channel 1 of the master videotape cassette or into the digital editing system.

On the editing control unit, activate only AUD-1 on the top row, center section of the editing control unit. You'll have black on the video channel of the tape, and the reporter narration in AUD-1.

When the narration ends, stop the edit and get ready to insert the soundbite. Take out the narration cassette from the playback deck and load the field cassette that contains the soundbite. Cue it up to the part you want to use. Set the in-point for the playback machine on the edit controller, and cue up the record machine with a natural pause after the end of the narration and set its in-point. Be sure the video switch in the recorder side of the edit controller is on, along with AUD-1 for the sound of the person.

Make the edit and press the "edit stop" button when you reach the end of the soundbite. When the soundbite ends, re-cue the record machine to the end of the bite, plus a natural pause. Take the field cassette out of the playback deck and re-load the narration cassette, cueing it to the next piece of narration to be laid down. Continue building the narration and soundbite or standup sections.

At this point your piece will have all the audio on channel 1, and video only in those places where you have soundbites, standups, or natural sound played as a soundbite. At times you'll want to use AUD-2 for special effects when you lay down narration, bites, and standups, but those are special circumstances and are best left until you have more experience manipulating the various audio tracks. The normal procedure is to keep all the primary audio on one channel because AUD-2 then can be used for the background sound and you don't risk messing up any of the primary audio by forgetting what is recorded where.

Fill in Cover Video

At this point, the master cassette still contains blank sections of video at places where only the reporter's voice has been recorded (see Figure 9.5). Appropriate visuals now are laid in against the prerecorded voice narration to fill the blanks. Normally the natural sound from the field scenes is used "sound-under" (Figure 9.6). Put all background sound on AUD-2, and lower the audio level so the background sound doesn't overpower the narration track and soundbites. If desired, add music or other sound under.

The most common practice is to put all narration, soundbites, and standups on one audio channel, and all background sound or special effects on the other. Sometimes, though, more involved audio track manipulation is used.

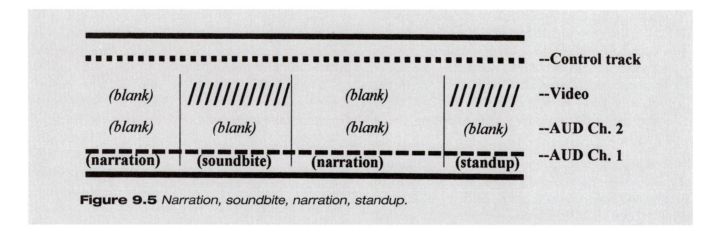

Figure 9.5 *Narration, soundbite, narration, standup.*

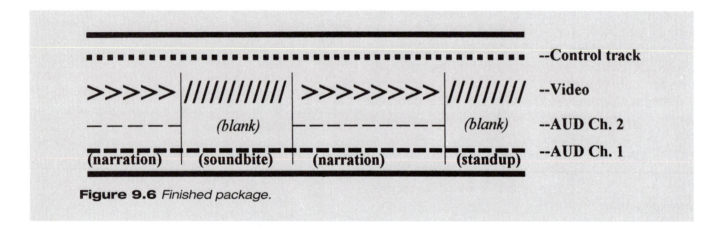

Figure 9.6 *Finished package.*

Add Graphics to the Package

If the reporter wishes to superimpose graphics (such as names and addresses) at any point in the video package, a log is made that shows that information as it should appear on the screen, along with start and stop times for the **supers**. Copies of this log are delivered to the studio technical director and to the character generator operator, who types up the supers and stores them in an electronic retrieval machine for call-up at airtime. If a character generator is part of the video editing console, graphics may be superimposed as part of the editing.

Pad Scenes to Avoid "Going to Black"

Include plenty of pad at the end of the edited package. Pad consists of approximately 5 seconds of picture after the last section of package that the home audience is to see or hear. The pad assures against the screen "going to black" the instant the package is finished. If the studio director momentarily misses the cue to punch up another picture source at the end of the package, the pad can continue playing until the director recovers.

Deliver the Master Cassette

Finally, the master cassette is delivered to the designated room, where tapes are played back at airtime.

Editing Tips

The following are some specific tips that will be useful to you as you edit.

Edit Point Errors. Video editing can be accomplished for the most part with frame accuracy, although edit points occasionally may slip. Professional editing units normally feature either 12/20 or 14/20 frame accuracy. An accuracy of 62 frames means that the edit point may begin or end within two frames from the desired point. An accuracy of 14/20 means that the edit may slip forward from the desired edit point as much as four frames, but that it will never begin earlier than the desired edit point.

To correct for the potential of edit points to "slop" forward (often with two or more frames of black between two scenes), most editors retard their desired edit-in points a minimum of four frames. In this manner, edit

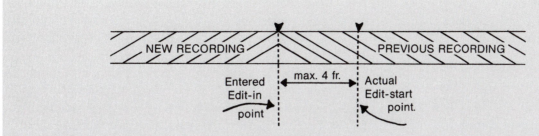

Figure 9.7 *Edit point retarded four frames to avoid possible incoming scene beginning in black.*

points that do slop forward are guaranteed not to extend past the exact point where the editor wants the outgoing scene to end (see Figure 9.7).

To retard the edit point, the editor enters an entry-in for the beginning of the next incoming scene, then retards it at least four frames by pressing the PLAYER button on the control unit and pressing ENTRY and M simultaneously at least four times. To meet FCC television standards, all edits on small-format (½-inch and ¾-inch videotape) must be free of flags, tracking errors, and time-base errors.

Flags. Flags often are evidenced as a series of black and white curved lines in the first frame of incoming video from a new scene. Possible causes include weak video levels when the scene originally was taped in the field, and field cameras that fail to produce a sufficient number of lines of video to fill the television screen. (At least one half-line of picture is lost each time video signals are dubbed from one tape to another, and

missing lines may appear as a dark bar at the top of the television screen.)

Tracking Adjustments. Whenever a tape is loaded in the player, a few scenes should be previewed prior to editing to determine whether tracking is acceptable. Tracking is the process by which the video head on a playback machine follows exactly the same path as the video head that recorded the signal. When tracking is bad, a herringbone pattern may appear on the monitor. If tracking errors appear, adjust the TRACKING control on the player until the scene clears.

Time-Base Corrector. Almost all small-format video media must be time-base corrected, either during editing or during actual newscast transmission, before it is suitable for use. The time-base corrector (TBC), a small box filled with complex electronics, enhances the picture and other electronic information stored on video

Flags at the edit point between scenes are evidence of an unacceptable edit.

Entering correct time codes is crucial for efficient video editing, and especially important when working against a tight deadline.

media. A critical role of the TBC is to improve synchronizing information on a control track, which in turn helps to eliminate picture jitter and breakup.

SMPTE Time Codes. The Society of Motion Picture Technicians and Engineers (SMPTE) Time Code helps editors conserve valuable time. Displayed on television monitors only during editing, the SMPTE Time Code appears in a small inset as a series of numbers that show accumulated hours, minutes, seconds, and frames of video. In- and out-points for each scene to be used can be noted simply by jotting down the **time code** at each of these points on a master shot sheet. Thanks to time codes, tape of events shot simultaneously by two or more cameras can be located quickly, and scenes of action recorded simultaneously from different camera angles can be match-cut with frame accuracy.

Time codes also allow editors to write detailed cutting instructions for a news package so engineering technicians can edit the tape later with no reporter present. In this way, scenes fed live to the newsroom for recording and later editing can be "shot-sheeted" even as they are being recorded.

Another advantage of the time code is that reporters in the field can synchronize tapes with their watches. As the photographer shoots various scenes, the reporter can consult a watch and jot down the times that important scenes were taped. During editing, these scenes can be retrieved with speed and precision from a reporter's shot sheet constructed in the field.

With digital editing systems, all information can be seen in time code and by frame number, as in Figure 9.8

Tape Crease. Occasionally during playback or recording, video media with physical damage emit an unusual noise — something like the sound of a zipper closing — as it moves past the rotating video heads. At the same time, a noticeable disruption in the picture will move vertically across the television screen. If creasing (also called wrinkling) appears, the offending videocassette should be replaced.

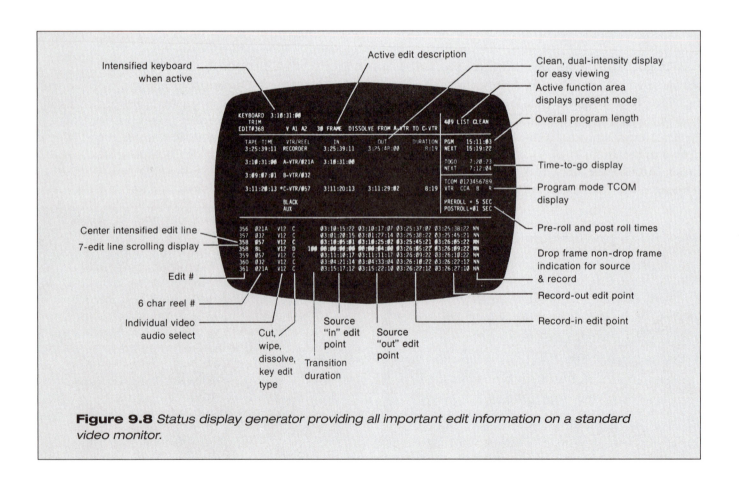

Figure 9.8 *Status display generator providing all important edit information on a standard video monitor.*

EXERCISE 9A: Newscast Story Selection

Name _____ Date _____

Consider that you have the following stories you could broadcast live via ENG equipment on the ten o'clock newscast. Because you have only one ENG van in this instance, determine which story you would cover, and defend your answer.

1. A city councilman has called a late evening news conference following the city council meeting to announce he is running for mayor.

2. A train carrying dangerous chemicals has derailed about 20 miles outside of your city. No chemicals have leaked out of the train, but officials are evacuating surrounding homes as a precautionary measure.

3 │ The citywide high school basketball championship game is tonight. You will be able to broadcast the closing minutes of the game and interview the coach live during the ten p.m. newscast.

4 │ A celebrity who grew up in your city is opening a restaurant downtown in support of your city's efforts to revitalize downtown.

5 │ The governor of your state is in your county holding a meeting to promote a new highway tax. Some of the revenues of the proposed tax will help upgrade a highway passing through your city to interstate standards.

Critical Thinking Questions

Directions: The following questions are provided to help you examine the deeper meanings and complexities of the various issues under discussion. Answer each question to the best of your ability after a thoughtful review of the subject at hand.

1. Nowhere in the journalistic world does teamwork count more than in electronic field reporting. Assuming a role of your choice (reporter, producer, photographer, etc.), what are your obligations and responsibilities to all other team members with whom you will associate as a working professional?

2. Would you prefer one long news package in a newscast, or more but shorter packages? Explain all the content and storytelling tools you would use to attract and hold larger audiences with longer format packages. Also address any aspects of news philosophy and subject matter that influence your thinking.

3. What types of news packages require that you disclose what happened in the anchor lead and/or the package open, and what kinds of stories are most effective when the outcome is delayed until the package ending?

4. We "see with our ears." Consequently, nat sound adds an essential sense of realism to news reports. What steps will you take while in the field, when writing the script, and during the editing process, to create reports in which "sound is the other half of the image?"

5. Audiovisual media do not create an actual reality but, rather, a reconstruction of reality. If you place one image (a snake) next to another image (a baby crawling on the ground), the viewer will create a mental concept (baby in peril) that is not contained in either image. What, then, are the responsibilities of the scriptwriter and the editor in fashioning news reports out of images? Explain the idea that "audiences remember what they see, not what they hear."

6. In an ideal world, would you prefer to create news packages by editing storytelling pictures and sound first, then writing the voice track to fit the images, or would you prefer to write the voice-over script first, then edit picture and sound to fit your words on the narration track? Explain why.

7. Which, in your view, is most important — telling viewers what happened, or allowing them to see what happened, using words only as necessary to interpret and explain? Discuss any exceptions that may contradict your point of view.

8. After reflecting upon your lifetime of reading books, watching films and television, listening to music and radio, surfing the Internet, and conversing with friends, how would you view the importance of the moving image in communicating the context of human life and the realm of ideas, values, and spirituality?

Self-Review Questions

Directions: Each of the self-review questions below addresses information contained in this chapter. Answer each question to the best of your ability, then review the chapter as necessary to further strengthen your understanding of each concept or issue.

1. What is the difference between linear and non-linear video editing?

2. What minimum capabilities are required of a "one-person band?"

3. What are the duties of a field producer?

4. In what essential ways does a news photographer or photojournalist differ from a "camera operator?"

5. What basic types of stories (news conference, live reports, etc.) do you expect to encounter in the field? How might the nature of each impact news content and treatment in your reports?

6. What is the basic structure of a news package? What guidelines do the reporter, photographer, and editor have to take into account when producing a package?

7. What is the basic video editing process involved in creating a news package, whether using a linear or a non-linear system?

8. What is the difference between an insert and an assemble edit?

9. What is the control track on videotape, and what is its function?

10. Explain in a paragraph or two whether you view video editing as primarily a technical skill, a creative story-telling skill, or a blend of both.

## CHAPTER TEN

Live Field Reporting and Storytelling

5:48 p.m. — 12 minutes before airtime for the six o'clock news in Minneapolis–St. Paul. An airliner carrying 300 passengers is closing in for an emergency landing. Air traffic controllers confirm that a crash is possible, and reporting crews speed to the airport in vans equipped with electronic news gathering (ENG) equipment. The crews set up television field cameras, video recording and playback units, and microwave transmitters that can beam signals live through the air to be recorded for later retransmission, or rebroadcast instantly to viewers' homes.

News directors monitoring the developing story now are faced with a tough decision. If they opt for live coverage, viewers may witness an event in which up to 300 persons will die before their eyes. One news director orders live coverage. Another news director balks at the story's potentially overwhelming impact. He orders his crew to record video of the landing for later editing and playback, either in a special report or on the regular 10 o'clock newscast. Finally the plane appears on the horizon. It lands safely without event. The television crews leave, and soon the airport is back to normal.

BREAKTHROUGHS IN ELECTRONIC JOURNALISM

In the strictest sense, there is no such thing as "electronic journalism." For all the marvelous gadgetry and electronic technology that the audio and video news media enjoy, no machine in the world yet generates news stories without human input.

Journalism remains today, as it always has, a process by which news events are reported and, sometimes, interpreted. The process involves the reporter's judgment, perception, creativity, language and visual skills, integrity, intellect, and hard work, and some means to deliver the finished story to an audience.

That concept of journalism has not changed much over the centuries. What has changed is the incredible progress in making the story more immediate, in the rapidity with which the story can be covered in the field and delivered to homes around the world. The importance of this technology was evident all over the country a few years ago. Following the September 11, 2001, terrorist attack on the World Trade Center, all major broadcast news networks shifted into high gear for continuous

Live news coverage can be the best choice for bringing news to viewers as it is happening, but it is important to use such technology only when the story justifies "going live."

coverage and live reports from Ground Zero. Americans were glued to their television sets and computers to see what was happening at the sites of the tragedy. In the initial hours after the attack, networks scrambled to get live coverage of the biggest story in American history.

An interesting dilemma developed: While the country could not get enough information about what had happened, why it occurred, who was responsible, and who was affected, viewers also were aware of the personal tragedy involving thousands of Americans and did not necessarily want live coverage that would focus on families and friends of victims during some of their most difficult and private moments. These ethical issues will be discussed in more depth in Chapter 14, but a short discussion is warranted here.

Live news coverage is a powerful reporting tool that helps involve the audience, but potential abuse requires deliberate use of the technology. Just because a television news station can do a live report does not mean it is always the best decision. But many times, live coverage does enhance a story and add a dimension that no other medium can offer.

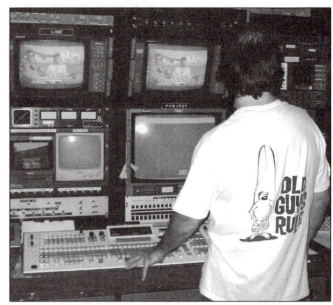

Satellite feeds allow fast transfer of news from far away, making it easier for local stations to cover national and international news.

ELECTRONIC NEWS GATHERING (ENG)

Behind this ability to report stories almost instantly are the technological breakthroughs that have resulted in **electronic news gathering** (ENG) or (EJ), through **satellite news gathering** (SNG), and **audio and video streaming** via the Internet.

Because ENG has the capacity to make audiences eyewitnesses to the news, the delivery vehicle that takes them to the scene of breaking news first has a distinct competitive advantage. The real competitive value of EJ is in enabling the organization to fulfill audience expectations. Once a strong loyalty develops, audiences expect their favorite outlets to have the important news, and to have it first. Promotional efforts help to project that image. If the organization is aggressive in covering the news, hiring good people, and using the latest technology to help improve its reporting and presentation, it has a good chance to be number one in the market, or at least to make a strong showing in the market.

Beware, however, that the predisposition to think of the audience as a "mass" results frequently in "pack journalism," wherein most journalists cover the same story, with the result that it dominates the news everywhere for a time. The technology of a given medium has a tremendous effect on what it covers. If it involves pictures, a story can generate enormous coverage though it is little more than visuals. Context and deeper meaning can be lost in a sea of images.

Satellite Newsgathering

Another technological revolution is the advent of **satellite newsgathering** or **SNG**. Through microwave and satellite technology, local news operations can cover stories live from anywhere in the world. No longer must local news audiences depend upon network news anchors and reporters for national and international news. Today they can receive those same stories via satellite, as reported by reporters from their favorite local station. This national and even global newsgathering capacity often is made possible through cooperative networks of local stations, which make their satellite uplink dishes, helicopters, and mobile studio vans available to member organizations.

For a station in Seattle, this means that local coverage of hurricane damage at a Houston shipping port is as simple as flying a reporting crew into Houston. The crew then can uplink reports to Seattle using a cooperating station's satellite facilities in Houston. Although this reporting flexibility does not guarantee better television news, it does offer that potential. Viewers throughout the country need to know how distant stories affect them. Businesses in Seattle may need locally tailored reports that tell them about effects of the hurricane on shipping throughout the Pacific Basin. Those same businesses may want to know how Pentagon deficits are likely to affect an economy heavily dependent upon aircraft manufacturing.

Audio and Video Streaming on the Internet

Technology also allows for virtually instantaneous streaming of audio and video via the Internet. Even live broadcasts are possible. As more bandwidth becomes available to Internet subscribers, ever larger and sharper images become possible. Some Web sites allow users to place video stories offered on the Web in a preferred order, then stream them as a "consumer-produced" newscast, either to the computer screen or to a high-definition monitor elsewhere within the subscriber environment. Such technologies have the potential to compete with, and one day to replace, traditional cable and over-the-air broadcasts.

BAD AND GOOD LIVE REPORTS

Viewer expectations often remain unrealized because the ability to "go live" is simply that — an ability. Not all stories warrant live coverage, and those that do may not break at times when they can be broadcast live. The exceptions are the highly visual and dramatic stories that deserve live coverage because of their significance — important resignations, strikes, major crime, disasters, and other so-called crisis stories. Run-of-the-mill stories might better be recorded and brought to the audience at a more sensible time, after reporters have had a chance to research the story and edit it into a more thoughtful and comprehensive package.

Frequently, big names in politics, sports, and business, hoping to use the station for free publicity, arrange their airport arrivals conveniently just in time for live coverage during the 6 p.m. newscast. Journalists who are forced to cover an important story live because of someone else's schedule have lost control of the story. They have no chance to check accuracy, no time to assure that the story is balanced.

Further, live interviews, when present, must run as is with no time for editing, no time to probe beneath surface answers. A skillful interviewee can talk nonstop during the minute or so available and project an image of righteous indignation when cut off because the time allotted for the story has run out.

Except for extremely newsworthy events that are highly dramatic and visual, most stations rarely interrupt normal entertainment programming for live reports.

One reason is that live inserts throw off the programming schedule and may preempt lucrative commercials. Live inserts also may drive viewers away from the station when their favorite programming is interrupted. And always the question must be asked: Will viewers be exposed to possible violence, bad taste, or obscenity?

Anyone who has watched the news very much can recall instances in which the reporter of a live story should have stayed home. Examples of stories that should not be covered live include everything from the aftermath of a mattress fire (in which no one is injured or available to be interviewed) to the reporter standing on a pier as she describes a hurricane miles away and out of sight over the horizon. Equally arcane are the live weather reports from the local botanical garden or the live standups in which the reporter describes barely visible scenes over his left shoulder.

SPOTLIGHT

Qualities of a Good Live Reporter

Journalists who do live reports cover stories into which they suddenly have been injected, sometimes without the benefit of adequate preparation, research, or insight. To do the job effectively, they need to know a little about almost every subject under the sun, to think quickly, and to have such a solid foundation in reporting skills that they can simply react when they do not have time to think.

They need extraordinary abilities to ad-lib, to draw solid answers from strangers they encountered only minutes before, and special gifts of perspective to help the audience understand the causes of the event they are reporting.

"To be successful at live reporting, individuals must have some very basic traits that have nothing to do with education," says Roger Ogden former General Manager of KCNC Denver. "They must be able to think on their feet. They must have a sufficient vocabulary, and they must have an analytical mind so they can quickly weed fiction from fact."

Covering an event live is difficult to do well, especially when it is a tragedy. The reporter must remain a neutral observer who can deliver a concise and informative report on the fly while maintaining composure.

Good live television, by contrast, contains strong elements of visual interest and dramatic significance. Reports such as these — the successful rescue of trapped miners, or on-scene reports of a threatening flood — offer a compelling reason to go live. They allow the audience to witness history in the making or to participate in an unusually dramatic story that touches many lives as it develops. Stories that lack visual impact and substance serve only as contributions to weak reporting.

LIVE INTERVIEWS AND INTERVIEWERS

Legitimate live interviews provide interest and mood available from no other source. Each day, hundreds of people tell their stories with more enthusiasm, conviction, and drama than journalists could ever accomplish through written, third-person accounts read on camera. It is one thing to hear the reporter's account of an air disaster and quite another to hear an observer's still strong impressions of a mid-air collision. The best interviews do more than deliver facts. They provide the credibility, mood, vivid details, and unexpected insights that help give news reports authenticity and vitality.

Typical Problems

Since the advent of live reporting, the interview has taken on a new and sometimes unwarranted function: It goes beyond enhancing live reports to sometimes substituting for the story itself. Reporters who have just arrived on the scene with instructions to "go live immediately" seldom have time to research the event adequately and prepare a reasoned report. They are forced instead to rely on a few seconds of on-camera introduction to the event, an interview that forms the main body of the report, then a few seconds of on-camera close, in which the implication is, "There you have it, folks."

In reality, what the folks at home receive is not a report but, instead, a headline service that contains hurried interviews with one or two people who give their sometimes inexact versions of what happened. The approach works at times, but often it fails because the interview, at its best, doesn't stand alone as the entire story. In its finest form, the interview proves the rest of the story and helps the report achieve at least the illusion of immediacy.

The Reporter Is Not the Story. Over time, the television news personality, whether anchor person or field reporter, inescapably assumes a certain "star quality." Seen frequently on screen, in promotional advertisements, and on billboards around the city, the reporter becomes a public figure. Instant public recognition

becomes a feature of everyday life that is established further by station surveys of how well the reporter is recognized in the market and how well viewers like the reporter's on-air personality.

As subjects of so much attention, on-air reporters may begin to think their presence on camera is the story. Journalists who fall victim to this syndrome refuse to let the story tell itself. They dominate interviews with long-winded questions, appear on screen more frequently than necessary, and fail, in the end, to take advantage of the visual media's strongest assets: storytelling images, good natural sound, and meaningful interviews and soundbites. Even though television reporters can't help but become personalities, their first obligation is to remain competent journalists. The best journalists know when to step aside and let the story tell itself.

The Soundbite Versus the Talking Head. A soundbite (a topic of Chapter 7) is the point of emphasis that proves the story and what's been said about it both visually and in the reporter's narrative. Frequently the soundbite is nothing more than that little moment of drama that elevates the story into a believable, interesting, and sometimes more dramatic report. By contrast, a **talking head** is radio with the picture of a

IMPROVING LIVE REPORTING SKILLS

Live reporting demands individual traits that include personal resources such as a quick and analytical mind, the ability to speak extemporaneously, a well-developed vocabulary, good judgment, and a sixth sense for what makes news. But even these traits can be improved further through training and practice.

Some news directors cite the desirability of news experience in radio, a relatively instant medium that requires the ability to present frequent live, ad-lib reports. Other stations cite the benefits of general assignment reporting, a job in which the reporter learns to identify and develop the sources that make news and also becomes an expert in covering a vast array of news topics. Individuals in the position learn, as well, how to meet people, how to conduct meaningful interviews, and how to present themselves on-camera.

Beyond such experiences, the live reporter has access to that old maxim: "Practice makes perfect."

moving mouth that spouts meaningless information. It is the interview that substitutes for the story and induces droopy eyelids in viewers.

Journalists who scorn the talking head argue that because television is visual, it should show the news, not merely tell it. Abstract or complex ideas, however, cannot always be visualized, and the rush to keep television news visual often deprives viewers of the critical statement or the complex explanation from a knowledgeable expert. When these interviews are used, they are kept to minimum length so as not to confuse or bore viewers. The argument is that television (and its viewers) prefers the dramatic and that print, not visual media, is the best way to deliver complex facts and ideas.

To a great extent, that point of view is valid but often is espoused by journalists who consider all interviews to be mere "talking heads." A telling distinction exists between the so-called talking head and a legitimate soundbite.

Former CBS news executive Fred Friendly told the story of government hearings at which learned experts testified on the maximum weight that postal workers would be allowed to carry on their daily rounds. The hearings droned on until a mail carrier stepped to the microphone to testify why the weight of his daily loads should be reduced. "I'll tell you why it matters," he said. "What matters is Tuesday. Tuesday is the day I gotta climb 13 floors with 122 pounds on my back, because Tuesday is the day *Life* magazine comes." The point is made, and the story enhanced, all because this brief moment of sound put into perspective the entire hearing and the issues that surrounded it.

Challenges of the Live Interview

Among the most difficult interview forms, the live interview is something of a juggling act. The reporter must elicit a statement, in the brief time available (often a minute or less), that really says something about the story, and be able to bring the interview to a smooth close in the allotted time. The longer the interview, the easier it is to zero-in on subject matter and to elicit meaningful responses from the interviewee.

"On the types of stories I cover," says NBC news correspondent Bob Dotson, "I can burn 40 minutes of tape if I have to. The person I interview knows I will pick out the meaningful responses so he can tell me now or he can tell me later."

In live reports, by contrast, the most important newsmakers often become performers over the years. They know the clock is in their favor, and they can talk for three minutes and still not give meaningful answers to the reporter's questions.

Reporters who conduct live interviews must have the background necessary to make live news reports interesting and meaningful. They must be able to meet people easily and have the capacity to help interviewees forget the pressure of the moment. They must be instant students of people and, regardless of the situation, unflappable. They also must have a certain amount of grit, so when interviewees try to seize control by running out the clock, they can adopt their best Mike Wallace style,

HOW TO CONTROL A LIVE INTERVIEW

To meet the challenge of producing a quality live interview, on-air journalists use a variety of techniques.

- Prior to on-air broadcast, the person to be interviewed can be given a predetermined cue signaling that the interview must end within 15 seconds. The cue may be something as simple as a touch on the knee (off-camera) or a prior cue to the interviewee: "When I ask you this question, that will be the end of the interview."

- Some interviewees will talk nonstop unless the interviewer finds some way to cut them off. When these people stop to breathe, the interviewer should be ready to jump in with a new question. In normal conversation, the interruption might be considered rude. On television, the same interruption may be barely noticeable to home viewers.

- In extreme cases, interviewees talk over a question as the reporter tries to move the interview in a new direction. To regain control, the interviewer's only recourse is to become more assertive and jump back into the interview with a question that begins something to the effect, "Forgive me, but ....."

- A smooth exit line, thought out in advance, can bring the live interview to a smooth close. The exit line may be something as simple as, "Dr. Steele, thank you very much," as the reporter takes a step away from the interviewee and faces the camera to wrap up the story from the scene. The exit line also can serve as a prearranged signal for the sound person to cut the interviewee's microphone and for the camera operator to zoom to a tight shot of the reporter, eliminating the interviewee from screen.

THE ABCs OF ENG: FASHION FOR THE FIELD
by Dana Rosengard

In local television news, the reporter is part of the image that viewers judge in their homes. What you wear contributes to how you are perceived. As young reporters, it is particularly important that you learn to dress more like the network correspondent or executive you may hope to become, rather than like the small-market, one-man-band reporter you may well be at first.

Let caution and restraint be your wardrobe watchwords. Ignore labels and trends. At the beginning of a career, it is much more important that you dress modestly and professionally than it is to look like a magazine advertisement. The only logo you should display on clothing while on the job should be that of your station or network. As you consider your clothing options, be sure you are not attracting too much attention to what you are wearing. Instead, look to leave viewers able to concentrate on what you are saying.

Men

For men, this goal is easier to achieve than it is for women, mostly because their choices are fewer. Starting underneath it all, literally, men should wear crewneck, plain, white t-shirts under shirts and jerseys. Another sweeping generality of good style is that shoes, belt, and watchband should all match, certainly by color, and ideally by material or fabric.

On to the more obvious fashion choices: Do not be a "three-solid man" — don't wear a solid suit (or sports coat) with a solid shirt and a solid tie. At least one of those three items should have a pattern or design. Remembering to err on the side of conservative, it's most likely the tie will carry the bulk of the style statement, matched with a solid shirt under a solid, subtly striped, or patterned suit.

Two tie guidelines to keep in mind: Avoid small and busy patterns, which often are distorted by the video or digital camera; and devise a plan of rotation so you do not wear the same tie any more often than is necessary. In general, the simpler the shirt, the more complex the tie can be. A solid shirt can handle any tie, keeping in mind that your ode to the Beatles or The Grateful Dead may be better saved for a social event than put on display during a newscast.

Finally for men, over-the-calf socks are strongly suggested. Nothing will embarrass a man more than a reverse wide two-shot that shows a reporter flashing skin and hair from crossed legs not properly, professionally, sheathed in socks, which should be chosen to match the slacks, not the shoes, and should almost always be solid.

Women

The watchword for the women: Safe is the better choice when choosing what to wear. Professional is the preferred look. Sexy and suggestive are best saved for Saturday night social engagements.

Suits should be simple and tasteful, with skirts approaching knee length, if not at the knee. A blouse or a lightweight sweater should be worn under all jackets. Sweetheart necklines or anything lace is not going to get a beginning reporter the respect she should hope to command from an official, a colleague, a competitor, or the public.

Dresses should also be the most modest length you can tolerate. As with neckwear for men, a simple or subtle pattern or design is much preferred to anything busy or distracting. Also beware the placement of buttons. They can pose problems for lavaliere microphones and appear to be extensions of body parts to which you should not be drawing attention.

Pants are entirely professional, matched with jackets or sweater sets or just a plain blouse. Get whatever style best suits your figure. Typically, the broadcast reporter can be seen only from the waist up, so basic pants or skirts can be repeated with a new top for a whole new look.

Shoes should be tasteful, comfortable and not hinder mobility. Heels should be reasonable, sensible, and chunky enough to support an on-the-go reporter on a mild run if necessary.

For men and women alike, jewelry should be kept to the barest of minimums. Actually, for men, a wedding ring and a watch are the only possibilities. Women can add perhaps one more ring, a necklace and, of course, a pair of earrings. These last two items should be kept small and simple, as any movement or reflection of light in this area will distract from the story you are trying to tell. Avoid bracelets, as they tend to clank against stick-mics and the anchor desk.

Videographers

Although this advice speaks primarily to the on-camera talent, videographers also should meet certain standards. Typically, individual newsrooms will have guidelines for them. Remember you are

(continued)

no longer in school, are being paid, and are every bit as much representatives of the station as are the reporters. Wear clean clothes without logos, suitable to step into a house of worship if you have to get a quick bite from a religious leader.

For the would-be television journalists, avoid white. Instead, go with ivory. The videographer will thank you. Also avoid small, high-contrast patterns (houndstooth check, seersucker, other small stripes). Neither videographers nor cameras like them. As you can never be sure what the day and assignment might bring, always have jeans and boots and a station logo sweater, sweatshirt, or jacket with you at work for fires and car wrecks. It's easier to dress down than up.

Dana Rosengard is an assistant professor in the Department of Journalism, University of Memphis. In addition to nearly a decade of work in network affiliated television newsrooms, he holds a Ph.D. in journalism and mass communication, as well as several years of fashion retail experience. Used by permission.

interrupt, and say, "You're evading the question. What were you doing on the night of March 23?"

ON-CAMERA APPEARANCE

Reporters should dress appropriately for on-camera appearances. The clothes to wear to cover a mountain rescue or a mine disaster obviously would be different from those for an interview with city officials or the opening of a symphony concert. Most stations offer guidelines on appropriate dress for on-air and field talent, and most discourage casual dress except in extenuating circumstances. The bottom line is: Dress to fit the scene.

When covering a combat zone in a war, a coat and tie would look out of place. The same is true when doing a standup story on a farm drought with a field being plowed as the background. Conversely, an open-collared sport shirt would look wrong in a standup on an economic story with the New York Stock Exchange floor as the background. Reporters should fit the scene and ambiance of the story.

PERSONALIZING THE STORY

Television news can capture the colors, sounds, and emotions of news happenings, and you can personalize the story by giving the viewer real human beings to relate to. Say you've been assigned to do a feature on Mother's Day and you wish to personalize the story. You might want to begin with shots of busy operators at the telephone company, then interview a couple of operators to see how many calls they've handled, go from there to shots of telephone lines reaching to the far horizon, and over these shots play some prerecorded conversations between mothers and their children. Throughout this story, the emphasis is on people — people who are special to each other. By emphasizing people, the audience can identify with the story.

Or take another happening — heavy rains that are keeping farmers from planting spring crops. To personalize the story, you will talk with the farmers who are unable to plant, learn their feelings, and find out how the rains will affect their income. Talk with food experts to learn whether delayed planting will affect supermarket prices. Talk with weather experts to find out when the project the rains to end. Again, you are personalizing the story by giving your viewers real human beings with whom to relate.

EXERCISE 10A: Covering Stories

Name _____ Date _____

As an individual written assignment, consider which stories you would report live and which you would record for later transmission. For each story you would transmit at a later time, explain how you might cover it and whether you would include interviews and standups or use only silent shots and voice-over narration.

1. After a series of high-rise apartment and hotel fires around the country, city inspectors find that only two buildings in your city meet current fire safety codes. The fire department is pressuring city officials to require that all existing buildings be upgraded to meet safety codes. Officials say other high-rise buildings already under construction may not meet national safety codes.

2. Workers at a local soft drink bottling company are picketing local supermarkets, trying to discourage shoppers from buying the bottling company's products. The picketers carry signs, and a spokesperson says the major issue is equal job opportunities for minority workers. Supermarket managers also are available for comment.

3. Proposals are being made to have Congress designate a local river as wild and scenic, a designation that would protect the river from further commercial or agricultural development. Environmentalists say the river is the last in the state that could be so designated and they want the river protected in its current condition for future generations to enjoy. State officials say local agriculture will be seriously jeopardized if the river's waters do not remain available for irrigation.

| 4 | A truck carrying radioactive materials has just overturned on an interstate highway outside the city. Officials are trying to determine whether the site is contaminated, the governor has been notified, and National Guard troops are guarding the area while traffic is rerouted. All officials at this hour are refusing comment. The truck driver cannot be located.

| 5 | Police say a young boy, possibly between 12 and 14 years of age, has robbed a convenience store and escaped with an estimated 1,000 dollars or more in cash. The store clerk was forced to lie on the floor while her hands and feet were bound with adhesive tape. Police are on the scene and are interrogating the store clerk.

| 6 | At two p.m. you learn that the School District will cancel all after-school recreational programs for elementary school students at community centers within the district. The decision will impact families with latchkey children significantly. The story could be aired first at five p.m.

EXERCISE 10B: Wire Copy Editing

Name _____ Date _____

Consider the following news service reports. If these were news stories in your city, how could you make them live reports? Include from where you would report, whom you would interview, and what you would wear on camera. Also list three questions the anchor in the studio could ask you for a live exchange.

NEW YORK – The new manager for the New York Mets is leaving a team just 30 minutes away. But moving from Yankee Stadium to Shea will be a whole new world for longtime Yankees coach Willie Randolph. And as the first black manager of a New York Major League Baseball team, Randolph does not lack for challenges.

-30-

CHICAGO – A tornado rips through the east side of Chicago this morning, damaging scores of apartment buildings and leaving thousands of residents without water, power and in some cases, a roof. So far officials are reporting no casualties as a result of the twister, but there is significant damage.

-30-

ORLANDO – Florida's Secretary of State's office is declaring the 2004 election a victory for voting officials who

vowed their state would not be the center of controversy four years after being publicly embarrassed in the 2000

presidential election between George W. Bush and Al Gore. Florida Republicans are elated with the outcome of the

election and relieved the state was a decisive victory.

-30-

ASSIGNMENT 10A: Field Reporting

Name _____ Date _____

Develop a reporting beat that you will visit at least once a week for four weeks. Each week, as a standing class assignment, write at least one story suitable for broadcast from the beat source you visit, and submit the copy you generate to your professor. You will have to visit the beat source in advance, introduce yourself, and secure permission to stop by weekly. It should take you only a few minutes each week to question your beat source about recent happenings, with perhaps another half to full hour to go through records and other documents as you research facts for your stories. Possible beat sources are listed below, with additional spaces provided for other beat sources in your area.

University Police Office

City Police Department

State Patrol Offices

Municipal Court

County Court

District Court

Fire Department

Sheriff's Department

Local Park or Forest Service Offices

School Board

City Building Department

City Council

Municipal Planning and Zoning Department

County Commissioners Office

Other (please identify)

_____

_____

_____

Critical Thinking Questions

Directions: *The following questions are provided to help you examine the deeper meanings and complexities of the various issues under discussion. Answer each question to the best of your ability after a thoughtful review of the subject at hand.*

1. Audiences like to watch things for themselves. Live reporting and "being first" offer news organizations important competitive advantages. What negative influences of live reporting may also impact viewers?

2. What are the relative merits and disadvantages of satellite newsgathering, which allows local news operations to cover stories live almost anywhere in the world?

3. How can public figures and special interest groups use live reports to gain control of the reporting process, and what can you do as a journalist to avoid this outcome?

4. Assuming the role of news director, what types of live coverage (tragic natural disasters, wars, violent demonstrations, etc.) would you censor or "sanitize?" Explain your reasoning in sufficient detail to serve as a recommendation from you, the news director, to your organization's general manager.

5. Taking a news director's point-of-view, how should a college student prepare to become a competent live reporter prior to applying for a position in market size 75–125?

6. What is meant by the notion that "the reporter is never the story?" How can failure to honor this maxim impact on the reporting process?

7. What are the distinctions between the soundbite and the talking head? How will your understanding of the two influence your reporting style when you enter the profession?

8. Explain how you might effectively use a live interview in the following scenarios. (If you don't think a live interview is appropriate, please explain why.)

a. Your local school board held a public forum about getting rid of sexually explicit books from the high school library.

b. A tornado ripped through town two hours ago and has left a path of destruction.

c. A local resident has just won the state lottery worth six million dollars.

Self-Review Questions

Directions: Each of the self-review questions below addresses information contained in this chapter. Answer each question to the best of your ability, then review the chapter as necessary to further strengthen your understanding of each concept or issue.

1. What are ENG and SNG? How do the two differ?

2. What is the pro and con of competition on the news gathering and reporting process?

3. What qualities does a good live reporter have?

4. In what ways can journalists improve their live reporting skills?

5. What are the essential content differences between live and prerecorded interviews?

6. What is the meaning of the phrase, "The reporter is never the story."

7. What are the major challenges of the live interview? How can these be met successfully?

8. How do the soundbite and the talking head interview differ?

9. What are the most important considerations that govern a reporter's on-camera appearance?

10. In what ways can a reporter legitimately personalize otherwise purely factual or institutional stories?

11. List two fashion do's and don'ts for both men and women appearing on television.

## CHAPTER ELEVEN

Producing Across Electronic Technologies

The chef and the electronic journalist share a common circumstance: What takes them hours to prepare is devoured in minutes. Dozens of people invest hundreds of hours in the average newscast or Web site news publication. Then, when the 30 or more stories they have taken hours to prepare are consumed in radio, television, or the Internet, they are rapidly absorbed and go into oblivion.

Each day the process is the same: Write another newscast, shoot another videotape, edit another story, create another link, and always hurry. The clock never stops. News happens fast, is covered and reported fast, and is consumed fast.

FORMAT AND PRESENTATION

The format is the form in which you serve up the news. In earlier times the TV news format was simple. The half-hour was divided into three segments—news, weather, and sports. Each night the pattern was the same. National and international news came first, followed by local news, then weather and sports. The news was delivered straight to the camera, formally, without "happy talk" or other diversions by the news personalities.

Today, regardless of whether it is broadcast, video and/or audio streamed on the Internet, or delivered through some other conduit, the emphasis is on a floating format with (in the case of TV) two

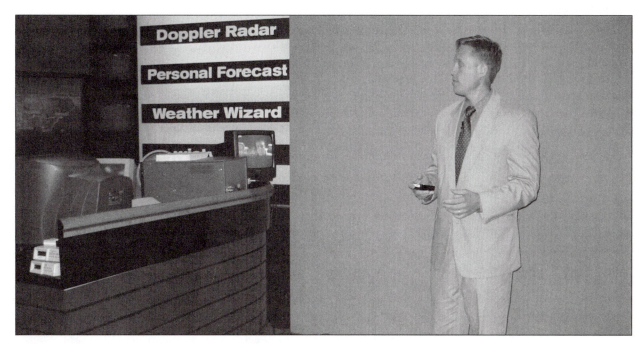

Weather news is often the most important to viewers, and in recent years, television stations have recognized this by offering more frequent weather reports within the newscast and have spent many dollars acquiring high-tech radar equipment.

221

dominant anchor personalities working in tandem to tie the entire newscast together. The news "floats" in the sense that given stories can be placed anywhere within the newscast, depending upon the news, sports, or weather day. In this way, emphasis is placed where it should be, irrespective of whether the news is local, regional, or international. If major weather is the big news of the day, the newscast might begin with a brief report by the weathercaster, who then admonishes the audience to stay tuned for more weather details later in the regular forecast. If a major sports story dominates the day's news, it, too, can be placed higher in the newscast.

Connecting the TV newscast are the two news personalities, who do hand-offs to sports and weather and occasionally or regularly may engage in brief conversation with other reporters.

As was discussed in the first chapter, the essential jobs in news work have remained much the same over the years, though we have migrated through technological developments from pure radio through television and into the complexity of the Internet. As you will read at the end of this chapter, the next step is a "converged" newsroom where one team is working to produce news stories in a variety of media formats. Though duties within the newsroom shift somewhat, the concept will be the same: Get as much useful but still accurate information to the public in as short a time as possible.

The job of shepherding the newscast into a finished unit falls to the news producer. The producer is concerned with the total content of the news — the organization, length, visuals (in the case of TV and Internet), which stories to add, shorten, or drop. In any newsroom the producer's job requires intimate knowledge of journalism, writing, production, and showmanship.

Every component of the TV newscast, from script and visuals to talent and timing, must be orchestrated into a smooth-flowing presentation that builds logically throughout the half hour. The newscast must maintain audience interest, end within a few seconds of the exact time allotment, yet look so professional that what in reality is a complicated orchestration appears so simple that anyone could do it.

The following discussion addresses the particulars of first radio, then television, then Internet news production. Although there are differences, primarily as a result of technology, the basic content is created in much the same way. Like the chef baking a cake, the ingredients are similar from one to another, though the presentation may be very different. A wedding cake and a plain chocolate cake look very different for different events, but they both have eggs, flour, and frosting.

THE RADIO NEWSCAST

"Rip and read" is a method of producing a newscast by selecting stories off the wire and reading them on the air. The newscaster might be a disc jockey who is on the air at the time, or may be a station employee whose part-time responsibility is being the news director. The wire services allow stations on a tight budget to provide their audiences with regional, state, national, and international news. If the station buys both a wire service and its accompanying audio feed, the newscast can provide the added dimension of actual comments from sources, known as **actualities**.

Wire services might provide the only news a station uses, and they also can be an integral part of a full-time news department's newscast. News directors read the wire service copy before each newscast, looking for important stories. If they find one, they might rewrite it to fit the length or station's "sound," or they might assign a reporter to find a local angle for tomorrow's newscast. Wire services can be a radio news department's most valuable tool in the battle to serve the community's news needs.

Wire services are not the only resource option the news director has. The station might belong to a network that provides regular newscasts that are fed to their subscribers at scheduled times during the day. A news director might opt to do a newscast just before or just after the network feed. Because the network news

A radio news anchor delivers the day's news from the announcer's booth.

covers national and international news, the station's news department is able to concentrate on local news. A station that has enough financial resources might subscribe to a network, a wire service, an audio service, and a feature service.

Of course, all those options won't replace the reporter covering local news. News directors still have to rely on their reporters to collect information, check the facts, conduct the interviews, recheck the facts, write the stories, edit the tapes, recheck the facts, and do the follow-up, if necessary. In journalistic circles the word **lead** has three basic meanings:

1. It may mean the first sentence of a story.

2. It may mean the first story in a newscast.

3. It may mean the idea for a story.

Preparing the Radio Newscast

Story coverage begins with following up this last kind of lead. Story leads come in many disguises. You may find a lead in the local newspaper classified ads, on the bulletin board at the laundromat, in conversation with a police officer, in the court records, or in the mayor's indiscriminate remarks during a heated discussion at the city council meeting.

A reporter must be alert to leads. If the station has a scanner, and if you pay attention to it, you can get some leads directly from the police and fire dispatchers.

The story lead is only the beginning. Once you get your lead, you have to decide whether you can do the story. Whom do you need to contact to get information? Can you reach the people who have the information while the story is still timely? Are ethical considerations involved? Is the story a hard news story or a soft news story? By answering these questions, you will have begun organizing your story.

In part, you will have defined what you want to write about and how you will have to proceed. These are the same questions your news director will ask if he or she has any doubts about the story.

Begin by investigating your lead. This is just the beginning. You will want to keep defining the story to make sure you actually have a story. Who were the key figures? What was the most important thing that happened? How did that affect the community? Why did it happen? Who will be the best sources to contact? Is the story news?

Certain aspects of writing tend to be consistent from story to story and station to station: Set margins for a 65-space line, and double-space the copy. Using this guide, the average broadcaster will deliver at a rate of about 16 lines a minute. If your story has to be 30

Table 11.1 *A Guide to Radio Newscasts*

Newscast Length	Minutes of Commercials	Number of Stories	Number of Actualities
5 min.	:60	10	2
10 min.	1:20	18	3
15 min.	1:20	25	5

seconds, you know you will have to write an eight-line story. If your news director has only five minutes to put together a newscast, this line-count technique can speed the writing process.

You can use the guide in Table 11.1 to help organize the newscast. To get all ten stories into a five-minute newscast, your stories must average 30 seconds in length, including the two actualities. This underscores the importance of writing for time rather than writing for space. It also demonstrates how valuable a tool the line-count technique can be.

Once you have the margins set and you know how long your story must be, you will have to provide some non-copy reference information — information that won't be read on-air. This information helps journalists plan the newscast. No single format is used by all stations, but most stations recognize certain information as being important. If your news script is formatted, it might look like Figure 11.1.

The non-copy reference information is a valuable planning tool. At a glance, information is available about story length, content — called a **slug** — and the time of day of the newscast for which the story was written. This information is important in planning the upcoming newscast and subsequent newscasts for which the same story may have to be rewritten. The station also may use the non-copy reference information to create a reference file of its newscasts for the week, the month, or the year.

Putting It On the Air

Once the story is written, a newscast must be put together. Stories will be selected according to which will be most important and interesting to the audience. In the last few minutes before a newscast, the newswire and the weather wire will be checked one last time. You may have to recheck the story by phoning your source for any last-minute developments. If your station has a mobile van out on the road, the news director or assignment editor might call the reporter, on the two-way radio, to see if he or she has anything to report or is ready for

NEWS

REPORTER: S.K. OOP

NEWSCAST: 4:00 PM

DATE: NOV. 16, 1987

SLUG: AIR CRASH

LENGTH: :30

TEXT

Federal Aviation Administration investigators are at the scene of this nation's latest air disaster. A Denver bound Airward flight 21 carrying 85 people crashed into a wheat field near Goodland, Kansas after colliding with a jet fighter. F-A-A spokesman Howard Friese (FREEZE) says the crash raises some serious questions.

FRIESE CART :05 "IT'S A MYSTERY WHY . . . AS A COMMERCIAL AIRLINER."

Names of the crash victims are being withheld this hour pending notification of relatives.

Figure 11.1 *Format of a radio news script.*

the regular live report. The newscaster also will select a couple of stories as **pad**, which will be used if the newscaster still has time to fill after reading the last regular story.

With that done, the stories will be placed in a specific order based on the relative importance of the stories and which commercials are scheduled during the newscast. The newscaster will pre-read the stories for content and pacing. Back-timing the last couple of stories that will air after the final one is normal practice. Back-timing allows the newscaster to end on time. If the local newscast must end at a specific time, say 5:05, so the station can join the network newscast, the newscaster must wrap up the local news at exactly 5:04:59. Back-timing is further discussed later in the chapter.

As the station comes out of the last commercial, the newscaster will check the time. If it is 5:03:29, he or she knows that one minute 30 seconds remain to finish the newscast. Because the newscaster back-timed the last two stories and found that they will take one minute 15 seconds, 15 seconds will remain for sign-off.

Even before the newscast is over, reporters will be calling their contacts for new leads, and the news director will be checking the wires for those big stories. Reporters with a serious commitment to bringing the world closer to their audiences thrive on the fast-paced schedule of a radio news department. At first, having to tell a story in less than a minute seems futile, but with practice you

A radio broadcast engineer monitors voice levels at the master control board during a live in-studio interview.

will discover just how much you can pack into 30 or 40 seconds. If you develop the skills and talents necessary for good storytelling, you will discover how memorable your stories can be to your audience. You also will find out how important those storytelling skills are to building an audience that will think of your station first whenever it's time for "the latest in news, weather, and sports."

Radio Delivery

You can do a few things to be more professional in delivering radio news.

1. You need to come across as if you're having a conversation with the listener. Rather than "announce" to the person, chat with the person.

2. You will want to sound conversational, as if you are not reading copy, even though you are. It takes practice to learn to read as though you are just chatting.

More specific tips:

- Speak at a comfortable pace as though you're telling your story to a friend rather than reading it to strangers.
- Vary your speaking pace slightly as you read, and avoid rhythmic reading patterns.
- Relax and concentrate on enunciation.
- Try to keep your voice in a register as low as you are comfortable with.
- Be interested in the subject matter; audiences can tell if you're just going through the motions.
- Avoid movements or mannerisms that might take your mouth away from the direction of the microphone or create unwanted noise in the studio.
- If you make a mistake with a word or phrase, correct it quickly and pleasantly without calling undue attention to your mistake.
- Be sensitive to people who are involved in the stories you are reading, as well as the people who are listening to you.
- Pause between stories to let your audience know you are changing subjects.
- Avoid opening and closing your mouth at the end of each sentence.
- If you must clear your throat or cough, hit the "kill switch" for the microphone.
- Whenever you're in front of the microphone, remember that you are a professional.

THE TELEVISION NEWSCAST

The concept of producing television newscasts flowed, historically, from what worked on radio. Like radio, the television newscaster is sitting with viewers in their home or office having a one-way conversation. The addition of visual elements in TV makes successful television presentation much more complicated than radio.

Formats are critical in television because it takes a large number of people all doing the right things at the right time to get the newscast on the air.

The Script

No television newscast would be possible without a script. The script (see Figure 11.2) is the foundation of your newscast and is most commonly is written in split-page format. On the left half of the page are instructions that will be carried out in the control room by the director — who will call up shots from the various studio cameras, create special effects, and orchestrate the various sources of sound and visuals that make up the newscast — and by other personnel responsible for the audio (live mics, sound tracks from videotape, cartridges, cassettes), name supers, still pictures, graphics, and charts. On the right half of the page is the actual story that will be read by on-air talent. Clearly, the script is the heart of the newscast — essential to a professional presentation.

The Visuals

Visuals in a television newscast come from many sources. The most common forms often are used in combination with each other, so a still picture behind the newscaster might precede a videotape, which then might give way to a live, in-field report that is aired during the news.

Video. Video usually refers to pictures and sound from the scene. In most operations it is in the form of videotape (**VTR**), but it can be digital video stored in computers. Normally it has been edited for air presentation, but sometimes is broadcast "raw" — uncut just as the photographer shot it. Video content might be a prerecorded insert from a reporter, recorded either in the field or in the studio; a previously recorded story from the network or syndication service; or a story "lifted" from the early evening network news.

All the visual stories to be used in a newscast can be edited onto separate cassettes for maximum flexibility in the news line-up. Within the newscast a story often is referred to as **VO** (meaning it will be "voiced-over" by the anchor) or **SOT** (meaning it will be used with the sound up full, as in a soundbite or reporter package report). (Chapter 3, "Writing to the Medium," introduces newscast formats.)

Graphics. Computer-generated graphics are created and stored in an electronic storage system, then recalled as needed throughout the newscast. Staff artists and photographers may prepare supplementary charts, graphs, still photos, and artwork. One type of graphic is

Slug: Six kids   Story Time: 1:46
Writer: Smith
Date:

AB/Box: Medicine

                                                          (AB)
                                                          It's a medical breakthrough a lot of
                                                          us are going to appreciate. Scientists
                                                          today announced the isolation of a
                                                          natural pain killer.
                                                          The substance is endorphin, an
                                                          amino acid found in the brain. It
                                                          appears to be 50 times more effective
                                                          than morphine.
                                                          TV-9's Kristy Martin has more on
                                                          the way American and Scottish scientists
                                                          found it.

SOT
                                                          (SOT)

   CG: Kristy Martin Reporting

   CG: University of Tennessee
         Medical Center, Memphis

   AT: 31 CG: Dr. Beaufort T.
                Farnsworth Research
                Chemist

   Outcue:". . . Kristy Martin reporting
            for TV-9 News."

TRT 1:28 + pad

AB/Box: Medicine

                                                          (AB)
                                                          And, Kristy reports, along with
                                                          fighting pain, endorphins may be
                                                          another weapon in the fight against drug
                                                          addiction. Regular doses keep addicts
                                                          from getting a high from heroin.
                                                          # # #

Figure 11.2 *TV script format.*

a still-frame of a scene shot in the field. These often are stored in computers and called ESS, which means "electronic still-store." When a graphic is used with the anchor on-camera, it usually is put in a box or an electronic frame beside the anchor's head. Graphics however, can be used full-screen or by themselves.

One example of full-screen graphics is the weather forecast. When the weather person is standing on camera pointing around at the map, the map is really an electronic graphic with the weather person superimposed on top. In the studio, the weather person usually is looking at a specially colored blue or green Chromakey wall, figuring out where to point by watching on-air monitors outside the camera range.

Some newsrooms don't require the scriptwriters to indicate where the special effect is coming from, as that is a concern primarily of the technical crew. In those cases, normal scripting includes the anchor's initials, a slash (/), and a one- or two-word indicator of what the graphic representation should look like. Thus, "AB/Downtown fire," would be appropriate.

Other newsrooms require more detailed instructions for the special effect source — for example, AB/Box: fire; AB/ESS: Fire; AB/Graphic: Fire; AB/Card: Fire. Refer to Figure 11.2 for an example of scripting the visual elements in the director's column (the left side). For more discussion of newscast scripts, see Chapter 3, "Writing to the Medium."

Producing the Half-Hour TV Newscast

The specific steps discussed next usually happen concurrently but are separated here to clarify the newscast production process.

Determine the News Hole. The challenge of filling a 30-minute telecast with 20 to 30 or more news stories is compounded as you subtract time for commercials, weather, and sports. An average half-hour newscast usually breaks down to fewer than 15 minutes of actual news time. To begin with, most television stations use commercial end breaks which take 30 seconds or more out of each half hour. You rarely get control exactly on the hour or the half hour. The real "half-hour" newscast starts with only about 29 minutes of actual program time.

Consider the list of items in Figure 11.3, which must be subtracted to determine the **news hole,** or total time, the producer can fill. The mathematics are easier if you begin with the "out" time of the program, because that's the largest number, then subtract the "in" time, and work on down through the things that have to be subtracted to get the news hole. Also note that the time subtracted for the internal breaks includes :05 pad for each break.

Switching commercial inserts always consumes a little time, so four 30-second commercials take just a touch longer than that to actually run on the air. You always can fill a few extra seconds of program time, but never run over, so we suggest that you figure every 2:00 break at 2:05. As a rule, any break over 1:00 in length should have the extra :05 added for producer pad. Actual producing experience has shown this to be an excellent "real life" factor to keep you out of time trouble.

Some producers insist that 20 to 30 items be used in the time left for news in a half-hour newscast, to give the newscast a faster pace and the illusion of more news content. Because the time is inflexible, however, the more stories that are added, the shorter they must become.

Program "out" time	10:29:30
Less Program "in" time	−10:00:30
Determines total program to fill	= :29:00
Less four internal breaks of 2:00 (2:05) each	− 8:20
Less 4:00 for sports	− 4:00
Less 3:30 for weather	− 3:30
Less :30 "chit-chat" for tosses to sports & weather	− :30
Determines news hole for story scripting	**12:40**

Figure 11.3 *Determining the news hole*

That's one reason many stations produce capsulized summaries, under promotional names such as "World in a Minute," wherein quick snippets of video are cut to fit a rapid-fire compilation of six to eight headlines that the anchor reads. With a lot of pictures, and some headlines from around the nation or world, the illusion of a lot of information is created with little information in reality.

Block the Newscast. Once you have figured out your news hole, you can go to work putting together all the elements that ultimately will comprise it. Consider this scenario:

It is 6:30 p.m. on a weeknight. Your early evening newscast has just finished, and now you must think ahead to the late evening news. In national news today, the President announced a major tax cut; OPEC raised crude oil prices; a Supreme Court justice was admitted to the hospital; a nonspecific terrorist threat was received, and the network has advised you it will feed a special live report at 10:03:30 p.m. on today's Senate debate over the future of Medicare.

In local news, police have tipped you that they will raid a meth lab operation at nine o-clock; you have videotape of a gigantic traffic snarl that occurred when a bridge collapsed during rush hour (four persons killed); inspectors say local restaurants are among the most unsanitary of any in the state; and you have videotape of the capture and arrest of two suspected bank robbers.

Besides these stories, a stringer has sent you home video of efforts to recover the bodies of two children who drowned in a nearby lake. You are inundated with news service copy and have prepared several strong feature stories that have not been aired and are becoming less timely as the week progresses. As usual, you have more news than you can air. Selection begins at this point as you decide which stories to drop and which to air.

As a producer, you have several things to do. First, you have to figure out the news hole (Figure 11.3). Then you look at the day's budget of news and consider the mixture of visual stories (those with supporting video from the field or special graphics) that can be used to illustrate the stories. You then plan the newscast as a series of logical segments separated by commercial breaks on a Newscast Format Sheet (Figure 11.4). A typical newscast rundown appears in Figure 11.5 to help you understand the way in which a newscast is produced. In this example, the specific story slugs are only to illustrate how a newscast looks on paper as it evolves throughout the evening to just before airtime.

During the process of newscast development, the producer does several things at once. You have to figure out how much time you have; how to set up the segments to give the program a nice, even feel; how to get the commercials on the air where they are supposed to run; budget the times for every element of the newscast, assign all the people in the newsroom (writers, anchors, reporters, yourself) to the various things that have to be scripted, and time the program. In most newsrooms, producers use a form, either printed or in their computer software system, to organize the newscast and keep track of everything. We will use the typical form in Figure 11.4 to build our newscast.

Fill in the Newscast Format Sheet. The most convenient road map in producing a television newscast is the **format sheet** or a computer-generated **news line-up**, a guide that shows you each element of the newscast, its length, accumulated or elapsed time after each story in the newscast, and in what order the stories will appear. It is referred to commonly in newsrooms as the **rundown** or the **line-up** and is generated by the newscast producer at the beginning of the shift. From that point, all concerned with the newscast use it to write the assigned scripts and produce the necessary elements that come together on-air to make a complicated process look simple. It keeps everyone together and organized. It usually is an evolving document, having a basic framework at the beginning of the shift, and then pieces are added or removed until the news actually goes on the air.

The format sheet indicates the writer, source of visuals, and who will deliver each story in the newscast. A quick glance shows the producer the relationship of each story to the next, as well as commercial lineup and placement. Line-ups in computerized newsrooms normally appear on a computer screen at each desk in the newsroom and can be printed as needed. News programs generally are organized in one of two ways.

1. The producer simply numbers each item/story consecutively throughout the newscast; or
2. The producer organizes the program in blocks that commonly are identified by the letters A, B, C, etc.

When letter segments are used, the pages are numbered from 1 on, within each segment. Thus, you'd have A-1, A-2, A-3, and in the next segment B-1, B-2, B-3, for example. Segments can be as long or as short as necessary. This numbering scheme, discussed in full in Chapter 3, generally is best for longer programs with more than one commercial break, because this system

Newscast Format Sheet

DATE:_____

Producer:_____   Anchor: _____

Writer:_____   Anchor: _____

VIDEO: Blank = anchor on camera

VO   = anchor voice-over

SOT   = sound on tape

V-S-V = VO-SOT-VO

PKG   = reporter SOT report

Live   = live remote report

Out time: _____
– In time: _____
= Program: _____
– Spots, wx, sports: _____
– Pad: _____
= News hole: _____

Back Time	Slug	Writer	Anchor	Video	Budget Time	Actual Time	Remarks

Figure 11.4 *Typical television news rundown format sheet.*

enables you to flip segments more easily if something is not ready on time.

Figure 11.5 is an example of a newscast blocked according to the lettered segment approach. The newscast format sheet is filled in partially with a pre-show tease, the station end-break or close, and a newscast with five segments. The "Remarks" column is for anything extra that doesn't fit anywhere else. In Figure 11.5 the producer has indicated, near the right margin, special graphics for some items. Some newsrooms don't put on the rundown the actual on-camera graphics superimposed behind the anchor That is a function of the director and technical crew in their control room preparations. Sometimes, however, producers want to make sure that certain things are used. The notes are placed at the right margin so they'll stand out, and to save room for front-timing (discussed shortly).

This is a typical ten o'clock newscast. Although some newsrooms do not include the pre-show tease as part of the actual newscast production, we have done so here to show how the length of the end-break affects program time and how the front-timing and back-timing work out. In this practice version of a newscast format sheet, we have included a boxed area for you to figure the news hole to be scripted. Also, in the upper right corner is a list of the common video source abbreviations. In most newsrooms those two things are not printed on the newscast producing forms because experienced producers are familiar with these items and require no printed reminders.

Decide Story Order. You have major stories and major visuals, which may or may not be equally important. The biggest story of the day, especially if it breaks late in the evening, might have no visuals at all, and you will have to lead your newscast with copy read live on camera. Some producers insist on leading with a dramatic tape story to catch and hold the viewers' interest, often cutting to it within ten seconds after the newscast begins. The technique of hitting viewers hard and quickly with dramatic footage is used to lessen the chance they will leave the room or switch to another station.

The same reasoning lies behind the use of teases and headlines that promote the upcoming newscast throughout the evening or just before the commercial break that precedes most newscasts. Viewers who have just finished their favorite program have momentary inertia. If you can tickle their interest with a tease before they change channels, you may be able to hold them throughout the entire newscast and count them in your ratings.

In its most effective form, the tease intrigues viewers about a story in the hope they will stick around until the story airs. Teases may drive part of your audience away from a broadcast, however, if viewers don't care about the latest in French fashions, for example, or how many frogs are marching on Miami tonight. The same considerations hold true for teases within the newscast that are read just before commercial breaks.

Pace the Newscast. Good producers always are aware of the program's pacing. When blocking the newscast, the producer must be careful not to end up with a couple of commercial breaks back-to-back. When you go especially long with a segment, because much of the day's news seems to be related and the content flow is best that way, you have to figure out how to keep from having an inordinately long, combined commercial break. During a four- or six-minute series of spots, your audience may switch to other newscasts. You can drive away the audience through poor pacing.

A good way to estimate how long your segments should be, based solely on the time at hand, is to divide the news hole by the number of segments. Thus, if you have a news hole of ten minutes, with five segments to be built, you know most will be about two minutes long. Usually, the final segment in a newscast is shorter, and that time is transferred to the earlier, hard news segments.

A lot of behind-the-scenes work during a half-hour newscast goes on to make sure it runs smoothly, but the best precaution is to spend time prior to air-time to ensure good pacing and logical placement of stories and natural transitions.

Newscast Format Sheet

DATE: _____

Producer: Diana McKibben   Anchor: Janet Smith

Writer: Dave Knopik   Anchor: Bob Thomas

VIDEO:
Blank = anchor on camera
VO = anchor voice-over
SOT = sound on tape
V-S-V = VO-SOT-VO
PKG = reporter SOT report
Live = live remote report

Out time:	10:29:30
– In time:	9:58:10
= Program:	31:20
– Spots, wx, sports:	18:55
– Pad:	1:00
= News hole:	11:25

Back Time	Slug	Writer	Anchor	Video	Budget Time	Actual Time	Remarks
	Pre-show tease	JR	JS	VO	:15		9:58:10
	PRE-SHOW BREAK				3:05		
	A-0 Open			SOT	:10		
	A-1 Airline crash	JR	JS/BT	V-S-V	:45		(Crash)
	A-2 Inflation	WD	BT		:15		(Dollars)
	A-3 Demonstration	WD	JS	VO	:30		(Protest)
	A-4 Recount	TL	BT	LIVE	1:30		(Ballot)
	A-5 Family hour	JR	JS		:20		(TV)
	A-6 Tease	WD	JS/BT		:10		(Bumper)
	BREAK #1						
	B-1 Tower	BT	BT	V-S-V	:35		(Tourism)
	B-2 Eagle point	JS	BT/JS	V-S-V	:40		
	B-3 Bus driver	JR	JS	VO	:25		(Highways)
	B-4 Accident	JR	JS	PKG	1:40		
	B-5 Tease	WD	JS/BT	VO	:15		
	BREAK #2						
	C-1 Toss to sports	DD	3-shot		:10		
	C-2- (sports rundown)	DD			4:00		
	C-9 Toss back	DD	DD/BT		:10		
	C-10 Tease Weather	JR	JS/BT		:10		
	BREAK #3						
	D-1 Toss to weather	CB	3-shot		:10		
	D-2- (see weather)			maps	3:30		
	D-9 Toss back	CB	3-shot		:10		
	D-10 Tease	JR	JS/BT	VO	:15		
	BREAK #4						
	E-1 Faces & places	JS	JS	VO	:30		(F&P)
	E-2 Belly dancing	BT	BT	Pkg	1:30		(Dancer)
	E-3 Reax ad-lib/Bye	JR	JS/BT				
	E-4 Close			SOT	:30		
10:29:30							

Figure 11.5 *Typical TV news rundown.*

So you could have the first two, in this example, with 2:30 of script time and the last segment only 1:00 including a kicker and "goodbye."

Scheduling breaks around news flow is advisable when it can be done without moving a break more than a minute or so from its intended position. Taking more time than that should be avoided, as it causes enormous time problems later in the program and, besides, some advertisers buy specific quarter hours for their commercials. Sliding a break past the quarter hour could result in a summons by the news director or general manager. The TV organization might lose several thousand dollars because a spot was not played where the advertiser paid to have it aired.

Many producers have come to understand the importance of building segments like they are mini-newscasts. Each segment should have a strong lead that is significant to the intended audience and will encourage the audience to engage with the newscast. Then the segment moves from strong and powerful stories through stories that are of interest but less dramatically compelling and ends with something positive. Research has indicated that news viewers get tired of too much negative news. It's depressing, and often the viewers are left feeling helpless regarding events they can do nothing about.

Therefore, at the end of the segment, you finish with something that's more uplifting. For example, if you had a segment starting with a bludgeon murder that was particularly gruesome, you might flow out of that into a story about increasing neighborhood patrols, then a sidebar about a citizen's crime-watch effort at self-policing a local neighborhood, and finally a story about a criminal being arrested in another case, or someone being sentenced. In this crime block, the negative news of the murder and necessity of more police patrols is tempered by the sense of citizen involvement in the crime-watch story. And at the end of the segment, the story about an arrest or sentencing provides a positive sense about something in law enforcement going right.

You must work with the news of the day, but how you do that can help the viewer put the various events into a personalized context. News, by definition, is the exceptional, the out of the ordinary. So when we cover crime, it often is because it is unusual or shocking. That can lead to the misimpression that it is worse than it is. As responsible journalists, we want to reflect reality, not distort it, so having some balance of positive and negative news is essential in our effort to serve our audience.

Determine the Visuals. Assuming that you have visuals for all major stories you will air, you have to decide their order and choose the copy that will be read live to accompany them.

Insert Commercial Breaks. Lay in commercials where they interfere least with news continuity. Some stations have rigid requirements for commercial placement — Break #1 at 10:07, Break #2 at 10:12, etc. — but this practice artificially restricts how you play the stories and how long the news segments can run between commercial breaks. A better guide is to let the news determine placement of commercials.

You will find all commercials listed and identified in the station's daily program log, which lists all commercial breaks, station IDs, program elements, their running times, and sources for the entire broadcast day. The log should be consulted before each news program to identify commercial sponsorship. In this manner, for example, if you report the story of a major airline crash on a day an airline commercial is scheduled, you can pull the conflicting spot in time to avoid embarrassment. Some advertisers, including airlines, have in their advertising contracts a provision whereby the commercials are pulled if a disaster occurs.

If you have significant theme-related news on a given day — international news, domestic politics, or major local crime, for example — you may want to span a break with that topic instead of delaying the break artificially. Usually, however, you should not extend a news topic past a break, then begin another unrelated group of stories (from local crime to Mideast peace talks, for example).

Anchors often pause during commercial breaks to discuss what is coming up next.

Occasionally you may have to break up a single story with a commercial, but few stories warrant such length. Stories that might warrant extended coverage of this nature include major disasters, historical developments, or assassinations. If you use commercial breaks as natural transitions in the newscast, the broadcasts will look smoother and more professional. Think of the commercial break as yet another production tool to help set up the pace of the newscast.

Assign Copy to Writers. The format, or news line-up, sheet includes space to identify which writer will prepare each story. So far, you have identified the following local items that must be written: meth lab raid, bridge collapse/traffic jam, unsanitary restaurants, and the capture of two suspected bank robbers. Reporters just back from the field may write their own copy; staff writers may write and rewrite other copy; and air talent and the producer may write still other stories.

In all cases, the producer assigns maximum length to each story that is to be prepared, although negotiations between the producer and reporters might result in somewhat different times than assigned originally. Usually the reporter thinks a story is worth more time than the producer does, and negotiations begin from that point.

Decide Whether to Script Commercial Breaks and Teases. Whether to script commercial breaks is a matter of taste and judgment. Few professional TV journalists mention a product name. Most say, "We'll have more news in a minute." To say more than this, they believe, is to place themselves in the role of salesperson and their feeling is, "Who wants to hear a pitchman giving the news?"

Lead-ins to commercials take several distinct forms. The simplest lead-in is a direct cut from news to the commercial without a transition of any kind. This method works well some of the time but causes trouble when, for example, a news story is so similar in content to the commercial that it becomes difficult to tell where the news ends and the commercial begins. The direct cut also is obvious and awkward when the story just before a beer commercial is about a brewer's strike.

A simple fade-to-black between news and commercials provides slightly more separation. This technique interrupts the pace of the newscast momentarily and tends to appear somewhat awkward to the viewer at home. More professional and conducive to station identification is the **bumper** graphic that appears on the screen momentarily between the last news item and the commercial. The bumper usually identifies the station or news team, sometimes with a short slogan against artwork, and provides distinct separation between news and commercials.

A similar device uses a live studio shot of the news set, with talent in place, over which is superimposed a short headline teasing the next story that follows the commercial break. Frequently the talent will voice the tease as a two-shot, with both anchors on camera, or with voice-over video of the major story in the next segment.

Prepare Hand-off Transitions. You also may wish to script the ad-lib transitions, or hand-offs from news to sports and weather, and back again to news, if your station requires interchanges among personalities. We don't mean that you should script the transitions verbatim, because to do so will sound stilted and contrived. Rather, you can consult with news, sports, and weather personnel (including field reporters who will be delivering "in-studio" reports) to determine what brief conversation they might engage in as the newscast switches between news personnel and from news to weather and sports.

Some stations consider brief, light-hearted banter — sometimes even serious discussion about important topics — as a way to help the news team appear more cohesive, friendly, and competent, if the banter is not overdone. This concept was imitated widely after it was introduced by WABC-TV, New York, and represented one more step in television's search for new ways to present the news.

Time the Newscast. The producer now determines actual total length for each story (lead-in plus taped story length and tag, etc.) and accumulated or elapsed time following each element in the newscast. Precise arithmetic is necessary when newscasts must end exactly on time so the station can join a network or other program that begins at a set hour. Often the director has as little as ten seconds' leeway between the end of the newscast and the start of a new program. Frequently, running times for each videotape are not determined, nor is the tape edited until the talent has written or timed all copy that will accompany the tape.

Timing stories against a stopwatch may not reflect the altered rate at which voice-over copy is delivered during the actual broadcast, so most editors automatically add five seconds of a scene to the finished length of the visuals. This protects the newscast from "going to black" on the air in case the newscaster stumbles, hesitates, stops to cough, or otherwise alters the on-air delivery rate.

The producer often times the newscast two different ways, at two different times in the evening. Called front-timing and back-timing, these are discussed in-depth in the following section. Basically, the producer uses front-timing once the newscast is **blocked**, using the "budgeted," or estimated, times the producer hopes the stories will run. The producer starts with the "in" time of the newscast and adds all the budgeted times, in order, to see if everything will fit. Then, just prior to the actual newscast, the producer subtracts every item's "actual" time, in reverse order beginning with the end of the newscast, from the final "out" time when the newscast must be finished (back-timing).

Front-Time, Back-Time, and Prepare Pad Copy. In the last few minutes before airtime, most good producers double-check their timing. Even with computer systems that time the newscast as it is produced, this is necessary because the computer systems use line counting to figure out how fast an anchor reads. Normally the anchor has been timed months ago in the middle of the day, not during an actual newscast, and that factor has been entered into the computer. Anchors don't always read the same, though, and producers need to know exactly where they are at every minute of a newscast.

How do you know you are running late when you are just five minutes into an hour newscast? The only way is with front-timing or back-timing. Even though most computerized newsroom systems do this, you can't trust the machines and should do it yourself. Machines are literal; people are not. When the day has been slow and the anchors have had a nice, relaxing dinner with some wine, they'll read more slowly than the computer timed them earlier. And when their adrenaline gets going with a lot of breaking news, they'll read a lot faster. If you have timed your scripts exactly with anchors reading the copy aloud during the shift that day, you'll know where you are and not become the victim of a computer, wondering what happened.

Basically, front-timing and back-timing are the reverse of one another. In **front-timing,** the producer simply starts out with the "in" time from the log when the program is to start. Front-timing often is done early in the producer's shift, after the program is blocked, to make sure the newscast will work as budgeted. In Figure 11.6, you can see that time, 9:58:10, was entered in the "Remarks" column at the top, straight across from the "Budget Time" of the pre-show tease. That is the time when the item is to begin.

The producer adds the budget time for each item to the beginning time for the previous item, in turn, and

ends up with a column of clock-times indicating when each item should start. In effect, we "add-up" through the newscast from the "in" time to the end.

At the bottom of the "Remarks" column, you can see we ended up with a final time of 10:28:20, noted after the E-4 Close finishes. That is 1:10 less than the actual "out-time" shown in the block in the upper left corner of the form we used to determine the news hole. That's the time cushion that producers refer to as pad. Your newscast should have some pad time because things have a habit of happening, which eats up any extra time. Filling in a few seconds of pad with the anchors chit-chatting just before they say "goodbye," or some wire copy "fill" (also referred to as "pad copy"), is much easier than running short and having to jump out of the middle of a final story in a herky-jerky fashion that looks unprofessional. As you can see, the times in the back-time column are different. These will be discussed later in the chapter.

Stack the Newscast Script. Next, assemble all pages of the newscast in consecutive order.

The process of physically stacking the newscast scripts usually occurs all day long as the various pieces of the final program are finished. A half-hour or so before airtime, any final scripts are added and the completed script set is double-checked. Most newsrooms operate from a rundown, as discussed earlier, wherein stories are assigned a number before they are physically ready for the final script. Those who are assigned to write those stories put the appropriate number on them before they turn in the stories. In some operations, and when things get wild with breaking news or with small newsbreaks in the evening, numbering may be done just before the final scripts are handed out to those who need them. Numbering usually is in the upper right corner of the script.

Formerly, news copy was typed on special carbon packs that yielded from five to seven copies — one each for newscasters, director, producer, audio person, and TelePrompTer operator. Now, the necessary hard copies often are run off in a copy machine or simply printed through the newsroom computer. Additional copies may be necessary for the computer graphics operator, who types out, on a special keyboard, name supers and other information that will be displayed electronically on the television screen during the newscast. Each page of the script must be numbered in consecutive order. Then, if the script is dropped or otherwise shuffled out of order, it can be reassembled quickly.

Despite the growth of newsroom computer scripting, many people in the newscast process still use physical

Newscast Format Sheet

DATE: _____

Producer: Diana McKibben   Anchor: Janet Smith _____

Writer: Dave Knopik _____   Anchor: Bob Thomas _____

VIDEO: Blank = anchor on camera
VO = anchor voice-over
SOT = sound on tape
V-S-V = VO-SOT-VO
PKG = reporter SOT report
Live = live remote report

Out time:	10:29:30
– In time:	9:58:10
= Program:	31:20
– Spots, wx, sports:	18:55
– Pad:	1:00
= News hole:	11:25

Back Time	Slug	Writer	Anchor	Video	Budget Time	Actual Time	Remarks
9:58:26	Pre-show tease	JR	JS	VO	:15	:18	9:58:10
9:58:44	PRE-SHOW BREAK				3:05	3:05	9:58:25
10:01:49	A-0 Open			SOT	:10	:10	10:01:30
10:01:59	A-1 Airline crash	JR	JS/BT	V-S-V	:45	:40	10:01:40 (Crash)
10:02:39	A-2 Inflation	WD	BT		:15	:12	10:02:25 (Dollars)
10:02:51	A-3 Demonstration	WD	JS	VO	:30	:33	10:02:40 (Protest)
10:03:24	A-4 Recount	TL	BT	LIVE	1:30	1:34	10:03:10 (Ballot)
10:04:58	A-5 Family hour	JR	JS		:20	:35	10:04:40 (TV)
10:05:33	A-6 Tease	WD	JS/BT		:10	:08	10:05:00 (Bumper)
10:05:41	BREAK #1					2:05	10:05:10
10:07:46	B-1 Tower	BT	BT	V-S-V	:35	:41	10:07:15 (Tourism)
10:08:27	B-2 Eagle point	JS	BT/JS	V-S-V	:40	:37	10:07:50
10:09:04	B-3 Bus driver	JR	JS	VO	:25	:18	10:08:30 (Highways)
10:09:22	B-4 Accident	JR	JS	PKG	1:40	1:31	10:08:55
10:10:53	B-5 Tease	WD	JS/BT	VO	:15	:11	10:10:35
10:11:04	BREAK #2					2:05	10:10:50
10:13:09	C-1 Toss to sports	DD	3-shot		:10	:10	10:12:55
10:13:19	C-2- (sports rundown)	DD			4:00	4:25	10:13:05
10:17:44	C-9 Toss back	DD	DD/BT		:10	:10	10:17:05
10:17:54	C-10 Tease Weather	JR	JS/BT		:10	:10	10:17:15
10:18:04	BREAK #3					2:05	10:17:25
10:20:9	D-1 Toss to weather	CB	3-shot		:10	:10	10:19:30
10:20:19	D-2- (see weather)			maps	3:30	3:30	10:19:40
10:23:49	D-9 Toss back	CB	3-shot		:10	:10	10:23:10
10:23:59	D-10 Tease	JR	JS/BT	VO	:15	:12	10:23:20
10:24:11	BREAK #4					2:05	10:23:35
10:26:16	E-1 Faces & places	JS	JS	VO	:30	:41	10:25:40 (F&P)
10:26:57	E-2 Belly dancing	BT	BT	Pkg	1:30	1:53	10:26:10 (Dancer)
10:28:50	E-3 Reax ad-lib/Bye	JR	JS/BT			:10	10:27:40
10:29:00	E-4 Close			SOT	:30	:30	10:27:50
10:29:30							10:28:20
							1:10 pad

Figure 11.6 *News rundown with actual story times and final back-time.*

copies of the script. That's because having pages in your hands sometimes is easier than trying to find things in a computer program. Also, computers go down. Nothing is worse than being in a computerized newsroom when the computer dies just before the news is to go on. That actually happened to a station in the early days of newsroom computers. It was impossible to do the news, so a filler program had to be aired instead.

Finally, having physical copies is particularly advantageous for anchors. They can use them, along with the TelePrompTer, to deliver the news better, as well as provide a backup if the TelePrompTer malfunctions or a last-minute item has to be ad-libbed into the midst of the newscast while on the air.

Assemble Visuals in Order. Late in the newscast production cycle, the video editors and technical crew will have completed most of their work. Just before going on the air, all visuals should be in order. The visuals include all graphics, still art, pictures, character generator information, and videotape. Visual elements are numbered sequentially, just as the script is numbered.

At this point, you can check the copy against the order of the visuals and the line-up of all other elements in the newscast. The one time you fail to compare copy against the line-up of all visuals is inevitably the time an out-of-order newscast falls to pieces before a trusting audience of thousands.

Proofread and Time the Final Script. As the script begins to flow in from writers, reporters, and newscasters, it should be edited, checked for obvious errors, and timed for final length. All scripts should be checked for length against the original times assigned on the format sheet. If the copy contains mistakes, this will be one of the last chances for correcting them. Also, reading the copy aloud at this point is a must. Consider the poor newscaster who, without benefit of rehearsal, comes across the following sentences that she must read aloud to her audience: "Swarms of pro-Castro crowds swarmed the city street."

Again consider Figure 11.6. We've finished everything, and the "actual times" are noted on the rundown. These are the true "read" times for each element. This example shows you the reality of producing. When a producer blocks a story early in the evening, the budget time is what that producer thinks the story is worth compared to everything else in the program. It is a "guesstimate," and all the people writing and producing

stories for the program try to make their items come in at the budgeted time. The reality of creative work, however, means that most won't be exactly the same time that was budgeted.

That's why, on this training form, we have included the "Actual Time" column. As the stories come in and we have final times for them, these are penned into the column. You can see that the newscast was three seconds long from the start because the pre-show tease runs :18 instead of the budgeted :15. As you look down the column, note that some stories are longer, some shorter, than what was budgeted.

In back-timing, the producer simply works in reverse order, using the "out" time at the bottom of the newscast and working back up to the top. This is done only when everything is completed. Back-timing with rough estimates of how long things will run doesn't do much good. What you are after when you back-time is absolutely the last moment an item must begin for you to be on time.

In our example (Figure 11.6), look at the first column on the left of the page, titled "Back Time." At the bottom of the column, you can see that the producer started with the final "out" time taken from the program log, which indicates when the newscast has to be finished. Then each "actual" time of every item in the newscast was subtracted from that "out" time, and the resulting final time when the item must begin, at the very latest, was penned in beside that item's slug in the "Back Time" column. The producer works in reverse order, beginning with the last item in the newscast and subtracting all the way up to the beginning, penning in the latest possible start time for each item in the newscast.

At the top of the "Back Time" column, when all the times have been calculated, you can see that the pre-show tease must begin no later than 9:58:26. Comparing that to the log time when the newscast should begin (noted in the boxed area where the news hole was computed), you can see that this newscast has a real pad of just :16. The producer originally set up the newscast and front-timed the elements early in the evening with 1:10 of pad, but that evaporated as stories came in at slightly different times from the original budget. If this producer had not back-timed, she would think, as the news began, that the program had plenty of slack. Having back-timed, however, she knows that with only :16, she's got to keep the anchors reading briskly.

Traditionally, before newsroom computers, producers back-timed on their copy of the newscast script after it was completed and distributed. That is still done by many producers, who want the last possible start times on each page of a hard copy script. On the last page of the script, the "out" time of the newscast is penned at the bottom. Then the length of the last item is subtracted and that time is written at the top of that page so the producer can see, at a glance, the last moment when that item should begin. If the "out" time on the final script page was 10:29:30 and that last item was an anchor-read kicker lasting :30, the time for that story to start at the top of that page would be 10:29:00.

The producer continues the process of subtracting each item back up through the newscast and writing the times on the tops of the pages. Thus, if a producer back-times on the script, every page will have a clock time that is the latest that item can begin without being late.

The advantage of back-timing is that it works back from the absolutely last moment, when the newscast must end. Any time during the newscast, a simple glance at the back-time for a story, as the anchor begins reading it on the air, tells you if you are late, early, or exactly on time. In this newscast, the producer sitting in the control room while it is on-air could glance at her back-time at 10:05. If the A-5 "Family hour" story was just starting, she'd know she was okay. If the anchor was just beginning the A-2 "Inflation" story, she'd know something was wrong and immediately begin analyzing the situation and planning what to drop later in the newscast to make up the lost 2:21.

One additional encouragement to use back-timing: Most stations get a little off their log time during the day. When that happens, the only way to make it up is in the live newscasts, which have some flexibility. A producer often gets the newscast a few seconds, or even a few minutes, later than the log says. If you've back-timed, you immediately know exactly how much you have to drop. If you've only front-timed, you'll have no idea.

We strongly recommend back-timing. The greatest sin in broadcasting is going long. When you do, commercials have to be dropped and the television operation loses money. If you are a little early going into sports and weather, the anchors can eat it up with some extra chit-chat, but when you're late, you can do nothing to keep from looking bad. Particularly when a newscast has a visual story, such as a feature package, at the end, you must hit that item exactly on time. If you realize you're running late after the story starts, dumping out will look terrible on the air. The only way to be sure of your timing is to back-time. Many producers front-time as they build the newscast and then back-time as a cross-check just before they go on the air, much as we have done in the example in this chapter.

Rehearse and Adjust the Newscast. In this discussion, rehearsal means a full run-through of the newscast, not simply reading through the scripts to get familiar with the copy. All on-air personnel should informally practice before any live appearance.

Two schools of thought govern rehearsals before airtime:

1. Rehearsal time polishes the newscast and builds confidence in the talent and technical staff; or

2. First runs usually are the best, because rehearsals destroy the energy and vitality that otherwise would be expended in front of the audience during the actual broadcast.

Regardless of which method you prefer — rehearsal or straight-from-the-cuff presentation — be certain that you are prepared as fully as possible when the magic moment of airtime arrives and it's "News, weather, and sports — coming right up."

INTERNET NEWS PRODUCTION

The job of producing Internet Web site news involves transferring radio and television into a new channel for consumers to use. The fundamentals of presenting important information, setting up newscasts to flow logically, and providing visual and audio support at the right time are the same. Some differences in writing copy are unique to the Internet because the audience is looking for news on the Internet with a slightly different mindset. For example, stories on an Internet news site have bulleted lists of information rather than lengthy paragraphs, and they highlight key phrases that can become hyperlinks to other pages within the site or other sites for more detailed information. Headlines and subheads for other stories are crucial to keeping the attention of the news surfer. (For more on Internet news writing, see Chapter 8.)

But most of what you have learned for radio and television news producing applies to the Internet. The big difference is that the Internet knows no boundaries in terms of when the Internet user engages a newscast, story, or interview.

Most Internet news operations provide regular newscasts, and within them may have separate hyperlinks for consumers to go to certain stories, issues, audio or video streamed material, and so on. But, from a production standpoint, facts still are gathered, stories have to be well written, and any audio or video presentations have to be produced.

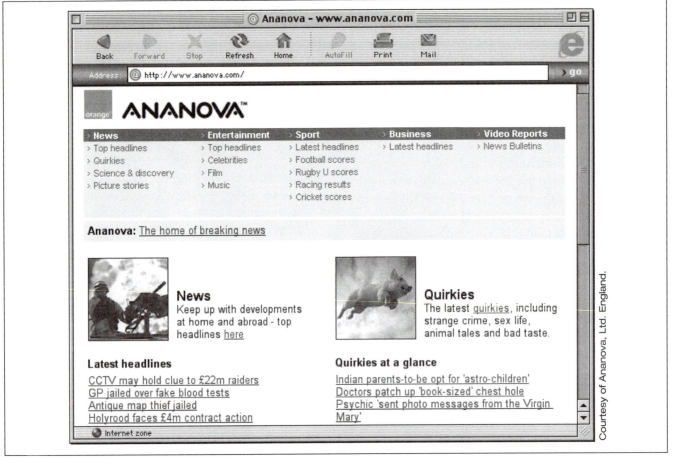

Ananova was the first news operation to launch a "virtual" news anchor, which aired for the first time April 2, 2000. Despite the innovative idea, it never caught on with mass appeal.

Interview with Terry McElhatton

The following interview with Internet news executive Terry McElhatton[1] demonstrates that the reporting, writing, and storytelling skills needed in good broadcast journalism are just as important, if not more, on the Internet.

Question: How is producing news different on the Internet?

McElhatton: It's more of a creative environment, where people are always looking for better ways to do things. We look for a person who is looking for new and better ways. There's a premium, in the emerging media, for new ideas and people who are always trying to push the envelope to find something new and different.

Question: So what would you tell students in a college journalism class that they need for successful careers in the years ahead as technology continues to accelerate and change the world?

McElhatton: I would tell them that in the "brave new world" of modern journalism, they need to learn basic journalism skills. Those are transferable. Integrity, honesty, and the check-your-facts focus of good journalism all translate across the board. But you need to learn how to apply those fundamentals within the various forms we use to convey information in the Internet, including print, audio, and video. In other words, you need to learn television — how television and the visual process works. But you need to learn radio, too. A lot of what we do is not just video, but streamed audio. And you have to have a sense of the print media so you can work with a basic Web page layout that is primarily text-oriented.

Consider this: Somebody wants to hear exactly what Bill Gates says in a major computer technology announcement. We have a headline and a short synopsis on our Web site. But the person coming to us wants to hear everything Bill had to say. In a regular commercial television newscast, you'd get, maybe, a 30-second soundbite. But we can put an entire hour or an hour audio file on the Web so individuals can listen to it at their convenience just like they would a radio program. We can do the same thing with video streaming, though current technology is a little slow with such complicated files to be transferred. You know, the video often looks a little jerky depending on how fast a connection the computer user has. So you need to learn how to do TV, how to do radio, and how to do print in the Web format because the Web is a hybrid, bringing together all three. The media are no longer segmented by technology, but merged with it.

Question: So some broadcast students, who have thought it was better for them because of less emphasis on spelling, grammar, and punctuation, have to rethink what skills they need, because part of it is going to be text. And, likewise, print journalists need video and audio skills.

McElhatton: The Internet journalist, in a way, is technologically more of a complete journalist using whatever appropriate storytelling form fits. And often you use all three — print, audio, and video. I think text is going to continue to be an important part of it. Our research has found that people like short, succinct things — maybe more than a headline, but not a long, involved story. They want to scan and pick out what to get into with more depth.

So, as an Internet journalist, you need to write short, concise copy, and it has to be both factually and grammatically correct. I think of it as print journalism in more of a broadcast style than the other way around. Because if you can't write a grammatical sentence, or your spelling is really bad, a lot of people will quickly see that in text and discount you. Credibility is lost if you make obvious errors that people interpret negatively.

Question: Would you agree, then, that this is almost the age of the expert storyteller, with more tools for the journalist to effectively convey meaning to an audience? Some critics believe we lost real storytelling as an art form in TV news, to a large degree in recent years, because local TV news got to be so "live shot"-oriented and focused on relatively trivial, but more entertaining fare. But in the Internet journalism arena, if you're going to hold the attention of bright people on the 'net seeking various, personally defined information agendas, you've got to be a good storyteller to draw them and hold their attention. Would you agree?

McElhatton: Yes. What happens is that the reporter will write a long, fairly involved sort of story — an intelligent story. Like all stories, it has various layers to it. So on the main Web page there's a headline with a short synopsis. That's all some people want, just like the way they scan and pick stories they're interested in from the daily newspaper. If the story on the Internet grabs you, you'll jump into the full story. It appears that a lot of people go to the full story about something that interests them and then print it out. They'd rather read it as text than read it off the computer screen.

People also build their own clip files from the Internet and can really organize them on their computers to use later. So an Internet news site is both a "keep up with current events" kind of tool for people, and a research one they can use to build knowledge or depth understanding over time. You can't do that with commercial TV news. You watch it and it's gone.

But the Internet is like saving up your old newspapers; only you can easily copy and paste it into your latest corporate report, a letter to a friend, or whatever. As I said before, it merges old technologies and then makes it easy for the consumer to use them. The power in the Internet is with the person clicking a mouse, not really with the news provider anymore.

Question: It sounds like the traditional boundaries that separated print and electronic journalism are rapidly eroding so that producing Internet news requires students to be good at all of them. In effect, you need to be a journalist able to write for and publish in all three contexts — print, radio, and television.

McElhatton: Yes. Electronic journalists still do stories with basic TV and radio formatting — you know the split-page kind of scripts with director commands down the left, and anchor copy, or soundbite text on the right side of the page. But once you've produced that story, you have to turn around and set up headlines and introductory text on the Web page. It really is more along the lines of a newspaper model, but it's more flexible. We use boxes for bulleted facts that are interesting from a story, or maybe pull-quotes we set up to help draw an Internet user further into a story.

So it's important for a broadcast journalist to understand what a pull-quote is, and for a print journalist to understand what a soundbite is. You need to be more of a generalist than a specialist in this new model. Part of that is that we all work across boundaries in these Internet newsrooms. They tend to be high-tech-driven with very well paid people and few, if any, union rules. So jobs are not narrowly defined. You jump from one thing to another and need a wide understanding of how it all knits together into this electronic tapestry we call an Internet news site.

Question: So, really, in Internet news you write, say, three stories. There's a short one that will be a headline and a brief synopsis of a couple of sentences. Then you have a jump to the second story; which is more of a depth piece that may be the equivalent of a reporter package. It might include streaming audio and/or video that would run, say, a minute and a half or so. Then you might have another jump the Internet user could click on that would take the person to a real depth piece like you'd find in *The New York Times* or the *Wall Street Journal*.

McElhatton: Right. And somewhere in all of that would be a link to the entire interview or a clip of a person in the story. The great thing about the Web is that you can link just about anything. So you can use all kinds of things in audio, video, or text and combine it all into a story presentation. A well-written story translates anywhere. You know, if you can write a story that is tight and compelling, we can use, in the Internet, whatever formatting tools work best to get it to the consumer, in several different versions that fit the individual user's needs and desires.

Question: But you've still got to have that sort of broadcast passion, more of a conversational style and energy, don't you?

McElhatton: Right. On the Web, reading off the screen, if it gets long and involved and arcane, you get bogged down very quickly. Then you click off. The attention span is getting shorter and shorter. And if people decide, in the middle of the copy, that this isn't going anywhere or it's not of interest to them, they're gone. On the Internet we have a pretty high churn rate. The last research I saw, the typical user of our Web site stayed with us only about 12 minutes. It's similar to CNN Headline News, where people check in, get a sense of what's going on, and then go off to other things.

Question: Where does all this go in the near future?

McElhatton: The Internet news scene seems to have settled down a bit in the last couple of years. But it's still very free-form. Different Web sites have different styles, and there is no "one size fits all." I think that will remain. We're not in the same narrow confines of other media. We don't publish one big paper once a day. We don't have just a few newscasts during the day where they can make room for us among the soap operas of evening comedies and dramas. Anyone can create a Web site, and it's more of an infinite media where maximum variety is not only possible but also desirable.

Internet users pick and choose what they want. I surf around the 'net, and I look at a lot of different news sites. The newspapers have been doing their sites usually in a newspaper format. They, frankly, *look* like newspaper sites. The same is true of TV station sites. But the pure Internet sites tend to make everything as user-friendly as possible without any sort of pre-set idea of what format or layout is best. They're really flexible, change frequently, and are very open to trying new things. It's still experimental. I do think once broadband really takes off, and people have a chance to find out what works for them, the industry will begin to settle down. The problem right now is the bandwidth is not there. In television, the video is always jerky to some degree. When you have really good, fast connections I think everything will end up in one flat panel display on your wall and everything that you want will be there.

Question: There seems to be a lot of similarity between the Internet news evolution and how radio and television news began. With new technology, the creative side always seems to dominate at first, which is what makes it take off. Then, after a while, it becomes a big business driven by corporate goals, people in suits with MBAs, and the profit mentality squeezes out a lot of the entrepreneurial attitude that drove the new technology to begin with.

Radio and TV were very exciting in their youth, but then they matured and got bogged down with formula approaches in programming, consultants providing schemes to draw more audience, and profit psychosis. Radio and TV were no longer inventors' toys but became big business bogged down in spreadsheets, quarterly reports, and corporate owners that didn't necessarily fully understand the original inventor's dream.

McElhatton: Yeah, they said, "We can make money off of this."

Question: So, can the Web avoid falling into that same trap that has caused a loss of ingenuity in every other media form as they have matured?

McElhatton: I think it will, at least for quite a while, because of the nature of the Web. It's still the "wild Web," and I think it will stay that way for a while. You know, it's open architecture. It's a different medium. In television, somebody decides, "This is what we're going to do" and "this is what you will see." They decide content for you. But the Web is a whole different animal. It's interactive. It puts the power of choice in the hands of the user, whereas in television you can choose which channel you watch, but within a channel it is pre-processed for you.

What I'm hoping — and a lot of other people are hoping — is that we don't just end up with television on the Web. I'm sure it will be co-opted in some way, but I hope that's a long way away. We have an opportunity to do great journalism in the widest possible sense of the word — plenty of variety, layers of knowledge depth, all tailored by the news consumer to fit his or her information needs. It's not really a "mass" medium, as newspapers, radio, and television have been where everything is done as though millions are engaged with the product at a time. It's the ultimate personalized journalism technology where, literally, everyone's plate of news contains things they really want to consume, not things that are force-fed to them by some gatekeepers deciding what people should have access to.

Photo by John McClelland of Roosevelt University in Chicago

The IFRA Newsplex, a Columbia, SC-based center, is dedicated to researching the direction of news media convergence and training journalists to adapt to this new media framework.

MEDIA CONVERGENCE

A likely scenario for the future is the trend toward convergence. Rather than replacing human journalists with virtual ones, news organizations will require journalists to have a variety of multimedia skills so they can report stories in more than one media format.

Media convergence is a buzzword that has infiltrated news organizations with great vigor in the past few years but without much real understanding. In common use, media convergence refers to individual news organizations crossing their traditional broadcast or print borders to incorporate text, audio, and video components in their delivery of news, most likely via a Web site.

Although this is a typical — though simplistic — understanding of media convergence, it does not explain actual convergence. In fact, the reason this textbook is still an electronic media text and not a converged media text is because only a handful of news organizations in the United States are really attempting convergence. As you will see, the few American news organizations dabbling in convergence are still doing so rather conservatively by maintaining a traditional approach to news delivery while experimenting with some elements of convergence.

What Is Media Convergence?

Media convergence is not merely the production of multimedia stories, although that is a common outcome of convergence. Practically speaking, media convergence can be defined as one news organization producing content for multiple media sources in a variety of media formats.

Currently, when news breaks, each medium covers the story according to its established parameters. Television news focuses more on the visual elements, highlighting the drama and emotion involved. Newspapers seek background and explanatory information. Public radio and news magazines tend to focus on analysis. Internet news organizations provide information in brief format, using lists and hyper links to help news consumers find the latest and most relevant information quickly.

In a converged media world, an integrated approach to news would dominate. For example, an organization operating from a physical newsroom in one city could conceivably have reporters all over the world ready to report various pieces of information. A newsroom manager would be in charge of considering all possible angles for the story. A researcher would be on-hand to begin looking up important supplemental information for a variety of reporters. Journalists in the field would be gathering information with a variety of media technology to be produced in several formats — such as basic information for immediate updates distributed via e-mail; audio and video for soundbites online and perhaps in a package story to be streamlined on the Web; photos for a slideshow as well as a main picture online and in print; map and timeline information for graphics to be used on the Web and in print. (For specific duties of various convergence journalists, see "A Different Kind of News" sidebar on page —.)

This kind of integrated effort by one organization is the goal of media convergence.

How Convergence Is Being Practiced Now

One journalism professor describes media convergence as a continuum, in which news organizations gradually move from one phase to the next. Dr. August E. Grant, associate professor of journalism at the University of South Carolina, says convergence occurs at three levels — cross-ownership, cooperation, integration.

Cross-Ownership. Cross-ownership of news organizations allows different media to more easily incorporate content from one medium into another. A newspaper and television news station owned by the same corporation can more naturally partner with each other to pool newsgathering resources and exchange some content without feeling threatened by a competing medium. This kind of sharing is happening informally across the United States increasingly but is still not a widely accepted practice for two reasons: competition among journalists and restrictive federal regulations.

Most broadcast and print reporters still have considerable ownership over their stories and view the

---

SPOTLIGHT

Newsroom of the Future

The following job descriptions reflect ideas and concepts developed from The Newsplex — a prototype multiple-media micro-newsroom for demonstration, research, and training in next-generation newsgathering tools and techniques. It is designed as a model to show the possibilities of the future. As you read each job description, consider which one fits your talents and interests, then make a list of how you can prepare yourself to be ready for such a career. For more on media convergence and the changing roles of journalists, see www.newsplex.org. Also visit the Morton Publishing web site for interviews with Newsplex Director Randy Covington and Academic Coordinator Augie Grant.

NEWSFLOW MANAGER

This person is similar to managing editor/news director of today's news media. The newsflow manager looks at the "big picture" of the entire news product, considering all stories being covered for the day plus follow-up content and on-going projects. The newsflow manager must be concerned about how all the individual pieces fit together and pay attention to what type of media formats are being used to deliver the most important information of the day.

STORY BUILDER

This person is similar to an assignment editor/section editor in today's media. The story builder oversees content gathering for a single story — including text, audio, video, photo — and determines the best ways to deliver the content (video news report, bullet info listed on Web, in-depth story in print the next morning, interactive map, timeline with photos and soundbites, photo slide show, etc.)

NEWS RESOURCER

The news resourcer replaces the librarian/information specialist from traditional newsrooms. This person is responsible for finding all relevant info for a variety of stories being pulled together for the day. Some information may be just for reporter background, but most should be gathered with the audience in mind. The news resourcer must be familiar with a variety of electronic research techniques, such as computer-assisted reporting, and know how to search government documents and electronic databases, as well as perform advanced Internet searches. The news resourcer may also be in charge of uploading much of the content online.

MULTI-SKILLED JOURNALIST

In this simulated newsroom of the future, journalists must have the same newsgathering instinct as currently is required. The difference will be how their information is used. Because it is going to be dissected for use in various media formats — video, print, audio — journalists must be prepared to gather information with that in mind. One person will not be expected to do it all, but will be expected to be able to do it all at different times. Likewise, copyeditors and designers will have to be able to work across platforms, understanding trends and conventions for electronic, online, and print presentations.

other strictly as competition — an attitude that does not bode well for sharing information. But in some instances a print reporter may appear on the television broadcast of a station owned by the same parent company and a broadcast reporter may write a story for the newspaper.

The Federal Communications Commission, which oversees television network airwaves, has placed strict limits on the number and type of media organizations one company can own within particular markets. Once concerned about monopolies, the FCC has prohibited companies from owning a newspaper and a television or radio station within the same market unless such ownership existed prior to the FCC regulation. So far, the FCC has been unable to relax its own standard — something it has been trying to do in recent years before a federal appeals court quashed such attempts in June 2004. The battle is not over, however, because the FCC is expected to continue pushing for more lax ownership regulations.

In the meantime, Media General in Tampa, Fla. — which owns *The Tampa Tribune*, *WFLA-TV*, and *Tampa Bay Online* — is the best example of convergence via cross-ownership. Scholars and professionals are heralding this effort as a step toward the future of journalism,[2] but it is still too early to label it a converged newsroom.

Cooperation. Cooperation is the logical result of cross-ownership, though it is not likely to be an easy transition. As noted, journalists who have traditionally competed against each other for the news audience are reluctant to share resources. But as the world continues to become more complex and as local communities grow, journalists are realizing that there is more than enough information to go around. The opportunity to pool resources to gather a more complete story can eventually overcome initial hesitation to work together.

Under cross-ownership, journalists may keep their name with a story but share it in a different medium. In cooperation, a journalist in one medium may offer information to a counterpart in another medium. For example, a broadcast reporter getting video and soundbites on the scene of a news story may give the text information to a print reporter who might otherwise be unable to track down the source for a quote. Likewise, either one may write/produce a brief to be placed online immediately, which can be updated in the news broadcast later. Separate stories are produced, but each is more complete than might have been possible initially and independently.

Integration. Ultimately, news organizations will reach true convergence as they become more comfort-

able with sharing resources. Rather than independent print, broadcast, and online media organizations producing content unique to their media, one organization with journalists trained across media will produce content in a variety of formats. The format will be determined by the goal of the information rather than by the capability of one medium. In this way, information dissemination in converged newsrooms can be content-driven rather than technology-driven. But there are many challenges still to tackle before this becomes a reality in American news media.

Current State of Convergence

Students of electronic media need not panic that the traditional radio and television news station is disappearing. Despite examples of some crossover in American newsrooms, the dominant reality is still very separate news operations. Few job descriptions currently ask for reporters to have skills across media, though journalists with multiple skills will be more attractive to any type of news organization.

As the United States catches up to the rest of the world in media convergence,[3] journalists increasingly will be expected to gather information in a variety of formats and be comfortable producing and delivering information in multiple ways.

Students currently in electronic news media programs have a unique opportunity to be prepared for the age of convergence and even help bring it to U.S. news organizations. For most college students, the easiest part is mastering the technological skills. Most likely, you are already familiar with many of the latest communication technologies — from sending and receiving text and visual information through your cell phone or e-mail to creating and designing advanced Web pages and possibly some digital video editing.

But, as we emphasize here, the technology involved in convergence is merely a mode for dissemination. The more important element — and hence the more challenging obstacle — is to comprehend the concept and its advantages for helping audiences receive and understand the plethora of information at their disposal.

Fortunately, the concepts already outlined in this text for creating a worthwhile news product still apply. Actually, they become even more important.

The ultimate advantage of converged media is a more content-rich product that better informs the public. Rather than getting essentially the same information from different sources, different media now can coordinate their information to offer a complete package that takes advantage of the strengths of various media.

This makes it even more crucial that journalism students understand the difference between *information* and *news*. In an information-saturated society, your job of filtering the most important information and presenting it to the audience in a meaningful way is crucial. Only an astute student of global, national, and local politics, culture, social aid, science and technology, economic trends, business, military strategy, and history will be able to make real sense of the information.

The world of media convergence has the potential to improve the current state of journalism — particularly electronic journalism, which has fallen prey to focusing on entertainment rather than news. Qualities and skills necessary for the journalist in the age of convergence include:

- *Having strong writing skills.* Students sometimes have the misinformed perception that electronic media journalists do not need to know how to

A DIFFERENT KIND OF NEWS

In a converged news organization, the format of news delivery is a combination of broadcast and print possibilities. The technology is already in use, and many news organizations are dabbling with some of these formats on a limited basis, but most have only begun to think about the possibilities. The following are some of the more likely news story formats that we will see consistently from a converged news organization.

E-mail/Cellphone news updates: Rarely, nowadays, does one find someone who doesn't own a cellphone, a palm pilot, or some handheld device able to connect to the Internet and send/receive messages. This trend will only increase, and the technology become more sophisticated, as our global society becomes more mobile and relies on information from these devices. News organizations likely will consider e-mail updates prior to any other story formulation, as that will be the best way to get information out immediately.

Streamed broadcast: This is not a new practice, as many local, network, and television news organizations have been streaming some stories on their Web sites. But as digital technology advances and society becomes even more mobile, consumers are likely to seek entire newscasts online.

Slideshows: More and more newspapers are utilizing electronic news capabilities by putting together short (2–3 minutes) slideshows of photos, video, and soundbites while narrating a short story. Additional text is included with each frame. *The New York Times* is incorporating slideshows regularly, especially with foreign correspondent reports (see www.nytimes.com), and the site www.interactivenarratives.org features slideshows from a variety of sources.

Interactive features: These are already popular on many news Web sites in the form of interactive polls. But they are becoming more sophisticated and newsworthy as tech-savvy reporters recognize ways to tell their stories better with such technology. The Citizens Union Foundation in New York City, for example, hosts www.Gotham Gazette.com to discuss New York City news and policy issues. The site offers interactive features to help educate New York citizens about issues in the city. Feature have included planning a park in downtown, the Republican National Convention in New York City, and the economy in the city.

Mobile Web Logs: Known in cyberland as "blogs," these are gaining popularity with news consumers and gatekeepers alike, though they have their share of detractors as well. Blogs were designed to be outlets for the general population to weigh in on the day's events or a specific subject of choice with their opinions. Considered a true outlet for the "marketplace of ideas," blogs represent the evolution of traditional letters to the editor and computer chatrooms. Some sites post the exact statement from a blogger who sends in a comment. Other sites request commentary on given subjects. Some sites send reporters to get statements, and perhaps accompanying photos or audio and video. In many instances, news organization columnists/reporters merely summarize statements from various contributors and offer general comments. There has been a lot of debate about the newsworthiness of many blogs, but the fact remains that this media form allows more participation by the audience and can be a good barometer for the issues about which the public is most concerned write. As emphasized early in this book, however, a good broadcast report begins with good writing. And coordinating text with visual elements is a difficult skill to master, but it will become more important in a converged newsroom where one story will have many elements of both.

- *Having intuitive reporting/newsgathering skills.* A good news story, no matter what the format, must be supported by facts from solid sources. Although there is a host of information online, nothing beats old-fashioned reporting for getting necessary information from people and hard-to-find primary documents. This information will be more easily missed from a converged news report that boasts being a complete package.

- *Knowing various writing styles, vocabulary, advantages/disadvantages, potential, and the like of all news media formats* (print, broadcast, online). To avoid missing the convergence train when it rolls through your news organization, you should be familiar with basic writing and reporting styles of each medium.

- *Being able to conceptualize visual, audio, and text elements for all stories.* Because you typically will be gathering information for multiple formats, you should train yourself to think about possibilities for each, even in your current news organization. Too, this will help you consider the best method for getting the information to the public. Sometimes a traditional broadcast package is necessary, but other times perhaps a visual timeline on the Web site will suffice with a few soundbites included. Thinking this way also will help you lead your news organization into this new era.

ENDNOTES

1. Used by permission. Copyright © 1995, 2000, 2004 by Terry McElhatton.
2. B. Garrison & M. Dupagne (2003 November), *A Case Study of Media Convergence at Media General's News Center in Tampa, Florida.* Paper presented to Media Use in a Changing Environment, Columbia, S.C.
3. S.Quinn (2003 November). *Lessons from the Edge: Convergence Outside the United States.* Paper presented to Media Use in a Changing Environment, Columbia, S.C.

ASSIGNMENT 11A: Formatting a TV Newscast

Name _____ Date _____

Format a complete half-hour television newscast, using the format sheets provided immediately following this assignment.

1 Assume you are formatting your newscast for a metropolitan audience.

2 You have seven minutes of commercials to slug.

3 Weather lasts three minutes.

4 Sports, with intro, lasts 4½ minutes.

5 Your newscast begins exactly at ten p.m. and ends at 10:29:30.

6 Follow the guidelines in this chapter as you prepare your format sheet.

7 To the following list of available stories, feel free to add any eyeball copy you wish, with or without graphics. Identify with an asterisk any copy you add.

PKG., 1:09: Some area restaurants said to be among the most unsanitary of any in state.

SOT bite, :45: President signs major tax increase bill into law.

PKG 1:15: (from CBS) Saudi Arabia raises crude oil $3.20 a barrel.

Reader: U.S. Congressman arrested on homosexual charges (graphic available).

PKG 1:40: This area threatened briefly today by minor radioactive leak at nearby nuclear generating plant.

Live net feed, PKG 1:20: Today's Senate debate over future of Medicare. Will begin at 10:03:30.

Live feed and videotape to cover live report any time during the ten p.m. newscast: Police raid a meth lab at nine o'-clock. —Arrests expected — This is the start of a statewide crackdown on drug dealers and producers. Good visuals expected.

Giant traffic snarl that occurred when Cherry Creek bridge collapsed during rush hour this afternoon, four persons killed. Good video. You decide time.

Two suspected bank robbers arrested, video of both arrest and capture. Not aired at five p.m. You decide time.

VO of recovery efforts for the bodies of two children who drowned today in nearby lake. You decide time. Story used at five o'clock, ran :38 seconds.

Senior citizens rally at State Capitol for support of a threatened Meals-on-Wheels program.

A high school student speaks against violence in her school. PKG (feature) 1:30 as is. Can be recut to 1:10.

Do high food prices deprive you of a nutritionally balanced diet?

Bomb squad almost blows up briefcase with man's lunch. VO-SOT-VO; soundbite with bomb squad technician, sheepish to say the least.

Public hearings in State Senate on hunting controversy. Governor appears to recommend that all hunters must pass hunting safety course, regardless of age. Cover footage available of hunters, today's hearing, and Governor's statement that too many people are being killed in hunting accidents. Calls it a crisis. You decide length and treatment. You have VO and SOT bites that can be run separately, or as a produced VO-SOT-VO.

Two-man burglary and robbery team broken up in robbery attempt last night in which one of the men is shot dead. PKG used at noon and five p.m. but fresh info on identities and the fact that both men operated together.

PKG, 1:09 + Druggists are often robbed following major drug busts.

Reader: Airline pilots and technicians begin work slowdown tonight at Airport to protest threatened wage and benefit cuts. PKG may be available by ten p.m.

Reader: Fluorescent lights may cause cancer. You decide length of story.

Reader: Number of teenage pregnancies is on the rise again. You decide length.

Reader with graphic: Metro transit drivers may strike for more pay. You decide length.

Reader with graphic: GM is recalling three million cars and trucks with defective suspension systems. You decide length.

Reader: Someone is stealing pet rabbits all over town. One resident lost eight rabbits and five feeding dishes last night.

VO-SOT-VO of recovery efforts for the bodies of two children who drowned today in nearby lake. You decide time. Story used at five o'clock, ran :38 seconds.

Senior citizens rally at State Capitol for support of a threatened meals on wheels program.

Supreme Court Justice admitted to hospital

Newscast Format Sheet

DATE:_____

Producer:_____ Anchor: _____

Writer:_____ Anchor: _____

Out time:	_____
– In time:	_____
= Program:	_____
– Spots, wx, sports:	_____
– Pad:	_____
= News hole:	_____

VIDEO: Blank = anchor on camera

VO = anchor voice-over

SOT = sound on tape

V-S-V = VO-SOT-VO

PKG = reporter SOT report

Live = live remote report

Back Time	Slug	Writer	Anchor	Video	Budget Time	Actual Time	Remarks

Newscast Format Sheet

DATE:_____

Producer:_____ Anchor: _____

Writer:_____ Anchor: _____

VIDEO: Blank = anchor on camera

VO = anchor voice-over

SOT = sound on tape

V-S-V = VO-SOT-VO

PKG = reporter SOT report

Live = live remote report

Out time: _____

– In time: _____

= Program: _____

– Spots, wx, sports: _____

– Pad: _____

= News hole: _____

Back Time	Slug	Writer	Anchor	Video	Budget Time	Actual Time	Remarks

Newscast Format Sheet

DATE:_____

Producer:_____ Anchor:_____

Writer:_____ Anchor:_____

VIDEO: Blank = anchor on camera
VO = anchor voice-over
SOT = sound on tape
V-S-V = VO-SOT-VO
PKG = reporter SOT report
Live = live remote report

Out time: _____
− In time: _____
= Program: _____
− Spots, wx, sports: _____
− Pad: _____
= News hole: _____

Back Time	Slug	Writer	Anchor	Video	Budget Time	Actual Time	Remarks

ASSIGNMENT 11B: Writing and Delivering a TV Newscast

Name _____ Date _____

As a class project, write and deliver a half-hour television newscast complete with commercials, sports, and weather. Follow the steps outlined in this chapter. Follow the outline given below only as practical, according to facilities available for your use.

Step 1: Assign personnel to the following positions:

NEWSCASTERS

1.

2.

COPYEDITORS

1.

2.

WEATHERCASTER

1.

FIELD PHOTOGRAPHERS & EDITORS

1.

2.

3.

4.

SPORTSCASTER

1.

STUDIO PERSONNEL (floor directors, video, audio, prompter, playback, etc.)

1.

2.

3.

4.

5.

NEWS PRODUCERS

1.

2.

3.

GRAPHIC ARTISTS

1.

2.

SCRIPT WRITERS

1.

2.

3.

Step 2: (Due_____, _____)
              Write Copy day date

Each member of the class should submit a minimum of three stories (five copies of each) suitable for broadcast. One or more of the stories, at your instructor's option, should be accompanied by a graphics card.

Step 3: Decide story order.

Producers should list all stories available for broadcast, assign stories that remain to be covered locally, then determine story line-up for the entire newscast. Late-breaking stories within the community can be covered just before the newscast is aired on a particular day. Don't forget commercial placement in the line-up.

Step 4: Prepare format sheet.

The producers should assign final length for each element and story in the newscast, and channel all copy that must be rewritten to the writers. Provide at least five copies of each story.

Step 5: Time and block the newscast based on "budget" timing. Producer front-times to determine pad.

At this time, producers should determine the accumulated time of the newscast following each element in the newscast.

Step 6: Editor: Begin to edit videotape.

Step 7: Script commercial breaks and hand-off commentary between newscasters and sports and weather talent.

Step 8: Prepare visuals.

Graphic artists prepare all graphics and other still visuals to be used in the newscast. All visuals are numbered and stacked in order.

Step 9: Edit, proof, and time copy.

Talent edits, proofreads, and times all copy against a stopwatch.

Step 10: Producer: Back-time the final newscast with "actual" times of all elements.

Step 11: Produce and videotape commercials.

(Note: Many TV stations will make old commercials available for your use. Contact the general manager or program director of the station.)

Step 12: Stack newscast.

The producer and on-air talent stack all copies of the newscast in order and number pages.

ASSIGNMENT 11B:
Writing and Delivering a TV Newscast *(continued)*

Name _____ Date _____

Step 13: Assemble graphics and other visuals.

All visuals are assembled in order. Number each graphic in consecutive sequence.

Step 14: Check copy against visuals.

The producer and on-air talent check copy against graphics, VTR, Vidifont, and the line-up of all other elements in the newscast.

Step 15: Back-time finishing copy and prepare pad copy.

Writers are responsible to prepare pad copy while the producer back-times all finishing copy with assistance from on-air talent.

Step 16: Prepare TelePrompTer copy.

A volunteer from class now can prepare TelePrompTer copy if a prompter machine is available.

Step 17: Distribute copy and rehearse newscast.

Copy is distributed to the TelePrompTer operator, audio person, director, anchor talent, and producer, and the newscast is rehearsed.

Step 18: Present final newscast.

Finally, it's airtime, and the newscast is presented for videotaping, playback, and final critique by the class.

ASSIGNMENT 11C: Evaluating Local TV News

Name _____ Date _____

The following assignment is a class project intended to involve all members of the class in a critical evaluation of local television news programs in your area. The emphasis is on developing sensitivity to news programming techniques by deciphering news treatments that reflect the station's desire for higher ratings and by becoming aware of the probable stimulus of news consulting firms. From the list of topics below, choose one or more categories to investigate, then make an informal report of your findings to the class.

Because television market size varies from area to area, you may have only one station in your community to investigate, or as many as three or more stations. If only one station is available for analysis, the class should monitor the station for as long as a week — each student taking one or more categories on successive nights so that all students are involved in the exercise.

CATEGORY 1:
Reporter Involvement
In class, determine which students will investigate examples of reporter involvement on the TV stations in your community.

1. _____ (Channel _____)
   (student's name)

2. _____ (Channel _____)

3. _____ (Channel _____)

4. _____ (Channel _____)

ASSIGNMENT 11C: Evaluating Local TV News *(continued)*

Name _____ Date _____

Channel monitored_____

Date Monitored _____

CATEGORY 2:

Story Breakdown

Each student who signs up for this category should take note of the following elements:

1. Total number of stories in the late newscast of the station of choice.

2. Subject matter for each story.

3. Average length of each story (total number of stories divided by total news time available, less commercial and weather/sports).

Story Breakdown	Actual Length	Visuals Used in Story
Story # 1 _____ (subject)		
# 2 _____		
# 3 _____		
# 4 _____		
# 5 _____		
# 6 _____		
# 7 _____		
# 8 _____		
# 9 _____		
#10 _____		
#11 _____		
#12 _____		
#13 _____		
#14 _____		
#15 _____		

Story Breakdown	Actual Length	Visuals Used in Story
#16 _____		_____
#17 _____		_____
#18 _____		_____
#19 _____		_____
#20 _____		_____

Use bottom of page for additional stories, if necessary.

Average length of each story: _____ seconds.

For reference: Other students doing this assignment.

1. _____   (Channel _____)
                      (student's name)

2. _____   (Channel _____)

3. _____   (Channel _____)

4. _____   (Channel _____)

ASSIGNMENT 11C: Evaluating Local TV News *(continued)*

Name _____ Date _____

CATEGORY 3:

Visual Content and Sources

In this category, observers should identify the number of videotape stories that appear in the early or late evening newscast. For each story that uses videotape, jot down the subject matter and total screen time of visuals.

Visual Content

1. _____ (Channel _____)

   (student's name)

2. _____ (Channel _____)

3. _____ (Channel _____)

4. _____ (Channel _____)

ASSIGNMENT 11C: Evaluating Local TV News *(continued)*

Name _____ Date _____

CATEGORY 4:

Commercial Time and Content

List each commercial within the newscast, including sports and weather, its running time, and the sponsor. (Identifying products and sponsors will help you determine audience makeup for that particular newscast. You may notice, for example, that pantyhose commercials appear in the sports portion of the newscast — a tip-off that many women are watching the sports). Record and add up total time the newscaster's face is on the screen during the news, and total times that sports and weather talent appear on the screen.

1. _____ (Channel _____)

                (student's name)

2. _____ (Channel _____)

3. _____ (Channel _____)

4. _____ (Channel _____)

As part of this assignment, determine percentage of commercial time versus total news time including sports and weather.

ASSIGNMENT 11C: Evaluating Local TV News (continued)

Name _____ Date _____

CATEGORY 5:

Soft News Content

Determine the number of non-hard news stories that appear in each newscast. List specific stories and the length of each story. Into this category fall feature stories, all "happy talk" or banter between anchor talent, etc.

Soft News Content

1. _____ (Channel _____)
                  (student's name)

2. _____ (Channel _____)

3. _____ (Channel _____)

4. _____ (Channel _____)

ASSIGNMENT 11C: Evaluating Local TV News *(continued)*

Name _____ Date _____

CATEGORY 6:

Sports and Weather
Determine average length of sports and weather shows. List and time each story in sports, and make a log of videotapes that appear in sports. Determine average length of any sports interviews that appear and identify interview subjects. Use the log that follows.

SPORTS	Subject	Length	Length	Visuals	Interview
Story #1					
#2					
#3					
#4					
#5					
#6					
#7					
#8					
#9					
#10					
#11					
#12					

Average length of sports programs you watched this week on Channel ____. Average number of tapes used in (#)_____ sportscasts this week. Average length of weather newscast _____ minutes (less commercial time).

For Reference:

Other students engaged in this observation are:

1. _____   (Channel _____)

                   (student's name)

2. _____   (Channel _____)

3. _____   (Channel _____)

4. _____   (Channel _____)

ASSIGNMENT 11D: Determining the News Hole

Name _____ Date _____

Do each of the following problems to determine the news hole. Use the following items in each of your program solutions. Include in your calculations any pad you think might be appropriate, based on what you studied in this chapter.

Commercial breaks = 8:00 (4 breaks of 2:00 each)
Sports segment = 4:30
Weather segment = 3:30

	Problem#1	Problem #2	Problem #3	Problem #4	Problem #5
In time	10:59:30	4:47:52	10:01:12	4:58:30	10:00:03
Out time	11:27:06	5:58:09	10:36:31	5:29:30	10:32:13

ASSIGNMENT 11E: Calculate News Time

Name _____ Date _____

This assignment provides practice in calculating the news hole for a newscast. Given the following beginning and end times for the news program, and the indicated mandatory items, determine the amount of time left that you, the producer, has to fill with news. Note that this is a Friday night newscast during football season, so we have a longer than usual sports segment, as well as long credits that run every Friday night as a positive, team-building tool for the station.

Time in	9:59:47
Time out	10:33:16
Commercials (6 breaks of 2:00 each)	
Produced newscast open	:18
Sports	5:30
Weather	3:30
Weekly consumer report	2:45
Long credits (it's Friday)	:24

ASSIGNMENT 11F: Back-Timing Your Newscast

Name _____ Date _____

This is a back-timing exercise. It should help you see how working back from the end of the program to "out" time works. Back-timing begins by looking at the program "upside down." The producer subtracts each item from the last to the first up to the beginning. To help you see how back-timing works, the newscast is listed from the end of the program, at the top of the list, down to the newscast open at the bottom of the list. For reference, we have done the math for the first two items. For this newscast, the following apply.

In	10:00:00
Out	10:20:30
Sports	2:30
Weather	2:30
Three breaks at 2:00 each	6:00
Credits (preproduced)	:30
Newscast open (preproduced)	:10

Item	Time	Back-time (latest possible item start)
Program "out" (from log)	10:20:30	
Newscast credits	:30	*10:20:00*
Bye bye	:10	*10:19:50*
Kicker	1:10	
Break #3	2:05	
Weather	2:30	
Break #2	2:05	
Sports	2:30	
Break #1	2:05	
Car wreck	:30	
Shooting	1:25	
President on crime	:45	
President's budget	:30	
City budget	:45	
School budget crisis	1:30	
School maintenance cost	:25	
School test scores	1:00	
Newscast open	:10	
Pad left in newscast		

Critical Thinking Questions

Directions: The following questions are provided to help you examine the deeper meanings and complexities of the various issues under discussion. Answer each question to the best of your ability after a thoughtful review of the subject at hand.

1. What are the similarities between the half-hour newscast and the news package?

2. Assume you are producing a late-night newscast. What sources of news and information would be available to you for your newscast in a large-to-medium market?

3. Given that a 30-minute telecast contains fewer than 15 minutes of actual news time, what do you believe to be an optimum number of stories, and average story length, on an average news day?

4. Discuss in detail how a news Web page can combine the best from radio, television, print, audio, still photography, and information graphics to report a story.

5. To what extent, if any, should journalists be involved in the marketing and promotion of news? Include appropriate examples to support your point of view.

6. It has been said that "good writing is rewriting what you have rewritten." What is the importance of proofreading, rewriting, and editing copy before airtime? Who must be involved in checking final copy?

7. Explain how a "multi-skilled" journalist working in a converged newsroom might approach a story about the upcoming elections for your state legislature.

8. Television news is often criticized for being too shallow. Explain how broadcast news might be improved through delivery via a Web site instead of over airwaves during a 30-minute newscast. In your discussion news hole, be sure to include time, advertising, and new technological capabilities.

Self-Review Questions

Directions: Each of the self-review questions below addresses information contained in this chapter. Answer each question to the best of your ability, then review the chapter as necessary to further strengthen your understanding of each concept or issue.

1. Explain and provide a detailed example of a half-hour news format.

2. What is the job of the news producer?

3. What approaches can be taken to improve radio delivery?

4. What are the primary components of a television newscast? Define each of them.

5. What are the primary components of an Internet newscast? Define each of them.

6. What are the main considerations that govern how a newscast is blocked?

7. Provide an example of a news format sheet. Explain its various components and their purpose.

8. What is the importance of pace in a television newscast? What pacing elements can a producer use to better manage pace?

9. What is a news "tease?" What are your reactions to typical teases you encounter when you watch television newscasts?

10. Discuss the idea of news media convergence and its potential to replace news delivery as we know it now. What are the obstacles? What will have to change for convergence to be a reality?

## CHAPTER TWELVE

Research, Ratings, and Promotion

Although journalism is among this society's most valuable philosophical estates, it is irrefutably a business as well. The paychecks that keep the journalist's mortgage and utility payments up-to-date come from advertising revenue. Revenue derives from sponsors who buy advertising at rates determined by the number of households reached and by the composition of viewers within those households. Newscasts create audiences. Stations sell the audiences to advertisers.

The stakes are huge. Today, nearly every home in the United States has at least one radio receiver and 98 percent have at least one television set. More than three-fourths of these homes have more than one TV set; the average number of TV sets in these homes is between two and three.[1] About 70 percent of all homes have cable and 16 percent have satellite.

Use of the Internet has grown rapidly in the past few years as more than half the nation is online. More than 150 million Americans access the Internet, and research suggests that the number of new users is growing about two million per month.[2]

Given the nearly universal use of electronic media, ratings systems are essential to determine who is watching what and how is it being delivered into the home. Over the past half century, these systems have grown to include telephone surveys, viewer diaries, electronic meters, and people meters that identify who is watching a program or news item at a given time. The resulting audience ratings and demographic profiles are among the most important measurements in determining a program's value and profitability. They also play an essential role in helping media organizations market and promote themselves and their programming.

THE NEWS PRODUCT

Most journalists would contend that if they produce any "product" at all, it is the news story or newscast. Station managers and owners, however, are more likely to think of their news department's "product" as the viewing audience. And, though journalists tend to think of their primary audience as viewers, in a real sense the station's paramount "audience" is made up of paying advertisers. The business of electronic media consequently revolves around efforts to attract the largest possible audience and then to measure how well the effort has succeeded. Toward that end, audience research and news promotion are critical to the continued success of most news operations.

RATINGS

Stations and Internet sites live and die by the ratings book, the report card that tells organizations the size and composition of their audiences for specific programs. Ratings are statistical estimates of the number of households tuned to a program or Web page and the types of people within those homes. Given the nearly 50 million Internet households and the 110 million TV households in the United States,[3] it would be impossible to survey each home individually, so ratings are based upon samples of the population at large.

Two companies best known for national broadcast ratings and research studies are Arbitron (radio, cable, telecommunications, direct broadcast satellite, online and new media industries) and Nielsen Market Research (national broadcast and cable networks, regional networks, syndicators, television stations, local cable TV systems, satellite distributors, online and new media industries). These companies use a common sampling technique called **area probability**

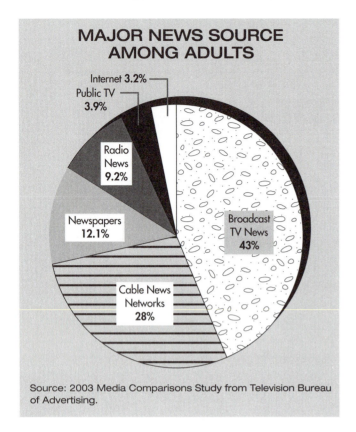

MAJOR NEWS SOURCE AMONG ADULTS

Internet 3.2%
Public TV 3.9%
Radio News 9.2%
Newspapers 12.1%
Broadcast TV News 43%
Cable News Networks 28%

Source: 2003 Media Comparisons Study from Television Bureau of Advertising.

of your vegetables should roughly match the ratios of the entire pot of soup. Again, this is the aim in sampling.[4]

Nielsen Media Research uses several methods to monitor viewership of television, including household meters, personal diaries and people meters.

Household Meters/Diaries

The market, or boundaries of the survey area within which the primary viewers of a station are located, is designated as the area of dominant influence (ADI) by Arbitron, or as the designated market area (DMA) by Nielsen. In larger markets, electronic set-tuning meters measure viewing activity in major local markets every day of the week.

Meters are installed on television sets in hundreds of households throughout each market to record when the TV set is on and what channel is selected. Subscribing advertisers, television stations, and networks receive overnight rating reports of viewing activity ("overnights") based on data these meters provide.[5] To be certain the meters are statistically accurate, other families are asked to fill out diaries that provide additional information such as the respondent's age, education, ethnic origin, occupation, product use, and the like.

The Nielsen Television Index (NTI) provides continuous audience estimates for all national broadcast network television programs. Minute by minute, a small electronic box stored inconspicuously in a household closet or basement records and stores tuning activity, including on-off activity and channel selection, for each television receiver in the home. Computers retrieve the data via phone lines. To provide crosschecks of statistical accuracy, viewers in other households are recruited to keep diaries that indicate weekly viewing activities for each person.

Another Nielsen service, the National Station Index (NSI), measures local market television. This service offers continuous metered market overnight measurement in 55 major markets and diary measurement in more than 200 Designated Market Areas (DMAs). But Nielsen is looking to phase out this method of audience surveying in favor of its local people meters, which are being tested in the top 10 markets between 2003 and 2006.[6]

People Meters

Audience measurements sometimes rely upon **people meters** — first introduced in the mid-1980s by Arbitron-Time Inc., Nielsen, and AGB Television Research, Inc. — which are now becoming the favored survey method.[7] The people meter is a small unit placed on or near the television set. Directly or via remote control, household family members indicate their presence as viewers by

sampling. This means that individuals who comprise the samples are chosen in proportion to their distribution within the population at large. For example, if the Boston area comprises 4 percent of the national population, 4 percent of the national survey population will be drawn from the Boston area in numbers that reflect a representative profile of viewers in the area according to considerations such as sex, age, income, and ethnic diversity.

Commonly, the sample size is surprisingly small. An average local sample might consist of anywhere from 200 to 500 people, and a national sample representing viewing activity in 100 million homes might contain 1,500 to 5,000 households. Though 5,000 out of 100 million may seem small, Nielsen Media Research likens the sampling process to making vegetable soup. You can eat a cup of soup to know what kind it is. But you also must stir the pot often enough to get a sample of all the vegetables.

The same is true with research sampling. The entire population is not needed to study a particular behavior, but it is important to get a sample that resembles the population and its demographic ratios. Using the vegetable soup example again, suppose carrots make up half the vegetables, celery 20 percent, potatoes 15 percent, green beans 10 percent, tomatoes 5 percent. If you stir the pot often, when you scoop a cup of soup, the ratios pushing a lighted button on the meter. Data are stored electronically and polled periodically using telephone lines.[8] People meters potentially are more accurate than hand-written diaries, as respondents can watch television without having to remember which channels they tuned in, at specific times, or to write it all down. People meters identify which family members view television and keep tabs on what they watch, how often they switch channels, and which commercials they avoid. People meters measure nationwide audiences only. Another benefit of the people meter is its ability to link viewing behavior with limited demographic information. With household meters and diaries, the viewing habits were not tied to the types of people watching.[9]

As an alternative to punching in personal codes, some people meters allow ratings companies to identify viewers and watch their viewing behavior even as viewers watch their favorite programs. For example, Nielsen Media Research developed a "passive people meter" that knows, second by second, whether viewers are watching TV or have turned away from the screen. A scanning camera hooked to a computer is programmed first to detect human presence in the room, then to scan for progressively higher resolution until it matches the facial characteristics of household members to those stored in its memory. [10]

Nielsen began its rollout of **local people meters** in New York City, Los Angeles, and Chicago in the fall of 2004. The ratings giant faced severe opposition from a variety of groups, including the National Association of Broadcasters, Fox News Corporation, and a host of minority broadcasting organizations. These opponents argued that the LPMs were not accurately recording minority viewing habits through their market sampling. But Nielsen President Susan Whiting argued in a Senate hearing that the real complaint for these groups was media market research showing a loss of viewers in the market.[11]

Because the local people meters can measure demographics better, as well as determine electronically when viewers switch channels and to which other channels, experts predict that research will show more viewers turning to cable than local broadcast. During testing in Boston between 2002 and 2003, for example, initial reports showed a drop in viewers for early morning and late evening newscasts. Anticipation of similar findings is fueling much of the debate over implementation.

In spite of the crossfire, few in the industry disagree that local people meters (LPMs) will be a more accurate measure of viewership for ratings than the diary/meter system. Some in the industry are predicting that LPMs could end the traditional "sweeps" weeks for broadcast news. If accurate ratings are available daily, there is no need for local and national news to inundate viewers in their market area with their best stories. "It will force programmers to think beyond sweeps," says Andy Donchin, senior vice president and director of national broadcast, Carat.[12] In fact, by the close of 2004, a few news directors were doing just that. Frank Comerford, president and general manager of WNBC in New York, said he does not look at sweeps anymore but instead looks at the daily data from people meters.[13]

SPOTLIGHT

Measuring Internet Use

Nearly two-thirds of the U.S. population age 12 and older were online as the 21st century began, or some 105 million people using the Internet in 38 million homes.* Internet research tracks these audiences and user activity to help advertisers target messages to specific users.

Ever since the Internet grew into a serious consumer resource, however, automated Web pages have used programs that continuously measure "hits," or page accesses. In addition, most Web audit services provide reports that tell where the people hitting a Web page are located.

Webmasters receive totals by country, state, even individual communities. Use can be tracked all the way down to the individual Internet Service Provider. Webmasters then can adjust their sites to encourage people to jump further into subpages, and track their consumer preferences.

Thus, you can tell if your news organization's Web site holds Internet users for a while, or if they just check in quickly and move on. You can try to make it more dynamic and exciting, and you can make decisions about how much streaming video and audio to provide and whether what you are doing on the Web site is really working in terms of attracting users.

For fun, log your own use of three different news Web sites. How many times do you click on a link within one story? How many elements do you search through on a home page? What section are you most interested in reading?

* From AC Nielsen News Release, "AC Nielsen Survey Finds Nearly Two Thirds of U.S. Population Age 12 or Older Are Online, May 2000, via http://www.acnielsen.com/news/american/us/2000/2000508.htm

Online Databases

In addition to data contained in the rating book, which represents as little as one-third of all the data obtained during a survey, the major research companies maintain online databases that provide client access to the remaining data. This information can indicate the number of people who watch both the station's early and late evening newscasts, for example, thereby indicating whether news content should be altered significantly to avoid repetition between the early and late shows or whether the advertiser is reaching similar or radically different audience profiles.

Data also can be customized for clients according to the customer's own research needs. The research staff can help interpret survey results and monitor more closely the attitudes and viewing behavior of individuals who kept diaries, for example.

Tracking Surveys

Every market has something of a life of its own. Audience turnover is inevitable as viewers come and go. Attitudes and behaviors within the market shift to reflect the spontaneous happenings and ongoing concerns within the community. To discern shifts in viewer and community attitudes, **tracking** research is used to gather information in regular, ongoing "waves." If comparisons are controlled tightly and are of adequate sample size, the station can better ascertain changes over time in viewer reactions to diverse concerns such as its coverage of major news events, changes in news personalities within the market, and the effectiveness of its promotion efforts.[14]

Focus Group Research

Stations hire consultants to conduct **focus group** research to pinpoint viewer attitudes and other information specific to a specific market. Viewers from a broad cross-section of the community are recruited to discuss their opinions about local television newscasts in the presence of a trained interviewer or moderator. The meetings typically are held in a hotel conference room or other public place, and recorded. The resulting information can be incorporated in reports that recommend specific action to the clients' TV station. Qualifying panelists are paid a fee averaging about $25 for their participation. The value of focus group surveys is their ability to unearth and refine highly specific information regarding what viewers most like and dislike about newscasts in their community.

Telephone Surveys

Consultants conduct periodic telephone surveys in client markets. For fees of more than $1,000 per survey minute, trained telephone interviewers query viewers in specific markets about their viewing habits and preferences. Thus, to conduct a 15-minute telephone survey of 400 respondents, a station might pay $15,000 or more.

In-House Research

Stations sometimes conduct their own in-house research on an interim basis to supplement major research from their consultants and ratings services. Specialists at area colleges and universities frequently are recruited to assist in designing questionnaires, statistical sampling, data processing, and analysis. In-house research, though possibly less accurate than national surveys, allows stations to test for reactions to programs, often more quickly and at lower cost than for contracted services.

Rating and Share Defined

From the data amassed through survey activities, rating and share percentages are determined and published in a ratings book, which tells the station how it is doing as compared to its competitors in the business of attracting viewers to its programs. **Rating** is the percentage of households watching a station compared to all households with television sets, whether they are in use or not. **Share** is the percentage of households watching a given station, in comparison to all households using television at that time.

THE DIFFERENCE BETWEEN RATING AND SHARE

Rating: Households watching a given station as a percentage of total households with a TV

Share: Households watching a given station as a percentage of households using television

To understand the difference between rating and share, assume a market with 1,000 television households, in which 600 households are watching television. Further assume that 240 of those households using television (HUT) are tuned to your station. That means the station has a 24 rating (24 percent of the total number of households with television), and a 40 share (40 percent of the households using television.)

A large rating is better than a large share because it means the station is reaching a large percentage of the total potential market audience. Although large share numbers are important, they may not add up to a large number of viewers. A late night show in a market of 1,000 television households might have a 50 share but only a 5 rating. That would be the case in the following example, which assumes that 100 households are viewing television:

$$\frac{50 \quad \text{Households watching station}}{100 \quad \text{Total households using television}} = 50 \text{ Share}$$

$$\frac{50 \quad \text{Households watching station}}{1,000 \quad \text{Total households with TV}} = 5 \text{ Rating}$$

How Ratings Translate into Profit

How much a given station gets of all its money depends upon the size of the audience it amasses. A station with 200,000 viewers might charge $2,800 to air a 30-second commercial, whereas a station with 500,000 viewers could charge $7,000 for the same 30-second commercial.

Despite increasing competition from other media, electronic media comprise a huge business. Advertising revenue for broadcast and cable was more than $56 billion in 2003, the most among other media.[15] Advertising on the Internet increased more than 20 percent between 2002 and 2003, raking in more than $7 billion in revenue.[16]

Clearly, the stakes are high. Figure 12.1 shows a Nielsen ratings page for Pittsburgh, Pennsylvania, reflecting viewership patterns for various demographics for the city's eleven o'clock newscasts and other programs.

Demographics

Although anyone is welcome to watch a newscast or an Internet transmission, some viewers can produce more profits because of their attractiveness to advertisers. Whether the advertiser is a travel company, a hard rock promoter, or a farm equipment dealer, it strives to reach an audience of potential customers. The luxury car dealer who reaches viewers with household incomes mostly below $25,000 is wasting money. Demographic studies help advertisers direct their messages at target audiences.

Demographics are the vital statistics of the community, expressed by age, race, sex, income, occupation, and place of residence. Demographics give the advertiser information such as marketwide indications of incomes and breakdowns of viewers according to age and sex, buying patterns on large-ticket items, and the size and distribution of minority audiences within the market. Most coveted among the age groups are viewers 18 to 49 years of age because they tend to earn and spend more money than those in other age groups do. For non-news programming, other age groups can be lucrative — among them, children with large allowances, teenagers, and the well-to-do retired set.

Within the 18- to 49-year-old viewing group, broadcasters have long coveted 18- to 34-year-old-female viewers. Women, regardless of education or economic status, spend more than any other age or gender group. They also make or influence the major buying decisions in their households. In the United States approximately a third of people 18 years of age and older are between 18 and 34 years of age.[17]

To lure more women in the 18–34 group from entertainment programs — which they tend to watch more frequently and with greater loyalty than news — some stations target their news specifically to this group. This narrowly focused approach accentuates "lifestyle reporting," with greater emphasis on news reports and features about women's issues, family, health, and entertainment, and less overall emphasis on traditional hard news and political reporting. To avoid excluding conventional audiences, which tend to be older and predominately male, the station must strive to offer stories that appeal to everyone: "How you can spot Alzheimer's in your parents, and what you can do about it." This trend that emerged in the late 80s continues today, particularly in local television news as they have added earlier newscasts to appeal to very specific audiences.[18]

Consultants

For most businesses, research and development are part of becoming number one in the marketplace. The same considerations hold true for electronic media. Research helps the station assess viewer attitudes and position itself against the competition. Because the research, management, marketing, and processes are so complex and the financial stakes are so high, hundreds of stations employ the services of national news consultants.

For contract fees based on market size, consultants conduct market inventories that include the strengths and weaknesses of the client station and its competitors, and analyze viewing patterns and trends within the market. A standard two-year consulting contract might call for an account executive of the consulting firm to visit the station every other month, and to initiate research about viewer attitudes and behavior. Separate fees may be charged for additional services such as talent coaching, set design, seminars, and specialized research.

PITTSBURGH, PA

WEDNESDAY 11:00PM - 1:00AM

METRO HH		STATION / PROGRAM	DMA HOUSEHOLD RATINGS WEEKS				MULTI-WEEK AVG	SHARE TREND				DMA RATINGS PERSONS											WOMEN							MEN						TNS	CHILD	
RTG	SHR		1	2	3	4	RTG/SHR	NOV'94	MAY'94	FEB'94	2+	18+	12-24	12-34	18-34	18-49	21-49	25-49	25-54	35+	35-64	50+	18+	12-24	18-34	18-49	25-49	25-54	WKG	18+	18-34	18-49	21-49	25-49	25-54	12-17	2-11	6-11
1	2		3	4	5	6	7 / 8	11	12	13	15	16	17	18	19	20	21	22	23	24	25	26	27	28	29	31	32	34	35	36	37	38	39	40	41	42	43

R.S.E. THRESHOLDS 25+% (1 S.E.) 4 WK AVG 50+%

11:00PM

HH RTG/SHR	STATION	PROGRAM	WK1	WK2	WK3	WK4	R/S	NOV	MAY	FEB	Persons...
17/33	KDKA	EYEWIT NWS-11	15	17	13	15	15/31	28X	36	43	8 10 2 4 5 6 6 8 12 9 16 ...
1/2	WPGH	MARRIED-CHLDRN	2	1	1	<<	1/2	3	4	2	1 1 1 1 2 1 1 1 ...
<<	WPTT	NORTHRN EXPSRE	1	<<	<<	<<	2	1			...
13/26	WPXI	CHNL 11 NWS-11	12	14	12	7	12/24	20X	15	18	7 8 3 5 6 7 8 9 9 9 9 ...
<<	WQED	AVG. ALL WKS	<<	<<	<<	<<	<<				
<<		HEALING-MOYERS					<<		1		
<<		GRT PERFRMNCES		<<	<<		<<				
<<		INSIDE STORY			<<	<<	<<				
1/2	WQEX	HONEYMNERS	1	<<	1	1	1/2	1X	1	1	
13/27	WTAE	WTAE 4 NWS 11	11	13	16	14	13/27	30X	29	23	8 9 2 4 5 7 7 8 11 11 11 ...
50		HUT/PUT/TOTALS*	47	53	50	44	48	45	52	53	28 34 10 18 21 26 28 31 39 37 45 ...

11:15PM

HH	STATION	PROGRAM	WK1	WK2	WK3	WK4	R/S	NOV	MAY	FEB	
16/33	KDKA	EYEWIT NWS-11	14	16	12	14	14/30	28X	35	42	
1/3	WPGH	MARRIED-CHLDRN	2	1	1	<<	1/3	3	4	2	
<<	WPTT	NORTHRN EXPSRE	1	<<	<<	<<		2	1		
13/26	WPXI	CHNL 11 NWS-11	12	14	12	7	11/24	20X	15	19	
<<	WQED	AVG. ALL WKS	<<	<<	<<	<<	<<				
<<		HEALING-MOYERS					<<		1		
<<		GRT PERFRMNCES					<<				
<<		INSIDE STORY			<<	<<	<<				
1/2	WQEX	HONEYMNERS	1	<<	1	1	1/2	1X	1	1	
13/26	WTAE	WTAE 4 NWS 11	11	12	14	15	13/27	29X	29	24	
49		HUT/PUT/TOTALS*	46	52	48	43	47	44	51	52	

11:30PM

HH	STATION	PROGRAM	WK1	WK2	WK3	WK4	R/S	NOV	MAY	FEB	
12/33	KDKA	D LETTRMAN-CBS	9	12	10	10	10/30	28X	33	38	
1/2	WPGH	AVG. ALL WKS	1	1	<<	<<	1/2	3	4	3	
2/5		NEWZ	1				1/5				
1/2		NIGHT COURT		1	<<	<<	<<				
<<	WPTT	NORTHRN EXPSRE	1	<<	<<	<<	<<	3	5	2	
8/23	WPXI	TONITE SHW-NBC	8	10	7	5	8/22	16X	13	16	
<<	WQED	AVG. ALL WKS	<<	<<	<<	<<	<<				
<<		HEALING-MOYERS					<<				
<<		THREE DANCES			<<	<<	<<				
<<		INSIDE STORY			<<	<<	<<				
1/2	WQEX	WAITNG FOR GOD	1	<<	<<	1	1/2	24X	2		
7/20	WTAE	ABC-NITELINE	6	7	8	6	7/20	24X	23	25	
35		HUT/PUT/TOTALS*	32	39	36	31	34	31	39	38	

11:45PM

HH	STATION	PROGRAM	WK1	WK2	WK3	WK4	R/S	NOV	MAY	FEB	
8/31	KDKA	D LETTRMAN-CBS	7	8	8	6	7/29	29X	29	39	
1/3	WPGH	AVG. ALL WKS	1	1	<<	<<	1/3	2	4	3	
1/6		NEWZ	1				1/5				
1/2		NIGHT COURT		1	<<	<<	<<				
<<	WPTT	NORTHRN EXPSRE	1	<<	<<	<<	<<	3	6	2	
5/20	WPXI	TONITE SHW-NBC	5	6	5	3	5/19	13X	13	15	
<<	WQED	AVG. ALL WKS	<<	<<	<<	<<	<<				
<<		HEALING-MOYERS					<<				
<<		THREE DANCES			<<	<<	<<				
<<		INSIDE STORY			<<	<<	<<				
<<	WQEX	WAITNG FOR GOD	<<	<<	<<	1	1	19X	2		
5/17	WTAE	ABC-NITELINE	4	5	5	3	4/17	19X	20	22	
27		HUT/PUT/TOTALS*	24	29	27	21	26	24	30	31	

12:00MD

HH	STATION	PROGRAM	WK1	WK2	WK3	WK4	R/S	NOV	MAY	FEB	
7/39	KDKA	D LETTRMAN-CBS	7	7	8	3	6/36	35X	37	42	
<<	WPGH	PAID PROGRAM	<<	<<	<<	<<	<<	X			
<<	WPTT	PAID PROGRAM	<<	<<	<<	<<	<<	X			
3/18	WPXI	TONITE SHW-NBC	4	4	1	2	3/16	12X	14	15	
3/16	WTAE	CHEERS	2	4	2	2	3/15	12X	16	16	
18		HUT/PUT/TOTALS*	16	20	17	13	17	15	20	20	

12:15AM

HH	STATION	PROGRAM	WK1	WK2	WK3	WK4	R/S	NOV	MAY	FEB	
7/39	KDKA	D LETTRMAN-CBS	7	6	7	3	6/35	35X	37	41	
<<	WPGH	PAID PROGRAM	<<	<<	<<	<<	<<	X			
<<	WPTT	PAID PROGRAM	<<	<<	<<	<<	<<	X			
3/16	WPXI	TONITE SHW-NBC	3	3	1	1	2/14	11X	14	15	
3/16	WTAE	CHEERS	2	4	2	2	2/16	12X	14	15	
17		HUT/PUT/TOTALS*	15	19	16	13	16	15	19	18	

12:30AM

HH	STATION	PROGRAM	WK1	WK2	WK3	WK4	R/S	NOV	MAY	FEB	
4/38	KDKA	INSIDE EDITION	4	4	5	2	4/36	33X	27	42	
<<	WPGH	PAID PROGRAM	<<	<<	<<	<<	<<	X			
<<	WPTT	PAID PROGRAM	<<	<<	<<	<<	<<	X			
1/11	WPXI	C O'BRIEN-NBC	2	1	1	<<	1/10	9X	12	10	
1/8	WTAE	JUDGE-YOURSELF	1	1	1	<<	1/9	9X	16	9	
11		HUT/PUT/TOTALS*	10	12	11	7	10	11	13	13	

12:45AM

HH	STATION	PROGRAM	WK1	WK2	WK3	WK4	R/S	NOV	MAY	FEB	
3/34	KDKA	INSIDE EDITION	3	3	4	2	3/33	29X	25	44	
<<	WPGH	PAID PROGRAM	<<	<<	<<	<<	<<	X			
<<	WPTT	PAID PROGRAM	<<	<<	<<	<<	<<	X			
1/8	WPXI	C O'BRIEN-NBC	<<	1	1	<<	1/8	8X	9	6	
1/9	WTAE	JUDGE-YOURSELF	1	1	<<	<<	1/7	9X	11	9	
9		HUT/PUT/TOTALS*	8	10	10	6	8	9	11	11	

WEDNESDAY 11:00PM - 1:00AM

Nielsen has been advised that a station(s) conducted a special promotional activity. See page 3.

Figure 12.1: A Nielsen ratings page for Pittsburgh, Pennsylvania.

NEWS CONSULTANTS

News consultants help stations better understand viewer attitudes and behavior within the market, help develop anchor and reporting talent, and help the clients position themselves better against competitors. Following are some of the consultant's activities.

- Determine viewer preferences in news and talent.
- Predict and respond to audience behavior.
- Perform statistical and audience analyses.
- Originate research designs and perform analyses.
- Conduct image and personality research.
- Develop marketing and promotion strategies.
- Conduct workshops and seminars.
- Develop communication skills.
- Do talent consulting and coaching.
- Do wardrobe, hairstyling, and makeup consulting.
- Do placement services.
- Develop franchises (specialized segment reports such as Weather Watchers, Health Beat, Spirit of Texas).
- Design newscast formats.
- Design weather, sports, and news sets.
- Bring the client station into closer contact with its viewers; represent viewers and their interests to the station.

Commonly, consultants conduct research to determine who is available to view the station, and which of those viewers (by age, income, sex, address, and occupation) are watching. Consultants also help determine how often viewers watch the station, including the number of viewers who watch both the station's early and late newscasts. Still other surveys help to determine how well reporters and anchors are recognized in the market, what people like and don't like about TV news in their viewing area, and everything from the personal performance and style of the station's talent to surveys of which anchors are most likeable and personable. Through this research, consultants can determine which anchors and newscasts are the personal favorites among viewers and track attitudes about the station's reputation within the community.

Consultants work for the station manager, or the station owners, not the newsroom. And, though consultants may make recommendations that extend to what times newscasts should be aired and whether to hire or fire anchors and reporters, the station is under no obligation to act on their recommendations. The consultant is a partner in research and development, not a replacement for the judgment of station management or newsroom employees who have more intimate knowledge of the marketplace and its viewers by virtue of their residency in the community.

Using News Anchors to Attract Audiences

For nearly three decades, audience researchers have documented the role of newscasters in attracting audiences to particular newscasts. By the early 1970s, researchers had discovered at least four levels of characteristics that influence audience perception of television personalities. In 1973, Herschel Shosteck ranked these clusters, in order of importance, as:

1. Voice and speech (pleasant voice, good speaking ability, good use of grammar)

2. Professional attributes (knowledge of subject, intelligence, level of awareness about events, good analytical ability)

3. Personal attributes (good personality, appealing as an individual, a demeanor of warmth and concern)

4. Appearance (dresses properly, attractive).

Personal qualities alone, however, seldom can both attract and hold audiences Shosteck noted that, although news personalities with high personal appeal definitely draw viewers, news content and presentation format also can help make television newscasts substantially more appealing.

Audience studies continue to reflect that many viewers choose what newscast to watch based on the anchor rather than solely upon news content or presentation formats. Nearly 45 percent of viewers in one market selected their news program because of an anchor. Viewers cited characteristics such as "he seems like one of the family," to professionalism, credibility, intelligence, knowledge of subject matter, delivery skills, and physical appearance, including dress and cosmetic appearance. Other important attributes included the newscaster's gestures, voice, and warmth.[19] Our own informal surveys of consulting companies and newscasters themselves expand the list to include honesty, integrity, curiosity, calmness, objectivity, good reporting skills, empathy, compassion, and community involvement.

PROMOTION

The increasing emphasis on news research and promotion has paralleled the growth of television news. As the profitability of news became apparent in the 1970s, marketing the news received greater emphasis. Even then, news executives tended to view marketing as something that belonged more in show business than in journalism on the grounds that the product is news, not soap.[20] Then, in the 1980s, came the realization that news departments have to be promoted. Even the best news presentation in the world is irrelevant if no one is watching.

The essence of promotion is the drive to motivate more viewers to switch to the organization's newscasts and become loyal viewers or listeners. The foundation of this promotion effort is market research to help the station determine its strengths and weaknesses, as well as those of the competition. The station looks for vulnerabilities in the market and seeks to fill a niche no other station has filled. The approach is similar to the garment retailer who discovers that women executives want wider selections in business attire and opens a store to serve them.

Once the station has decided how it will identify its "brand" and what niche or position it wants to occupy within the market, viewers have to be told. Branding an organization is essential to help differentiate it from the competition.

Community Involvement

Perhaps market research shows that news viewers want a station that's involved with the community and are concerned about local issues but they can't name a station that really stands out. The station then might seek to position itself in the market by becoming more involved and concerned about the community than any other station, and by demonstrating that involvement tangibly and visibly at every opportunity.

The station will not succeed merely through promotion that says it is now involved in the community. It must become what it purports to be, through its public service and community relations, through issue-oriented and consumer reporting that reinforces its involvement in the community, and through its sponsorship of activities such as Crime Stoppers, canned food drives, adoption-placement services, and expanding the weather to provide regional coverage. Yet another aspect of community involvement may mean satisfying viewers who want more local sports coverage. In this case, the station might decide to beef up its sports staff and promote the fact that it provides more local sports coverage than any other station.

Promoting Strengths, Not Weaknesses

Always, the essence of promotion is to promote strengths, not weaknesses. If market research shows that an anchor is perceived to lack authority, the station may work to promote strengths that will overcome viewer objections to the anchor. If the anchor is a strong field reporter or interviewer, perhaps these attributes can be brought to the viewer's attention through promotion. The anchor might even be asked to do more field reporting and interviews to demonstrate desirable anchor attributes more tangibly.

Quality Reporting

Although promotion is critically important, quality in news reporting can be its own reward. "Good reporting is its own promotion," says Mike Beecher, director of news and public affairs, KFVS-TV, Cape Girardeau, Missouri. "Beyond helping attract and hold loyal audiences, good reporting can help win awards that earn the station valuable recognition that can itself be promoted."[21] Even though promotion can help attract viewers and reinforce the station's image, every station first must develop something worthwhile to promote.

Promotion Off-Screen

Throughout the broadcast day, stations use every conceivable device to promote their news. Motorists on the local freeways are exposed to billboards, taxi and bus signs, and radio ads that promote talent and invite citizens to watch the station's news. Throughout the year, viewers in the community are invited to attend health screenings and fairs that the station sponsors. Stations know that for the TV news program to be accepted, they must become involved tangibly and visibly in the community, and it must keep the community aware of its efforts.

Elsewhere to be seen are the station's satellite trucks, and perhaps a helicopter with the station logo flying overhead toward some news story, or landing at elementary schools so the photographer can shoot pictures of the school children and transmit them at the close of the newscast that night. Additional promotions are aired throughout the broadcast day at commercial breaks: "Tonight on the late news, learn CPR techniques that could help you save the life of someone you love" or "This evening at the Kiwanis banquet, you can hear the station's lead anchor deliver the keynote speech."

Stations also try to lure viewers by promoting "exclusive" reports or "breaking news" on the evening newscast. Sometimes these promotions are legitimate and sometimes they are more hype than substance. Watch a week of the same newscast and determine how often they promote their upcoming stories and later newscasts. How often are these legitimate stories?

Sweeps

Although stations constantly invite people to watch their programs, they ask most insistently during the survey periods called **sweeps**, conducted in February, May, July, and November. Year-round, Nielsen Media Research constantly tracks TV households with people meters, homes using set-top meters in local markets, and during sweeps Nielsen collects information from families who keep diaries of their viewing habits. But as mentioned previously in this chapter, sweeps periods may become less important to news stations as the local people meters, which provide feedback daily, gradually replace household meters and diaries in all markets.[22]

In sweeps periods, stations strive to build audiences with the best news reporting, entertainment programs, and promotion they can muster. Viewers are treated to first-run movies, the best entertainment programs, and lavish specials. News departments trot out their best mini-series and ratings-related features. They do special reports on everything from teen sex to how to check your credit rating. Some viewers are even tempted with prospects of free vacations and cash prizes. Because the results of sweeps survey periods will influence the station's ratings for months to come, stations usually offer their strongest and most tantalizing programs during these periods.

Between sweeps, the fare is likely to be far more pedestrian. In response to what critics call "**front-loading**," the Federal Trade Commission has issued "Guidelines Regarding Deceptive Claims of Broadcast Audience Coverage." These guidelines state that television stations ". . . should not engage in activities calculated to distort or inflate such data — for example, by conducting a special contest, or otherwise varying . . . programming, or instituting unusual advertising or other promotional efforts, designed to increase audiences only during the survey period."

Ultimately, as technology advances, daily measurements in all markets may one day render sweeps periods unnecessary. Daily measurements may be the only solution to end the hype to which viewers are now periodically exposed.

Image Advertising Versus Product Promotion

Typically, news promotion distinguishes between image and product promotion. Image advertising is staged and highly produced to project an impression of the news operation as the station would like itself to be perceived (warm, caring, friendly, believable, comprehensive). "Image advertising traditionally shows reporters jumping in and out of helicopters, the lone anchor at the typewriter in a dimly lit room, or the anchors dressed in casual clothes swapping wieners with indigent children in the park," says Bill Brown of The Coaching Company.[23]

In product promotion the news product is its own advertising. The footage seen in promotional spots comes from actual news reports, and whenever anchors and reporters are shown on screen, they are doing their jobs, not playing themselves or acting out their roles as they would in image advertising. At Christmas time the anchors seen in product promotion spots don't just ride in a sleigh with disadvantaged kids. They also work to raise money to send these children to college.

The philosophy governing the spots is that there's no need to stage what already exists. "Often there is little justification to go out and hire a production crew at great expense to re-create what's already there," says Brown. He offers the example of a simple product promotion spot that illuminated the work of Herb Dennenberg, former consumer reporter at WCAU-TV, Philadelphia:

> Senior citizens saw their dream vacation become a nightmare when, without warning, their travel agent went bankrupt. Herb Dennenberg learned of their story, helped organize a trip to Florida, and gave them a vacation they'd remember all their lives. Herb Dennenberg's consumer investigations make good things happen for people. They're part of what makes Channel 10 News, News Plus.[24]

The alternative to this approach — image advertising — would be to show Herb Dennenberg waving to the camera from a sailboat or some other similarly contrived spot that focuses on image rather than true performance. In addition to its credibility, an advantage of product promotion lies in its potential effectiveness at low cost. A station can spend tens of thousands of dollars on image promotion, or for a minimal fee, can produce a taped spot in which parents thank an anchor for a Wednesday's Child segment that introduced them to their adopted child.

Image promotion tends to be more effective among people who are already loyal viewers. Consequently, an image spot portraying an anchor or a reporter as warm or caring may have its greatest influence on those who already are loyal viewers. "People who recognize image promotion are the people who already use your product," says Brown.[25] The phenomenon is not unlike soda drinkers who tend to focus on soda ads. The billboards that people recognize, and where they are and what they say, most likely are either very penetrating for some creative reason or they happen to be products that those people already use, says Brown. Image promotion serves the station best on some occasions, but even then the news product may be sufficient to promote the image.

Topical Promotion

Every day, viewers who never or seldom watch a station's newscast tune in throughout the broadcast day to watch other parts of that station's program schedule. As viewers watch the station's other programs, they can be exposed to **topical promotion** — spots that invite viewers to tune into the news for interesting news stories and series reports:

> Project Abuse continues Monday night with a special program for parents . . . helping them understand the threat of sexual abuse their children may be facing. Our adult program offers advice on talking to children about sexual abuse and what to do when children are being abused. For the sake of your children, join us Monday night at eight for a special program for parents, a part of Project Abuse on WCCO Television.[26]

Also known as episodic promotion, or tune-in, topical promotion is effective because nearly all viewers tune away from their favorite news station occasionally, whether to watch another station, even a station they don't prefer, simply for content. Once viewers begin to watch another station, their viewing may become a habit and they may switch loyalties altogether. Raw material for the spots commonly are excerpts from the news reports or are prerecorded specials themselves. Whether the spot amounts to a statement about the station's aggressive news coverage ("you saw it here first") or a series to help women prepare to reenter the workforce, implicit in every topical promotion is the lure, "See what we just did" or "look what we're about to do" (or show you). "Try us — you'll like us."

In their topical promotions, stations strive for subjects that appeal to men and women alike, ideally in as broad an age range as possible. Health and consumer reports that address topics such as car repairs, safe sexual practices, and how to perform the Heimlich maneuver, provide grist for topical promotions that may help generate far larger audiences for the nightly newscasts.

Proof-of-Performance Advertising

The most obvious promotion is to remember to tell people you're doing a good job in ways that benefit the audience. This promotion can be accomplished through spots that show an audience something you've done, such as a helicopter rescue of flood victims, or a mention during the lead-in to an investigative report: "So far

this year, Channel 9 has exposed more than a dozen consumer frauds in the area." Among the most powerful of these tools is the **proof-of-performance** (or proof-of-benefit) spot reminding viewers that the station is living up to its promises. Perhaps the station has carved out a niche as the best spot news station in the area or has positioned itself as the station with the best sports coverage. Thereafter, every time the station scoops the competition with a hot spot news story, or airs outstanding sports coverage, proof-of-performance spots are aired to remind the audience that the station is being faithful to its stated commitment.

In this promotional spot by KOTV-TV, Tulsa, following Memorial Day flooding in Oklahoma, the station strives to illustrate the extent to which it is involved with and concerned about the community.

> These pictures were taken by a stringer (that's a freelance cameraman) of a rescue during Memorial Day weekend flooding. A KOTV cameraman was also on the scene, but he wasn't shooting these pictures. He was the one driving the Eyewitness News truck that was pulling the victim out of the water. It's nice to work somewhere where the priorities are right.[27]

As self-serving as these efforts are, the audience needs to know about the station's significant achievements. A station doesn't have to hide the fact that it's doing a good job. If self-service becomes the news station's primary product, however, audience erosion is inevitable.

Other Promotional Devices

Another promotional device is the news **tease** :

> The city's leading mayoral candidate says she may quit the campaign. The exclusive story tonight on Channel Two at eleven.

Also important is the graphic display of talent credentials, such as the Seal of Approval from the American Meteorological Society, and frequent mention of temperatures and weather conditions gathered from throughout the viewing region by station-recruited "weather watchers" to help establish a greater regional presence. Graphic elements also are crucial to the station's promotion efforts. Consistent graphics showcasing and using theme music as the show opens and closes and at commercial breaks help give the station an easy-to-recognize identity.

CONTENT: THE NEW BATTLEFIELD

Talent, both primary (anchors) and secondary (field reporters), are among any station's most important assets. "Talent glue," the sheer charismatic quality of some anchors, can hold a newscast together even when other elements are less than ideal. Researchers at Kent State University found that viewers who regard the newscasters as "friends" watch the local news more often and perceive the news as more important and realistic than viewers who don't think of the newscasters as friends.[28] It follows naturally that recruiting and developing talent is a high priority at most stations. When programming is mediocre, the most immediate, if short-term, financial return may be gained through talent development and promotion.

In the past, sales and promotion departments sought to build a news image based upon the anchor personalities, with the assumption that audiences judge the newscast by its anchors. Today, though, researchers have reported a gradual drop in the percentage of viewers within news audiences who watch a news show primarily because of an anchor. Today, at most stations, talent alone may not be enough to win the battle for ratings. In part because of the national news consultants, local newscasts have become more homogeneous and more difficult to differentiate from one station to the next.

Although talent provides one way to differentiate the station's look, the industry has awakened to the fact that no matter how you tell it, who tells it, how graphically well it is done, what you tell is important, says Steve Ridge, manager of TV consultation for Frank Magid Associates.[29] Given this view, levels of consistent excellence in all areas of the newscast may be the accurate predictor of long-term audience loyalty — a concept

On-air talent is one of the main sources for a news station's image, but the ultimate test is to provide news that matters to the community.

that holds no one individual as indispensable and that viewers must be offered meaningful, informative, and interesting news content, told in a clear, understandable manner, that they can relate to their own lives.

Typically, the newsroom and the sales department have been deliberately separated. The credibility of news, it is argued, would be damaged irreparably if news content were to be subject to the whims of advertisers. The philosophy was enunciated in a memo that William Paley, founder of CBS, issued to the network in 1954: "An advertiser who sponsors any type of information program produced by us does not thereby purchase or in any way gain, any rights to control the contents of the program."

Yet today, as broadcasters compete for more elusive advertising dollars, some stations, at the request of advertisers, have begun to create news segments and informational broadcasts as vehicles for commercial messages. A health segment that emphasizes jogging and walking is created for a sport shoe manufacturer, for example, or a financial report is sponsored by an investment banking firm.

Targeted Broadcasting

As audiences become fragmented and more viewers drift away from traditional local and network news sources, advertisers hope to reach specific profiles of viewers through an approach called **targeted broadcasting**. Rather than using mass media to reach an entire audience of women aged 25 to 54, advertisers might try to reach only the most affluent women in the group, perhaps 8 or 10 percent of the total population of this group of women. If this most profitable group watches the Arts and Entertainment Network with greater loyalty than either local or network news, advertising dollars will be shifted from news to the A&E Network.

Further, advertisers are more likely to use **bundled media**, incorporating specialized magazines, special-interest TV, and books rather than traditional mass media, to reach these audiences, thereby diverting ever more advertising dollars from mass to specialized media.[30] Inevitably, the mass media themselves are eroded, and by definition become specialized media when they fail to attract at least 40 percent of the available audience.

Another trend is **narrowcasting**, in which stations target their broadcasts at narrowly defined audiences to meet advertiser goals, as when the broadcaster creates a business traveler's weather report for sponsorship by an airline company.[31] Activities such as these prompt fears of possible conflict of interest. Will stations dare to follow the airline-sponsored report with stories that indict the sponsor as the airline with the highest number of late departures and arrivals in the industry?

Psychographics

Advertisers also rely on **psychographics** to determine the values and attitudes of specific audience segments. Rather than lump male viewers demographically into an 18- to 34-age category, for example, market researchers study the individual attitudes and values that drive people to buy specific products. No longer are viewers' age and sex used as the sole predictors of consumer buying choices and behaviors.

Psychographics (or socio-psychographics) include additional variables such as the viewer's lifestyle, self-esteem, religious and political affiliations, and shared values within primary demographic groups. Advertisers use this information to help design commercials that reach specific target audiences, based on their psychographic profile. Program originators also can use psychographics to help identify more effective station promotional campaigns and programming schedules.[32]

MARKET RESEARCH PROBLEMS AND TRAPS

Media organizations use the material covered in this chapter to define themselves, their products, and their markets. Market analysis does have some pitfalls, though. If the basic methodology is flawed, no research is worth the time to print the results on paper. The point of doing research is to get an accurate picture of whatever you are studying. If you approach the problem incorrectly, flawed decisions will be based on illusions.

As a media organization employee, you need to understand what to consider when people start saying things such as, "Our research shows . . ." or, "The research we have clearly demonstrates. . . ." Frequently, market research does not provide finite answers but, rather, strong indications. Also, those doing the research may have a vested interest in a specific outcome. For example, if a news consultant really believes that some news packaging technique or approach to producing newscasts is the best, that consultant may, consciously or subconsciously, skew the research design or resulting data.

Communities vary considerably from one region of the nation to another. Therefore, formula approaches to news may provide quite different results in viewing patterns from one market to another.

Problems with Focus Groups

As discussed earlier in this chapter, many media organizations use focus groups to determine what audiences want in newscasts. The problem arises when media managers develop the incorrect impression that focus groups are decision-making tools. A focus group is useful only in gathering preliminary information so other research techniques, such as telephone or in-person survey interviewing, can be used to probe the identified areas further. Focus groups are only a first step in market research.

Broadcasters, for example, often contract with a consultant to conduct a series of focus groups — perhaps 15 to 20 — all set up to generate audience information. Focus groups do not provide statistical data, though, so the number of focus groups held doesn't mean much in terms of validity of the result.

In addition, focus groups are susceptible to the way the focus group leader, or a particularly strong personality among the participants, guides the discussion. Group dynamics come into play, and some individuals withhold their opinions if they are contrary to the group leader's perceived point of view. Thus, focus groups provide tenuous data, at best. In a broad research program, they are useful in gaining an understanding of the general concerns circulating within a community, but focus groups don't go much further.

Problems with Telephone Surveys

Perhaps the most common research technique used in American media today are telephone surveys, often used to follow up focus group work. Phone surveys are generally inexpensive, fast, and easy to use when targeting specific parts of a community. Where telephone surveys break down is the difficulty of getting what is called "qualitative" data, the kind of thing you learn when you ask a person to "tell me what you think of TV news in Dallas." Open-ended questions like this may generate a wide range of descriptions with nuances of meaning that are not easy to break down into simple categories.

Statistical evaluation is more difficult because complicated answers are difficult to code numerically. Therefore, telephone survey researchers like to use simple questions that ask respondents to agree with one of three to five statements written by the researchers. Although the respondents actually may fall somewhere among the various answers, the forced choice makes them take a position that is somewhat like the way they feel, but not exactly. In survey research, then, the study can be easily skewed at the outset because of the forced choice of answers created by the researchers.

The greatest "real world" methodology problem for telephone surveys is the tendency to limit the research to people who describe themselves as news viewers. That means the research applies only to those people, not to

Television news stations constantly view their competition on TV monitors in the newsroom.

individuals whose viewing habits differ from the researchers' predetermined classification. This gets people into big trouble in the fragmented world of television viewing.

In one major market, a telephone survey was conducted in which respondents were prequalified. People were asked at the outset, "Would you describe yourself as a regular viewer of local television news?" If the answer was "yes," the interview continued. If "no," the person was thanked and the interview was terminated. Initially, some 600 people were called, but after eliminating those who said "no," some 450 full interviews were completed. Statistically, that is a large enough sample to provide useful data.

Results of this survey were curiously parallel to what the Nielsen ratings for the market showed. In fact, the research results virtually mirrored the rating book. Why would that be the case? Because only people who already described themselves as being committed news viewers were included in the survey. And these people naturally agreed with statements describing their favorite station.

The flaw in the research was that it threw out the people who did not describe themselves as regular viewers of local television news. In the market in question, a full 40 percent of viewers at ten o'clock (when the major local news programs aired) were watching other, non-news programming, according to the Nielsen ratings. The research project asked only those who already were fans of specific newscasts to describe what they liked — and they liked what they watched.

The irony in this study is that the viewers who didn't consider themselves regular viewers of local television news are the ones who should have been analyzed. With 40 percent of viewers in that market selecting other programming during newscasts, a substantial uncommitted market remains to be tapped. And, in the case of the market involved in this study, only 10 percent of those uncommitted viewers would have been enough to move the number-three station up to number one. Uncommitted viewers are the easiest ones to get to sample a newscast. Getting loyal viewers to switch from their favorite newscast to another is most difficult.

What's more, you can learn a great deal from people who don't buy your products or, in the case of television programs, tune in. Maybe some of those viewers just don't care about what's going on, but they may have other reasons for not watching local news programs. Viewers who de-select may not think existing local newscasts offer much "news." But how would you know why viewers de-select local news if you don't ask them? Some viewers clearly prefer to watch snakes hatch on the Discovery Channel. Other viewers tune out of local news because it doesn't fulfill their information needs. If they represent a significant number of people, the station possibly can provide for their information wants and needs and win the ratings battle with them.

Whenever you exclude respondents through some qualifying question, you may jeopardize your study seriously. For example, if you were doing a telephone poll late in the last Presidential campaign, would the following be a good thing to have your telephone solicitors ask?

[When respondent answers, ask] "Do you plan to vote for President?"

[If "no," discontinue interview]

You can see that this would give you no information on why a person did not plan to vote, which could tell you a lot about the effectiveness of campaign tactics being used.

Or think about this situation: You work for Pepsi Cola and are trying to figure out how to gain more market share against your arch rival, Coca Cola. You start a telephone survey interview with this prequalification question:

[When respondent answers, ask] "Would you describe yourself as a regular Coke drinker?"

[If "yes," discontinue interview]

That would eliminate all self-described "Coke drinkers" from your sample. If you are doing this survey in the South, that means almost everyone. In that region of the country, "coke" is a generic term that means just about any soft drink available. If you don't do follow-up questions asking what kind of "coke" the person likes, you'll never find out what you really need to know.

In another news study, a national television news consultant asked people to indicate their content preferences for the newscasts they watched. The station involved then was provided a list, in descending order, with the most frequently mentioned preference on top of the list. The station news director then put up the list on large signs at strategic points around the newsroom, including the wall of the conference room, where producers and assignment editors met twice a day to discuss coverage and newscast design. It was titled, "They want . . . ," indicating that the viewers wanted these items in their newscasts.

The news director also sent a memo to all producers indicating that they should try to get at least five items from the list in each of their newscast blocks outside of the time set aside for sports and weather. The topic lists often reflect specific regional concerns. For example, some communities are more concerned than others about weather (number one on the following list). Weather is a bigger deal in North Dakota, Chicago, or Florida during hurricane season than it ever is in Hawaii, where the temperature doesn't change much during the year.

Viewers want:

1. Weather
2. Local issues (stories about neighborhoods)
3. National issues
4. Positive stories
5. Live remote reports during the news
6. Sports stories
7. Needs of the elderly
8. Crime
9. Economic and business stories
10. Medical information
11. Education
12. Consumer stories
13. Investigative reports
14. State government
15. City government
16. Editorials

The problem with this kind of approach is not one of identifying subjects for which a given audience may have a preference. The problem is in attempting to force the findings of a relatively broad research project into story selection for daily newscasts. If you were a producer working in this newsroom, having received the memo and seeing the sign in the conference room, your tendency would be to put a weather story in the top two

news segments of every newscast. But weather comes and goes as a news topic. Many days it's not news. Some days it's very big news.

Trying to do weather as "news" all the time would make you look silly. The same is true of most such topics. Further, when a producer of a half-hour newscast, with a news hole of about ten minutes (after subtracting commercials, sports, and weather) blocks out time for five stories from the list, limited time remains for the rest of the day's events.

The result can be the invention of news. If nothing is going on at five, but we must have a live remote in every five o'clock newscast because the research shows that viewers like live remotes, we end up with reporters standing in front of empty buildings reporting news that happened there three hours earlier. When the gathering market research results in inventing "news," media organizations have moved from reporting to creating events, controversies, and community concerns. Rather than reflecting reality, they become manufacturers of something that may not exist except in the minds of those trying to satisfy viewer expectations and preferences.

News As a Perishable Commodity

As a final consideration regarding research: News is a perishable commodity. It's what is happening today as the course of human events evolves, often unpredictably. Market research is limited by when it is done. After the field information is collected, it is tabulated and analyzed. Weeks after the respondents actually told field workers what they thought about something, it gets to the news director in the form of a consultant's report. That time lag can render even the most rigorous research meaningless.

Consider the example of terrorists who flew passenger jets into New York's World Trade Center towers. Prior to this event, if you had conducted a national survey of Americans with a huge number of respondents, say 10,000, you probably would have elicited little interest in learning more about the political climate in Afghanistan, the threat of terrorist acts on U.S. soil, or a man named Osama bin Laden. When the attacks occurred, however, media coverage created near-instant awareness of the issues, terrorist groups, and personalities.

If you had taken another national survey of Americans in the days following 9/11, again with a huge sample of 10,000 respondents, a significant number of respondents surely would have indicated a desire to know more about the forces behind this story. The course of events clearly has everything to do with what people say they want to know more about.

Reasons for Watching the News

People engage with specific newscasts for many reasons:

1. They like the presenters.

2. They believe a certain station will give them the news they need to know quickly.

3. They trust a specific news source when something vital to their concerns happens, turning to their so-called station of record.

4. They prefer how the station packages and reports the news.

All these things tend to fluctuate, depending on the context of daily life. Market research can provide solid evidence of past performance and a good indication of what probably will help build audience in the future. Researching news audiences, however, is complicated by the very nature of news as being fluid and dynamic.

In sum, any research is only as strong as the methodology used. Looking for the holes in research projects is important. Also important is determining whether the consultants who do that research have any internal agenda. Statistics is a science of using numbers to draw inferences. Playing loose with the numbers is easy, particularly when most people who read the results are not expert statisticians.

When you are faced with a piece of research that makes you wonder about its validity, a good place to check it is your local university. Find a statistician who has no vested interest in the research. Ask that person to look it over and tell you whether it's solid. Those who provide market research commercially do so as a business, and customers may get what the salesperson thinks they want so more business will be forthcoming. That is not to say that market research is always flawed. It is to say that market research always should be questioned, especially when it seems to provide simple answers to complex problems.

WHAT LIES AHEAD?

The "business" of journalism impacts news content and the role of journalism itself. Concern increases as the drive to increase profitability leads stations away from serving the traditional but generic "mass" audiences in favor of content that will attract narrowly defined target audiences. We are already witnessing somewhat of a decline in the appetite for traditional journalism — which historically has addressed society's problems and issues and sought to give a broad understanding about world happenings — as we watch younger generations flock to the Web log (blog) for information of their choosing,

usually focused on entertainment and scandal. What youthful, affluent audience would seek stories about poverty in Third World countries, the aging of America and its impact on the economy, or long-term effects of ignoring environmental issues?

Or perhaps we fail to give viewers enough credit. Perhaps narrowly focused stories will become just one more resource for audiences that seek information in all its diversity. Given the audience research and promotion techniques available to today's communicators, electronic media will continue to changes in both style and substance. As always, it will fall to the journalist — not the advertiser or the general manager — to protect a profession whose stock in trade always has been fairness, accuracy, and balance. Without the traditional integrity of journalism, news media will fail not only as a vehicle for information but as a vehicle for advertising, as well.

ENDNOTES

1. Nielson Media Research, "Trends in Television 2004" via http://www.tvb.org/nav/build_frameset.asp?url=/rcentral/index.asp.

2. "A Nation Online: How Americans Are Expanding Their Use of the Internet," National Telecommunications & Information Administration Report, Feb. 5, 2002 via http://www.ntia.doc.gov/opadhome/digitalnation/.

3. Neilsen, A. C., "US Broadband Penetration Jumps to 45.2% — US Internet Penetration nearly 75% — March 2004 Bandwith Report" http://www.websiteoptimization.com/bw/0403/

4. Nielsen Media Research, "What Ratings Mean, and Other Frequently Asked Questions," May 2000, via http://www.nielsenmedia.com/whatratingsmean/.

5. Nielsen Media Research, "What is a Metered Market," taken from "Frequently Asked Questions" via http://www.nielsenmedia.com 2004.

6. McClellan, Steve, "Fuzzy Math: People Meter Tests Fail to Score with NYC Broadcasters," *Broadcasting & Cable*, March 8, 2004.

7. Nielsen Media Research, "How do you figure out the ratings?" taken from "Frequently Asked Questions," via http://www.neilsenmedia.com 2004.

8. Stevenson, Richard, "The Networks and Advertisers Try to Recapture Our Attention," *New York Times*, Oct. 20, 1985, p. 8E.

9. Downey, Kevin, "Coming to LA, local people meters," Media Life Magazine, Aug. 3, 2003, via http:// www.medialifemagazine.com/news2003/aug03/aug25/2_tues/news3tuesday.html.

10. "Brother Nielsen is Watching," *Time*, June 12, 1989, p. 61.

11. Eggerton, John, "D.C. Not High on Regulating Nielsen," *Broadcasting & Cable*, July 15, 2004.

12. McClellan, Steve, "Fuzzy Math," Note 6.

13. Gough, Paul J. "LPMs have altered the face of local TV business," *The Hollywood Reporter*, December 2, 2004.

14. Sell, Suzanne, "Research: Tracking the News Audience," *RTNDA Communicator*, November 1986, p. 33.

15. "Advertising, Specialty Media and Marketing Services," in the 2004 Veronis Suhler Stevenson Communications Industry Forecast & Report.

16. "Advertising, Specialty Media and Marketing Services," in the 2004 Veronis Suhler Stevenson Communications Industry Forecast & Report.

17. Population Estimates Program, Population Division, U.S. Census Bureau, Washington, DC, via http://www.census.gov/population/estimates/nation/intfile2-1.txt.

18. Cummings, Gary, "Soft-Pedaling the News for Women," *Washington Journalism Review*, August 1986, p. 10.

19. Pfister, Nancy, "Anchors Key to News Program Choice," *Journal of Arkansas Journalism Studies* (Little Rock, AR: University of Arkansas, Department of Journalism), 2:2, Fall/Spring 1985-86, pp. 9–10.

20. Kellogg, Stuart, "The 50 Percent Solution: Marketing Your TV News Product Effectively and Efficiently," RTNDA 40th Annual International Conference, Nashville, TN, September 11–14, 1985.

21. Kellogg, "50 Percent Solution," Note 20.

22. Trigoboff, Dan, "Nielsen Grows Local People Meter: Measurement will be in top 10 markets by 2005" *Broadcasting & Cable*, March 3, 2003.

23. Kellogg, "50 Percent Solution," Note 20.

24. Kellogg, "50 Percent Solution," Note 20.

25. Kellogg, "50 Percent Solution," Note 20.

26. Kellogg, "50 Percent Solution," Note 20.

27. Kellogg, "50 Percent Solution," Note 20.

28. "Making Friends With Your Audience," RTNDA Intercom, 3(4), February 1986, p. 4. (Project conducted by Dr. Alan Rubin and Robert Powell, School of Speech Communications, and by doctoral candidate Elizabeth Perse.)

29. Cummings, Gary, "TV Consultants Earn Their Keep," *Washington Journalism Review*, 42, December 1986.

30. Levine, Joshua, "The Last Gasp of Mass Media?" *Forbes*, Sept. 17, 1990.

31. Cummings, Gary, "The Watershed in Local TV News," *Gannett Center Journal* (Gannett Center for Media Studies, Columbia University), Vol. 1, No. 1, Spring 1987, pp. 40–41.

32. Sherer, Jill, "Psychographics Define Audience's Values," *Electronic Media*, Dec. 18, 1989, p. 70.

EXERCISE 12A: Television News Research

Name _____ Date _____

1 As part of a class discussion or assigned paper, share your views about whether broadcast news is an "information service" or a "consumer product." Contrast your view with the notion that the news department's "real product" is the viewing audience and that the station's "true audience" is made up of paying advertisers.

2 Prepare a paper on the primary research methods and hardware that research companies use to determine broadcast audience size and composition.

3 Discuss the difference between audience rating and share. Tell which is most desirable, a large rating or a large share, and explain why.

4 Explain the role of news consultants in helping a broadcast organization attain ratings dominance in news. As part of your explanation, include a discussion of the anchor's role in attracting and holding an audience.

5 Describe news sweeps, and explain the potential impacts of sweeps, both negative and positive, on news content and promotion.

6 Consider the various methods research companies measure television use (market share, personal diaries, people meters). Which method do you think is the most effective and why? Is it possible to really know exactly what people are watching and what just may be turned "on" on the television? Explain your answer.

7 Describe the differences between image advertising and product promotion, including as part of your response an evaluation of the relative costs involved, the probable impact, and the audiences most commonly reached with each form of promotion.

8 Describe and provide examples of all proof-of-performance advertising you observe while watching commercial television news stations in your area over a one-week period. Discuss your findings in class.

9 Discuss the approaches called narrowcasting and targeted broadcasting, and examine their potential impact on traditional local and network news programs.

Critical Thinking Questions

Directions: The following questions are provided to help you examine the deeper meanings and complexities of the various issues under discussion. After a thoughtful review of the subject at hand, answer each question to the best of your ability.

1. Journalists and managers differ in their definitions of "product" and "audience." Journalists view their "product" as reporting and their "audience" as viewers. Managers and advertisers, on the other hand, commonly view their "product" as audience and their audience as "advertisers." What, in your view, are the proper definitions for "product" and "audience?"

2. What are the positive and negative influences of ratings and circulation upon American journalism? What is the value of ratings and circulation to news readers and viewers?

3. How accurate can national ratings surveys be when a few thousand respondents represent millions of media users? Explain in detail.

4. If a news organization follows the desires of its audience for content, it runs a risk of "creating" news to appeal to the public. Explain what this means and why it can be a serious problem.

5. To what extent do you believe news organizations have an obligation to serve their audiences, even if it means earning little or no profit. What scenarios can you imagine when a station does not profit from airing a program or report?

6. What positive and negative effects do recommendations from news consultants have on news content, treatment, and selection? What influence do personalities have in news presentation?

7. What is the nature of news marketing and promotion? How do they differ, if at all, from the marketing and promotion of other consumer goods and services? As part of your answer, include whether news is simply an information product or a consumer service, and justify your viewpoint.

Self-Review Questions

Directions: Each of the self-review questions below addresses information contained in this chapter. Answer each question to the best of your ability, then review the chapter as necessary to further strengthen your understanding of each concept or issue.

1. What are the roles of commercial newscasts, respectively, as a "product" and as a "service?" Provide examples to support your observations.

2. How can a sample of a few thousand people accurately reflect the viewing habits of millions of people? Explain specifically.

3. How are local people meters likely to change the traditional "sweeps" periods?

4. How is Internet use measured?

5. How is focus-group research conducted? What is the value of this research?

6. What is the difference between rating and share?

7. Which would yield a larger total audience, a high rating or a high share? Why?

8. What are the news consultant's various activities, and what probable positive and potential negative outcomes do these activities have?

9. What is the role of news anchors in attracting and holding larger audiences?

10. What is the role and impact of news marketing and promotion upon news selection, treatment, and presentation?

## CHAPTER THIRTEEN

Legal Considerations

To understand the legal framework of electronic forms of journalism requires a sense of the industry's major historical developments. Related considerations are those of ethics and professionalism, discussed in Chapter 14, which give the industry credibility, and encompass privacy, fairness, and personal conduct.

Regulating the electronic media today is more complicated because of the Internet. While print media have enjoyed less government interference, broadcast media have remained on a rather tight leash. And just where the Internet fits into the legal framework of the "press" has frustrated the government, legal experts, and communications industry executives alike.

HISTORICAL BACKGROUND

Electronic media never have been as free from government regulation as the print media. Although some restrictions of broadcast media were swept away in the 1980s, many remain. The rise of cable television in the last two decades, along with the evolution of the Internet, has changed the debate surrounding electronic media forms. Regulation of the technical side of new media forms is one arena of concern. Another is how, or whether, to regulate content.

> *A word is not a crystal, transparent and unchanged; it is the skin of a living thought and may vary greatly in color and content according to the circumstances and time in which it is used.*
>
> JUSTICE OLIVER WENDELL HOLMES
> Town v. Eisner, 245 U.S. 418, 425 (1918)

In the pre-cable and pre-Internet days, the rationale for governmental involvement in broadcasting grew literally out of the air. The justification for strong government regulation came from the assumption that the airwaves are public property in much the same way as a river or a public park. Given the limited number of frequencies available for broadcast signals, government therefore had a responsibility to act as a representative of the public. By Congressional mandate, government regulators were required to license those broadcasters who best served the public "interest, convenience, and necessity."

The Communication Acts

The first major attempt to regulate came in the wake of the Titanic's sinking in 1912 amid reports that shipboard wireless operators might have summoned help earlier and loss of life would have been less dramatic if the airwaves had not been jammed. The Radio Act of 1912 gave government the right to allocate licenses and wavelengths to anyone who applied. Yet, the law gave the Secretary of Commerce little enforcement power if stations did not stick to assigned frequencies.

The woman evangelist Aimme Semple McPherson, for example, operated a pioneer radio station from her temple in Los Angeles during the early 1920s. The station wandered all over the dial. After repeated warnings, a government inspector ordered that the station be closed down. Secretary of Commerce Herbert Hoover received the following telegram from McPherson:

> Please order your minions of Satan to leave my station alone. You cannot expect the Almighty to abide to your wavelength nonsense. When I offer my prayers to Him, I must fit into his wave reception. Open this station at once.

Unlike McPherson, a number of early broadcasters asked for government regulation when radio was still in the experimental stages. Broadcasters wanted a traffic police officer, someone to bring order out of the engineering chaos caused by wandering signals. The radio audience never knew if the station it wanted would be disturbed by another station's signals. To make radio profitable for advertisers that were increasingly interested in the new medium, broadcasters requested stronger regulation.

The result was the Radio Act of 1927, which became the foundation for the Communications Act of 1934, the law governing contemporary broadcasting. The Communications Act transferred the regulation of broadcasting from the Department of Commerce to a new, independent regulatory agency, the Federal Communications Commission. The FCC would regulate communication sent by wires, cables, or radio. The agency had much broader powers to cover additional broadcasting technology.

The Telecommunications Act

Since 1934, numerous congressional amendments have been added, culminating with the 1996 Telecommunications Act, which sought to minimize government interference in the broadcast communications industry. With the exception of the Communications Decency Act, which attempts to establish boundaries on sexually explicit and violent material accessible to children via the electronic media, the 1996 law adopted a "hands-off" approach to government regulation.

The Scarcity Doctrine

While Congress has struggled with legislation regarding electronic media regulation, the courts have played their part in the confusion over the past few decades. In 1969, the U.S. Supreme Court issued its **scarcity doctrine,** which justified government regulation of the broadcast media because of scarce availability of the airwaves.[1] But four years later, in *CBS v. The Democratic National Committee,* the Supreme Court considered broadcast news to be as worthy as print news of full First Amendment protection. Justice William O. Douglas wrote for the majority:

> My conclusion is that the TV and radio stand in the same protected position under the First Amendment as do newspapers and magazines. The philosophy of the First Amendment requires that result, for the fear that Madison and Jefferson had of government intrusion is perhaps even more relevant to TV and radio than it is to newspapers and other like publications.[2]

Deregulation

As the 1970s came to an end, the FCC realized that the courts were not sympathetic to complete government control over the electronic media, so it began moving in the opposite direction, making the 1980s a decade of deregulation. At the same time, the Commission encouraged the development of new electronic media, such as direct broadcast satellite, multi-channel distribution systems, and low-power television.

Despite these moves, the Supreme Court showed it was not ready to relinquish total control of the electronic media. In 1984, Supreme Court Justice William Brennan noted:

> The prevailing rationale for broadcast regulation based upon spectrum scarcity has come under increasing criticism. . . . We are not prepared, however, to reconsider our longstanding approach without some signal from Congress or the FCC that technological developments have advanced so far that some revision of the system of broadcast regulation may be required.[3]

The Entrance of Cable TV

When cable TV entered the broadcast scene in the early 1980s, the courts were faced with a broadcast system that did not use the airwaves, thereby killing the scarcity rationale for regulation. In 1979 the FCC tried to exercise editorial control over cable channels by requiring that cable companies set aside certain channels for public access programming. The U.S. Supreme Court sided with the cable companies but chose not to address First Amendment implications in its opinion. Instead, the Court argued that the FCC had no power to impose "common carrier" status on cable or broadcast communications.[4]

A similar issue with cable regulation appeared again in the 1990s, forcing the Supreme Court in 1995 to determine whether cable belonged to the print model or the broadcast model for legal matters. In the fall of 1992, Congress passed the Cable Consumer Protection and Competition Act, which, among other things, required cable companies to carry all local broadcast signals. Turner Broadcasting — owner of CNN, Headline News, and TNT — immediately challenged the **must-carry rules.** These regulations reduced the number of channels available for cable networks.

The U.S. District Court upheld the must-carry rules despite Turner Broadcasting's claim that the must-carry provision is content-based and favors one speaker (broadcasters) over another (cable operators). In a 5–4 decision, the U.S. Supreme Court supported the theory behind the must-carry rules but remanded the case to the lower court for factual development. Justice Anthony Kennedy said the lower court must compile

The Federal Communications Commission was successful in arguing that the scarcity-of-airwave spectrum necessitated regulatory control over broadcast media, but it has had difficulty extending such control to cable and satellite media because "airwaves" are not an issue.

evidence that without the must-carry rules, cable operators would drop broadcast stations. The government's justification for the regulation is the potential monopoly of cable stations to prevent subscribers from access to other broadcast programming.

In this age of speedy, high-tech access to information, the law inevitably lags behind its development and implementation. The government and judicial system, working within the confines of bureaucratic protocol, rarely can keep pace with the evolution of communications systems. This chapter highlights the major developments, past and current, in the regulation of the telecommunications industry.

THE FAIRNESS DOCTRINE

From 1949 until 1987, the **Fairness Doctrine** required broadcasters to devote reasonable time to covering controversial issues of public importance, and to do so fairly by providing a reasonable opportunity for contrasting opinions to be aired on those issues. This was one of the major regulatory statements of the FCC that affected working broadcast journalists. In essence, the FCC said that, to operate in the public interest, a station had to report on important controversial issues and had to do so fairly.

The FCC regulated content with the Fairness Doctrine for nearly 40 years. In its 1985 Fairness Report, however, the agency indicated that it wanted to abolish the doctrine. The FCC got the green light to move ahead with its plan when the D.C. Court of Appeals ruled in 1986 that Congress had "permitted" fairness regulations but had not "mandated" them.

In 1987 the FCC ruled the Fairness Doctrine obsolete because of the massive number and variety of other information sources. FCC commissioners decided they no longer needed to monitor the editorial decisions of broadcasters by outlining how to air diverse views, a policy upheld by the U.S. Supreme Court in its 1969 Red Lion case. In 1989, the U.S. Court of Appeals for the D.C. Circuit agreed with the FCC's decision to drop the Fairness Doctrine.[5]

A federal appeals court in 1993 narrowly affirmed the FCC's position that abolishing the Fairness Doctrine meant that broadcast stations no longer had to provide equal coverage for ballot issues.[6] The Committee Against Amendment 2 complained to the FCC that KARK-TV in Little Rock had not sufficiently covered the opponents of a 1990 ballot proposal to change interest rates for consumer credit and loans. The FCC said that, even though it had not mentioned referenda or initiatives

> *I am returning herewith without my approval S742, the "Fairness in Broadcasting Act of 1987," which would codify the so-called Fairness Doctrine. . . . This type of content-based regulation . . . is, in my judgment, antagonistic to the freedom of expression guaranteed by the First Amendment.*
> RONALD REAGAN, U.S. PRESIDENT, 1987

specifically when it first abolished the Fairness Doctrine in 1987, it concluded that the doctrine hampered broadcasters in discussing controversial public issues, which would include ballot issues.

The Committee and the Arkansas AFL-CIO appealed the FCC's ruling to the Eighth Circuit. The majority opinion said elimination of the Fairness Doctrine was under the FCC's authority because it was a commission policy, not a statutory requirement. Ever since the FCC abolished the Fairness Doctrine in 1987, Congress has tried to counter the action by amending the text of the 1934 Communications Act. In 1987 President Ronald Reagan vetoed such legislation.

New language again was rejected in 1991 after the Senate introduced a bill designed to make the Fairness Doctrine law. A 1994 congressional campaign to add the Fairness Doctrine was halted after pressure from listeners of talk shows and religious broadcasts. Conservative talk show host Rush Limbaugh helped defeat the campaign when he told listeners the measure would cripple talk radio and force political correctness.[7]

Despite the end of the Fairness Doctrine, two sections of the 1934 Communications Act remain, dictating the amount of freedom that broadcast stations have when it comes to political programming. Section 315 outlines equal opportunity rules for political candidates, and Section 312 stipulates that stations must provide reasonable access for political candidates.

POLITICAL CANDIDATES AND EQUAL OPPORTUNITY

Section 315 of the Communications Act specifically concerns fairness in political broadcasting, and it gives precise regulations of that content. The major thrust of the section says:

> If any licensee shall permit any person who is a legally qualified candidate for any public office to use a broadcasting station, he shall afford equal opportunities to all other such candidates for that office in the use of such broadcasting station, provided that such licensee shall have no power of censorship over the material broadcast

under the provisions of this section. No obligation is hereby imposed upon any licensee to allow the use of its station by any such candidate.

This law applies to both free and commercial time given by a station. The rules for what constitutes a "legally qualified candidate" include announcement of intention to run, qualifications for holding the office for which the candidate is running, and either qualification for the ballot or a "substantial showing of being a bona-fide candidate." Furthermore, if one candidate uses the station's facilities to produce a program, any other candidate for the same office has the same right. This section applies only to the political candidates and not the candidates' spokespersons.

The FCC has said the law requires equal opportunities, which may not be the same as equal time. The time of day, as well as the amount of time, must be considered because of differences in audience size and makeup. Section 315 does not require broadcasters to provide any time at all, nor does it require broadcasters to notify legally qualified candidates of their opponents' broadcasts. Instead, the candidate must ask for time within a week of the first appearance by the political opponent.

There is also no right of censorship under Section 315 even if content is racist, vulgar, or libelous. Although broadcasters cannot be held liable for remarks over which they have no control, candidates themselves can be held legally accountable.

An Atlanta television station discovered the rigidity of this "no censorship" provision in 1992 when it aired a candidate's graphic anti-abortion message in the early evening. The station refused to air a responding 30-minute video, "Abortion in America — the Real Story," the following Sunday between 4 and 5 p.m., but the station agreed to air the program after midnight. Though the FCC and the U.S. District Court sided with the station's decision because the material was indecent, the District of Columbia U.S. Circuit Court of Appeals reversed, saying the station was violating the "no censorship" rule of Section 315, as well as the candidate's right of access provided in Section 312.

Section 315 is predicated upon "use" of the airwaves, but what constitutes "use" under the law has sometimes been a tricky decision. The FCC considers any presentation that features a candidate's voice or image to be "use." Simply stating a candidate's record or stand on the issues is not considered use. Neither is the use of a candidate's image or voice in an opponent's ad. Most other appearances, however, count as use, including appearances on TV sitcoms, feature films, or entertainment talk shows.

During the 1980 and 1984 presidential campaigns, for example, any movies with actor-turned-President Ronald Reagan were considered "use" and other candidates were required to be given that much free airtime. Similarly, movies starring actor Arnold Schwarzenegger qualified as "use" when the actor ran for governor of California in 2003.

Congress has identified four exceptions to the meaning of the term "use" where political candidates are concerned. Appearances on bona fide newscasts, news interview shows, news documentaries, or broadcast news events are exempt from Section 315 requirements.

The FCC considers appearances on network news shows, local news programs and even interview shows such as "Oprah Winfrey" and "Montel Williams" to be legitimate newscasts and therefore not under Section 315. However, if a newscaster is running for political office, his or her appearance does constitute "use" and stations would be required to offer equal time to opposing candidates.[8]

A more troublesome category for the FCC is the so-called news interview show. The FCC has defined a bona fide news interview program as one that is regularly scheduled and is under the journalistic control of the producers. The "Donahue Show" sought and received an exemption from Section 315 requirements in 1984. The FCC based its decision on whether the show's host could control discussion. In Donahue's case, the agency agreed he could.

Likewise, candidates' appearances on "Meet the Press" would not be considered "use" because it is a regular program in which political figures appear with nationally known journalists to discuss news events. But a show created during political campaigning designed for the audience to meet various candidates would be considered "use" and subject to Section 315.

Any appearance at a bona fide news event is not considered "use" and does not invoke Section 315. A candidate who happens to be at the scene of a spot news story and is interviewed for a news story does not equal "use." The FCC considers political conventions, debates between political candidates, and press conferences to all be bona fide news events not subject to "use" under Section 315.

At first, only non-broadcast organizations could sponsor debates that would be considered news events. In 1983 the FCC broadened the exemption to include broadcaster-sponsored debates. In 1988, the FCC added debates sponsored by political parties, and a year later it added debates sponsored by candidates themselves, as bona fide news events exempt from Section 315.

In 1980, Sen. Ted Kennedy, challenged the FCC's rule that press conferences were news events. Kennedy, who was running against President Jimmy Carter for the Democratic Party nomination, argued that Carter's press conferences designated "use" and Kennedy should be given equal time. But the networks, the FCC, and the U.S. Court of Appeals agreed that a live press conference is a bona fide news event.[9]

POLITICAL CANDIDATES AND ACCESS

Section 312 (a) (7) maintains that broadcasters must allow candidates reasonable access to local airwaves. The requirement is meant to prevent broadcasters from refusing to sell advertising time as a result of their having to offer candidates the lowest advertising rate 45 days before a primary and 60 days before a general election under Section 315. Repeated violations of this candidate access law could result in loss of the station's license. Under Section 312 (a) (7), stations can give either free time or commercial time, or both, but they must make time available for political advertising during prime viewing or listening hours. The commission said, however, that stations do not have to ignore contracts with commercial sponsors to give candidates their choice of broadcast time, and they do not have to sell odd blocks of time to accommodate a candidate's message that would complicate the normal program schedule.[10]

In September 1999, the FCC required broadcast stations to allow political candidates to buy longer airtime so they could provide more detailed information about their campaigns. Previously, the FCC forbade political ads to be longer than commercial advertisements.

Political access to the airwaves has been somewhat hampered by campaign finance reform that went into effect in 2003. The primary purpose of the new law was to limit "soft money" contributions to political campaigns that were unregulated by the Federal Elections Commission. First Amendment advocates argued that the law's restrictions on soft money contributions used for political advertising is a free-speech violation. In a 5–4 decision, the Supreme Court said it believed the restrictions to be narrow and necessary for preventing political corruption in campaign finance.[11]

Without a doubt, no other regulatory statement has generated as much controversy as the Fairness Doctrine during its almost 40-year lifetime and in the decades since its demise. As recently as the 2004 election season, FCC Chairman and Senator John McCain (R-Arizona), called on the networks to expand their election coverage to include more reports on campaign issues and fewer stories on the latest polls. McCain even threatened to push for reviving the Fairness Doctrine if broadcasters did not improve their coverage of the presidential campaign.[12]

Those who oppose the Fairness Doctrine say it "chills" speech — the opposite of its stated intention — because broadcasters stay away from controversial subjects for fear of failing to represent all viewpoints. Those who favor the Fairness Doctrine and argue it should become a federal law insist that the regulation only told journalists to do what good reporters say they do anyway: Give the public balanced coverage of important, controversial issues.

STAGED NEWS

Staging news events — falsifying or re-creating an event for a newscast — has become more of an issue as competition among media has heightened. Ratings are ever-important, and without the "breaking news" or "special report" or "exclusive," television newscasts risk losing viewers. There has yet to be a staged event quite like Orson Wells's 1938 radio production on CBS of "War of the Worlds," which simulated an alien invasion in New York City. But staged news events unfortunately have been fairly common in broadcast news history.

In 1969, an FCC investigation of news staging held up the broadcast license renewal of the CBS-owned Chicago station WBBM-TV. A reporter filmed a "pot party" by Northwestern University students to show the prevalence of marijuana on a college campus. The reporter was a recent Northwestern graduate, and charges of staging were levied against the reporter and the station. A station ultimately is responsible for everything it airs except political broadcasts.

Generally, though, the FCC has tended not to be too hard on the station for what a reporter has done. Actually, the FCC usually tries to avoid involvement in staging or slanting charges. Although the FCC will investigate charges that tape has been edited to give a dishonest or false impression, considerable evidence of a deliberate attempt to stage or slant a news event is required before the FCC will become involved. The penalty for violation can be refusal to renew the station license — the most severe penalty the FCC can assess. In the case of WBBM, however, the FCC held up the license renewal for 18 months. Legal fees cost the station hundreds of thousands of dollars.

An investigative report on NBC's *Dateline* November 17, 1992, staged an explosion to show how easily a GMC truck could blow up if hit in a collision. *Dateline* reporters added explosives to speed up the effect for the television audience, and General Motors filed suit against the network. NBC News president Michael Gardner, who resigned over the incident, wrote an on-air apology that saved NBC from going to court but could not prevent it from suffering a credibility setback.

In January 1997, a federal jury in North Carolina awarded a $5.5 million judgment to the Food Lion grocery chain for a report that appeared on the November 7, 1992, broadcast of *Prime Time Live*. Although the report was not staged, two reporters pretended to be employees of the chain so as to secretly videotape unsanitary methods of handling meat and deli food.

CBS POLICY ON STAGED NEWS

CBS has spelled out in its 1971 "Operating Standards: News and Public Affairs" its policy against staging news events. The following excerpt is taken from that policy, which was submitted to Congress in 1972 during hearings in the House of Representatives regarding the rigging of programs on television.

"It is essential that CBS personnel not stage, or contribute to the staging — however slight — of any news event or story. Specifically, nothing should be done that creates an erroneous impression of time, place, event, person or fact.

There are some events such as, speeches, press conferences and demonstrations of various types which occur only because coverage by the press is anticipated. The sole factor that determines whether any such event shall be covered is, of course, the basic newsworthiness of the event. But personnel should be alert at all times to the possibility that attempts may be made to "use" CBS cameras and microphones.

Coverage should be as inconspicuous as possible. If, in the course of covering riots, demonstrations, rallies or similar events, it becomes obvious that, but for the presence of cameras, disorders would not be taking place, or would diminish sizably, or terminate, the cameras should be capped or removed. On-the-spot judgments by producers, correspondents, reporters or cameramen that a situation may be eased by capping or removing the cameras will be fully respected."

Inquiry into alleged rigging of television news programs (Serial No. 92-96). Hearings before the Special Subcommittee on Investigations of the Committee on Interstate and Foreign Commerce, House of Representatives, Ninety-Second Congress, Second Session, May 17, 18, and 23, 1972. Washington, DC: US Government Printing Office.

Despite the truth in the investigative report, the jury found ABC liable for fraud.[13] However, the 4th Circuit Court of Appeals threw out the $315,000 reduced judgment, arguing that no fraud existed because Food Lion could not prove injury over the reporters lying to get hired.

LIBEL

Traditionally, **libel** laws have been among the most pervasive of all the restraints on broadcast news. The courts have defined libel as published defamation that damages the reputation, not character, of an individual. In all libel cases, the person suing must prove that the media were guilty of some degree of fault.

Does "published" mean the broadcaster is exempt from this restraint? No. The courts have ruled generally that because a broadcast is disseminated to a mass audience and often is from a written script, it is libel. A study by the Media Law Resource Center found that libel suits against newspapers dropped in the last 25 years while the number of libel suits against broadcasters rose slightly over the same time period.[14] The good news is that, according to the study, the news media as a whole have been more successful in winning libel suits against them — from 35.6 percent of trials won in the 1980s to 54 percent of trials won since 2000.

Civil and, in some instances, criminal libel are covered by state law. Thus, each state has its own libel regulations. You should be familiar with the law in your state. State laws, however, must be in harmony with the U.S. Constitution as interpreted ultimately by U.S. Supreme Court decisions. These decisions provide guidelines for working journalists in all states. Knowing these general guidelines will help you to understand and avoid libel problems.

The plaintiff (the individual suing for libel) must prove at least four elements:

1. **Publication.** The report is communicated to a third party. With broadcast news, this is assumed.

2. **Identification.** The libel subject does not have to be named in order to be identified. A detailed description, a well-known nickname, or even the person's occupation could suffice. If a person is the only football coach in town, there is no question who is being spoken about. Likewise, a clear image of a person also be considered sufficient identification. This is particularly a problem when general video shots are used for footage with voice-overs that may refer to reputation-damaging behavior. For example, a story reporting increased drug use among white men in their 40s could be problematic if general video shown during statements about drug use corresponds with identifiable images of white men in their 40s. If any man in the video is identifiable to his community, and he can prove that the report implied he was among the drug users, the station is likely to lose a libel suit.

3. **Defamation.** A person's reputation — not his/her character — is damaged by the report and can be proved as such. Character refers to who you are; reputation refers to who people think you are.

4. **Fault.** Public persons suing over stories about public issues have to prove actual malice by the journalist — knowing falsity or reckless disregard for the truth, a constitutional standard set forth in *New York Times* v. *Sullivan*, a landmark case that will be discussed later in this section. States are allowed to determine the degree of fault a private person must prove, as long as the courts do not impose liability without some showing of fault. In most states, private individuals must prove simple or gross negligence, which is defined in various state libel cases.

Usually, plaintiffs bringing a libel suit must also prove the information is false. A plaintiff considered to be a public person — such as a government official, a celebrity, a prominent community leader — must prove the statement is false. But a private person usually has to prove falsity only if the statement involves a matter of public concern.[15]

Libel can be of two types:

1. *Libel per se* — words that are damaging on their face (e.g., thief, liar, traitor). There is no universal list of words considered defamatory, so courts must consider the specific words and context within each situation. Precedents will exist within communities or states or circuits, but times change and the meaning of words can change.

2. *Libel per quod* — damage by extrinsic circumstances not included in the story or by innuendo. In a Tennessee case, a reporter wrote that a woman shot her husband, who was in the home of a woman who lived next door. The reporter did not include the fact that the woman's husband and several other persons also were present. The sexual innuendo amounted to libel per quod.

New York Times v. Sullivan

The single most important requirement coming out of the 1964 Supreme Court ruling in *New York Times* v. *Sullivan* is that the defamation of a public figure must be made with actual malice.[16] This means that the First Amendment will protect even false and defamatory statements made about a public official's public conduct unless the official can prove that the media defendant published the material with knowledge that it was false or with reckless disregard to finding the truth.

The *Times* case involved L. B. Sullivan, Montgomery Police Commissioner in the early 1960s, who said he had been defamed by an ad in the *Times*. The full-page editorial advertisement, titled "Heed Their Rising Voices," said thousands of civil rights activists were being met with police brutality, citing numerous incidents that involved the Montgomery police. Sullivan, though not named in the ad, brought a libel suit in Alabama and won in state supreme court.

The *Times* appealed to the U.S. Supreme Court, which reversed in a landmark decision. Justice William Brennan said Alabama's libel law was unconstitutional because it relied on the rule of strict liability, which did not require a showing of fault but, instead, required only that the statements were published and that they were about Sullivan. The ruling acknowledged that some of the statements in the ad were incorrect, but the Court stated that some false claims would be allowed in the interest of promoting open, robust debate on matters of social and political importance, such as civil rights and brutality being committed against blacks in the South.

The significance of *Sullivan* is that the Court recognized the key issue: Public officials were criticized for their handling of civil rights efforts, and the state courts were trying to punish the press for this public embarrassment. So the Supreme Court contended that to keep open and robust debate and to allow the press its constitutional freedom from fear of censorship, criticism of public officials must be guarded. So the Court created the "actual malice" standard, stating that a public official was maliciously libeled by the press.

Actual malice is defined as journalists printing known falsities or failing to investigate the truth prior to publication. This actual malice standard applies to public officials, public figures, and limited public figures. **Limited public figures** are individuals who could be considered public figures in a limited context or who have voluntarily placed themselves in the public limelight for a specific issue.

Whether the actual malice standard applies to private plaintiffs who are suing mass-media defendants depends on state law. In most states, private persons are only required to prove negligence, but a few states require private plaintiffs to prove a higher degree of fault — such as gross negligence or even actual malice — if suing over a matter of public interest.

In addition, state courts often cannot permit recovery of presumed or punitive damages (usually the larger damage awards) unless the plaintiff proves actual malice. A private figure who fails to meet this tougher standard of fault can collect damages that compensate him or her only for actual injury. You can search the latest Supreme Court libel ruling in your state to find out fault requirements for private individuals.

Libel Defenses

Some situations may exonerate the communicator of libel. The three principal libel defenses are truth, privilege, and fair comment.

Truth. Truth is the best defense possible, but this defense is not always usable because it is so difficult to prove. Proof of truth comes mostly from people who are not connected with the station, because journalists seldom witness the actual event. The journalist must be able to use sources to prove the truth if needed. Thus, doctors, lawyers, and ministers might prove to be dangerous sources because they would not have to testify about information obtained from a client's privileged communication.

In using the truth as a defense, objectivity is tested. A journalist who fails to cover both sides of a story or to check information thoroughly runs the risk of showing carelessness and indifference to others' rights. Journalists cannot afford such negligence.

Privilege. Of the three principal defenses, privilege is the most complicated because what is privileged material in one state may not be in another. Members of the judicial, legislative, and executive branches of government at all levels are granted an "absolute privilege" of protection for any libelous statements and documents used in official proceedings. This protection does not exist in unofficial forums and for certain records. For instance, police dockets in some states are not privileged.

Journalists are granted "qualified privilege" for fair, accurate, and complete accounts taken from an official record or proceeding, even if libelous. Journalists sometimes err by reporting defamatory comments made outside the official meeting — for instance, in a hallway during a court proceeding. Even though some courts have allowed the defense of privilege at open public meetings involving unions, political parties, chambers of commerce, and the like, in which public issues were discussed, there is no guarantee of privilege in these instances. If journalists consider airing potentially libelous material from these forums, they should exercise caution and seek legal counsel first.

Fair Comment. Journalists traditionally have criticized the actions of people and institutions affecting the public's interests. Entertainment activities such as plays, concerts, political addresses, and sporting events have been written and talked about in a variety of ways. And the Supreme Court has ruled that statements of pure opinion on matters of public interest are protected by the First Amendment.[17] Since the emergence of this constitutional protection of opinion, the use of the common-law fair comment defense in libel suits is less powerful but is still a defense. The fair comment defense requires the court to ask three questions:

1. Is it an opinion statement (a statement that can be proved true or false)?

2. Does the statement focus on a subject of public interest?

3. Is there factual basis for the comment?

A good rule for journalists is to always bolster reports and commentaries with facts. If a commentary contains a libelous remark, courts will be more likely to consider it "fair comment" if it included statements of facts as evidence of the opinion.

PRIVACY

A much more recent concept in terms of legal development is privacy law. Privacy, the concept that a person has the right to be left alone, began evolving in the 1880s but was discussed first in a Harvard Law Review article by two young Boston lawyers, Louis Brandeis and Samuel Warren, in 1890. Their article was a reaction to snooping and prying by the press into private lives of prominent Boston citizens, themselves included. New York state enacted the first privacy law in 1903, but the concept was slow to catch on in many states. Now, however, almost all 50 states and the District of Columbia recognize a legal right to privacy — either through statutes or through common-law precedent.

Four areas of privacy concern people working in the media.

1. *False light* involves distortions or fictionalizations that would be highly offensive to a reasonable person. This could happen by running a videotape of a person without his or her permission, to illustrate a story that has nothing to do with the individual. Another way this type of invasion of privacy might occur is by embellishing the facts. False-light invasion of privacy sounds a lot like libel and requires the plaintiff to prove actual malice when the story is a matter of public concern.

2. *Publication of embarrassing private facts* is a tort still not recognized in some states. This type involves the broadcast of non-newsworthy, private,

embarrassing facts that are highly offensive to a reasonable person. One such case involved a man who deflected the gun from a person attempting to shoot former President Gerald Ford. Later news stories referred to him as a homosexual, and he sued for publication of embarrassing, private facts. He lost the case, with the court noting that he had been involved prominently and publicly in gay rights activities in San Francisco. Facts that an individual already has made public willingly cannot be considered private. Journalists, however, must be careful to weigh the news value of potentially embarrassing facts about the lives of private individuals.

In another case, a Pittsburgh Steelers fan convinced a *Sports Illustrated* photographer to take his picture during a game but sued the publication for embarrassing private facts when the published photo revealed that his fly was open. The district court ruled against the fan because he was in a public place and had asked for his picture to be taken.[18]

A more serious situation involves publication of rape victims' names. Though many news media organizations have specific ethical policies on what to do with such information, their legal right allows publication or broadcast of names found on official government documents such as police reports or court records. The Supreme Court made this clear in a 1975 case involving an Atlanta television station. Though four states at the time, including Georgia, had statutes making it illegal to reveal the names, the Supreme Court said the press is not invading an individual's privacy when it reports information that is already part of the public record.[19]

3. *Appropriation* involves taking a person's name or likeness for commercial purposes without the individual's consent, which usually occurs in the context of advertising. The area in which this invasion of privacy issue affects broadcast news the most is through local and network news self-promotion. For example, when a local news station puts together a one-minute promo of its 10 p.m. newscast and news team, it typically shows shots of reporters and anchors in previously aired news reports.

The Booth rule, as courts have called it, allows news media to have clips that include individuals who were part of the news that is being referenced in the promotion without calling it an invasion of privacy through appropriation.[20] News media are barred from implying such individuals endorse their product or broadcast without permission, but the mere use of a previous news story in promotional media is not a violation of appropriation.

4. *Trespassing* or intrusion may occur as a result of a journalist's conduct in newsgathering. A journalist can be found guilty whether he or she actually airs any information or footage obtained. The act of intruding, either physically or with a hidden camera or microphone, may be enough to convict. In deciding these cases, courts will look at the place where the intrusion is claimed to have occurred. A person's home is considered more private than an office. Courts also will ask whether the journalist received permission to enter the plaintiff's private property. But even that must be considered carefully.

SAMPLE NEWS POLICY GUIDELINES

1. *Using news media for personal gain:* An employee will not, directly or indirectly, seek publicity through the press, radio, or television.

2. *News media credentials:* Representatives of the news media who produce credentials will be admitted to coverage of any scene or disaster, crime, accident, or similar occurrence, when cleared by the officer in charge of same.

3. *Interviews with news media:* Representatives of the news media are authorized to interview any member of this department on a person-to-person basis, regardless of rank; but this privilege shall not extend to any act that may in any manner jeopardize the investigation in progress or a future court proceeding.

4. *Courtesy of news media:* All courtesies will be shown to news media in the field, as well as within the facilities of this department. An employee, in turn, should expect members of the news media to extend like courtesies to which members of this department are entitled in the exercise of their duties.

5. *Preferential treatment:* No preferential treatment will be shown to any representative of the news media.

6. *Photographing prisoners:* Photographing any individual in the custody of this department by the news media will not be authorized within the confines of the sheriff's department building. Federal prisoners in the custody of the department may be photographed by news media only upon authorization by the arresting federal agency or the U.S. Marshal. When escorting a prisoner outside the facilities of this department, photographing by the news media will not be restricted.

7. *Releasing names:* An employee will not release the name of a person killed by a criminal act or accident until identification has been verified and an earnest effort has been made by the coroner's office to notify next of kin; however, if the next of kin has not been notified after a reasonable time, this information will be released.

8. *Information that will be released:*

   a. Victim's name, address, age, sex, race, occupation, and next of kin.

   b. Description of subject(s) involved in the crime.

   c. Amount of money taken (if any), except in robberies, in which the amount should be withheld.

   d. Weapon used (if any).

   e. Type of force used.

   f. Injuries suffered by victim(s) or subject(s).

   g. Facts and essential circumstances of any arrest or incident, which includes name, address, sex, race, occupation, age, and, if over 18, charges.

   h. All events occurring in the judicial process.

   i. Accident reports, miscellaneous incident reports, arrest reports.

   j. On rape or sex offenses, only the age, race, and general location of the incident.

   k. Witnesses' names on drownings, accidents, etc.

9. *Information that will not be released:*

   a. Names, addresses, and exact location of female victims of sex offenders.

   b. Names and addresses of witnesses to Class 1 crimes.

   c. Statements made by subject(s) after arrest.

   d. Names and addresses of subject(s) wanted for crimes, unless help is wanted from the news media in an effort to locate subject.

   e. Details of subjects' previous arrest record.

   f. Juvenile offenders' names and addresses.

10. *Police lines:* At the scene of a major crime incident or disaster, police lines are set up to control crowds and preserve evidence. Representatives of the news media with proper press credentials will be allowed past lines, where the preservation of evidence and order will not be affected.

A North Carolina jury in 2003 agreed that an Asheville television reporter was not guilty of trespass, with a story about patient care at an assisted living facility, because the reporter had permission of an on-duty supervisor. The attorney for WLOS-TV, however, noted that individual shots of mentally ill patients at the facility did raise concerns of privacy.[21] The trend among state and federal courts has been to favor privacy over access, so journalists have to be careful in their newsgathering.

As more emphasis is placed on privacy rights, journalists should not assume that private property becomes public because something newsworthy occurs there. As in all invasion of privacy suits, defenses include arguments that the disclosure was not highly offensive to a reasonable person, that the disclosed material was newsworthy, or that the plaintiff gave consent.

CONTRACTING WITH A SOURCE

The difficulty of bringing a libel or invasion of privacy case against a journalist does not mean the journalist cannot be held accountable for breaking a promise to a source. The issue often can be one of breaking a contract. One case involved two rape victims who agreed to be interviewed for a news series. The station promised the women that they would not be identifiable on air, but the lighting used during the interview did not mask the victims' features adequately. What's more, no attempt was made to disguise their voices.

When a promotional announcement aired on the station the weekend before the series began, the employer of one of the rape victims recognized her. She also received telephone calls from others who saw her in the promo. When she complained to the station, she was promised that she would not be recognizable in future segments. When the next segment aired, however, people who knew the two rape victims could identify them readily, and the face of one victim was clearly visible at one point in the program. One of the women never had told her family that she had been raped, and both claimed that the failure of the station to maintain their anonymity caused them great distress.

They sued for breach of contract, negligent infliction of emotional distress, and intentional infliction of emotional distress. The appellate court ruled that the station was guilty of breach of contract and negligence in not taking adequate steps to fulfill its promise to maintain anonymity. The intentional infliction of emotional distress claim was denied because that requires "severe mental pain or anguish . . . inflicted through a deliberate or malicious campaign of harassment or intimidation."[22] Clearly, this was not a libel case because

the truth of the facts broadcast by the station was not disputed, but the station made a promise, did not fulfill the terms of that promise, and was held liable by the court for the harm its broadcasts caused.

This case emphasizes two important aspects of journalism. One is that the people we use in our stories are, in a very real sense, our victims. We put them on television and get them to say things that sometimes cause them a lot of trouble. That goes with the territory of covering news. When a journalist receives a promise from a journalist, however, that promise must be kept. It is a contract.

The second point this case underscores is how careful television journalists must be when dealing with promotion producers. Most stations hire people specifically to promote what those stations are doing. Those people frequently have no journalism background, and their job is to make people want to watch the newscasts. Sometimes the promos do not accurately represent the stories being promoted in the effort to hype them, and that distortion can affect the journalist's reputation and legal liability.

One way to prevent promotional distortion is to provide promotion producers only the edited story, not the raw field tapes. In the case of stories involving sensitive topics, the raw field tape may include scenes that the reporter and photographer know can't be used but that a promotion producer might use in ignorance. For example, a judge issued a restraining order against publication of the names of ten sexual child abuse victims. During the 10 p.m. news, the reporter covering the trial that day told a videotape editor to use a wide shot of the courtroom, including a large card with the children's names listed. On a normal television set the names could not be read, but on a large-screen television, the identities were clear. The district attorney filed contempt of court charges, and the parents of the children involved threatened substantial lawsuits. Three station employees were fired, two others were disciplined, the station incurred considerable legal costs, and its reputation as a news organization was tarnished seriously, all because of one shot in a news story lasting about five seconds.[23]

CONTEMPT OF COURT

The power of the courts to regulate news reporting involves two major areas: free press versus fair trial, and the right of reporters to protect their news sources.

Free Press Versus Fair Trial

Free press versus fair trial discussions get quite involved, as they bring into conflict the First, Sixth, and

Fourteenth Amendments to the Constitution. Why the conflict? Journalists are concerned with crime news. Journalists believe citizens need to know what is going on in their city or town for safety reasons. They also believe citizens should know what goes on in their courts so they can see the fair administration of justice.

Media critics worry that the media place too much emphasis on crime. They believe that excessive publicity interferes with the judicial process and emphasize that the Sixth Amendment's guarantee of a fair trial means an impartial jury that has not been prejudiced by media accounts.

Ever since the Sam Sheppard case in 1966, both the press and the bar have been more acutely aware of how harmful excessive publicity can be to the rights of the accused. Sheppard, a physician, was convicted of the July 4, 1954, murder of his wife. Sensational news coverage characterized the arrest, investigation, and trial. One television broadcast interviewed the judge, and television stations showed video of the jury, judge, and Sheppard going in and out of the courtroom nearly every day of the trial.

After 12 years in prison, the Supreme Court overturned the conviction because of a biased trial caused in part by media coverage. The Court acknowledged that Sheppard was not denied due process "by the judge's refusal to take precautions against the influence of pretrial publicity alone . . . but we believe that the arrangements made by the judge with the news media caused Sheppard to be deprived of that 'judicial serenity and calm to which [he] was entitled.'"[24]

Although the media still are confronted with restraining or "gag" orders in connection with judicial proceedings, Supreme Court rulings have given more assurances of open criminal proceedings over the past two decades.[25] The landmark Richmond Newspapers case in 1980 recognized that the media and the public have a First Amendment right to attend criminal trials.[26]

Also as a result of two fairly recent Supreme Court rulings, both *voir dire* (juror examinations) and preliminary hearings before a magistrate are presumptively open unless a compelling need for closure can be proved by the parties wishing to exclude the media.

Although the Supreme Court has not applied its rulings specifically to civil cases, lower federal and state courts have considered such trials to be open to the public. Journalists should respond to attempts at closure the same as they would in criminal proceedings: Identify themselves as members of the press, state their objections to being excluded from the proceeding, and respectfully request the judge to hold a hearing. If that request is denied, journalists should request a recess to

Although cameras can go almost anywhere in public can, allowing cameras in the courtroom has been a major issue in the free press, fair trial debate. Today nearly two-thirds of states allow cameras in a public trial.

contact their news directors and the stations' attorneys to appeal the closure formally.

Even though more recent Supreme Court rulings have given journalists increased access to criminal proceedings, access to information is still curtailed. Restraining orders are placed on witnesses, attorneys, police officers, and other officers of the court to prevent media representatives from talking with these individuals.

In many states, the bench, press, and bar have worked together to draft guidelines that will preserve a defendant's right to a fair trial, as well as the public's right to be informed about operation of the criminal justice system. The guidelines suggest types of material that can be released without harming the judicial process. They also list types of information that can hinder the defendant's right to a fair trial. Because these are voluntary agreements, they work well only in communities in which all sides of the free press–fair trial controversy demonstrate a spirit of cooperation.

It is important to understand the difference between allowing reporters to attend trials and allowing them to record proceedings. For the broadcast journalist, access to the trial is not as useful if video and audio recording are not allowed. Cameras in courtrooms gradually became the norm, but not without a struggle. Canon 35 of the American Bar Association banned cameras and other electronic equipment in courtrooms for years following the outrageous conduct of photographers in the trial of Bruno Hauptmann, convicted of kidnapping the infant son of Charles and Anne Lindbergh.

Again in 1965, cameras were deemed an impediment to a fair trial, according to the Supreme Court in the trial of Billy Sol Estes, a Texas financier charged with theft, swindling, and embezzlement.[27] The *Estes* decision justified camera bans in courtrooms for years, but as photographic equipment became less intrusive and disruptive, some states began to permit telecasts and broadcasts of criminal trials. In the early 1970s, several states — Alabama, Georgia, Florida, Indiana, Washington, and Nevada — began experimenting with the use of cameras in the courtrooms. Alabama established a rather progressive precedent when the news media in Mobile and 13th Circuit Judge Robert H. Hodnette, Jr. joined together in drafting a plan for using cameras in court.

A breakthrough for cameras in the courtroom came in a 1981 case out of Florida involving two Miami police officers who argued that they had not received a fair trial because the presence of cameras had been psychologically disruptive. The Supreme Court ruled in *Chandler v. Florida* that the mere presence of cameras in the courtroom did not interfere with a fair trial and refused to place a ban on their use. Instead, the Court said states could adopt their own rules regarding courtroom cameras.[28] The American Bar Association ended its opposition to cameras in court with a 1982 resolution supporting "unobtrusive use of cameras."

Although cameras can be used to some extent in almost two-thirds of the states, federal courts are still struggling with the issue. In 1994, the U.S. Judicial Conference voted to continue a ban on cameras in federal courtrooms despite success with experimentation in the early 1990s. Judges voted in 1995 to allow the 13 circuit courts to permit televising civil cases, but since then, only two circuits have done so. In 2002, the news media petitioned U.S. District Judge Leonie Brinkema to allow cameras during the trial of Zacarias Moussaoui, suspected of terrorism against the United States. Brinkema refused, saying cameras could pose a security risk and intimidate witnesses.[29]

The Supreme Court has been even less responsive to allowing cameras in the courtroom. It has released audiotapes in a few rare instances of oral arguments presented to the Court — including the December 2000 argument regarding the presidential election recount in Florida and the Spring 2003 argument regarding affirmative action policies at the University of Michigan.

Shield Laws

The relationship between journalists and sources has taken a strange twist in recent years. Normally, the discussion centers on the journalist's need to be able to assure his or her sources that their names and other information will be kept confidential. This promise of confidentiality is necessary, reporters contend, to get certain types of information not otherwise obtainable. For years, journalists assumed they had a First Amendment right not to reveal their sources — until the 1971 *Branzburg v. Hayes* case (actually three cases in one). Here, a divided Court said journalists are like all other citizens and must testify when summoned before a grand jury. The decision left lower courts to decide, on a case-by-case basis, whether a limited reporters' privilege exists.

Nearly every state has given some protection to reporters against revealing their sources or information obtained during newsgathering, either through state **shield laws**, state constitutional amendments, or common law (except in cases involving grand jury hearings, as mentioned in *Branzburg*.) In making the determination, courts usually take into consideration whether the person seeking the information has shown that the reporter has knowledge relevant to the case at hand, whether the information goes to the heart of the matter, and whether it could be obtained elsewhere. A reporter generally will have more protection for names of his or her sources than for things the journalist might have witnessed personally.

Although the laws vary from state to state and some observers believe they are not very useful or strong enough to stand up against judicial determination to overturn, others believe shield laws may at least make some officers of the courts more reluctant to subpoena a reporter. It is noteworthy, though, that in our post-9/11 environment, courts are less likely to honor shield laws and more likely to require disclosure if they believe the information is at all relevant to security. The other side of the confidentiality controversy is demonstrated in this question: Can a reporter be held liable for violating a promise of confidentiality to a source?

This question has arisen before, but it reached the Supreme Court for the first time in 1991.[30] The case involved a local political campaign worker in Minneapolis who lost his job after local newspapers printed his name as the source of damaging information to his candidate's opponent. Dan Cohen sued the newspapers for breach of contract of confidentiality. The Court held that journalists do not have a right to disregard promises that otherwise would be enforced by law.

ACCESS

All states now have open records and open meetings laws. Most of these are patterned after the Federal Freedom of Information Act (FOIA), covering records, and the Federal Sunshine in Government Act, covering meetings. It is important for journalists to know how to request public information through both state and federal open records statutes. You can find sample FOIA letters on a variety of Web sites, including state press association sites, the Society of Professional Journalists (www.spj.org), Investigative Reporters and Editors (www.ire.org), and the Reporters Committee for Freedom of the Press (www.rcfp.org).

In addition, all journalists should research their own state statutes governing open records and open meetings so they will know what they are entitled to under the law. In addition to legal access, reporters should try to develop sources of information within government offices. Both the legal and the informal approaches are necessary to get the best possible information.

Many times, government agencies also place restrictions on employees about how they are to handle the media. As you gather spot news, you will deal with the full spectrum of public officials. Many of them, especially in law enforcement, work under news policy guidelines similar to those in the boxed example. As you read these guidelines, consider the types of news coverage they might restrict.

Since the September 11, 2001, terrorist attacks, journalists have seen their rights of access dwindle. The Reporter's Committee for Freedom of the Press put together a report in 2003 detailing the impact of increased national security regulations on newsgathering. "The White Paper," for example, cites the USA Patriot Act — adopted just six weeks after the trade center attacks — as an attempt to expand the FBI's ability to get records through secret court orders.

The major potential danger to journalists, according to the report, comes in Section 215, in which the FBI could request things such as books, records, papers, or documents related to terrorism. Though the Privacy Protection Act of 1980 clearly spells out the limited circumstances in which authorities can conduct a newsroom search, theoretically the Patriot Act would allow such action. Complicating the issue, investigative journalists cannot find out how often records have been obtained through this new measure. In addition, the Patriot Act makes it easier for investigators to eavesdrop on a terrorism suspect's telephone calls and e-mail communications with so-called "roving" wiretaps. Therefore, journalists have an increased risk of having their telephones or e-mail conversations with sources intercepted by government agents if those sources are considered a threat to the U.S. government.[31]

An additional complication for journalists in newsgathering has been HIPPA (Health Insurance Portability and Accountability Act), enacted in 1996. In the first federal privacy protection of health records, journalists have been voicing concerns over its abuse by local, state, and federal officials who often refuse to disclose patient information. But it is important to know that the law does not prohibit disclosure of directory-type information of a patient, such as name, location in the hospital and condition. This is particularly important to news organizations that report on accidents and other disasters in which they need to report injuries and deaths. HIPPA also always permits disclosure of individual health information with the consent of the patient, the legal guardian or a family member of a deceased patient. Finally, the law does permit disclosure of private health information if it is necessary for public health issues.[32]

COPYRIGHT

The Copyright Act of 1976 replaced the outdated 1909 statute to conform to recognition of electronic media. The act says that film, videotape, and photographs may be **copyrighted**. In 1998, the Sonny Bono Copyright Extension Act added 20 years to copyright protection — from 50 years beyond life of the author to 70 years beyond life of the author for all works created after January 1, 1978. For works created prior to 1978, copyright protection lasts a total of 95 years from the date of creation.

Prior to the 1976 copyright law, works were protected for 28 years with a chance to renew for another 28 years. If a work created before 1978 was in its initial 28-year copyright, the author could renew it for an additional 67 years, protecting it for the maximum 95 years. If a work created before 1978 was in its second 28-year term, it would also be protected for a total of 95 years.

Portions of a work may be used under fair use guidelines, the most important of which is whether the use adversely affects the market value of the work. People working in broadcast news should know that copyright protects the method of expression — the sound or pictorial recordings themselves — but not the idea of creating that expression or the facts contained in it. News events are not copyrightable, but the way facts are put together in a news story — the presentation and style — can be copyrighted.

If you air an exclusive interview with a prominent figure, other journalists can certainly report about the statements from the interview because you have no copyright on the information. But another station could not replay your interview, nor could a newspaper reprint a transcript without copyright permission from your station because the story itself is protected. It is important to emphasize that broadcast news journalists working for a local affiliate, network, or cable news operation do not own their works; the copyright belongs to the news organization. The same is true for journalists working in print or online.

Freelance journalists own a copyright on their work but often have to relinquish some rights in order to get published. A freelance journalist has several options, including selling complete ownership of the report or video. Generally, however, freelancers opt for **one-time rights,** in which they sell their work to a publisher for one-time use but there is no guarantee that the work has not been published somewhere else first. A freelancer also may choose **first serial rights,** which allow a publisher the opportunity to be the first to put the story in the public's view but still gives the freelancer the right to sell the work again. This has become slightly more complicated with the Internet. The Supreme Court ruled in a 2001 case that publishers must seek additional copyright permission for any subsequent publishing of the same story on a Web site. So if a television station buys rights to air a freelancer's video news report on a tornado in a nearby county, the station must get additional copyright permission for the work to be added to the station's news Web site. The freelance journalist could legally charge the station twice for those two uses.[33]

Copyrighted works can still be used by others but only in a limited manner. Such limited use is guided by fair use provisions outlined in the law. Fair Use has become harder to police as the Internet has made information widely accessible, but is still strictly enforced. The concept behind fair use is that portions of copyrighted work may be used without permission for purposes of comment, criticism, news reporting, teaching, scholarship, and research.

To determine whether a particular use is fair, the law considers four factors:

1. *Purpose and character of the use.* This is related primarily to the types of uses listed above. Works used in a non-commercial context are more likely to be considered fair use.

2. *Nature of the copyrighted work.* Courts tend to look at what the purpose of the copyrightable work is. If it is meant to be something used just once like a workbook, it is less likely to be fair use if copied without permission. If the work is more creative in nature, such as a poem or a novel, it is less likely to be fair use than if it is informational, such as a news story. Whether the work has been published or not is crucial for courts; generally, courts are highly protective of rights of first publication to the creator

3. *Amount of work used.* The total amount of a work used is not as important as the portion of a work used. If a two-minute clip of a 60-minute documentary is used, that is less troublesome than a one-minute clip of a 1:20 minute news story.

4. *Effect on the market.* The creator of a work must prove that the widespread use of his or her work could negatively affect the potential for profit. Courts generally have been sympathetic to the creators of the work on this point if they can show any adverse affect on the potential market.[34]

To notify that a work is copyrighted, it must contain the copyright symbol © followed by the word "copyrighted," the year, and the owner's name.

FEDERAL REGULATION

The FCC has been active in regulating many areas of broadcast, including obscenity / indecency and violence. In addition to traditional broadcast media, such regulation extends to cable, telecommunication, and cyberspace.

Obscenity and Indecency

Although the FCC spent much of the 1980s and 1990s abandoning restrictions on the electronic media, it has not backed down on the issues of obscenity and indecent programming. But the regulation of broadcast obscenity and indecency is a particularly tough one, as the FCC and courts must reconcile Section 326 of the 1934 Communications Act, which prohibits FCC censorship, and Section 1464 of the U.S. Criminal Code, which bans obscene language in radio or television broadcasts.

Section 326 states:

> Nothing in this chapter shall be understood or construed to give the commission the power of censorship over the radio communications or signals transmitted by any radio station, and no regulation or condition shall be promulgated or fixed by the commission which shall interfere with the right of free speech by means of radio communication.

Section 1464 reads:

> Whoever utters any obscene, indecent or profane language by means of radio communication shall be fined no more than $10,000 or imprisoned no more than two years or both.

In addition, the FCC has interpreted Section 326 to mean no censorship of specific programs, but does not prevent it from punishing broadcasters for questionable decency. One of the first cases testing this interpretation involved George Carlin's "Filthy Words" comedy routine. In this 1978 decision, the Supreme Court insisted that the two statutes did not conflict and determined that the FCC did have power to regulate the broadcasting of indecent programming. The Court determined that the content was indeed vulgar and offensive and, because television is pervasive and easily accessible to children, regulation is not a First Amendment violation.[35]

Test of Obscenity. Part of the ambiguity in regulation of obscenity stems from the inherent problem of defining what is obscene material. In *Miller v. California*, the Supreme Court said local **community standards** should be used to determine whether something is obscene for that specific community.[36] It emphasized that standards in Las Vegas will not be the same as standards in a small town in Utah. According to *Miller*, a work is obscene according to the following three-pronged test:

1. Would a person, applying contemporary, local community standards, find that the work, taken as a whole, appeals to prurient interests (morbid interest in nudity, sex, or excretory functions)?

2. Does the work depict in a patently offensive way sexual conduct defined specifically by applicable state law?

3. Does the work in question lack serious literary, artistic, political, or scientific value?

Regulation of Indecent Programming. The *Miller* test outlined material that would be obscene and, therefore, unconstitutional. But material that is merely "indecent" becomes more problematic and often falls to the whim of societal norms — or at least the politicians and lawmakers in charge of setting some of those norms. Indecent programming has been the bane of the FCC as the liberalizing of American society has continued to test the limits of broadcasting, and particularly the tastes of politicians.

In 2001, the FCC issued a new statement regarding its position on indecency that was first defined in its 1978 case against George Carlin. This FCC standard for **indecency** is any programming considered patently offensive according to community standards for the average broadcast viewer, and any material depicting or describing sexual or excretory activities.[37]

When Janet Jackson's decorated nipple was exposed on primetime television during the 2004 Super Bowl — one of the most-watched televised events every year, with more than six million viewers — few Americans, by the next morning, had escaped being exposed to or hearing about the national drama. The FCC and Congress were ready to combat what they considered evidence of the unraveling of morality in America. Capitol Hill moved almost immediately for increasing fines to stations for indecent programming from $27,500 per

incident to as much as $500,000 per incident, sending a clear message to broadcasters that censorship was to take a backseat to obscenity and indecency.[38]

Janet Jackson and Justin Timberlake issued a public apology for an incident they first claimed was an accident. NFL Commissioner Paul Tagliabue apologized for allowing MTV to produce the show. Viacom President Mel Karmazin pleaded with lawmakers not to punish the industry for an incident he considered just as reprehensible as they did.[39]

The FCC is winning the public opinion battle, and broadcasters are paying the price — a big one. Even though new laws in regard to fines had not passed in Congress by end of 2004, the FCC was still handing out hefty fines. Viacom was expected to be slapped with a $550,000 fine for each of its local CBS stations that aired the Super Bowl halftime show.[40] CBS reported that it would appeal the fine, even if it means going to court.[41]

The aftermath of the Super Bowl incident was a renewed crackdown on indecent programming in television and radio. NBC got caught in the new smut policing when the FCC publicly chastised the network for a spontaneous comment from U2 lead singer Bono during the 2003 Golden Globe Awards. In March 2004, the FCC decided not to fine NBC or Bono for his comment "f***ing brilliant" on primetime television, but the Commission made it quite clear that it would impose the fine the next time. In addition, the FCC put all broadcasters on notice that the f-word is officially indecent and will result in FCC fines for its use.[42] In October 2004, the son of Nascar legend Dale Earnhardt remarked to reporters after his Talladega win that his accomplishments did not mean sh** compared to his father's. The FCC went on the offensive again, fining the network and suggesting a time delay in all live sporting and entertainment events to allow for editing such comments.

Clear Channel Communications was among the first to actually feel the financial sting. The nation's largest radio chain paid a record $755,000 fine for sexual comments made on its Florida-based "Bubba the Love Sponge" show. A week later, Clear Channel was fined $247,500 for sexually explicit content involving porn star Ron Jeremy. In response to the FCC's actions, Clear Channel fired the "Bubba" host and pulled shock jock Howard Stern from six of its major markets.[43]

This recent wave of fines is not new but, rather, the continuation of a trend that gained steam in the mid-1990s with the proliferation of radio shock jocks. The FCC cracked down on radio stations airing the "Howard Stern Show," doling out $1.9 million in fines to stations airing the Stern broadcasts that included material deemed indecent. But Stern has maintained his fight against such actions and has found some champions. Though Clear Channel cut his program in six markets, Infinity Broadcasting Corporation was adding Stern in nine markets, including four markets where the show had been yanked by other broadcasters. As of summer 2004, Stern's radio show was airing on 45 stations.[44]

In 1990, the U.S. Court of Appeals in Washington blocked an attempt at a round-the-clock ban on indecent broadcasts. Two years later, in the Public Telecommunications Act of 1992, Congress permitted indecency between midnight and 6 a.m. for all broadcast stations except public radio or television stations that signed off the air before midnight. Those stations could air indecent programming beginning at 10 p.m. When the Act was challenged in court, the U.S. Court of Appeals for the D.C. Circuit threw out the double standard and set the safe harbor for all stations from 10 p.m. until 6 a.m.[45] In its 2001 indecent programming policy statement, the FCC restated its insistence on this safe harbor time period.[46]

In the spring of 2000, the Supreme Court once again looked at indecent programming and struck down Section 505 of the 1996 Telecommunications Act. The case involved Playboy TV, a cable channel with 24 million subscribers. At issue was the ineffectiveness of scrambling the channel to non-subscribers. The government was hoping Section 505 would shield children from hearing sexually explicit content on the channel despite not being able to see it. The provision stated that a channel dedicated to primarily sexual content must limit its hours to times when children were not as likely to be watching — 10 p.m. to 6 a.m. — or pay for the expensive technology to scramble the channel so no sounds or visuals were recognizable.

Although the Court recognized a need to protect children, it determined Section 505 to be too restrictive of protected speech. Justice Anthony M. Kennedy wrote for the majority: "This history of the law of free expression is one of vindication in cases involving speech that many citizens find shabby, offensive or even ugly. . . . The citizen is entitled to seek out or reject certain ideas or influences without government interference or control."[47]

Regulation of Violence

With almost as much rigor as it has attacked indecency, the FCC of late has renewed its interest in curbing television violence.

In May 2004, FCC Chairman Michael Powell agreed to a request from a U.S. House of Representatives committee to study violence on the airwaves. Specifically, the committee asked the FCC to address harm that comes to children who watch excessively violent programming.[48] Despite thousands of published papers from media scholars on this topic, which has generally found that some children when exposed to some violence may sometimes act aggressively, Congress asked for an FCC report by January 2005.

In early 1996, Congress did revise the 1934 Communications Act to require the **V-chip**, following a Senate vote in 1995 to establish a ratings system for violent programming on TV. The four major television networks had agreed, in 1994, to supply an advisory to parents in newspapers and the *TV Guide*, warning of violent programming. In February 1995, the Department of Defense, the U.S. Postal Service, and Amtrak decided not to advertise during any television show with excessive violence, excluding documentaries, sports programs, and news. The three spent a combined $68 million on television advertising in 1994.[49]

In summer 2004, the Federal Trade Commission reported that violent advertising was still being marketed heavily during shows that children are likely to watch In particular, the FTC cited violent films, music with explicit lyrics, and violent video games as prevalent products advertised during shows catering to children.[50]

Regulation of Cable / Satellite / Telecom

Ever since deregulation of the telecommunications market was completed through the 1996 Telecommunications Act, the name of the game has been media consolidation. The thin line separating the cable, telephone, satellite, and broadcast industries has continued to blur, leaving a handful of multibillion-dollar media conglomerates that offer duplicative services.

Most of the current debate centered on mandated **"must carry"** rules. The torturous history of these provisions dates back nearly 50 years to the 1960s, but the major battles have been waged in the last ten years with the introduction of the 1992 Cable Act. This law foresaw the potential market monopoly of cable companies as most Americans used cable for their programming. To preserve competition in the telecommunications market, Congress told cable companies that they must carry local broadcast stations on cable.

Recall, in our earlier discussion about the regulation of broadcast, that the airwaves have a limited spectrum, allowing for only so many available channels. Cable, however, offers programming through coaxial cable wire, providing for essentially unlimited space. The proliferation of satellite programming has offered even more channel possibilities, so in 2002 Congress added satellite carriers to the list of those required to carry local broadcast programming. However, satellite carriers such as Direct Broadcast Satellite were not required to carry local broadcast programming across the board. But if they offered subscribers in a certain market any local stations in that market, they had to offer all local stations within that market.

Not surprisingly, the cable industry has opposed these moves, arguing it is an infringement of their free speech rights to force companies to carry local signals instead of the programming of their choice. But the Supreme Court has found the must-carry provisions to be constitutional despite the burden on free speech rights.[51]

The latest battle in this war stems again from a Congressional mandate that all broadcast programming must be in digital format by 2006.[52] Currently, most broadcast programming is analog. The switch to digital will allow for much improved visual and sound quality with high-definition programming and also will provide more spectrum space for programming offered in standard definition. During the transition within markets, broadcasters will offer both analog and digital programming.

Because cable companies currently must carry all local broadcast programming, the National Association of Broadcasters argues that it also must carry the digital programming during the transition period. Cable operators believe this is a gross violation of the First Amendment to be forced to carry more local broadcasting. Free speech arguments aside, the major worry for both cable and broadcast is loss of its place in the programming market. Consumers will have to buy a high-definition television set or a converter — thus far, pricey — and broadcasters are worried that they will lose customers during the transition. Cable operators fear the same problem if they are forced to carry too many broadcast signals.[53] The next few years will be revolutionary for the quality of programming offered via television, as well as for the laws that will be governing that programming.

The last few years have seen a variety in services by communication industries. Cable companies are offering high speed Internet connections that allow long-distance phone calls via a computer for no more cost than that of the monthly service; cellular phone companies are making long distance charges a thing of the past and are including World Wide Web service, e-mail, text messaging, and picture sharing through wireless technology. As these things will only increase in the coming years, the courts will have to decide if the telecommunications industry remains a common carrier and is not responsible for content.

America's new love affair with cell phones and wireless technology has potential legal implications. With the ease of a taking a picture virtually anywhere and sending it to anyone without being noticed could have severe legal implications. The potential for invasion of privacy and the temptation of news organizations to assume that photos or videos sent from a consumer are true events are potential problems that courts will likely be wrestling with in coming years.

THE INTERNET

Over the years, radio and television added new challenges to questions of libel, copyright, and obscenity. For the last decade, cyberspace has been charting new territory in these legal matters.

Cyberspace encompasses the Internet, World Wide Web, online service providers such as America Online, Yahoo, MSN, and Hotmail, and browsers such as Netscape and Microsoft Internet Explorer. With a heavy reliance on textual information, the Web initially looked more like a print medium, just in electronic form. But as individual webmasters and organizations have become more Web-savvy, their sites have become sophisticated multimedia presentations with streamed audio and video, regular interactive features, and infinite links to other information.

What legal model do regulators follow — print or broadcast? Who owns the rights to the published work — the individual? the online service? Who is responsible for defamatory statements? Who is the "community" when determining whether material is obscene based on "community standards?" Answers to these legal questions are still in progress as courts and government officials battle to monitor cyberspace (if that is possible, much less reasonable), but some standards are evolving as the two entities fight to catch up with technology.

The 'Net and Libel

Two main issues surface when dealing with libel on the Internet — who is responsible for the libel, and what jurisdiction applies? Print and broadcast news organizations are responsible for libel because they control the message sent to the public. Common carriers such as telephone companies, however, are not responsible because they have no control over what is communicated.

Courts have applied the same rationale within cyberspace. Content providers — including sites controlled by an individual or an organization such as a news media Web site — are responsible for any libel that is published. Common carriers — referring primarily to Internet Service Providers [ISPs] such as AOL and MSN which host sites for users — are not responsible for libelous material.

The prevailing case in this area stems from a 1998 case involving AOL and political gossip columnist

Matthew Drudge. AOL had been providing The Drudge Report free to subscribers since June 1997, in exchange for a royalty payment to Drudge. This agreement also stated that Drudge would create, edit, and update the report for AOL, but AOL maintained the right to remove content that it determined was in violation of the AOL guidelines governing its online service. When Drudge printed that Sidney Blumenthal, assistant to U.S. President Bill Clinton, had a history of spousal abuse, Blumenthal sued for libel. The court found Drudge liable for his defamatory statement and said AOL, in spite of its editorial agreement granting power of censorship over The Drudge Report, was in no way responsible for the libelous material.[54] Blumenthal and Drudge settled out of court in May 2002.

Congress had weighed in on the issue with its 1996 Telecommunications Act by establishing that no ISP should be treated as the speaker of any information from another content provider. It is unclear how much protection is given to Web site operators and individual subscribers under the law, but so far, most courts have been following this congressional standard.

When it comes to jurisdiction for libel cases, courts have been much less consistent. A plaintiff brought suit in Washington D.C. because the defamatory statements were available to more than 200,000 AOL subscribers in the nation's capital. But the court rejected the rationale, saying the original message was sent to Virginia and the subject had nothing to do with the D.C. area.[55] In another case, online articles from the *New Haven Advocate* reporting on the Virginia correctional system and its warden were found to have made enough impact in Virginia to allow a libel suit to be tried there.[56]

The 'Net and Obscenity

Material considered "obscene" is subject to regulation no matter where it occurs. But as pointed out in the earlier discussion on obscenity, the fine line between indecency and obscenity is tough to draw, so censoring questionable material on the Internet is a murky proposition. Besides the First Amendment questions involved, trying to determine liability for misconduct is a logistical nightmare. Should the content on the 'net be tightly controlled, such as radio and television, or should it be as unrestrained as magazines and newspapers?

Congress is 0 for 2 in its attempts thus far to legislate indecency on the Internet. Lawmakers passed the Communications Decency Act in 1996 as part of the most recent Telecommunications Act, only to be struck down by a unanimous Supreme Court decision the following year. The Court ruled against two provisions of CDA that sought to protect minors from "obscene" or "indecent" material on the Internet by prohibiting the "knowing transmission" of obscene messages depicting patently offensive material based on community standards.[57] Although the provisions sought to protect children, the Supreme Court believed the ban deprived adult viewers of their right to choose what content they would view on the Internet. Justice John Paul Stevens wrote, for the 7–2 majority, that the Court believed the CDA lacked the precision required under the First Amendment when attempting to suppress speech:

> "It is true that we have repeatedly recognized the governmental interest in protecting children from harmful materials. . . . But that interest does not justify an unnecessarily broad suppression of speech addressed to adults."

Congress attempted again in 1998 to curb children's access to sexually explicit material on the Web with its Child Online Protection Act. Among its stipulations, COPA imposed fines up to $50,000 a day to commercial sites that make porn available to children under 17 years of age.

In 2004, the Supreme Court again struck down the law as an unnecessary limitation on free speech.[58] But this time the Court split 5–4 and allowed Attorney General John Ashcroft another chance in federal district court to defend the constitutionality of government restrictions on Internet pornography.

Though the Court majority in the COPA case doubted that government controls on Internet porn would be better than filtering software, the Court did hint that COPA could ultimately be upheld. In the decision, Justice Anthony Kennedy said the Court did not believe "Congress is incapable of enacting any regulation of the Internet designed to prevent minors from gaining access to harmful materials."

The Third Circuit Court of Appeals had ruled against COPA in 2000, rejecting the statute's constitutionality because it could not enforce contemporary community standards over the entire Internet community.[59] If COPA were going to regulate the Internet as it proposed, the Third Circuit said it would have to do so using standards that reflect those of the community most likely to be offended by the material. This would place an impossible burden on Web publishers, who, to comply, would have to follow the most conservative standards within their states. Third Circuit Judge Leonard Garth said that, in his opinion, the community standards test is still viable for other media but has "no applicability to the Internet and the Web."

In his decision, Garth referenced one of the earliest cases to consider standards in a virtual community of users. That case involved two Californians who operated a Bulletin Board Service with images and words often involving bestiality, sadomasochism, and other sexual fetishes.[60] The U.S. District Court in Memphis, Tennessee, had convicted the couple, Robert Alan and Carleen Thomas, in 1994 on charges of conspiracy and interstate transportation of obscenity because they allowed users to download pictures of bestiality, torture, self-mutilation, rape, and the like, for a fee.[61] The Thomases argued that their "community" was all of cyberspace, but the Sixth Circuit Court of Appeals rejected this notion. The court ultimately relied on the fact that the Thomases, though operating out of California, knew they had a client in Memphis who was downloading the sexually explicit material, so local standards applied.

On review of the Third Circuit opinion of COPA, the Supreme Court disagreed that the community standards analysis was enough to make the statute unconstitutional, so it remanded the case back to appeals court.[62] On a second look, the Third Circuit maintained that COPA was unconstitutional because it did not meet the "least restrictive means" test for restricting speech.

Ashcroft's second appeal to the Supreme Court resulted in the most recent ruling striking down the law — at least temporarily. The Supreme Court kept in place a provision from the original 1999 district court ruling stating that the law cannot go into effect until its constitutionality is finalized. One scholar suggested that a national community standard may be on the horizon, given comments supporting such an idea by some Supreme Court justices in the COPA decision.[63] Though a national standard would have its own complications, it could be preferable to arbitrary local standards. Regardless, the one certain outcome is that this issue will get more attention in coming years.

The 'Net and Copyright

The Internet and online services deliver breaking news, manuscripts, photos, video, images, music and a plethora of other creative works that can be downloaded, stored and distributed easily and quickly. The accessibility to superb research resources and multiple dissemination opportunities increases the likelihood of piracy on the 'net. But all information in cyberspace is copyright-protected, even without the optional copyright notice, and journalists should not use material without permission.[64]

As a general rule, works posted to the Internet are no different from other published materials. Courts have struggled to apply copyright principles developed for traditional media to interactive, digital media. A federal court in California enjoined a Bulletin Board operator for managing illegal trading of Sega™ video games over

the Internet. Chad Scherman, operating as "Brujjo Digital," asked users to upload Sega™ software, and even charged to download the pirated material.[65]

In Florida, a federal court said a Bulletin Board operator could pay civil damages for copyright infringement even if the operator does not encourage or participate in illegal trading of copyrighted works. George Frena was guilty of copyright infringement when subscribers to his commercial Bulletin Board illegally downloaded pictures from Playboy Publications for a fee.[66]

One of the main concerns with copyright infringement is accountability. Content providers want Web site operators and access providers to be responsible, as finding individuals violating copyright provisions is extremely difficult. But Web site operators and access providers argue that if they are liable for third parties, growth of the Internet will be hampered.

The Church of Scientology's Religious Technology Center (RTC) in 1995 sued a former Scientology minister for posting excerpts of Scientology texts to his Web site. RTC also claimed copyright infringement by a bulletin board operator and Netcom, an Internet Service Provider.[67] Netcom fought its liability in the matter, and the court determined the ISP to be a "contributing" copyright infringer. Had Netcom been aware of the copyright infringement taking place through its access provisions, the ISP would have been liable for some copyright violations.

Congress attempted to address this liability issue with its Digital Millennium Copyright Act. DMCA generally states that ISPs do not violate copyright laws when they transmit, route, or provide infringing material if they did not initiate the transmission or routing. Likewise, if the ISP caches infringing material made available by someone else or provides links to infringing content unknowingly, the ISP is not liable.

Illegal downloading from the Internet has been one of the biggest copyright challenges. And nowhere is this problem more evident than with music. With the advent of compression technology in the late 1990s, downloading large MP3 files became much faster and, therefore, easier and more popular. Despite pleas from the recording industry to block MP3 player sales and use, a federal court ruled that the device was merely a method for storing portable files rather than using hard drive space and was not for commercial use.[68]

The Recording Industry Association of America was also leading a charge against individuals who would upload their own music collections and then share them with others on a peer-to-peer networking scheme. Of the several groups that provided this free exchange of music files, Napster was the most widely used. RIAA sued Napster in 2001 and won for copyright infringement. Napster argued that its software did nothing illegal, only allowed a path for sharing free music. The 9th Circuit Court of Appeals agreed with the recording industry that Napster and other companies were violating fair use provisions for copyrighted music available on the Internet.[69]

Since the Napster ruling, RIAA has become even more aggressive in going after music pirates. In spring 2003, the association went after four college students who were downloading thousands of songs, storing them on a central server and making them available to the university community through high-speed Internet networks on campus.[70] One student operating such a site from Michigan Technological University stored 650,000 songs, including nearly 2,000 songs from his own collection.

In summer 2004, a three-judge panel in the 9th Circuit Court of Appeals issued a blow to the recording industry with a ruling in favor of two companies that produce file-sharing software.[71] The court said Grokster and StreamCast Networks were not liable for aiding copyright infringement because they could not monitor how users of the software were exchanging music and movie files. Though the music and movie industries claim that most of the files shared using such software is illegal, the court maintained that the companies were not in control of the piracy.

The difference between this case and the Napster ruling, in which the 9th Circuit found the file-sharing software company guilty of copyright infringement, is in the networking. The 2004 panel said Napster was controlled from a central server that searched for available files for users; Grokster and StreamCast Networks, the court found, are decentralized without such control.

The possible outcome of this ruling is a more concentrated effort by the recording industry to go after individuals who are illegally downloading files and a stronger push for legislation that holds companies liable for aiding piracy. Congress stepped into the fray in the 2004 session with hints at a specific bill to curb online music piracy. Almost instantaneous criticism came from common carriers and Internet Service Providers that feared they would be held liable, too. The outcome of this kind of legislation is uncertain for now, but it is significant that lawmakers and policy wonks are considering prosecuting others than just the individuals who actually break the law.

Currently, the punishment for online music copyright violations is up to three years in prison and $250,000 in fines. Individuals also can be held civilly liable, costing perhaps as much as $150,000 per infringement. For the four college students targeted by RIAA, the association was seeking $150,000 per song downloaded. RIAA has launched an educational campaign to coincide with its legal veracity, including messages that pop up on users' screens when they are trying to illegally download music.[72]

The current remedy has come from companies including KaZaa, MusicNet, and iTunes, which provide for users to pay per song downloaded. So far this compromise has been acceptable. Individuals can pay the same price as they would for one artist's CD and get the songs of their choice; and the music industry is not losing profit on the sales of copyrighted works. The success of continued piracy investigations and convictions will determine whether this new system is as good as it promises to be.

ENDNOTES

1. *Red Lion Broadcasting Co. v. FCC*, 395 U.S. 367 (1969).
2. *CBS v. The Democratic National Committee*, 412 U.S. 94 (1973).
3. Footnote 11, *FCC v. League of Women Voters of California*, 468 U.S. 364 (1984).
4. *FCC v. Midwest Video Corp.*, 440 U.S. 689 (1979).
5. *Syracuse Peace Council v. FCC*, 867 F.2d 654, 16 Media L. Rep. 1225 (D.C. Cir. 1989) cert. Denied, 493 S.Ct. 1019 (1990).
6. *Arkansas AFL-CIO v. FCC*, 11 F.3d 1430, 22 Media L. Rep. 1001 (8th Cir. 1993) (en banc).
7. Cooper, J. "Talkers Brace for Fairness Assault," *Broadcasting & Cable*, Sept. 6, 1993, p. 44.
8. *Branch v. FCC*, 824 F.2d 37 (1987).
9. *Kennedy for President Committee v. FCC*, 636 F. 2d 432 (1980).
10. 1984 Political Primer, 100 F.C.C.2d, at 1524-25.
11. *McConnell, U.S. Senator, et al. v. Federal Election Commission*, No. 02-1674 (Dec. 10, 2003)
12. Eggerton, John. "Cable Key to Broadcast Election Coverage," *Broadcasting & Cable*, July 6, 2004.
13. *Food Lion Inc. v. Capitol Cities/ABC*, 194 F. 3d 505 (1999).
14. "Media Winning More Libel Suits," *Quill* (May 2004): 4.
15. *Philadelphia Newspapers, Inc. v. Hepps*, 475 U.S. 768 (1986).
16. *New York Times v. Sullivan*, 376 U.S. 254 (1964).
17. *Milkovich v. Lorain Journal Co.*, 110 S.Ct. 2695 (1991).
18. *Neff v. Time*, 406 F.Supp. 858 (1976).
19. *Cox Broadcasting Co. v. Cohn*, 420 U.S. 469 (1975).
20. *Booth v. Curtis Publishing Co.*, 11 N.Y.S. 2d 907 (1962).
21. Eggerton, John. "WLOS-TV Wins, but Lawyer Voices Caution" *Broadcasting & Cable* (Jan. 12, 2004): 11.
22. *Doe v. American Broadcasting Co.*, 543 N.Y.S.2d 455, 16 Med.L.Rptr. 1958 (App.Div. 1989)

23. Clayton, K. "News Story Leads to Station Firings," *Electronic Media,* March 1990, p. 8.

24. *Sheppard v. Maxwell*, 384 U.S. 333 (1966).

25. *Richmond Newspapers v. Virginia*, 448 U.S. 555 (1980).

26. Ibid.

27. *Estes v. Texas*, 381 U.S. 352 (1965).

28. *Chandler v. Florida*, 449 U.S. 560 (1981).

29. *United States v. Moussaoui*, 30 M.L.R. 1251 (2002).

30. *Cohen v. Cowles Media Co.*, 111 S.Ct. 2513 (1991).

31. The Reporters Committee for Freedom of the Press, "Homefront Confidential: How the War on Terrorism Affects Access to Information and the Public's Right to Know," September 2003. (http://www.rcfp.org/homefrontconfidential/index.html).

32. HIPPA Guidelines, 45 CFR Section 164.

33. *New York Times Co. v. Tasini*, 121 S.Ct. 2381 (2001).

34. *Harper & Row Publishers v. Nation Enterprises*, 471 U.S. 539 (1985).

35. *FCC v. Pacifica Foundation*, 438 U.S. 726 (1978).

36. *Miller v. California*, 413 U.S. 15 (1973).

37. In re Industry Guidelines on the Commission's Case Law Interpreting 18 U.S.C. Section 1464 and Enforcement Policies Regarding Broadcast Indecency, FCC File No. EB-00-1H-0089, 4/6/01.

38. Steinberg, Jacques. "Eye on FCC, TV and Radio Watch Words," *New York Times*, May 10, 2004.

39. Eggerton, John. "D.C.'s Indecency Frenzy," *Broadcasting & Cable*, Feb. 16, 2004.

40. McConnell, Bill. "Viacom Faces $550K Jackson Fine," *Broadcasting & Cable*, July 1, 2004.

41. "CBS Reiterates Jackson Fine Opposition," *Broadcasting & Cable*, Sept. 9, 2004.

42. Eggerton, John. "FCC Says F*** Is Indecent," *Broadcasting & Cable*, March 18, 2004.

43. "FCC cracks down with hefty fines," *Quill* (May 2004): 4.

44. Eggerton, John. "Stern Cleared on New Channels," *Broadcasting & Cable*, June 30, 2004.

45. *Action for Children's Television v. FCC*, 58 F.3d 654 (1995).

46. In re Industry Guidelines on the Commission's Case Law Interpreting 18 U.S.C. Section 1464 and Enforcement Policies Regarding Broadcast Indecency, FCC File No. EB-00-1H-0089, 4/6/01.

47. *United States v. Playboy Entertainment Group, Inc.*, No. 98-1682, May 22, 2000.

48. McConnell, Bill. "FCC Will Look at Violence," *Broadcasting & Cable*, May 20, 2004.

49. "Three Government Advertisers Pull Ads from Shows with 'Excessive Violence,'" *Publishers Auxilliary*, Feb. 27, 1995, p. 9.

50. McConnell, Bill. "FTC Sees Too Many Violent Ads," *Broadcasting & Cable*, July 9, 2004.

51. *Turner Broadcasting System v. FCC* (Turner II), 520 U.S. 180 (1997).

52. Advanced Television Systems and Their Impact Upon the Existing Television Broadcast Service, Fifth Report and Order, 12 FCCR 12809 (1997).

53. For a lengthy discussion on this debate, see Joel Timmer, "Broadcast, Cable and Digital Must Carry: The Other Digital Divide," 9 Comm. L. Pol. 101-150 (2004).

54. *Blumenthal v. Drudge*, 992 F.Supp.44 (D.D.C. 1998)

55. *Mallinckrodt Medical Inc. v. Sonus Pharmaceuticals Inc.*, DCDC Civil Action No. 97-1732 (PLF).

56. *Bochan v. LaFontaine*, 27 M.L.R. 2057 (1999).

57. *Reno v. ACLU*, 521 U.S. 84 (1997).

58. *Ashcroft v. American Civil Liberties Union*, No. 03-218 (2004).

59. *ACLU v. Reno*, 217 F.3d 162 (3d Cir. 2000).

60. Baird, Woody. "Memphis Compusex Case Has Online Fallout," AP story printed in *The Commercial Appeal*, Feb. 11, 1996, p. B1.

61. Kelly, M. "Banned in Memphis: City has High Profile in Obscenity Case History," *The Commercial Appeal*, June 1, 1995, pp. C1, C3.

62. *Ashcroft v. ALCU*, 122 S.Ct. 1700 (2002).

63. Cenite, Mark. "Federalizing or Eliminating Online Obscenity Law as an Alternative to Contemporary Community Standards," 9 Comm. L. & Policy 25-71 (2004).

64. Penchina, R. "Venturing Online: Protecting You and Your Product in Cyberspace," Editor & Publisher, June 24, 1995, p. 122.

65. *Sega Enterprises Ltd. v. Maphia*, 857 F. Supp. 679 (N.D. Calif. 1994).

66. *Playboy Enterprises Inc. v. George Frena et al*, 839 F. Supp. 1552, 22 Media L. Rep. 1301 (M.D.Fla. 1993).

67. *Religious Tech Ctr. v. Netcom On-Line Communication Servs., Inc.*, N.D. Cal. (filed Feb. 8, 1995).

68. *Recording Industry Association of America v. Diamond Multimedia Systems*, 9th Cir., No. 98-56727, 6/15/99.

69. 6 E.C.L.R. 144 (2001)

70. Gentile, Gary. "Music Industry Sues 4 College Students," Associated Press, April 2003.

71. Richtel, Matt. "File-Sharing Sites Found Not Liable for Infringement," New York Times, August 20, 2004.

72. Harmon, Amy. "Music Swappers Get a Message on PC Screens: Stop It Now," *New York Times,* April 30, 2003.

EXERCISE 13A: How Should You Respond?

Name _____ Date _____

For each of the following statements, tell what you are legally bound to do.

1. A candidate for mayor has asked to respond to an interview your reporter did with the incumbent mayor on his current budget requests. What are you required by law to do? What would you do as news director?

2. You have presented an editorial during the 10 p.m. newscast opposing expansion of the gas production facility near your city. Plant officials ask for time to respond. What must you do?

3. In an editorial, you have attacked the city manager for lack of good judgment in hiring building inspectors. What must you do?

4 In a political broadcast, one of the candidates accuses his opponent of forging tax documents. He doesn't produce any evidence of the charge. What can you do in editing the tape for broadcast tonight?

5 In a news story, the city attorney endorses a proposed ordinance to require property owners to pay for a new sewage system. An attorney for the homeowners association requests equal time on the news show to refute that endorsement. What will you do?

6 You and the photographer are sent to cover a story on a campus demonstration at the president's office. When you get there, the student leader has just finished his speech. The photographer suggests that you ask the student to give it again for the cameras. What do you do?

7 You produce a documentary on government graft in your county. The county welfare director had retired two years ago, but in the documentary, three people on welfare accuse the former director of requiring them to pay monthly kickbacks of $20 each to remain on the eligible list. The director denied the charges and threatened to sue for libel if the charges were broadcast. You have other witnesses who attest in writing to the graft but are unwilling to say so on videotape. What should you do? If you are sued, what defense do you have?

EXERCISE 13A: How Should You Respond? *(continued)*

Name _____ Date _____

For each of the following statements, tell what you legally are bound to do.

8. You mistakenly accuse Timothy Cornet of being the person arrested for kidnapping a four-year-old girl. The man accused was really Timothy Corinth. Mr. Cornet calls you immediately after the radio news broadcast accusing you of libel. Would he have a case? What should you do?

9. You are reporting the city council meeting. In your report you quote the council's denial of license renewal to one of the local restaurants. The council's report states that the restaurant has had numerous sanitary violations, some of which you note in your report. The restaurant manager calls your station soon after your report, complaining that it is erroneous. The council report made a mistake, he says, and it is another restaurant that is losing its license. Are you guilty of libel? What would be your defense? What should you do?

10. You are taping the arrival of the Queen of England at a local hotel. In your taped report, a prominent business leader in your community can be seen checking in at one of the hotels with a woman who is not his wife. He calls, trying to get you to discard the film, claiming his privacy as a private citizen has been abridged. Has it? What would you do?

11 You are doing a report on the nude bars in town. In editing the videotape, the editor cuts everything except tape of the dancers from the knees down. You are disappointed at the censorship. You check with the news director. What should the news director tell you?

12 You produce, on your own time, a documentary on welfare reform. Should you have it copyrighted? What protection would a copyright give you?

13 You falsely report that an individual has won $87,000 in the state lottery. Literally hundreds of opportunists call her, seeking her financial help. Does she have a case against you? Why or why not?

Critical Thinking Questions

Directions: The following questions are provided to help you examine the deeper meanings and complexities of the various issues under discussion. Answer each question to the best of your ability after a thoughtful review of the subject at hand.

1. What are the differences between the legal constraints that govern reporting in the various media — print, radio, television, cable, and the Internet?

2. In your view, should electronic media be held to different legal standards than print media? Explain the two models, the rationale behind each, and discuss why you agree or disagree with distinguishing between the two. Be sure to use legal arguments to support your position.

3. Section 315 provides for no right of censorship of political remarks over which broadcasters have no control, even if the content is racist, vulgar, or obscene. What are the potential benefits and harms of this regulation?

4. If any person or organization is allowed to censor electronic media content, who should it be? Under what circumstances?

5. What is the difference between staging a news event and motivating a news subject to perform an activity before the camera? Is either approach ethical? If so, under what circumstances?

6. How does the concept of libel apply to electronic journalists? Under what conditions, if any, is it permissible and legal to libel a news source?

7. Give three examples of electronic news reports that invade an individual's privacy and are not newsworthy. Use hypothetical or real-life examples to explain.

8. How is it possible for journalists to cover pre-trial criminal proceedings without jeopardizing the defendant's right to a fair trial? How far can you go in reporting information without harming the judicial process?

9. Most entertainment audiences are exposed occasionally to obscenity and sexual innuendo. What guidelines, then, should govern nudity and obscenity in news reporting?

10. How far should a news organization go in using graphic content in a news report where the content helps tell the true story, such as in reports about war or terrorism?

Self-Review Questions

Directions: Each of the self-review questions below addresses information contained in this chapter. Answer each question to the best of your ability, then review the chapter as necessary to further strengthen your understanding of each concept or issue.

1. What are the provisions of Section 315 and Section 312 of the Communication Act? What is the intent behind those sections?

2. What is "staged news?" Provide an example.

3. What is libel? What are the principal defenses against libel?

4. What four elements must a successful plaintiff prove in a libel trial?

5. What is the difference between libel *per se* and libel *per quod*?

6. What is the definition of privacy? How can the legal concept of privacy impact the reporting process?

7. What have courts said regarding downloading and sharing music files for free via the Internet? Under what area of communication law does this fall?

8. As a journalist, how can you balance the need for a free press against a defendant's right to a fair trial?

9. What are shield laws? How effective are they in protecting a journalist's right to report accurately and completely?

10. What laws help to protect the journalist's access to important public information?

## CHAPTER FOURTEEN

Ethics and Professionalism

Essential to the definition of professional electronic journalism is an emphasis on ethical standards. Legal standards (discussed in Chapter 13) protect society against unethical and abusive conduct, and if you, as a working journalist, have a strong commitment to professional ethics, most of the legal restrictions will be academic to you. Many of the ethical decisions you will make relate to the concepts of privacy and fairness, and to the specific codes and policies of professional conduct.

ETHICAL FOUNDATIONS

In the American model, the journalist is presumed to be a neutral observer of events who does everything possible to keep personal bias out of the news being reported. Many journalists aspire to that ideal with the belief that the public has a right to receive news and information free of political or other values that affect the way it is reported. In reality, however, we are all human beings and, thus, products of our past experiences. We are value-laden beings subject to perceptions of reality determined by the way we see the world. Our belief systems are constructed from early childhood through our relationships and experiences. Thus, "truth" often differs depending on one's background and perspective.

Intelligent journalists know where their opinions rest and work hard not to let them interfere with objective reporting. Sometimes, though, that translates to unfairness in reporting, not only for the side the reporter may disagree with but also one with which he or she agrees. For example, a reporter who is a political conservative may be harder on candidates with whom the reporter agrees because of a conscious effort not to favor them.

In addition, we tend to view the world based on our ideology. In the American concept of the world, hard work is supposed to produce success. When people work hard but still fail, we tend to see that as somehow unfair. But are homeless people always victims of an unfair system, or are they sometimes products of their own bad choices along life's road? When you do a story about the homeless, your values will greatly influence what and how you report that story. The way you perceive their world may not be the same way they do.

The U.S. Constitution was set up with a separation of church and state and also a separation of powers among the three major elements of our system: executive, legislative, and judiciary. When we report on events elsewhere in the world, we do so from an American perspective, and our cultural values influence our interpretations. For instance, in the Mideast one of the major religions does not embrace the concept of separation of church and state, nor is its military considered separate from the other two institutions. Indeed, the founder of Islam was a religious prophet, military general, and government statesman all wrapped up in one person.

How do you report objectively on another culture that has core values different from yours? When our values get mixed into our perceptions of objectivity, the question becomes an ethical one. This has to be a constant concern for journalists, for in human beings, perception is truth. Frequently truth is not a finite, easily definable set of facts but, rather, a complex set of beliefs steeped in our mythologies and experiences. Finding the "truth," therefore, is an unending pursuit that requires an always open mind and willingness to consider opposing points of view.

The Marketplace of Ideas

In 1644 John Milton delivered a speech to the British Parliament against licensing of the press, which later became the foundation of Western free press theory. In the *Areopagitica*, the **marketplace of ideas** was forged as a fundamental concept of finding truth. Within that concept, if all ideas are permitted to be placed in the market of public opinion, truth will prevail. The concept of the press being "free" to provide a marketplace of ideas was integrated into the U.S. Constitution as part of the First Amendment, which prohibits any abridgment of "freedom of speech, or of the press." The concept was a direct result of the European struggle for religious and political freedom, primarily in England from the reign of Henry VIII on.

A major flaw exists in the concept of the marketplace of ideas. The market is not an open one, in which all ideas are on the table. Rather, the marketplace of ideas is a fairly small arena in the modern context of mass media. It is generally confined to those who can buy their printer's ink by the 55-gallon drum or can afford to own a radio or a television station. To have an idea is not the same as being able to convey that idea to millions of people so they can consider its worthiness.

Some suggest that the World Wide Web is the great equalizer, making anyone with Internet access and a computer a potential publisher. Attracting readers to a Web site from among the millions in cyberspace still requires either an established brand name or significant financial resources to promote the Web address. This natural economic limitation, further complicated by technical limits of the radio wave spectrum (only a fixed number of possible radio stations is available on the dial), is the cornerstone of the debate about whether contemporary media represent all societal interests.

In advertising-driven media, the marketplace of ideas tends to be defined in terms of content worth selling to narrow economic and demographic categories. For example, tailoring newscasts to a target market defined as "single-family homeowners in the 18- to 49-year-old group with at least two children and more than $40,000 of annual income" clearly opens up considerable debate about whether media so focused can possibly serve the wider society.

Considerable research supports the view that the reverse may be true: Media generally support the prevailing middle-class ideologies with limited serious criticism of government policy and middle-class values. In addition, top-of-the-hour radio newscasts indicate little diversity of content or emphasis and strikingly uniform presentation of news.[1] Indeed, one could argue, the ideas of the contemporary media marketplace are not what rule it but, rather, the fairly uniform pursuit of narrowly defined audiences.

News Versus Entertainment

The ethical journalist faces never-ending questions about the how and why of coverage. Are marginalized social groups covered effectively? Do the media, anxious to please certain target viewers, tend to reinforce prevailing mythologies by producing programming that reflects those viewers "wants?" How does the structure of radio and television (economic and technological) influence coverage?

Consider the last question: Radio is a medium of sound, and television primarily a medium of pictures. Although some stories work well within the printed context of the daily newspaper, they are dull in electronic media. For example, video of the state legislature is usually boring stuff — just a bunch of people standing or sitting around. From the ideal of providing compelling video that will draw viewers into the newscast, almost nothing is worse than showing people standing around. In one major-market television newsroom, producers, reporters, and photographers were ordered, in a newsroom memo, to stop putting what the executive producer termed "BOPSAs" (a bunch of people standing around) on the air. Is it any wonder that much of television news focuses on dramatic events that are compelling visually but often of marginal social import in the greater scheme of things?

Television frequently has been criticized for lacking depth and follow-up and failing to provide a wider context to the sea of images it washes over the audience. That may be one reason television news ratings have declined in the post-cable era, when wide ranges of viewing choices are available. If some choice other than news programming is available, millions of Americans choose "other." Is that because they simply do not care about current events? Or might it be that what they see on television has little to with their personalized worlds? Or has television news been so captivated by entertainment values that it is more "infotainment" than journalism, and thereby has driven those seeking traditional news elsewhere to get it? The answer is probably a combination of those possibilities along with additional factors.

As news viewing has been eroded by competing media, many news organizations have sought to preserve market share by manufacturing a mass-mediated kind of reality through orchestrated "hot button" news series during major rating periods. When news departments create these series, with little relationship to the flow of current events, are the journalists involved being

How a news station chooses to cover certain stories may involve critical ethical questions. A story's framework often dictates how the public views the story and its subjects.

ethical? Are they ethical in producing newscasts with a great deal of emphasis on the "human" side without a wider context addressing the "why" and "what" of the situation?

Television tends toward the emotional. Pictures are powerful emotionally. But has television news gone too far with such fare in the seemingly endless parade of people weeping on the evening news for one reason or another? Has traditional current-events coverage about the greater issues of public policy been displaced by this fare because the audience doesn't want the former, or because television journalists have become hostages to their own technology? Interestingly, a 1999 study of local television news found that viewers want more in-depth local stories — from infrastructure to education to trends — and stations producing this sort of quality programming were more successful commercially than stations that filled their newscasts with crime, celebrity, and sensation.[2]

The following pages introduce some of the most pressing ethical dilemmas in electronic news media.

PRIVACY

The concept of privacy, which is legally defined in most states, has been interpreted variously in the federal courts. Besides the legal constraints of privacy law, critics often ask, "Do the media have the ethical right to invade a person's privacy even if the legal right is there?" Members of the public are concerned about media invasion of privacy.

Most networks and local news programs ran camera shots that peered through the hedges into Caroline Kennedy Schlossberg's yard at her home on Long Island as she and her young children awaited word in the wake of the plane crash of her brother, John F. Kennedy, Jr. In a survey done in the wake of his death, 86 percent of the polled American registered voters agreed that news organizations should not run a current photograph or image of family members who have lost a loved one within the prior week. And 80 percent agreed that photographers should not photograph children without permission.[3] Yet, typically, news crews are routinely assigned to stake out and photograph people caught up in the tragedy of loved ones. Sometimes they are celebrities, but often they are ordinary people who, except for the newsworthiness of the train wreck, airplane crash, or other disaster, would attract no media attention.

Clearly, there is a significant difference in attitude between media organizations and their audiences about what is appropriate and necessary to convey the meaning of a story. How far into a person's private life should an interviewer delve? Not very far, if you ask the viewing public. Many polls indicate that most people think invading the privacy of a person while gathering the news is wrong. But journalists must balance that criticism with the responsibility of the public's right to know. That balance must be struck with an acute sense of news judgment and fairness.

On the local level, journalists face these ethical questions almost daily. The TV reporter and videographer on assignment in San Angelo, Texas, faced a difficult decision when they followed police to do a report from inside a murder victim's house. The police allowed the reporter and videographer into the home, but the victim's husband requested that they leave. They did, but not until after they got the story. Did they invade the privacy of the husband even though police had given their permission? That's both a legal and an ethical question. The legal question was never answered because the husband who brought suit died before it came to trial. The ethical question is perhaps easier to answer in this case.

Maybe some of the tougher questions fall into a gray area. Consider these dilemmas:

- Should a drowning victim be shown being pulled from a lake?

- Should the reporter do a live interview from the hospital with the father of a flood victim?

- Should the names or visuals of juveniles who have committed a crime be used in a story? (Some states have legal restrictions regarding the use of juvenile names in a story, but many states leave this to the media's discretion.)

- Should the names of rape victims be made public?

- Should photos of coffins of combat victims be shown? (Photographers and videographers are not allowed to take pictures at military bases when soldiers bodies are being returned home for burial.)

Electronic media reporters and editors confront these and many similar questions daily.

FAIRNESS

Bias, or unfairness, often lies in the eye of the beholder, but it occurs in stories themselves whenever reports are false, are incomplete, omit an essential detail, or unfairly emphasize one point of view over another. But it also can occur in story choice. For example, a South Carolina news station followed a tip that a local college with only 500 students had no space for about 10 students who were signed up for on-campus housing. When the reporter met with the school administrator for an interview, the official asked the reporter if the station was *also* covering the housing problem with the nearby state university in which a few hundred students were beginning the year without a campus residence. Though the first story was accurate because the school was experiencing trouble with housing all of its students, it was not fair to single it out and not cover the larger university in which many more students were displaced. To be fair and accurate, the station should have covered both situations.

The key to **fairness** is not simply to report both sides of an issue but, rather, to report all points of view with equal energy. Political and religious bias may be present, either intentionally or unintentionally, whenever ideas, issues, and candidates receive unequal emphasis or unequal energy.

An 8-second soundbite with a politician may portray more emotional energy, conviction, and psychological heat than a similar 8-second bite with the opposition. The short bite may be superior even to a 35-second bite. One could argue that the 35-second bite gives one candidate more visibility and emphasis, but one also can argue that the 8-second bite gives the other candidate an unfair advantage because it is so compelling and memorable. Equal time does not automatically constitute fairness.

CBS News learned this hard lesson during the 2004 presidential campaign. In a "60 Minutes" report on Sept. 8, 2004, Dan Rather reported that new documents proved that George W. Bush's military service in the Texas Air National Guard was questionable. Immediately, conservative pundits hit cyberspace blogs with questions of legitimacy on the documents supplied by a former commander in the Texas Air National Guard. Rather and CBS issued a public apology in a Sept. 20 broadcast, saying they had made a mistake in judgment. During that broadcast, Rather interviewed the former commander, who claimed he did not forge any documents but did mislead the network on the name of a person who gave him the documents. Rather and CBS News said they could not verify that name and regret using the documents without being confident in their origin. "It was an error that was made, however, in good faith and in the spirit of trying to carry on a CBS News tradition of investigative reporting without fear of favoritism," Rather said in his statement.[4]

Something of a writer's personal sense of ethics and fairness show through in any story, in the writer's choice of words, the order in which the words are expressed, and what facts in the story receive the most emphasis. The late David Brinkley of ABC said that the journalist cannot possibly be objective in the sense that to be totally objective is to have no likes or dislikes, no feelings one way or another about anything. What is possible, Brinkley said, is to be fair — to make a totally honest effort to report the news event or the newsmaker as representatively as possible. Most stories are neither all black nor all white. They usually have more than two sides if the issue at stake is especially controversial.

To be fair in your reporting of such stories, you must report with equal emphasis all salient points of view, irrespective of your own social and political views and feelings. You must be, as former CBS News President Richard Salant said, "just as skeptical of those news sources we admire and of stories with which we agree as we are of those we dislike and the stories with which we disagree."

The difficult, if not impossible, goal of being totally objective does not overrule your responsibility to strive for fairness.

ELECTRONIC NEWSGATHERING (ENG)

Before the rapid evolution of electronic newsgathering (ENG), broadcast journalists faced fewer challenges, problems, and opportunities than are now commonplace thanks to electronic newsgathering. Broadcast journalists did not face the ethical dilemmas involved in deciding whether to telecast airplane crashes live and in color. They did not have to make instant news judgments, as developing stories were sent live to mass audiences.

Live coverage of dramatic events, such as an airplane crash or an apartment house fire, is more emotionally involving than reports shown after the fact. Live coverage offers the viewer more intense anticipation about the story's outcome and, hence, more suspense. But an additional element, not present even in live radio news coverage, is the possible visual identification of victims before next of kin can be notified.

Ethics in journalism implies a responsibility to be believable and to earn the public trust. No journalist can afford to compromise truth or good taste. To do so is to lose faith with the public and to bias the information upon which viewers form their opinions and decide courses of private and public action. Ethics (and professionalism) in journalism presupposes a belief in service to the public, a belief in self-regulation and autonomy in one's work. In some ENG broadcasts, those considerations are outweighed by the capability that ENG provides to go live almost at will.

Live Coverage

In the infancy of ENG, the tendency at some stations was to go live on every conceivable kind of story. We have the capability, the reasoning went, so why not use it? Suddenly reporters, unprepared for the consequences of this technology, were given the freedom to bury themselves in it. Viewers across the nation were assaulted with startling shots of plane crash victims receiving last rites on bloody landing strips, vulgar obscenities uttered unthinkingly and sometimes with calculation by news interviewees, the actual act of suicide by a man holding hostages in a sleazy bar, naked "streakers" and "mooners" flashing for the minicams at protest rallies, and acts of violence that included the assault of a social organizer who was struck in the head with a glass water pitcher as he delivered a speech.

The ability to broadcast live calls for a news ethic because a journalist seldom can "background" a live broadcast adequately. There is no lead time to bone up on the event, no leisure to reconsider a decision once it is made. By the time people see a story on their home screens, it is too late for the reporter to back down from a bad decision, or from a lapse in news judgment or good taste.

Just as ethics and good taste are a matter of individual judgment, so, too, are the considerations that dictate whether a given event should be covered live in the first place. Don Hewitt, former executive producer of CBS's 60 Minutes, maintains that, for the most part, live television is not good television. Hewitt believes the best television has drama that cannot be built into a live broadcast unless the event is dramatic in and of itself. And, says Hewitt, few events are inherently dramatic.

In this context, live coverage of people escaping from a flood-ravaged canyon is dramatic, whereas a meeting of city council might better be taped and edited into a solid story for later presentation. On the one hand, nothing is inherently dramatic in scenes of council members sitting around a table while a reporter tries to explain what they're doing. On the other hand, a 15-second "talking head" piece with the winning quarterback at the Super Bowl might be as dramatic as a live shot of an oil refinery explosion. The joy in a mother's face as she is reunited with her child who was lost in the mountains may be as valid for live coverage as the rescue of stranded motorists trapped on a snowy interstate highway. The point is that decisions about each story must be made on the basis of the unique conditions surrounding each event.

Consider the consequences of one station's decision in a Midwest TV market. The story began when police surrounded a local bar where an armed man had taken several patrons hostage and threatened to kill himself. ENG crews from several stations arrived almost simultaneously and worked their way to within feet of the doorway where the gunman was barricaded. A police negotiator tried to talk the man into peaceful surrender.

At that point, one station broke into regular programming with a live report from the scene. The gunman yelled to the camera crew, "If you don't get away from the door, I'm gonna' shoot myself!" Suddenly he did put a gun to his head and pull the trigger. The man died in full view of the camera and the thousands of viewers who were watching, many of them children who had tuned in to late afternoon programming. The other stations at the scene videotaped the story but did not broadcast it live. Viewer reaction to the event as broadcast live was immediate and irate.

Media Competition

Competition is intense in television news, particularly since FCC deregulation and the rise of cable television increased the number of competing channels markedly beginning in the mid-1970s. The pressure to generate ratings is ingrained in the television news business because of the combined forces of inherent journalistic competitiveness and the millions of dollars in advertising at stake.

Former Seattle television news reporter Julie Blacklow described the way ratings pressure affected the KING-TV newsroom in the early 1990s:

> The "ratings" system turned television news into a popularity contest, a full-fledged, knock-down, clobber-the-opponent competition.
>
> Being the best, being right, being thorough, and being responsible became less important than being number one. Advertising rates (how much your station can charge for a commercial) depended solely on your place on the Nielsen chart: The higher you ranked, the more advertisers paid to run their commercials on your station. News became, and remains, singularly dollar-driven and ratings-obsessed. And we began to watch very closely what the competition was doing on a nightly basis, to see what stories seemed to be drawing more viewers.

> With the posting every morning of "ratings" score sheets on newsroom bulletin boards, we were able to see exactly how many of you were watching. If a story on Satan-worship in Sultan played big, the other stations would copy it instantly.
>
> The effect of imitative behavior, coupled with the inexcusable power of consultants dictating to newsrooms what stories should be emphasized, is disconcerting and troublesome, to say the least. And these realities explain why television news is the way it is today: a daily dose of mostly meaningless, poorly researched, irrelevant and insubstantial "filler" pretending to be news; a series of "live shots" for no particular reason other than to justify the purchase of expensive technology; a recounting of every rape and shooting in our cities with none of the pain or humanity behind those horrifying acts.[5]

This view is extremely cynical, possibly a product in part of the disillusionment that comes to the serious journalist when the realities of news as a business settle in. Even so, that view of ratings as all-important and technology as a key to expand those ratings have created an all too common approach in many newsrooms of "live for live's sake." It means that each major newscast has a live remote broadcast within it regardless of whether news really is happening at broadcast time. As a result, in many American television markets, night after night, you see reporters standing in front of darkened buildings on the 10 or 11 o'clock evening news explaining "live" what happened earlier, or a 5 o'clock news "live shot" of something that happened early in the afternoon or even in the morning with only the reporter reporting the event actually "live" at five.

What's more, live remotes are extremely time-consuming. First you must have the anchor do a five- to ten-second toss to the remote reporter. Then the reporter talks for ten to 15 seconds to set up the package insert often used in live remotes. After the package is aired, the normal procedure is to come back out to the reporter live at the remote again. Another ten to 15 seconds are used to wrap up the story from the scene and do a toss back to the studio anchor. Then, to make the anchor look smart, he or she usually asks a brief question of the field reporter, followed by a quick answer. The question and answer usually are scripted carefully in advance to make sure that both reporter and anchor look intelligent. All of that eats up three or four minutes on something that otherwise would be a 30-second voice-over.

Because live shots take up so much time, other news cannot be covered within the tight time constraints of the newscast. Thus, the belief that audiences want to see live coverage contributes to manufacturing it at the expense of other coverage.

Camera Position

Camera position dramatically affects audience perception of news events. On the one hand, if the camera at a demonstration is shooting from behind demonstrators toward a police line, you'll see the faces of the police opposing the mob. Of the mob itself, you'll see only the backs of those involved and the featureless backs of heads. On the other hand, a camera shooting from behind the police would show only their backs but you'd see the angry faces of the demonstrators taunting the police, spitting at them, throwing things, and otherwise attempting to trigger a violent confrontation. Each camera position reveals things the other cannot. To get the full story of a confrontation, you need both points of view. Showing only one point of view clearly distorts reality to a substantial extent.

In the case of live shots, rarely is more than one camera available, so you are much a victim of your positioning. And people have become quite sophisticated in performing all kinds of dopey, and sometimes obscene, activities in the background of live camera coverage. One sportscaster in a major market was doing a live report from the local NFL team's locker room after a game when one of the linemen unwittingly walked into the background briefly without wearing a stitch of clothing, facing the camera. Suffice it to say that when you go live, anything can happen — and often does.

Benefit of Perspective

Newspaper reporters have the relative leisure to develop a perspective about the story that is being reported. The same is true, to a lesser extent, of the electronic journalist who prepares a delayed report to be played back later. This leisure of perspective occurs as notes are gathered, the reporter drives back to the newsroom, the story is typed, the copy is passed through editors and rewrite persons, and it finally emerges as a finished story. The process of the print story (or delayed newscast account) is more self-correcting than the instant report because it is the product of more reflective thought.

The leisure of retrospective analysis applies, of course, to the on-the-scene inspection of the event, the taking of notes, and the gathering of facts, but it also extends to the assimilation of the story by its intended audiences. Newspaper and traditional newscast audiences know that the story has evolved through time and

News stations sometimes fail to think about the angle of the camera shots, as well as background content. This can be particularly embarrassing during live shots. Notice here the videographer is careful to have a neutral background behind the reporter.

that its author has had time to analyze the event more thoroughly than the reporter of a live event. Audiences who witness live reports must assume more of the burden of making sense of news events.

With live ENG, television reporters are saying to their audiences, "Here are the facts, as best we can report them, as they are happening." This is a far cry from saying, "Here are the facts of what happened," because in the live report so little is known at that point about the happening. The emphasis is almost entirely on the "what," with little consideration, by necessity, of the essential "why" of the event or of its potential consequences.

A major ethical problem that television journalists have to reconcile is manipulation, aggravated by increasingly sophisticated people and organizations seeking coverage. Journalists always have been wary of — though not always perceptive about — those trying to use them. For example, a candidate for Congress in a major market recognized that the local stations didn't have much news to cover on the weekends, that their newscasts were mostly filler material. So the candidate carefully orchestrated rallies and other public appearances and campaign events to take place on Saturday and Sunday afternoons. The stations all showed up weekend after weekend to cover the only thing going on in town — the candidate's staged events.

The result was substantial audience awareness of the candidate, a major increase in public knowledge of the person, and myriad positive images of the candidate doing wonderful things. The candidate's opponent kept staging events during the week, when other events were going on that competed for space on the evening

VETERAN REPORTER TALKS ABOUT ETHICS IN REAL-WORLD JOURNALISM

When Christiane Amanpour walked into the CNN Newsroom more than 20 years ago, she had a bicycle, a suitcase, and 100 dollars. At the time, the young television reporter fit right in at CNN, where the cable news channel was a fledgling entity among big-time network news players. Because she was a foreigner, Amanpour was immediately assigned to the foreign desk, and the young reporter found herself in just about every war zone the United States paid attention to.

"Because CNN is seen all over the world, I'm so identified with war and disaster these days that wherever I go, people say jokingly — or maybe not so jokingly — that they shudder when they see me," Amanpour said.

It didn't take long for Amanpour to learn the ropes of her job, or to see the downside of being a television reporter. While covering the war and famine in Somalia in the early 1990s, Amanpour was doing a live shot while explaining on camera how ill one man was. During her report she realized that the man was actually dying.

"I didn't know how to break that moment, how to get the camera away, what to do that would not sully what was happening in real life," she said.

Amanpour discovered the power of the press again in Somalia after the video and photograph showing a dead American soldier being dragged in the street was publicized all over the world.

"That image — and I can tell you from experience — has haunted U.S. foreign policy since that day," she said. "Because the leaders are afraid of those kinds of pictures, because leadership can be painful, . . . because that image that we played over and over and over and over again forced a new president to pull out of Somalia, it has had a traumatic effect ever since."

One of the most difficult aspects of her job, Amanpour said, has been watching the demise of solid television news. Despite attempting to keep Americans informed about major developments abroad — often at the expense of the lives of foreign correspondents — Amanpour has seen television news networks air relatively insignificant stories instead of international developments because of the entertainment value for the audience.

"[Foreign correspondents] would go through hell to do their pieces only to frequently find the stories killed back in New York because of some fascinating new twist on 'killer Twinkies' or Fergie getting fatter or something," Amanpour said.

Despite her growing disappointment in television news of late, Amanpour is optimistic, because she sees how journalism is making a difference in many places around the world. "I'm a believer, and that's why I still do it," Amanpour said. "I believe that good journalism, good television, can make our world a better place. And I really believe good journalism is good business."

Based on remarks by Christiana Amanpour, Chief International Correspondent, CNN, Keynote address to the RTNDA Conference of 2000. Used by permission. Copyright © 2000, 2004 by Christiana Amanpour.

newscasts. As a result, the weekend candidate, who was less well known at the beginning of the campaign, won handily. The stations could argue that they were only covering the "news" that occurred on the weekend, but it was "news" created by and for a candidate engaging in the political business of manipulating voters — and using the media effectively to do it.

Public relations professionals can be effective tools for the journalist to use. They can be resources to get information that is hard to get elsewhere, and valuable contacts who can make available hard-to-get individuals. News and public relations professionals have a symbiotic relationship. Each functions partly because of the other. Maintaining neutrality, however, always must be at the forefront of the journalist's mind, and the recognition of the many agendas at work in the media message marketplace.

Instant News Policy

Television news operations traditionally employ far fewer employees than their newspaper counterparts. For that reason, television reporters typically conduct far less research than newspaper reporters do. TV stations may do only one or two stories per week, or at best a series on that one story. Often, fast-breaking news events preclude proper backgrounding, even for seasoned reporters. When events such as calamitous earthquakes and volcanic eruptions occur, reporters must react almost instinctively. Their primary concern is how to report the story as thoroughly as possible with little information available.

The demands of live broadcast do not lend themselves easily to treatment in a handbook of ethical guidelines because decisions are almost always situationally based. Therefore, policies must deal in broad generalities because, in news, few events can be dealt with in specifics. There is no way to know what to predict.

At some electronic news organizations, the problem is handled by designating certain key people as responsible for dictating "instant policy." Often, these individuals are the news director and the executive news producer. "When we have a major breaking story — a hostage situation or a plane crash — we call those people in," says Roger Ogden, former General Manager at KCNC-TV. "They make the kinds of decisions that can't be printed in a manual."

Even when guidelines exist, there is the real question of whether they can be implemented routinely. Nora Beloff, former reporter for the British Broadcasting Corporation and the Reuters news agency, says, "The life of a journalist has to be a series of compromises in which ethics is unlikely to be the overriding consideration."

The reason for this, simply put, is that there is no time to form ethical decisions while under the pressure of deadlines and instant reporting. These decisions, Edward R. Murrow once said, must be "hammered out by the individual on the anvil of experience."

"Our people, both in the newsroom and in the field, have to have a solid news or editorial philosophy to begin with, because broadcast news happens so quickly," adds former NBC Vice-President Thomas Wolzien. "When you're sitting in the newsroom or the control room at five-thirty or six o'clock, and you're going live somewhere, you have a real problem because you don't have time to think. You can purely and basically react."

SPECIFIC NEWS COVERAGE

How given news topics are covered on an ongoing basis deserves serious attention. We have discussed the various challenges with live coverage of news, but sometimes we are also complacent about how we are covering traditional news stories.

Crime coverage

Television newscasts typically provide abundant coverage of crime, but it is a specific kind of crime. So-called white-collar crime — accountants embezzling millions, people cheating on their income taxes — is hard to show on television. The visuals are boring shots of spreadsheets with lots of numbers, or the front doors of financial institutions. Blue-collar crime, the stuff of lower socioeconomic classes, is much more visual. Stick-ups of convenience stores, gang fights, a violent incident at a school — all provide strong pictures with emotional power — police cars with their lights flashing, angry or injured people with fire in their eyes, and blood on the street.

The result is that crime on television is not necessarily the kind that harms the nation deeply but, rather, is powerful superficially while usually involving only a few people. Those in the journalism business have called violent crime coverage, including war video, "bang-bang" news.

Crime is a staple in some news formats that emphasize primarily crime coverage that is visually powerful. This coverage frequently features minority groups because violent crime tends to be more common in among socioeconomically disadvantaged people. It may contribute to socioeconomic racial **stereotyping**. If most people involved in crimes shown on the evening news night after night are African American or Hispanic, the audience quite likely will consider people of those ethnic groups as more prone to violence. Thus, news coverage can affect stereotyping in a multicultural society that has had a history of polarization by race.

In addition, the intense coverage of crime is driven by television station marketing studies that show Americans are concerned about crime. That may distort the perception of crime in the society, though. When we see violent crime nearly every evening on the news, because "action news" emphasizes coverage of crime, does that, in turn, contribute to an increase in viewer fear and anxiety about crime?

For many people, the very definition of news means that it is the exceptional, the extraordinary. For something to be news, it has to be different. Does coverage of topics within the context of television news, therefore, create a kind of manufactured reality on the screens in our living rooms separate from the reality of most of our daily lives?

Reporting on Government

In the area of politics, evidence exists that television has changed the way national leaders come into prominence and policy is set. Television coverage has a tendency to reframe complex political discussions into simplistic campaign positions and pare down involved political arguments into superficial soundbites. Since television became an active part of political campaigning in the 1960s, there has been an increasing emphasis on the "image" of our political leaders. This is not inherently bad, but it should be a constant reminder that our news coverage must not be superficial. We should strive to give viewers useful information and not just provide an "image" that may not accurately reflect the candidates' political positions.

In the same context, it is extremely important for journalists to be aware of potential bias in favor of one candidate over another. Though the substance of the news coverage may not be negative, images and video that show one candidate looking unprofessional and idiotic while another appears slick and businesslike are not necessarily fair representations and, therefore, are unethical.

Economic Pressure

Unfortunately, sometimes our coverage is influenced by advertising and other economic pressures. We have to be wary of our news judgment failing because of outside financial pressure.

This problem was evidenced by a reporter who was assigned to do a seemingly innocuous five-part series on how to buy a car, for newscasts during a November ratings period. The series was conceived as a consumer-oriented series to help give viewers the feeling that the station was helping them cope with their world. The reporter found a dealer who would cooperate but required the interviews to be shot in such a way that the specific identity of the interviewee and the dealership involved would be kept confidential. The trade-off was full disclosure on the "tricks of the trade" of buying and selling cars.

The series proved to be a strong one, with solid consumer information on things like the "hand-off," in which the "greeter" in a dealership hands off the customer to a "closer," who actually does the hard selling. Tips were provided on how to counter high-pressure tactics by the "closer." Also included was specific information about how to find out the dealer's real cost for any vehicle, and how to bargain down the price through approaches such as asking for dealer financing (which often provides the dealer additional profit).

After the series aired, a local consortium of auto dealers, incensed at the television station's effort to inform customers on the ins and outs of getting the best deal, got all of its member dealers to cancel their advertising on the station — an annual loss of more than a quarter-million dollars. The reporter was not fired, but neither the reporter nor the television station involved has attempted another aggressive consumer series affecting such a crucial advertising clientele.

PROFESSIONAL CODES

Ethics can be divided into two major categories: professional ethics and personal ethics. During the 20th century — the era of social responsibility of mass communications — journalists initiated several codes of conduct. Among the significant codes are the Canons of Journalism and the responsibilities of a free press as recommended by the Commission on Freedom of the Press.

We have reprinted two major ethical codes in the Appendices D and E to this text. The RTNDA Code of Broadcast News Ethics Code provides guidelines for ethical conduct of radio and television journalists. The Ethics Code of the Society of Professional Journalists, with roots in the newspaper industry, is one of the best documents available to help define this challenging area of the professional behavior of working journalists. In addition, you can consult both codes on their organizations' Internet home pages, at:

RTNDA: http://www.rtnda.org/rtnda/
SPJ: http://spj.org.ethics

Media Organization Policies

In addition to industry codes, such as the RTNDA and SPJ codes, many media organizations have their own policies that specify certain conduct. The policy statements cover many facets of behavior expected of the organization and its employees. For example, a television station policy may cover how to handle sex crimes, other crimes, race, suicide, and people with disabilities. Policy statements also may cover aspects of the job relating to ethics. The guidelines may involve conflict of interest, moonlighting, political activity, and freelancing.

Professional Behavior

From a sociological perspective, professional behavior may be defined in terms of four basic criteria:

1. *Expertise*: specialized knowledge and skill vital for a newscaster; acquired through education, experience, and professional relationships.

2. *Autonomy*: use of one's own judgment without outside interference, which allows one to rise above the mediocrity of surrounding people and do what one thinks is the best action in any given situation.

3. *Commitment*: continued devotion to and pursuit of excellence within one's profession; working toward goals without detour.

4. *Responsibility*: maturity and devotion to benefit society.

Professional behavior encompasses the demonstration of intellectual competence, freedom from outside interference, and high ethical conduct. If you are to rise above mediocrity, you must develop a sense of professionalism that you will exhibit no matter where you work. Achieving professionalism is the best means to attain genuine job satisfaction in your career.

PERSONAL ETHICS

In journalism, ethical questions such the ones mentioned here arise every hour of every day. Although you may have to make a decision once or twice a day about the length and format of a story, everything you write, shoot, edit, and read on camera reflects your journalism ethics. If you were asked to write one or two paragraphs defining your personal journalism ethic, what would you say? What will you do as a journalist in the field when you are confronted with these ethical situations? Will you be willing to give up a nice car, a home in the suburbs, your children's college education, and walk out of a newsroom where what you see as unethical behavior not only is accepted but is encouraged?

Journalism ethics is not a simplistic set of finite criteria. It is a complicated area driven by ideals that emanate from the 17th century and continue to influence our concept of what it means to be a member of a free and democratic society. Maintaining journalistic ethics is a never-ending struggle with powerful influences. Despite professional codes and organizational guidelines, your choices as a professional journalist will come down to your own ethics, which should be guided by the highest standards within the news media.

Every day of your television news career, you will be covering events, putting together stories about what you see and find out, and attempting to build a relationship of trust with your audience. Some of the ethical questions raised in this chapter are overarching, philosophical issues regarding the way an entire industry perceives its role. It is an industry made up of many individuals doing their jobs day in and day out, but it has a special role in creating the fabric of American society, and within that special role rests great responsibility. The journalist must, at all times and in all ways, be honest, forthright, and uncompromisingly ethical.

In the final analysis, the individual's personal ethics will make the difference in a given situation. Although

TYPICAL POLICY GUIDELINES

1. *Sex crimes:* Handle with as much care as possible. State that the crime was committed, provide essential facts, but don't go into detail. Don't report the victim's name. For example, you might report a rape case like this: A 21-year-old Central Valley woman was raped early this morning as she returned home from work. Police are seeking a 6-foot man, weighing about 175 pounds.

2. *Crime stories:* Provide the facts, but don't sensationalize with morbid details. Avoid going into the "how" of the crime. Never use juvenile names without the court's permission. Don't report that a person is arrested for questioning. Report a suspect's name only after a charge has been filed.

3. *Race:* Unless the race is an important part of the story, don't mention it. If, John Smith is the first black mayor of Central Valley, though, use it. Sometimes in describing fugitives in crime stories, race is important.

4. *Suicide:* Don't say that someone committed suicide until the coroner has ruled the death a suicide. As in any crime story, state the facts simply without detail. Attribute the suicide ruling to the coroner.

5. *Disabilities:* Never joke about a disability. Don't mention a disability unless it is essential to the story.

professional standards cover major issues, in many cases the professional or station codes do not cover individual circumstances. One of the essential attributes of any occupation that makes it a profession is a code of ethical conduct. It is not the occupation itself that is professional, though; it is individuals within that occupation. For an individual to be professional, he or she must have, beyond an overriding sense of public responsibility, a keen sense of personal and professional ethics.

ENDNOTES

1. Washburn, P.C., "Top of the Hour Radio Newscasts and the Public Interest," *Journal of Broadcasting & Electronic Media* (1995), 39(1), 73-91.

2. Rosentheil, T., C. Cottlliev, and L.A. Brady, "Quality Brings Higher Ratings, but Enterprise is Disappearing," *Columbia Journalism Review,* Nov/Dec 1999, pp. 80-85.

3. Brill, S., "Curiosity vs. Privacy," *Brill's Content.* October 1999, pp. 98–103, 109, 127–129.

4. CBSNews.com, "Dan Rather Statement on Memos," Sept. 20, 2004

5. Blacklow, J., "No News Not Good News: 10-second Sound Bites May be the Undoing of Real TV Journalism," *Seattle Times,* (1992 February 9, p. A-19) Copyright © 1992.

EXERCISE 14-A: Writing Stories Involving Ethical Dilemmas

Name _____ Date _____

1. You are asked to cover a rape case for the radio newscast. You find out the following facts. Write your story from the facts.

Rape victim: 19-year-old sophomore at Central Valley University . . . she's from Miami, Fla. and is majoring in music . . . 5'8" and weighs 130 pounds. Her name is Dorothy Green.

Rape suspect: 35-year-old Tom R. Spencer, assistant librarian at the university. He lives at 3030 Concord and has been picked up by police for questioning.

Incident: Miss Green was studying late at the library. When it closed, she left to walk back to her dorm. She was wearing shorts and a halter top when her assailant grabbed her from behind and made her go with him in the trees behind the dorm. He tore her clothes from her, raped her at gunpoint, and let her go without further harm except a threat that if she tried to identify him, she would be "dead, dead, dead." She called women's crisis center immediately upon returning to her dorm at 1:20 a.m. Police picked up Spencer at his apartment about 3:15 a.m.

(Your story here)

EXERCISE 14B: Ethical Decisions in Broadcast News

Name _____ Date _____

1. You receive the following soundbite from the policeman investigating a murder at an exclusive mansion near the city. Would you have to edit any of it? If so, what would you delete?

> "I found Mrs. Davis lying in a pool of blood near the swimming pool, the machete-type knife still in her rib cage. It looked like she had been stabbed five or six times. It was the worst scene I've witnessed in my 26 years on the force."

2. How would you edit the following news story?

Mrs. Emily Jester, 64-year-old African American woman, committed suicide this morning in her garage. She lived at 4332 Chestnut Rd. A neighbor heard a shotgun blast about 10:30 this morning at Mrs. Jester's and went to check. A 16-gauge shotgun was found in the room with Mrs. Jester after the neighbor, Tina Willis, called police. The coroner, Dr. Tom P. Pratt, is investigating the incident.

3. As a reporter for Station XYYZ-TV, you are invited to cover the opening of a new educational service center. The center sells equipment to help children with learning difficulties. You have a child with a mental disability, and the public relations director offers to give you a reading machine while you are at the opening covering the story. What do you do?

4 You are a reporter with XYZ radio. You are offered a job working as a weekend weather person at the local TV station. It won't interfere with your radio work . . . at least the hours won't conflict. What should you do?

5 You are quite interested in politics and would like to work in the Democratic primary. Your station management is avidly Republican. What should you do?

6 You are assigned to cover the Democratic candidates for governor and lieutenant governor, but you really like the Republican candidates better. Should you do your best to be objective in your coverage, or should you ask for a reassignment?

EXERCISE 14B: Ethical Decisions in Broadcast News *(continued)*

Name _____ Date _____

7 You are covering an assignment at a solar energy research lab. After doing the story, you decide that would make a good feature story for a particular magazine. That night on your own time, you write an outline and query letter to the editor. Later you get a response from the editor. She says she would like the article and she'll pay you $500 for it. You then wonder, because you gathered the information while doing the story for your electronic media organization, if it's right to make money freelancing on this subject. What do you decide?

8 The police have arrested Paul Robbins, a local bank president, for questioning about embezzlement. They have not charged him but are holding him the 24 hours before they have to bring charges and are still questioning him. In your state, you can report the story legally. Do you think you should before charges actually have been filed? If so, why? If not, why not?

9 At least twice a week, you talk with Sarah Reinhart, public information officer for the State Department of Health, as part of your beat. She's always open and honest. This week she tells you the director is going to crack down on the state university cafeterias with surprise investigations next week. She asks that you not report anything until the inspections are done. What should you do? When should you keep information confidential, and when should you use it?

10 How should you, as a radio news director, respond to a request from an advertising salesman to do a live interview from the grand opening of a new restaurant in town?

11 Why is it unethical for journalists to receive perks?

12 Should the weekly public affairs radio program be produced live from a major restaurant in town each week? What might be the problem(s)?

13 Should your radio station have a policy statement permitting news personnel to do commercials? Why or why not?

14 Assume that you are assigned to cover a possible land fraud story. You enter a business with your camera running, and the owner chases you out. Should you use that tape on your news report this evening? Why or why not?

Critical Thinking Questions

Directions: The following questions are provided to help you examine the deeper meanings and complexities of the various issues under discussion. After a thoughtful review of the subject at hand, answer each question to the best of your ability.

1. What qualities distinguish law from ethics? What sanctions help to enforce each?

2. Discuss the notion that all individuals have the right to freedom of speech, but that nowhere in the Constitution is anyone guaranteed the "right to know" anything.

3. News finds its way to us from all points on the globe, but most commonly from an American perspective. What are the positive and negative impacts of this? What media alternatives offer other cultural points of view? How accurate do you believe the points of view of other cultures can be? What, in your opinion, is the best way to become accurately informed about important issues?

4. Under what circumstances do the media have an ethical right to invade a person's privacy, even if a legal right exists?

5. What essential considerations must a journalist follow to help assure fairness in news reporting?

6. Credibility of television news media has been jeopardized by unethical coverage in recent decades. What has contributed to this? What specific news examples can you give to support your answer?

7. Context and perspective are essential elements in news reporting, yet often are sacrificed in live reports. Under such circumstances, then, what are the journalist's responsibilities to the audience?

8. Construct a comprehensive set of personal ethics that can guide you as a working journalist.

Self-Review Questions

Directions: Each of the self-review questions below addresses information contained in this chapter. Answer each question to the best of your ability, then review the chapter as necessary to strengthen your understanding of each concept or issue.

1. What is the difference between ethics and law as they relate to the journalist?

2. Listen or more examples of unethical behavior as it relates to gathering and reporting the news.

3. Does giving equal time for various points of view guarantee fairness in news reporting? Why or why not?

4. How do the various technologies and forms of media impact a journalist's ability to be fair, accurate, and ethical?

5. How can competitive pressures influence ethical behavior during the reporting process?

6. How can professional codes of ethics help guide journalists during the reporting process?

7. What policy guidelines govern coverage of sex and crime stories, race, suicide, and disabilities? What changes, if any, would you suggest in existing guidelines?

8. How can camera position mislead the viewer's understanding of a news event?

9. What is your definition of news as it relates to your sense of ethical responsibility to a viewing audience?

10. What are the four basic criteria that govern professional journalistic behavior from a sociological perspective? Explain.

Web Sites for Electronic Journalists

Following are Web sites that may be useful in researching, writing, reporting, and producing the news. Some sites offer news and updated information of interest to professionals. Others may be useful to confirm information, locate and contact news sources, and even search for employment. Internet addresses change frequently. You may wish to update or correct the following information periodically, as well as add other sources you find useful. Be sure to verify any information from the Internet that you use in your writing, and remember to attribute your Internet sources as necessary.

http://airsafe.com
Air Safety Page

http://www.abcnews.go.com
American Broadcasting Company Home Page (ABC)

http://www.ajr.org
American Journalism Review

http://www.ap.org
Associated Press (AP)

http://www.bbc.co.uk
British Broadcasting Company Home Page (BBC)

http://www.beaweb.org
Broadcast Education Association (BEA)

http://www.BurrellesLuce.com
Burrelles Luce Information Service

http://www.cnn.com
Cable News Network Home page (CNN)

http://cbc.ca
Canadian Broadcasting Corporation (CBC)

http://www.crtc.gc.ca
Canadian Radio-Television and Telecommunications Commission

http://www.newschannel5.com
Channel 5 News in Tennessee. See "Scripts"

http://cbsnews.cbs.com
Columbia Broadcasting System Home page (CBS)

http://congress.org
Congressional Guide

http://cjwww.csustan.edu/cj/rframe.html
Criminal Justice Related Sites

http://www.c-span.org
C-SPAN

http://www.digitaljournalist.org
Digital Journalist (still and video digital photography and editing.)

http://www.editorandpublisher.com/eandp/classifieds/index.jsp
Editor and Publisher Classifieds

http://www.engsafety.com/
ENG Safety

http://www.espn.go.com
ESPN Sports

http://www.facsnet.org
FACSNET (research site for reporters)

http://www.faa.gov
Federal Aviation Administration

http://www.fcc.gov
Federal Communications Commission

http://www.law.emory.edu/caselaw/
Federal Courts Finder

http://www.ftc.gov
Federal Trade Commission

http://www.fedworld.gov
FedWorld (A program of the United States Department of Commerce)

http://www.findlaw.com
FindLaw (Search Engine for law information)

http://www.usdoj.gov/04foia/04_3.html
FOIA Guide

http://www.foxsports.com
Fox Sports

http://www.foxnews.com
FOX Television

http://www.tvspy.com/
Job "Pipeline" (Fee-based)

http://www.tvjobs.com/
Jobs in Television (Broadcast employment service)

http://newslink.org
Journalism jobs site

http://lii.law.cornell.edu
Legal Information Institute at Cornell University

http://www.tvjobs.com/msi/
Master Station Index for jobs in TV

http://www.nielsenmedia.com
Media research site

http://www.msnbc.com
MSNBC

http://www.mtv.com
MTV Online

http://www.nab.org
National Association of Broadcasters (NAB)

http://www.nabef.org
National Association of Broadcasters Education Foundation (NABEF)

http://www.nba.com
National Basketball Association

http://www.nbc.com
National Broadcasting Company (NBC)

http://www.nfl.com
National Football League

http://www.nhl.com
National Hockey League

http://www.nppa.org
National Press Photographers Association (NPPA)

http://www.npr.org
National Public Radio (NPR Online)

http://www.msnbc.com
NBC/MSNBC News

http://eclecticesoterica.com/news.html
The Newsroom

http://www.nilesonline.com/
Robert Niles Online (Reporter research site)

http://www.online-journalist.com
Online Journalist

http://www.ereleases.com
Press Release delivery service

http://media.prnewswire.com/en/jsp/main.jsp
PR Newswire for Journalists

http://www.pbs.org
Public Broadcasting System (PBS Online)

http://www.rtnda.org
Radio-Television News Directors Association (RTNDA)

http://www.reporter.org
Reporter Organization Investigative Reporting Site

http://www.rcfp.org
Reporters Committee for Freedom of the Press

http://www.tvrundown.com
The Rundown

http://www.spj.org
Society of Professional Journalists (SPJ)

http://www.totalbaseball.com
Total Baseball Online

http://www.upi.com
United Press International (UPI)

http://www.upn.com
UPN

http://www.usdoj.gov
U.S. Department of Justice

http://www.supremecourtus.gov/
U.S. Supreme Court

http://www.usscplus.com
U.S. Supreme Court Decisions since 1994

http://www.weather.com
Weather Channel

http://www.wunderground.com
Weather Underground

http://www.whitehouse.gov
White House

http://www.whitehouse.gov/news/briefings/
White House Press Briefings

INTERNET E-MAIL ADDRESS FINDERS

http://www.411.com/
411.com

http://iaf.net/
Internet Address Finder

http://www.whowhere.com
Lycos™ People Search

MULTI-ENGINE SEARCH TOOLS

http://www.altavista.com
Alta Vista

http://www.dogpile.com
Dogpile

http://www.excite.com
Excite

http://www.go.com
GO Network

http://www.google.com
Google

http://goto.myway.com
GoTo

http://www.hotbot.com
HotBot

http://www.lycos.com
Lycos

http://www.metacrawler.com
MetaCrawler

http://www.search.com/
Metasearch

http://peoplesearch.net/
PeopleSearch

http://webcrawler.com
Webcrawler

http://www.yahoo.com
Yahoo

The Linear Editing Process

The video editing unit at almost all television stations consists of four components:

1. Video player
2. Video player/recorder
3. Editing control unit
4. Television monitors that show scenes from both player and recorder.

VIDEO PLAYER AND RECORDER

The control unit operates the electronic and mechanical functions of the video player and recorder. Editing decisions are entered in the control unit, which in turn operates the player and recorder during actual editing. On some units the editing control is incorporated as a physical part of the video machine. All components — player, recorder, editing control unit, and the two television monitors — are fitted onto a movable rack known most commonly as the editing console.

A videocassette from the field, in brief, is edited in the following manner:

1. The cassette is loaded into the video player.
2. Scenes (and sound) on the cassette are transferred electronically to the video recorder. Signals fed from the player are re-recorded, in order, on a master cassette.
3. All instructions for the transfer of scenes and sound are performed by entering appropriate instructions in the editing control unit.

A tab or removable button on the bottom of some video cassettes provides a means to prevent accidental erasure of prerecorded material. If the button is removed, the cassette cannot be used for recording. Only when the button is in place is recording possible. The same precaution holds true when field-recording.

EDITING CONTROL UNIT

The exact layout of the editing control unit varies from one manufacturer to the next, but the schematic diagram shown in Figure B.1 represents the features found on most units. The editing control unit is divided into four distinct areas:

1. The controls that operate the player whenever actual edits are not being performed.
2. The controls that instruct player and recorder to perform actual edits of varying nature.
3. The controls that operate the recorder whenever actual edits are not being done.
4. Digital counters that display elapsed scene time in hours, minutes, seconds, and frames.

Player Controls

Referring to Figure B.1, the left row of player controls — REC, FW, REW, and STOP — is used much like the controls on audiocassette recorders. With these buttons the operator can record manually, fast-forward, rewind, and stop the cassette in the video player. Player controls in the second row marked PLAY, PAUSE/STILL, and SEARCH are used to play scenes from the raw field tape on the left monitor. When the PLAY button is pushed, scenes from the field tape play at normal speed. The PAUSE/STILL button stops the tape and displays a single still frame from the scene at that point. The SEARCH button activates the shuttle control, which allows the editor to view the tape at slower or faster than normal speed.

When the shuttle control is activated, the tape can be viewed at speeds ranging from a frame or

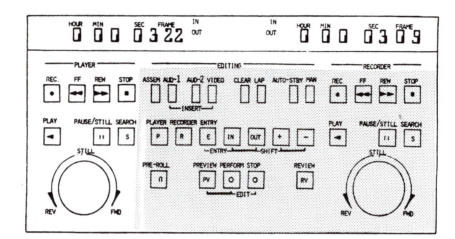

Figure B-1
Player controls.

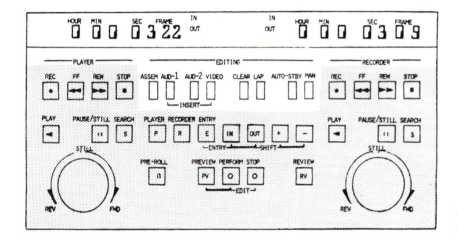

Figure B-2.
Editing controls.

two per second (each second of video contains 30 frames of picture) to as fast as five times normal speed (up to 20 times on some units). The shuttle control is a great time-saver when the editor must locate scenes that are separated widely within the 20-minute field cassette.

Recorder Controls

The controls that operate the recorder (on the right side of the editing control unit) are identical in function to those on the player side of the editing control unit. The only difference is that they operate the recorder, not the player. Scenes from the recorder are displayed on the right monitor.

Editing Controls

Three rows of buttons control all editing functions (see Figure B.2). The first row of buttons is marked ASSEM, AUD-l, AUD-2, VIDEO, CLEAR, LAP, AUTO- STBY [Standby], and MANUAL. The first four buttons on this top row are used to tell the editing control unit what type of editing is to be performed. The editor has two choices: (a) the Assemble (ASSEM) mode, or (b) the

INSERT mode (AUD-l, AUD-2, VIDEO). To understand the nature of each type of editing, we first examine a piece of videotape (Figure B.3).

1. The control track (CTL) consists of one electronic pulse for each frame of video and is necessary to regulate recording and playback speed. Film is controlled in much the same way except that film has physical, not electronic, sprocket holes.

2. The video track carries the picture information as electronic signals from the camera that are recorded magnetically on the videotape.

3. The address track accepts an optional time code, in hours, minutes, seconds, frames, or in real time. The address track requires an accessory time code generator that is used, for example, at sporting events where three cameras record an event simultaneously from different angles. The time code from the address track later can be displayed on the editing console, and the editor can select scenes from each tape based on the real time displayed from each tape.

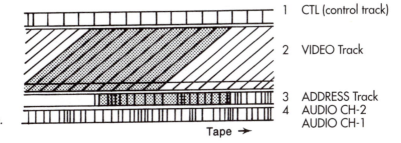

1 CTL (control track)

2 VIDEO Track

3 ADDRESS Track
4 AUDIO CH-2
AUDIO CH-1

Figure B-3.
A piece of videotape.

Tape →

4. Audio channels 1 and 2 carry the sound tracks. Normally, sound in the field (interviews, standups, wild sound) is recorded on channel 2, although some stations record sound on both channels. During editing, voice-over narration normally is recorded on channel one.

In the ASSEMBLE mode, all information on the field tape is transferred to the master cassette: video, address track, and sound on channels 1 and 2. At the same time, a control track (see the control track in Figure B.3) is laid down on the master cassette. Editing in the AS-SEMBLE mode is similar to splicing sound film in which sprocket holes, pictures, and sound are contained within each scene. In the INSERT mode, only the video track and/or channels 1 and 2 are transferred to the master cassette. No control track is laid down during insert editing, so a control track already must be present.*

Hence, if you intend to edit in the INSERT mode (for example, when you wish to lay down video only, or sound only on channels 1 and/or 2), you first must record a control track on the master cassette. Only then can you make insert edits. Without a control track, scenes on the master cassette will break up and will be unsuitable for use in a newscast. Continuing along the top row, the CLEAR button clears the digital counters on either the player display or the record display. The LAP button, when activated, tells the total time of the last edit in hours, minutes, seconds, and frames.

The three buttons, ENTRY, IN, and OUT are used in combination (see Figure B.4). These buttons tell the player and recorder to begin and end edits with frame accuracy. Touching PLAYER, ENTRY, and IN, for example, will enter an edit-in point on the player side. The scene will be transferred to the master cassette in the recorder beginning precisely at this point. Touching RECORDER, ENTRY, and IN will enter an edit-in point on the recorder side. The recording of a scene from the player will begin exactly at this point on the master cassette. Conversely, touching PLAYER, ENTRY, and OUT will tell the control unit the precise frame on which to end an edit. The out point also can be entered on the record side by touching RECORDER, ENTRY, and OUT.

Edit points, once entered, can be shifted forward or backward by touching the buttons marked 1 and –. To advance an edit point on the player, simultaneously touch PLAYER and the button marked 1 once for each frame of shift desired. Touch PLAYER and the button marked to retard the edit point. The same procedure is followed if you wish to shift an edit point on the recorder. Simply touch RECORDER and 1 or – as appropriate. Whenever entry in or out points are stored, lighted arrows appear next to the IN or OUT designation at the top of the control unit next to the digital frame counters.

The third row of editing controls is marked PRE-ROLL, PREVIEW, PERFORM, STOP, and REVIEW (see Figure B.5).

The first button, PRE-ROLL, backs up the videotape a predetermined number of seconds in anticipation of the next edit. Videotapes must be pre-rolled for three reasons:

1. *To avoid mechanical damage to the videotape.* Videotape heads spin against the tape at high speed and eventually put a small "dent" in the oxide when they are parked in still-frame "pause" for too long while the editor is searching for the next scene. Pre-rolling backs up the tape and also relaxes the tape tension around the recording heads.

---

* If the editor wishes to edit in the INSERT mode, a control track first must be recorded on the master editing cassette. Because the process differs from one editing unit to the next, we will not attempt to explain the proper procedure on a case-by-case basis. A simple process, however, is to drive both player and recorder with a sync generator or black burst generator. Even an older television camera that feeds an external sync pulse to both player and recorder will suffice. An uninterrupted control track then can be laid down on the master cassette by touching the following buttons (see Figure B.2): ASSEMBLE (on the first row), PLAYER and ENTRY and IN on the second row, and PERFORM on the third row. (Be certain the video player is in STOP position.)

When activated, the AUTO-STANDBY button automatically enters a new edit-in point and pre-rolls the master videocassette five seconds at the completion of the preceding edit. The button functions only during ASSEMBLE edits. It is inoperative during INSERT editing. When activated, the MANUAL button cancels the control unit's automatic editing capabilities, including the memory for electronic edit-in and edit-out points. The MANUAL mode is used rarely at most stations.

On the second row (see Figure B.4), the first button is marked PLAYER. When this button is activated, editing instructions that relate only to the player side can be stored in the editing control unit. When the RECORDER button is activated, instructions that pertain to the recorder can be entered.

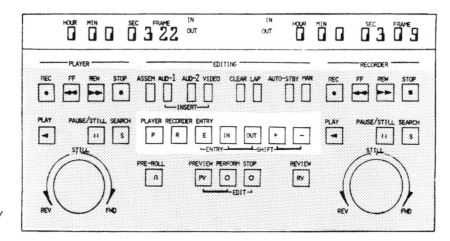

*Figure B-4.
Second row
of buttons.*

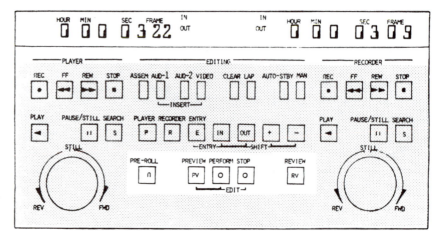

*Figure B-5.
Third row
of buttons.*

2. *To avoid electronic interference at the point of the edit.* Tapes that are not pre-rolled during the lengthy editing process may exhibit a moving line of electronic interference at the point of an edit — a phenomenon known among engineers as "creep."

3. *To allow the player and recording machines to reach full speed prior to making an edit* so electronic signals from the tape are stable or "locked-in" to produce a usable image.

To pre-roll tape on the player side, press PLAYER (on the second row) and PRE-ROLL. To pre-roll tape on the recorder side, press RECORDER and PRE-ROLL. As stated previously, the pre-roll is performed automatically on the recorder side when AUTO-STANDBY is activated in the ASSEMBLE mode only. Once edit-in and edit-out points are entered, the edit can be previewed before it actually is made. The PRE-VIEW button allows the editor to see how the edit will look without making an actual edit. The PERFORM button actually performs the edit. When this button is activated, signals are transferred from the player onto the master cassette. In addition, if the tape has not been pre-rolled prior to an edit, the PERFORM button will pre-roll both player and recorder automatically.

The STOP button ends edits that are in progress (signals that are being fed from player to recorder). It is not necessary, however, to stop an edit manually with the STOP button if an edit-out point has been entered on either the player or the recorder side. Once an edit is complete, it can be reviewed by touching the REVIEW button. This allows the editor to check the edit just made before going on to the next edit.

MAKING AN INSERT EDIT

When making an INSERT EDIT, any of the following combinations of sound and picture are possible:

- audio 1 only
- audio 2 only
- video only
- audio 1 and 2
- audio 1 and video
- audio 2 and video
- audio 1, audio 2, and video

To make an INSERT edit, follow these steps:

1. Be certain that the master recording cassette contains an acceptable CONTROL TRACK.

2. Press any of the three INSERT buttons you wish to use (Audio 1, Audio 2, and/or Video). In the INSERT mode, the assemble edit capability is canceled and the automatic standby feature is automatically defeated.

3. Find the scene you want in the player (use either PLAY or SEARCH mode).

4. When the scene is located, press the PLAYER button on second row, center section of the editing control unit, then press the EDIT button and the IN button simultaneously.

5. Enter an edit-in point on the recorder side by pressing the RECORDER button on the second row, center section of the editing control unit, then press the EDIT button and the IN button simultaneously.

6. Once an edit-in point has been entered on the record side, pre-roll the recorder by pressing RECORDER and PRE-ROLL. This step backs up the tape five seconds in anticipation of the edit and prevents damage to the tape when it is parked for prolonged times in PAUSE/STILL.

7. Play through the scene on the player side until you find the ending point. At the end of the material you wish to transfer, mark an edit-out point by pressing PLAYER, ENTRY, and OUT. During the actual edit, the edit will end precisely at this point (within two to four frames of accuracy on most systems).

8. To preview the edit, press the PREVIEW button on the editing control unit.

9. To perform the actual edit, press the PERFORM button on editing control unit. (Some units require that you press both PREVIEW and PERFORM at this stage.)

10. To review the edit you have just made, press the REVIEW button on the editing control unit.

11. Repeat procedures #3 through #9 to accomplish the next edit.

MAKING AN ASSEMBLE EDIT

To make an ASSEMBLE EDIT, follow these steps:

1. Press ASSEMBLE and AUTO-STANDBY on the editing control unit.

2. Find the scene you want in the player (use either PLAY or SEARCH mode).

3. After locating the scene, press the PLAYER button on the second row, center section of the editing the control unit, then press the PLAYER button and the IN button simultaneously.

4. Next enter an edit-in point on the recorder side by pressing the RECORDER button on the second row, center section of the editing control unit, then press the EDIT button and the IN button simultaneously.

5. Once the edit-in point has been entered on the record side, pre-roll the recorder by pressing RECORDER and PRE-ROLL. This step backs up the tape five seconds in anticipation of the edit and prevents damage to the tape when it is parked for prolonged times in PAUSE/STILL. Note: When the editing control unit is in the AUTO STANDBY mode, the manual pre-roll is necessary only at the first edit-in point. At the end of all subsequent edits, a new edit-in is entered automatically on the record side, and the recorder is pre-rolled automatically.

6. Play through the scene on the player side until you find the ending point. At the end of the material you wish to transfer, mark an edit-out point by pressing PLAYER, ENTRY, and OUT. During the actual edit, the edit will end precisely at this point (within two to four frames of accuracy on most systems).

7. To preview the edit, press the PREVIEW button on editing control unit.

8. To perform the actual edit, press the PERFORM button on the editing control unit. (Some units require that you press both PREVIEW and PERFORM at this stage.)

9. To review the edit you have just made, press the REVIEW button on the editing control unit.

10. Repeat procedures #3 through #8 to accomplish the next edit.

Digital Editing

Every year new software is developed that makes digital editing easier. Many computers come with some version of digital video editing software, such as iMovie on most current Macintosh computers. The most popular software being used at news stations and in journalism schools currently includes Media 100® and Final Cut Pro®.

Because Final Cut Pro is currently being adopted in many schools, we are including some helpful hints for using that program for digital editing. Many of the concepts are the same with all software, so these steps can be useful for a variety of programs.

GETTING STARTED

Final Cut Pro is an excellent video editing application, and can take you through projects from the novice to professional level. Just as with other digital video editing software such as Premier or iMovie, Final Cut Pro begins with your external hardware. It is important to have plenty of room on your hard drive because of the large amount of space video digitizing requires.

A digitized movie can range from 1 gig to 120 gigs or more. The size depends largely on the length of your movie and at what level of resolution you are digitizing. If your final product has to be broadcast or film quality, you will want to choose the highest audio and video settings for clear and crisp playback. If the final project is going to be distributed on the Web, however, a medium to low setting will be adequate. Also make sure you have plenty of RAM. Anything below 256 Megs of RAM is too low; 512 Megs of RAM and higher is suggested. This will allow faster rendering and smoother playback while editing.

A digital video camera is also necessary. A camera that takes mini DVC or Hi 8 film formats is suggested. But, as long as the camera has an ilink port that enables it to connect to your computer's FireWire port, there should be no problems. Connect your camera to your computer and turn it on, then turn on Final Cut Pro. Do it in this order so Final Cut Pro can recognize the camera as it is loading. If the camera is not being recognized, a prompt will be displayed stating that no camera is detected, and to either continue or try again. If this prompt pops up, turn off your camera and try again.

Set-Up

To get started in Final Cut Pro, go to the menu that says "Final Cut Pro" and choose "Audio/Video settings" or "Easy Set-Up." This part of the program allows you to choose various settings for digitization. For basic use, you will want to choose Easy Set-Up and follow the instructions. NTSC and PAL are video formats. NTSC is used in the United States, so if you set up Final Cut via Audio/Video settings, choose the NTSC settings for Sequence Presets, Capture Preset, Device Control, and External Video from the menu options. It should read under the Summary menu as follows: DV NTSC 48kHz Superwhite, DV NTSC 48 kHz, FireWire NTSC, and Apple FireWire NTSC (720 × 480). These settings are not set in stone and may have to be changed depending on the final media you are working with, but it will get you started and ready to work with broadcast and film-quality projects.

Under the Final Cut Pro menu, there is a heading for Preferences, which is also important to modify before starting your project. Upon opening Preferences, you will see a number of different

Prepared by Steffan Legasse, 2003. Used by permission.

settings, most of which you will not need to worry about for basic use. You will, however, want to set your scratch disk. If you have two or more hard drives, this is important because it will tell the computer where your digitized video will go. If you have only one hard drive, this step is not important because all video will go on your single disk. Under the General heading, it is important to set up auto saving features to the frequency of your choosing and audio playback quality, which will impact how quickly your computer will run during audio and video playback within Final Cut Pro.

Once you have done this basic set-up, you can go up to File menu and choose New Project. Give the project the name of your movie and press OK. Several screens will become visible. The top right is called your Canvas, which is the screen that allows you to view the entire movie as you have edited it. The screen to the left, called the Viewer, allows you to view the individual clips of your movie, edit them, and then enter them into the project.

The box below the Viewer, called the Browser, is where all of your original movie clips are kept and where you can select effects for your movie such as dissolves, filters, and text applications. Effects also can be selected under the Effects menu by choosing Video filters and Audio transitions.

The last box is the Timeline. It allows you to view the clips that you have selected, the effects you have applied, the audio and video edits and so on. When you play the movie from the Timeline, it will play in the Canvas and vice versa.

Digitizing

The next step is to get the content from your camera into your computer so it can be edited. To do this, again make sure your camera is connected properly and that Final Cut Pro has recognized it. Then go to the File menu and choose Log and Capture. A new box will pop up, allowing you to review your video and choose the clips you want.

You do not want to capture the entire video at once. For example, if you want something that occurs between 10 minutes and 34 seconds and 11 minutes and 15 seconds, you would enter those times. This is called entering Time Code. The Time Code is the portion of the tape that has video and audio on it and the amount of time it occupies on the tape. A Time Code break occurs when there is video, a blank spot, and then video again. The counter starts at the beginning of the tape at 0 hours 0 minutes 0 seconds. When a Time Code break occurs, the Time Code starts over.

This can be a problem for a number of reasons. Final Cut Pro can think you have two tapes, treating the video before the break as one tape and the video after the break as another. It also can digitize the wrong scenes from your tape. For example, if you have a scene you want to capture before the break that falls between 3 and 5 minutes, you could accidentally digitize the scene after the break that also falls between 3 and 5 minutes. If you have breaks, don't worry too much. Just be conscious of them and careful when you are digitizing your video.

That said, you can now start reviewing the material and entering the times of the clips you want to choose for your final broadcast news story. This is an important part of the editing process, so you want to choose the best clips that you might use in your project. Go to the text entry that says Reel and give your tape a name, then a description of the particular scene for which you are about to enter the Time Code.

After labeling the tape and clip, click on the Marker arrow. You will see two boxes with zeros in them, and this is where you will enter your Time Code. In the two other boxes below the viewing screen that say Not Set, enter the same time code as you enter into the Marker boxes. For example, if you have a news story about police giving more speeding tickets lately, you may name the Reel "Police Speeding." For video of a police officer walking up to a motorist from a long view, your description may be "officer walking, long." If the clip falls between 4 minutes and 16 seconds and 6 minutes and 56 seconds, you would enter 41600 in the first box and 65600 in the second box under the Marker heading. Final Cut Pro does not require the numbers to be divided with colons manually because it knows how to translate these numbers into 4:16:00 and 6:56:00 automatically.

You then repeat these entries in the boxes below Not Set and press the button that says "log clip." A red symbol with a line through it will appear in the Browser box. This means that the clip is logged but not actually physically captured on the computer. Only the coordinates for capture have been set thus far. You will go through the entire tape, entering the clips you want in this same manner.

When you are finished logging the clips, you should have a long list of offline media or clips that are set but not actually digitized in the Browser window. You can divide the offline media into different folders in the Browser to organize them more easily, or you can simply leave them as they are. Once you have logged everything you want off the tape and have organized the clips in the manner you desire, it is time to capture.

Capture

Capture is easy. If the Time Code has been entered correctly, all you have to do is select the offline files in the Browser and select Capture under the File menu. You can also right-click on the Browser and choose Capture. Final Cut Pro will communicate with your camera and take the clips of video that fall between the times you have entered. This is a good time to take a break because video digitizing can take quite some time.

Once the video has been digitized, you can actually watch the clips on your computer. You can now disconnect the camera, unless you have more tapes to digitize. (You don't have to disconnect the camera, and you may want to leave it connected so you can hook up a monitor to view the progress of your movie on a larger screen). If you have more tapes to digitize, repeat the steps above until you are finished.

All the files that were once offline are now online. You can edit them and enter them into the project.

Entering Audio/Video and Editing

Let's go back to our example of police giving more speeding tickets. Perhaps you want to open your news story with video of a police officer in his car on the interstate pulling over a motorist, and you want to use natural sound. Click on the file you have named "police pulls over," and look at it in the Viewer. If you want only a piece of the clip for your news story, move the slider to the point you want the clip to start and click the arrow button on the Viewer called "mark-in."

There is another button next to it called "mark-out." Press this button when you have the slider on the point of the clip where you want it to end. Click on the image in the Viewer itself and drag it into the Timeline. The part of the clip that you designated with the mark-in, mark-out points is all that will show up in the Timeline rather than the entire digitized clip called "police pulls over." You will see three channels in the Timeline now. Two will be your audio and one your video. You can click on this clip, move it around within the Timeline, delete it, add effects to it to experiment, and so forth, and none of this will affect your original digitized piece that is located in your Browser.

Follow these same steps with the scenes that follow, and begin to piece the various clips in proper order for your news story. When you piece one clip to another, the Canvas splits to show whether the scenes are connected. When you see a frame from each clip in the boxes on the Canvas, they are connected and you can now watch the clips as a seamless scene. You can also add music, sound effects, and voice-overs to your news story in the audio fields of the Timeline.

When you drag a new audio file into the Timeline, a new audio track is automatically created to contain it. The same occurs for video files. Music and sound effects must be imported into the Browser first, however, by right-clicking in the Browser and choosing Import file or folder (for occasions when there are numerous music or sound effect files). This also can be done through the File menu by choosing Import file or folders.

As you edit out what you want in the Viewer and then place those clips together in the Timeline, you will see your news story start to take shape. You can add music and sound effects and trim out what you don't want by simply opening that file again in the Viewer. If this is the case, make sure you do so from the Timeline clip and not the original clip in the Browser. You want to always keep your original digitized clip intact so you can go back and get more slices of it if necessary.

Importing

You can import all types of files in Final Cut Pro. The most useful are Bias Peak files (the audio software that accompanies Final Cut Pro 3), Quick Time files, iTunes files, pictures from a variety of sources including edited images from Photoshop, among others.

Rendering

To see an effect or transition fully and before exporting your final story to disk or tape, you must render your clips. Video effects such as transitions take the longest time to render, whereas audio renders relatively quickly.

The items in the Timeline that require rendering will have a red line above them. To render something and view it fully in the Timeline, you must make sure the Timeline box is selected, then go to the Sequence menu and click either Render Selection or Render All. You don't have to render everything at once, which can be helpful, as rendering may take more than an hour, depending on the length of your story and the number of effects included.

Transitions, Filters, and Effects

Transitions are helpful when trying to convey a passage of time, a change in mood, a change in location, and gradual fade in or fade out of credits, etc. The most useful transitions, effects and filters are listed below and can be found in the Effects tab in the Browser or under the menu tab labeled Effects.

Fade in Fade Out
Cross Dissolve
Time wipe
RGB Color Correction

Cross Fade (0db) under audio transitions

Text (for credits) accompany with a fade in fade out for a simple but effective display

Brightness contrast

Widescreen (not necessary but can be a useful cropping tool and adds a nice dimension to any project)

To enter one of these effects, simply click on the name and drag it to the desired clip. To view the effect, render it and then play it back on either the Viewer or Canvas.

Exporting Your Movie

Thus far, you have selected and edited all your clips, placed each in the proper order for your news story, entered any audio effects, and rendered the clips that require it. You should have a nicely polished piece of work. Now you are ready for the final step.

Final Cut Pro allows you to export your piece in a number of ways. The crucial factor for determining how to export your story depends greatly on your final media format, from Web-based video to high quality film as your final newscast production. For Web-based movies, you would go to the File menu and choose Export QuickTime Movie and choose a low-resolution file setting.

For videotape, you would choose Print to Tape from the File menu. This requires that you connect your camera back to the FireWire port and make sure it has been recognized by Final Cut Pro. If this is the case, make sure you have a blank tape in the camera and click Print to Tape. This will put your finished version of the movie on tape that you can later copy to VHS or some other form of media.

To put your final version on DVD, you would export the story as a Final Cut Pro Movie with the resolution, audio settings, and frame rate at their maximum levels. Once it is exported to your desktop, you can enter it into a DVD authoring program of your choice or simply put it on a DVD for backup.

END NOTE

Other than these beginning instructions and tips, you may want to experiment. Use what is included in this guide as a starting point, but don't be too cautious about exploring the software. It can seem intimidating at times, but many of the various components and features will not come up in a basic project, or even some advanced projects.

Code of Ethics and Professional Conduct of the Radio-Television News Directors Association

The Radio-Television News Directors Association, wishing to foster the highest professional standards of electronic journalism, promote public understanding of and confidence in electronic journalism, and strengthen principles of journalistic freedom to gather and disseminate information, establishes this Code of Ethics and Professional Conduct.

PREAMBLE

Professional electronic journalists should operate as trustees of the public, seek the truth, report it fairly and with integrity and independence, and stand accountable for their actions.

Public Trust

Professional electronic journalists should recognize that their first obligation is to the public.

Professional electronic journalists should:

- Understand that any commitment other than service to the public undermines trust and credibility.
- Recognize that service in the public interest creates an obligation to reflect the diversity of the community and guard against oversimplification of issues or events.
- Provide a full range of information to enable the public to make enlightened decisions.
- Fight to ensure that the public's business is conducted in public.

Truth

Professional electronic journalists should pursue truth aggressively and present the news accurately, in context, and as completely as possible.

Professional electronic journalists should:

- Continuously seek the truth.
- Resist distortions that obscure the importance of events.
- Clearly disclose the origin of information and label all material provided by outsiders.

Professional electronic journalists should not:

- Report anything known to be false.
- Manipulate images or sounds in any way that is misleading.
- Plagiarize.
- Present images or sounds that are reenacted without informing the public.

Fairness

Professional electronic journalists should present the news fairly and impartially, placing primary value on significance and relevance.

Professional electronic journalists should:

- Treat all subjects of news coverage with respect and dignity, showing particular compassion to victims of crime or tragedy.
- Exercise special care when children are involved in a story and give children greater privacy protection than adults.

- Seek to understand the diversity of their community and inform the public without bias or stereotype.
- Present a diversity of expressions, opinions, and ideas in context.
- Present analytical reporting based on professional perspective, not personal bias.
- Respect the right to a fair trial.

Integrity

Professional electronic journalists should present the news with integrity and decency, avoiding real or perceived conflicts of interest, and should respect the dignity and intelligence of the audience as well as the subjects of news.

Professional electronic journalists should:

- Identify sources whenever possible. Confidential sources should be used only when it is clearly in the public interest to gather or convey important information or when a person providing information might be harmed. Journalists should keep all commitments to protect a confidential source.
- Clearly label opinion and commentary.
- Guard against extended coverage of events or individuals that fails to significantly advance a story, place the event in context, or add to the public knowledge.
- Refrain from contacting participants in violent situations while the situation is in progress.
- Use technological tools with skill and thoughtfulness, avoiding techniques that skew facts, distort reality, or sensationalize events.
- Use surreptitious newsgathering techniques, including hidden cameras or microphones, only if there is no other way to obtain stories of significant public importance and only if the technique is explained to the audience.
- Use the private transmissions of others only with permission.

Professional electronic journalists should not:

- Pay news sources who have a vested interest in a story.
- Accept gifts, favors, or compensation from those who might seek to influence coverage.

- Engage in activities that may compromise their integrity or independence.

Independence

Professional electronic journalists should defend the independence of all journalists from those seeking influence or control over news content.

Professional electronic journalists should:

- Gather and report news without fear or favor, and vigorously resist undue influence from any outside forces, including advertisers, sources, story subjects, powerful individuals, and special interest groups.
- Resist those who would seek to buy or politically influence news content or who would seek to intimidate those who gather and disseminate the news.
- Determine news content solely through editorial judgment and not as the result of outside influence.
- Resist any self-interest or peer pressure that might erode journalistic duty and service to the public.
- Recognize that sponsorship of the news will not be used in any way to determine, restrict, or manipulate content.
- Refuse to allow the interests of ownership or management to influence news judgment and content inappropriately.
- Defend the rights of the free press for all journalists, recognizing that any professional or government licensing of journalists is a violation of that freedom.

Accountability

Professional electronic journalists should recognize that they are accountable for their actions to the public, the profession and themselves.

Professional electronic journalists should:

- Actively encourage adherence to these standards by all journalists and their employers.
- Respond to public concerns. Investigate complaints and correct errors promptly and as with as much prominence as the original report.

- Explain journalistic processes to the public, especially when practices spark questions or controversy.

- Recognize that professional electronic journalists are duty-bound to conduct themselves ethically.

- Refrain from ordering or encouraging courses of action which would force employees to commit an unethical act.

- Carefully listen to employees who raise ethical objections and create environments in which such objections and discussions are encouraged.

- Seek support for and provide opportunities to train employees in ethical decision-making.

In meeting its responsibility to the profession of electronic journalism, RTNDA has created this code to identify important issues, to serve as a guide for its members, to facilitate self-scrutiny, and to shape future debate.

SOCIETY OF PROFESSIONAL JOURNALISTS

Code of Ethics

Preamble

Members of the Society of Professional Journalists believe that public enlightenment is the forerunner of justice and the foundation of democracy. The duty of the journalist is to further those ends by seeking truth and providing a fair and comprehensive account of events and issues. Conscientious journalists from all media and specialties strive to serve the public with thoroughness and honesty. Professional integrity is the cornerstone of a journalist's credibility.

Members of the Society share a dedication to ethical behavior and adopt this code to declare the Society's principles and standards of practice.

Seek Truth and Report It

Journalists should be honest, fair and courageous in gathering, reporting and interpreting information.

Journalists should:

- ▶ Test the accuracy of information from all sources and exercise care to avoid inadvertent error. Deliberate distortion is never permissible.

- ▶ Diligently seek out subjects of news stories to give them the opportunity to respond to allegations of wrongdoing.

- ▶ Identify sources whenever feasible. The public is entitled to as much information as possible on sources' reliability.

- ▶ Always question sources' motives before promising anonymity. Clarify conditions attached to any promise made in exchange for information. Keep promises.

- ▶ Make certain that headlines, news teases and promotional material, photos, video, audio, graphics, sound bites and quotations do not misrepresent. They should not oversimplify or highlight incidents out of context.

- ▶ Never distort the content of news photos or video. Image enhancement for technical clarity is always permissible. Label montages and photo illustrations.

- ▶ Avoid misleading re-enactments or staged news events. If re-enactment is necessary to tell a story, label it.

- ▶ Avoid undercover or other surreptitious methods of gathering information except when traditional open methods will not yield information vital to the public. Use of such methods should be explained as part of the story.

- ▶ Never plagiarize.

- ▶ Tell the story of the diversity and magnitude of the human experience boldly, even when it is unpopular to do so.

- ▶ Examine their own cultural values and avoid imposing those values on others.

- ▶ Avoid stereotyping by race, gender, age, religion, ethnicity, geography, sexual orientation, disability, physical appearance or social status.

- ▶ Support the open exchange of views, even views they find repugnant.

- ▶ Give voice to the voiceless; official and unofficial sources of information can be equally valid.

- ▶ Distinguish between advocacy and news reporting. Analysis and commentary should be labeled and not misrepresent fact or context.

- ▶ Distinguish news from advertising and shun hybrids that blur the lines between the two.

- ▶ Recognize a special obligation to ensure that the public's business is conducted in the open and that government records are open to inspection.

Minimize Harm

Ethical journalists treat sources, subjects and colleagues as human beings deserving of respect.

Journalists should:

- ▶ Show compassion for those who may be affected adversely by news coverage. Use special sensitivity when dealing with children and inexperienced sources or subjects.

- ▶ Be sensitive when seeking or using interviews or photographs of those affected by tragedy or grief.

- ▶ Recognize that gathering and reporting information may cause harm or discomfort. Pursuit of the news is not a license for arrogance.

- ▶ Recognize that private people have a greater right to control information about themselves than do public officials and others who seek power, influence or attention. Only an overriding public need can justify intrusion into anyone's privacy.

- ▶ Show good taste. Avoid pandering to lurid curiosity.

- ▶ Be cautious about identifying juvenile suspects or victims of sex crimes.

- ▶ Be judicious about naming criminal suspects before the formal filing of charges.

- ▶ Balance a criminal suspect's fair trial rights with the public's right to be informed.

Act Independently

Journalists should be free of obligation to any interest other than the public's right to know.

Journalists should:

- ▶ Avoid conflicts of interest, real or perceived.

- ▶ Remain free of associations and activities that may compromise integrity or damage credibility.

- ▶ Refuse gifts, favors, fees, free travel and special treatment, and shun secondary employment, political involvement, public office and service in community organizations if they compromise journalistic integrity.

- ▶ Disclose unavoidable conflicts.

- ▶ Be vigilant and courageous about holding those with power accountable.

- ▶ Deny favored treatment to advertisers and special interests and resist their pressure to influence news coverage.

- ▶ Be wary of sources offering information for favors or money; avoid bidding for news.

Be Accountable

Journalists are accountable to their readers, listeners, viewers and each other.

Journalists should:

- ▶ Clarify and explain news coverage and invite dialogue with the public over journalistic conduct.

- ▶ Encourage the public to voice grievances against the news media.

- ▶ Admit mistakes and correct them promptly.

- ▶ Expose unethical practices of journalists and the news media.

- ▶ Abide by the same high standards to which they hold others.

From Society of Professional Journalists, 3909 N. Meridian St., Indianapolis, Indiana 46208, www.spj.org. Copyright © 2004 by Society of Professional Journalists. Reprinted with permission.

Glossary

A

Accuracy The state of being correct, factual, truthful, and honest in the presentation of information. (Ch 2)

Active voice A sentence structure in which the subject completes the action; something happens to somebody or to something. (Ch 2) *See also* passive voice.

Actuality An audio insert or sound cut played in a radio news story; similar in nature to the soundbite in television. (Ch 3, Ch 7) *See also* Soundbite.

Actual malice The act of journalists' printing known falsities or failing to investigate the truth prior to publication. This actual malice standard of law applies to public officials, public figures, and limited public figures. (Ch 13)

Appropriation With reference to right of privacy law, involves using a person's name or likeness for commercial purposes without his or her permission. (Ch 13)

Area probability sampling A survey method in which the individuals in the sample are chosen in proportion to their distribution within the larger population. (Ch 12)

AT Stands for "accumulated time," a term used in broadcast news story scripts to indicate how far into the story a soundbite appears on camera. (Ch 7)

Attribution Crediting a person or an entity as the originator of a statement, idea, or point of view. (Ch 2). *See also* Broadcast-style attribution; Newspaper-style attribution.

Audio Link A smooth transition between different cuts of a soundbite (SOT). *See also* 'Bridge'. (Ch 7)

Audio / Video Streaming The technology used for producing audio and video reports on the Internet. (Ch 10)

B

Blocking Grouping stories for the newscast into logical segments separated by commercial breaks. (Ch 11)

Bridge A smooth transition between soundbites (SOTs), often done with voice-overs or reporter standups. (Ch 7)

Broadcast-style attribution The conversational practice of identifying the originator of information at the beginning of a sentence, as in "The National Weather Service says heavy rains are falling across the Midwest at this hour." (Ch 2) *See also* Attribution; Newspaper-style attribution.

B-roll video Extra video shots filmed in case more video is needed during story editing. B-roll video is often included with video news releases. (Ch 8)

Bumper The graphic appearing on the screen momentarily between the last news item and a commercial; usually identifies the station and may contain a logo and slogan for the current news team. (Ch 11)

Bundled media Specialized media such as niche magazines, special-interest TV, and books that advertisers use to reach specific audiences. (Ch 12)

C

CART Signifies an audiotape cartridge, a term still used at some radio stations to indicate an actuality or a report on audiotape. The term originated before digital technology rendered the CART obsolete. (Ch 3)

CG Character generator, a computer that produces electronic type that will appear on the screen, often as a name superimposed over a speaker or as a graphic that provides supplementary text or statistics for a story. (Ch 3)

Clipping Losing a word or phrase at the beginning of a news story because the story was edited too close to the opening text. (Ch 9)

Cold cuts Abrupt endings of cuts within a news story in which sound and picture end suddenly before a new, unrelated picture appears. (Ch 9)

Community standards One part of the obscenity law for determining if something is obscene. If it would offend the (community) within which it is aired or published, it could be ruled obscene. (Ch 13)

Copyright The legal protection of original material, which belongs to the individual who created it. (Ch 13)

Cross-ownership An arrangement in which media companies own various types of media organizations, such as newspapers, radio stations, and television stations. (Ch 11)

CT An old radio term, Cartridge, with reference to a radio soundbite. The common reference in the industry now is SOT (Sound On Tape) or soundbite. (Ch 7)

D

Defamation With reference to libel law, information that is damaging to a person's reputation and can be proved. (Ch 13)

Demographics As used in viewer/listener surveys, variables including age, income, geographical location, and consumer habits. (Ch 12)

Dramatic conflict What happens between two opposing forces; one of the elements of newsworthiness. Also sometimes defined as the quest for a goal against opposition. (Ch 4)

E

Electronic or Satellite News Gathering (SNG) The capability of local news operations to cover stories live from anywhere in the world through microwave or satellite technology. (Ch 10)

Embarrassing private facts With reference to privacy law, this tort states that the publication or broadcast of non-newsworthy, private embarrassing facts about an individual is an invasion of privacy. This tort is not recognized in all states.

Ethics The personal or professional philosophy of what is right and acceptable as it governs the rules of living and behavior and the fulfillment of professional conduct. (Ch 14)

F

Fairness In the context of journalism, refers to reporting that adequately represents all viewpoints. (Ch 14)

Fairness doctrine A legal doctrine, almost never invoked now, requiring broadcasters to devote reasonable time to covering controversial issues of public importance. (Ch 13)

False light With reference to right of privacy law, involves distortions that are highly offensive to a reasonable person. (Ch 13)

Fault With reference to libel law, a journalist knowingly producing a false and defamatory story or producing a false story with complete disregard for finding out the truth. (Ch 13)

Feature story A news account that emphasizes the inherent human connection in a story rather than taking a purely factual, institutional approach. As defined by *New York Times* writer Bill Carter, a legitimate feature story is the serious journalistic treatment of emotional, personal stories that address larger issues. (Ch 6)

Feeding / Feeds Sending prerecorded news stories from around the country and globe to local television stations via satellite or wire services. This system — also done in print journalism with wire services — allows media outlets that do not have the necessary budget or resources to cover news outside the local market. (Ch 5)

First serial rights With reference to copyright law, rights that allow a publisher the opportunity to be first to use a copyrighted story. (Ch 13)

Focus group A research method in which a cross-section of the community is interviewed for opinions on a designated topic. (Ch 12)

Format sheet A list of the newscast line-up indicating each element of the program, including length of the segment, accumulated time after each story, and the order in which stories appear; often referred to as the rundown. (Ch 11)

Formula reporting The practice of structuring every story similarly, irrespective of subject matter or most appropriate treatment (VO, soundbite, standup, end-break/close, etc.), especially when under deadline pressure. (Ch 6)

Freak event lead Opening a feature story with a description of a bizarre or unnatural occurrence; useful if the event is highly unusual. (Ch 4)

Front loading The term referring to news stations adding special promotions to the newscast during a "sweeps" period — the time when Neilson Media Research surveys how many viewers are watching various broadcast stations. (Ch 12)

Front-timing Starting with the (in(time from the log when the program is to start. Front-timing often is done early in the producer(s shift, after the program is blocked, to make sure the newscast will work as budgeted. (Ch 11)

Futures File A simple filing system, such as an accordion-style folder with pockets for each day of the month or a computer spreadsheet to keep track of upcoming events or issues worth reporting. (Ch 5)

G

Graphics Supplementary visuals used in news reports. In electronic journalism, these might consist of charts, graphs, still photos, artwork, or still frames from video. (Ch 11)

H

Hand-offs Anchors' tossing back to a different anchor for another segment during the newscast, such as going from sports to weather to local news. (Ch 11)

Hard news Newsworthy information consisting of what people need to know to make decisions, take a course of action, or form an opinion; the information people expect to see and hear because it helps them in their everyday lives. (Ch 5)

Hard news lead A story beginning that reveals the essential facts of a timely, significant story; also called an informative lead. (Ch 4)

I

Identification With reference to libel law, a requirement that an individual be able to be identified by name or picture or description for the report to be considered defamatory to the person. (Ch 13)

Internet A global network of cables and computers made up of thousands of smaller regional networks that allows access to the World Wide Web. *See also* World Wide Web (WWW). (Ch 3)

Internet journalism The use of various forms of media, including computers, the Internet, audio, video, still photography, and graphics to research, gather, and report the news. Frequently, Internet presentations are interactive, meaning that audiences can communicate with reporters in chatrooms and seek additional information by following hyperlinks on the computer or television screen. (Ch 3, Ch 8)

Invasion of privacy Any intrusion such as trespass or publication of embarrassing facts, even if true, that violates an individual's right to privacy (the right to be left alone. (Ch 13)

Inverted pyramid A style of lead developed during the Civil War that contains as many of the five Ws (who, what, when, where, why) as possible; developed at a time of frequent interruptions in telegraph service as a way to ensure transmission of the story's essential facts. Though still in use, the inverted pyramid lead has little utility for writers in electronic media. (Ch 4)

ISP (Internet Service Provider) A company that provides clients with dial-up and/or broadband access to the World Wide Web, creates and maintains Web pages, and sometimes helps promote client Web pages. (Ch 1)

J

Jargon The specialized language of any special interest group or organization that is unfamiliar to the average layperson. (Ch 6)

L

Lead The sentence that begins a story; typically summarizes the essence of the story or reveals the heart of the story to come. The "lead" may also refer to the first story in a newscast or the main idea for a story. (Ch.4, Ch 11)

Lead-in The anchor copy that introduces the story and sets up the video package or prerecorded audio report in radio and television newscasts; also can refer to the sentence in the copy that leads into a soundbite in a radio or television report. (Ch 4, Ch 7)

Libel Published defamation that damages reputation (the person people think you are), but not character. (Ch 13)

Limited public figures Individuals who could be considered public figures in a narrow context or who have voluntarily placed themselves in the public limelight for a specific issue. (Ch 13)

Linear editing An editing process using two video recorders hooked together in which one plays and the other records; still the most common form of editing, though digital editing is rapidly becoming the preferred method. (Ch 9)

Line-up The order of stories in a newscast. (Ch 5)

Literary allusion lead A type of leads that references fictional or historical characters. (Ch 4)

Local People Meters (LPMs) Small units placed on or near a television set that can more accurately identify individual viewing habits because of its electronic information gathering. The LPMs were beginning to replace Nielson's previous "people meters" in the top 10 major markets in fall 2004.

Localizing The practice of emphasizing a national or an international story from a local community's point of view, generally by emphasizing a local connection. (Ch 4)

M

Marketplace of ideas A doctrine in First Amendment holding that no regulation should be placed on political speech because in the free market, only the ideas and insights that are worthy will survive. (Ch 13)

Media convergence The concept of one news organization producing the content for multiple media sources in a variety of media formats. (Ch 11)

Metaphor lead A type of lead that uses figures of speech to compare aspects of life with which the audience is familiar. (Ch 4)

Must-carry rule A legal doctrine mandating that cable companies must include some local programming. (Ch 13)

N

Narrowcasting Refers to news stations tailoring a newscast or news segment (such as weather or sports) to a specific audience demographic in order to meet advertiser goals. (Ch 12)

Natural sound stories Stories that rely only on images, soundbites, and natural sound from the environment to tell stories, with no reporter standups or voice-over narration. Also called "nat sound" stories. (Ch 6)

News hole The time remaining for news within a telecast after subtracting time for commercials, weather, sports, and internal news promotions. (Ch 11)

Newspaper-style attribution A form in which the speaker's identity is delayed until the end of the sentence, as in, "Heavy rains are falling across the Midwest, according to the National Weather Service." (Ch 2) *See also* Attribution; Broadcast-style attribution

Non-linear editing A computer editing process similar to word processing, with pictures. Images and sounds are recorded digitally on computer disks so they can be moved or shortened independent of one another in computer memory. Whenever an element is added or removed, the system automatically reconfigures everything before and after the change to maintain an exact match between video and audio. The final edited piece then is recorded to disk or videotape. (Ch 9). *See also* Linear editing

O

One-person band A person who photographs, reports, writes, and edits his or her own news stories. (Ch 9)

One-time rights With reference to copyright law, refers to creators of original works granting one-time use to another. (Ch 13)

Outcue The last three or four words of a soundbite, used in scripts to let the director know how the bite ends. (Ch 3)

Overlap In a video cut, sound extending past the video to help lead into the next video; a transition method between video cuts. (Ch 9)

P

Pad copy Supplementary copy for an anchor to read in case a newscast would otherwise end too early. (Ch 11)

Parody lead A form of story beginning that is a take-off on events and sayings currently in vogue and of widespread public interest. (Ch 4)

Parroting Wording in the lead-in to a soundbite that is nearly the same as, or identical to, the words in the soundbite. (Ch 7)

Passive voice A sentence structure in which the subject passively receives the action and the actor remains unidentified or is mentioned toward the end of the sentence. (Ch 2). *See also* Active voice.

People meters Small units placed on or near a television set, which directly or via remote control, identify viewers in the room and collect data about their viewing behavior for transmission to survey companies. (Ch 12). *See also* Local People Meters.

Phonetic pronunciation A means of indicating the pronunciation of a word by using sets of letters to indicate the sound in each part or syllable of a word, such as, (Hurricane Debby veered toward the Caicos (KAY-kos) Islands tonight. (Ch 2)

Product promotion In news, the use of footage from actual news reports to help promote a newscast. (Ch 12)

Prominence A notable, highly recognizable person or thing that attracts attention; one of the elements of newsworthiness. (Ch 4)

Proof-of-performance advertising A station's reminder that it has been faithful to promises made to its audience, such as exposing consumer frauds, providing the best local high school sports coverage, or helping to save viewers' money. (Ch 12)

Proximity Being close to the audience, whether geographically or emotionally; one of the elements of newsworthiness. (Ch 4)

Psychographics Variables such as the viewer(s lifestyle, self-esteem, religious and political affiliations, and shared values within demographic groups; used in connection with viewer research. (Ch 12). *See also* Demographics

Publication With reference to libel law, the published defamation of an individual. (Ch 13)

Publication of embarrassing facts With reference to right of privacy law, the broadcast of non-newsworthy information that would be highly offensive to a reasonable person. (Ch 13)

Pyramid A news story writing format in which information in the story builds to a dramatic conclusion; often used in the electronic media. (Ch 4)

Q

Question lead A type of lead that asks a question; a dangerous approach if the question lacks substance and fails to elicit audience interest. (Ch 4)

R

Rating The number of households watching a given telecast, expressed as a percentage of total households with a TV. (Ch 12)

Referencing Writing voice-over copy to match or reinforce what is begin seen on the screen; also called "audio-video linkage." (Ch 3)

Relatedness Relevance to the listening audience. (Ch 4)

Reporter enterprise The initiative a reporter exhibits in identifying and reporting original stories that otherwise would not be reported. (Ch 8)

Reporter Package A self-contained story that includes SOTs (Sound On Tape) from the reporter in addition to voice-overs and soundbites from sources. (Ch 9)

Reporter standups Prerecorded segments in which the reporter appears on camera within the news story. Generally the reporter is standing near a newsworthy location for the story. This video method is also used as a bridge, or transition, between soundbites and voice-overs in a news story. (Ch 7, Ch 9)

Rundown A format sheet, or a list of the newscast line-up indicating each element of the program, including length of the segment, accumulated time after each story, and the order in which stories appear. (Ch 11)

S

Satellite media tours Video News Releases (video forms of press releases) that often offer a spokesperson to be available via satellite uplink to do interviews with numerous news stations around the country. (Ch 8)

Scarcity doctrine A legal concept referring to the scarce availability of broadcast airwaves; used to justify more governmental regulation of the electronic media. (Ch 13)

Section 312 (a)(7) A section of the 1934 Communications Act that stipulates broadcast stations must provide reasonable access to political candidates, both free air time and commercial time. (Ch 13)

Section 315 A section of the 1934 Communications Act that mandates broadcast stations must provide equal opportunity for air time to all political candidates if it provides time to any candidate. Note that the section does not mandate the stations to offer time, merely that if they give it to one, they must offer it to all. (Ch 13)

Separateness The disconnect between journalists and the audience's perceptions and preferences; attributed to several conditions, including frequent job changes to new cities, odd working hours, and different cultural backgrounds. (Ch 5)

Share The number of households watching a given station, expressed as a percentage of households using television. (Ch 12)

Shield laws State laws that protect journalists from revealing sources to government officials. (Ch 13)

Significance The importance of a news story and who it affects most directly in some way; one of the elements of newsworthiness. (Ch 4)

Slug Brief information at the top of a script that indicates content and length of story. (Ch 11)

Soft news Information that is enriching and usually interesting but not necessarily pertinent. (Ch 5)

Soft news lead A story beginning that creates an emotional or philosophical outline and thereby helps create a human context for the story to come. (Ch 4)

SOT (Sound On Tape) Sound that is normally played at full volume while the anchor or reporter stops talking, such as a recorded interview, a news conference, or natural sound from the environment. The term is a holdover from the days before digital video but often is used interchangeably regardless of recording medium. (Ch 3)

Soundbite A short excerpt from an interview, news conference, or spontaneous comment aired as part of a broadcast news report. (Ch 3)

Split-page format A script in which instructions for the video editor and studio director are written on the left side of the page, with narration to be read by anchors/reporters on the right side of the page. (Ch 3)

Split-squeeze remote The technique of using two separate frames of video during a live remote broadcast, one frame showing the anchor and the other a reporter or news subject as they converse. (Ch 3)

Spoken copy A conversational-sounding script that closely resembles the sound of the natural spoken word as opposed to the sound of the written word spoken aloud. (Ch 2)

Spot news Hard news events, such as fires, explosions, airline crashes, and tornadoes, which often break without warning; a hallmark of many spot news events is their unpredictability. (Ch 5)

Staccato lead A summary lead with a series of short sentences; an effective type of lead for a number of related events or thoughts, such as actions at a city council meeting or various impressions of the day's weather. (Ch 4)

Staged news A news event that dramatizes, creates, changes, or otherwise alters a news event, and thereby produces a false or misleading portrayal of that event. (Ch 13)

Stereotyping Generalizing, usually derogatory in nature, expanded to a larger segment of the population based on the actions of one individual or a few individuals. (Ch 14)

Story budget A list of news stories for the day; used during planning meetings in newsrooms at the beginning of the day and often included when companies send several Video News Releases on one tape/DVD to news stations. (Ch 8)

Story follow-up The practice of following a story over time to keep audiences connected with stories that are process-oriented rather than event-centered. (Ch 8)

Story ownership The practice of making a story one(s own in a way that exemplifies superior knowledge, insight, and custodianship of the story from initial research to final transmission of the report to an audience. (Ch 8)

Stringer A non-employee who provides information, writes or reports a story, or shoots video for a news organization, either on speculation or at the organization's invitation, in exchange for a one-time payment. (Ch 1)

Summary lead A story beginning that indicates something about the story to come without revealing the heart of the story. (Ch 3)

Suspended lead The beginning of a story that delays the climax, or the essence of the news, until the very end of the story; one of the common types of feature leads. (Ch 4)

Sweeps Ratings survey periods, in February, May, July, and November, during which TV households are monitored for viewing behavior via people meters, telephone surveys, and diaries. During sweeps periods, stations try to build the largest audiences possible for sale to advertisers throughout the rest of the year. (Ch 12)

T

Tag A sentence or two that an anchor reads immediately after a news package has aired. Tags let the anchor add an important fact or two and help give the story a sense of finality. (Ch 3)

Talking head A derogatory term for the person delivering a boring soundbite. (Ch 10)

Target audience A bloc of individuals who share certain characteristics, such as age, economics, or lifestyle, that give it a somewhat common identity, such as "Women 18–34 earning more than $30,000 annually." (Ch 2)

Targeted broadcasting A technique for advertisers to reach a specific population demographic. (Ch 12)

Teases Brief copy spoken on camera, or voice-over copy with graphics or videotape, that motivates viewers to stay tuned for an upcoming story after a commercial break. (Ch 11)

Thematic blocking Grouping stories within a newscast by similar subject matter or any other means that emphasizes their relatedness. (Ch 5)

Time code The elapsed time on a videotape that is useful in editing so specific points on the video can be easily accessed. (Ch 9)

Timeliness The element of newsworthiness referring to events that occur now or will occur in the immediate future. (Ch 4)

Topical promotion Announcements of discretionary topics that are of particular interest to viewers; one device to help lure viewers to watch newscasts they normally don't patronize. Also known as episodic promotion or tune-in. (Ch 12)

Toss The transition statement made by an anchor to the reporter's story. (Ch 8)

Trespassing With reference to right of privacy law, journalists' illegally intruding onto the private property of an individual.

TRT Total running time of a video source; informs the director exactly how long an item runs. (Ch 3)

V

V-chip A device now built into television sets that provides a ratings system for all programs. (Ch 13)

Verb tense Any form of a verb that indicates time, such as past, present, future, immediate past, or immediate future. (Ch 2)

VNR (Video News Release) Raw or edited video footage of a story from a special-interest group, including script and sometimes voice-over narration, suitable to run within a newscast with few or no changes. (Ch 8)

VO (Voice-Over narration) A form of presentation in which the anchor(s or reporter(s voice can be heard (over(the pictures on the screen during live broadcasts or playback of news packages. (Ch 3, Ch 9)

VTR (Videotape Recording) A term sometimes used in scripts to refer to any source of video. (Ch 3)

W

Well-known expressions lead An opening sentence of a story that capitalizes on sayings that most members of the audience have heard before; should be used sparingly to avoid being cliché. (Ch 4)

White-collar crime Nonviolent crimes involving financial fraud that generally take place in a business or corporation.

World Wide Web (WWW) An information system that gives users on computer networks universal access to various media and a large universe of information. (Ch 3). *See also* Internet.

Index

access, as a legal concept, 307, 313, 315–316
accountability, 322, 370–371
accuracy, 25, 111, 295, 310, 336
"actual malice" standard, 310
"Actual Time," 236
actuality(ies), 57, 58, 59, 151, 156
advertising / advertisers, 54, 232, 295. *See also* commercials
and appropriation as invasion of privacy, 311
boycotts of violent programming, 319
-driven media, 334, 342
image, 289–290
and market research, 281, 284, 285, 291
political, 307
proof-of-performance, 290
AGB Television Research, Inc., 282
ages, style for, 27, 30
Amanpour, Christiane, 340
American Bar Association, position on cameras in court, 314, 315
American Journalism Review home page, 55
analog programming, 320
Ananova, 238
anchors, news, 2, 8–9, 58, 60, 64, 152, 160, 186, 188, 222, 236, 237
appeal to attract audiences, 287, 288
and graphics, 227
and live remotes, 338
and pads, 234
Arbitron ratings, 281, 282
area probability sampling, 281–282
Ashcroft, Attorney General John, 321, 322
assignment editors, 2, 9, 11, 172, 174, 186, 223
AT times, 58, 64, 160
attribution, 25–26, 31 (Figure 2.1)
audience, 85–86, 105, 107, 108, 171, 204, 224, 232, 295. *See also* communication; market
radio, 304
and ratings, 281, 285, 338
research, 295
target, 5, 24–25, 53
television news, 335, 339
writing to, 23–24
audio, 4–5, 8, 24, 53, 189, 193. *See also* sound
actuality example, 156
attribution in, 31 (Figure 2.1)
engineer, 191
link, 157
streaming, 22, 204, 205, 221, 237, 238, 320
tracks, 191, 193

back-timing, 224, 230, 234, 235 (Figure 11.6), 236, 237
balanced coverage, 295, 308
Bamber, James, 205

Beloff, Nora, 341
bias, 336, 342
black burst and fade to, 192, 193, 194, 233
Blacklow, Julie, 338
Bliss, Edward, 22
blocking
the newscast, 228, 230, 231 (Figure 11.5), 234
thematic, 109
blogs, 244, 295, 336. *See also* Web pages
Blumenthal, Sidney, 321
"Booth rule," in privacy law, 311
Brandeis, Louis, 311
Branzburg v. Hayes, 315
Brennan, Justice William, 304, 310
bridge
standup, 187
story, 157
Brinkema, Judge Leonie, 315
Brinkley, David, 337
broadcast journalists, 1, 2, 105, 107, 239, 337. *See also* journalists
broadcasting / broadcasters
government involvement in, 303
and libel, 309, 320
live, 341
targeted, 291
Brokaw, Tom, 171
B-roll video, 174
Brown, Bill, 289
Bulletin Board operators, legal rulings, 322
bumper graphic, 233
bundled media, 291
Bush, George W., CBS National Guard story on, 336

Cable Consumer Protection and Competition Act, 304, 319
cable TV, 304–305, 334
camera
in courtroom, 314–315
and ethics of live shots, 339
campaign finance reform, 307
Canons of Journalism, 342
Carlin, George ("Filthy Words" case), 317–318
CART, 58
Carter, Bill, 130
Carter, President Jimmy, 307
CBS
policy on staged news, 308
Rather report on President Bush, 336–337
Super Bowl halftime show, 318
CBS v. The Democratic National Committee, 304
cell phone news, 244, 320
CG (character generator), 58, 60, 64, 160, 195
Chandler v. Florida, 315
Child Online Protection Act (COPA), 321

Clear Channel Communications, 318–319
clipping, in playback, 192
closes, 206, 234, 235 (Figure 11.6)
CNN, 304
Christiane Amanpour comments about, 340
home page, 55
Cohen, Dan, 315
"cold cut," 190
color bar, 192
Comerford, Frank, 283
commercials, in TV newscast, 227, 228, 230, 232–233, 237, 292
Commission on Freedom of the Press, 342
communication, 23
components of effective, 92–94
conversational, 92
FCC regulation of, 304
relatedness of, 92–93
Communications Act of 1934, 304, 317, 319
Section 325 of, 306, 307
Communications Decency Act, 304
community involvement, station's, 288
community standards, 318, 320, 321–322
confidentiality, and shield laws, 315
conflict (news element), 85, 86–87
consultants, news, 285, 287, 292, 294
contempt of court, 313
contract, breach of, 313
control panel / track, 189, 190 (Figure 9.3), 191–192, 193, 194 (Figures 9.5, 9.6), 196
conversational
story structure, 90
tone / style, 173, 225, 240
Copyright Act of 1976, 316
copyright and copyright law, 316–317
and the 'net, 322–323
and Scientology Church case, 322
countdown leaders, 192, 193
crime coverage, 314, 341–342, 343
criminal proceedings, access to, 314
CT (prerecorded cartridge), 156
cyberspace, 320, 322, 334. *See also* Internet; Web pages

deadlines, meeting, 9
decency standards. *See* obscenity
defamation, 309, 310
demographics, and ratings, 283, 285
Dennenberg, Herb, 289
deregulation of electronic media, 304, 319, 338
Digital Millennium Copyright Act (DMCA), 322
digital video equipment and editing, 190, 191, 192, 196 (Figure 9.8), 225, 365 (Appendix C)
Direct Broadcast Satellite, 320
disclosure of private health information, 316
Dmytryk, Edward, 107

"Donahue Show," 307
Donchin, Andy, 283
Dotson, Bob, 132, 207
Douglas, Justice William O., 304
Drudge Report, libel case, 320–321

ear, 22, 94, 171, 189. *See also* audio; communication; sound
Earnhardt, Dale (indecency charge), 318
"echoes," 131, 135
editing, 134
controls, 360 (Figures B-1, B-2)
digital, 190–193, 196 (Figure 9.8), 365 (Appendix C)
for electronic media, 171, 185, 190
linear, 185, 190, 191, 192, 359 (Appendix B)
non-linear, 185
soundbites, 157
video, 190–191, 194, 236
wire copy, 172
editors, 186
assignment, 2, 9, 11, 172, 174, 186, 223
video, 188, 189, 190
electronic media, 1, 54, 86, 87, 151, 171, 203, 239, 243, 244, 281, 295
ethical standards of, 333
interviewing for, 153, 154
jobs in, 7, 11–12
regulating, 303
style guidelines, 28–29
Web sites, 355 (Appendix A)
writing for, 21, 22, 56, 93, 94, 173, 175. *See also* communication; news story
electronic news gathering (ENG), 10, 204, 208–209, 337
Ellerbee, Linda, 56
e-mail news updates, 244, 320
emotion, in reporting, 86, 130
end-breaks, 227, 230
ENG coordinator, 11
entertainment versus news, 334–335
equal opportunity, 306
equal time, 306, 307
ESS, 227
ethics in journalism
personal, 335, 337, 341, 343
professional, 342, 344, 369 (Appendix D), 373 (Appendix E)
executive producer (EP) position, 8
eyewitnesses, 157

fair trial versus free press, 313–315
fair use, 317, 323
fairness, 295, 303, 310, 336–337, 369, 369–370
Fairness Doctrine, 305–306, 307
features, 108–109, 129–130, 132
elements of, 133
interviewing for, 135–136
writing, 136

381

Federal Communications Commission (FCC), 304, 317
   and cable TV regulation, 304
   deregulation, 304, 319, 338
   and equal opportunity, 306–307
   fair harbor time period, 319
   Fairness Doctrine, 305–306, 307–308
   news staging investigation, 308
   and obscenity and indecency regulation, 317–319
   ownership regulations, 243
   and political advertising, 307
   and Section 315 of Communications Act, 306
   violence on television, regulating, 319
Federal Elections Commission, 307
feeds, story and network, 108, 222–223, 224
First Amendment rights and protection, 304, 307, 309–310, 311, 313, 314, 315, 318, 320, 321, 334
five W's / four W's, 90, 130
flags, 195
focus group research, 284, 292. See also market research
Food Lion Prime Time Live report, 308–309
Ford, President Gerald, 311
format sheet, 228 (Figure 11.4)
formats
   integrated, 243
   live-shot, 64, 67
   news story, 186–187
   newscast, 229 (Figure 11.4)
   on-camera reader, 60, 63
   on-camera reader with graphic format, 60, 62
   radio, 224 (Figure 11.1)
   reader (TV), 60–67
   split-page, 57, 225, 239
   TV newscast rundown, 228, 229 (Figure 112.4), 231 (Figure 11.5), 233
   TV script, 54–56, 57–59, 221–222, 226 (Figure 11.2)
Fourteenth Amendment, 314
frame editing, 194, 195 (Figure 9.7)
free press versus fair trial, 313–315, 342
free speech. See First Amendment
Freedom of Information Act (FOIA), 315–316
freelance journalists, 317
Frena, George, 322
Friendly, Fred, 207
front-loading, 289
front-timing, 230, 234, 236, 237
futures files, 108, 171

Gardner, Michael, 308
Garth, Judge Leonard, 321
government, reporting on, 342
grammar style for media, 35–36
Grant, Dr. August E., 242
graphics
   bumper, 233
   full-screen, 227
   as promotion device, 290
   in video package, 194, 225, 227
Grierson, John, 54
Grokster, court case involving, 323

hand-offs, 233
handles, 133, 135

hard news, 108–110
   lead, 89
Hart, John, 131
Hauptmann, Bruno, trial, 315
headlines, 132
Hess, Stephen, 172
Hewitt, Don, 337
HIPPA (Health Insurance Portability and Accountability Act), 316
Hodnette, Judge Robert H., Jr., 315
Holmes, Oliver Wendell, 303
Hotmail, 320
household meters / diaries, 282
human interest (news element), 85, 87, 89, 136

icons, in digital editing, 191
image advertising / promotion, 289–290
immediacy, 54, 153, 206
indecent programming, 317
   Bono and, 318
   Carlin, George, and, 317
   Earnhardt, Dale, and, 318
   on the 'net, 321
   regulation of, 318–319
   Stern, Howard, and, 318
Infinity Broadcasting Corporation, 319
information, 1, 5, 107, 244. See also news
"infotainment," 107, 334
interactive features, 244, 320
Internet, 334
   advertising on, 285
   and copyright law, 317, 322–323
   formatting, 54–55, 221–222
   high-speed, 320, 323
   journalism, 54, 172, 239, 240, 241
   and libel, 320
   and music downloading, 322
   news organization, 4 (Figure 1.2), 5, 6, 7, 241
   news production, 205, 221, 227, 237, 238
   news sites, 55, 239, 240
   numbers of users, 281
   and obscenity, 321–322
   pictures used on, 55
   piracy, 323
   regulation of, 303, 321
   reporter, 239
   streaming, 4–5, 8, 24, 188, 204, 205, 221
   use, measuring, 283
   writing, 175–176, 237
Internet and Broadcast PR News, 174
Internet Service Providers (ISPs), 5–6, 58, 320, 321, 322, 323
interviewer, 153–154
interviews and interviewing, 64, 132, 133, 135–136, 152–153, 154, 157, 193
   live, 206–207
   for localizing wire copy, 173
   news, and Section 315, 307
   telephone, 155
   tips, 154, 158
inverted pyramid news structure, 54, 90 (Figure 4.1), 91, 176
iTunes, 323

Jackson, Janet, 318
jargon, 108
Jeremy, Ron, 318
JIC, 108

journalism, 25, 86, 132, 203, 281, 295, 313. See also electronic media
   basic skills, 238
   ethics, 337, 343
   Internet, 54, 172, 239, 240, 241
   "pack," 107, 204
   personalized, 209, 232, 241
journalists, 1, 2, 105, 106–108, 175, 310, 313, 316–317, 337, 338, 339–340. See also interviewing; reporters
   under cross-ownership, 243
   electronic, 21, 54, 153, 203–204, 239, 339
   ethics of, 333, 340, 341, 343–344
   freelance, 317
   multi-skilled, 242, 243
   print, 21, 239. See also newspapers
   tasks of, 1, 6, 21
   television, 313
judgment, news, 105–107, 110
jump cut, 187

Karmazin, Mel, 318
KaZaa, 323
Kennedy, Justice Anthony, 304–305, 319
Kennedy, Sen. Ted, 307
Kennedy plane crash story, 335–336
Kinney, Don, 130
Kuralt, Charles, 93, 130

Landes, Mike, 91
Lansing, John, 136
Larson, John, 130–136
lead-ins, 156–157
leads, news, 21, 90, 109, 223, 232
   conversational (pyramid), 90
   electronic, 58, 108, 171
   freak event, 89
   hard news, 89
   inverted pyramid style of, 90
   literary allusion, 90
   metaphor, 89
   parody, 90
   question, 89
   relatedness of, 93
   soft news / feature, 89–90, 130, 136
   staccato, 89
   summary, 88–89
   suspended, 89
   throwaway, 89
   well-known expressions, 89
   writing, 88
libel and liability, 306, 309, 321
   ABC, for Food Lion report, 309
   AOL case, 320–321
   defenses, 310–311
   fair comment, 310–311
   fault, in, 309
   and the 'net, 320, 321
   New Haven Advocate suit, 321
   New York Times v. Sullivan, 309–310
Limbaugh, Rush, 306
limited public figures, 310
Lindbergh kidnapping case, 315
line-count technique, 223
line-up. See news line-up
linear editing, 185, 190, 191, 192, 359 (Appendix B)
listening, 135, 153, 154, 158
live
   broadcasts, 341
   interviews, 64, 206–207

remotes, 294, 338
   television coverage, 204, 205, 237, 337–338, 339, 340
live-shot format (TV), 64, 67
local people meters (LPMs), 283
localizing, 92, 111, 173, 175
log. See program log

market
   research, 288, 292, 294, 295, 342. See also advertising; ratings
   target, 334
marketplace of ideas, 344
mass media / communication, 8, 110, 291, 342
McElhatton, Terry, 238
McPhee, John, 131
McPherson, Aimme Semple, 303
meaning, conveying, 172, 191, 239
media. See also electronic media; organizations, media; print media
   advertising-driven, 334
   bundled, 291
   competition, 338
   conglomerates, 319
   convergence, 241–245
   digital media, 320, 322
   policy, 342–343
Media General, 243
Media Law Resource Center, 309
"Meet the Press," 307
message, writing, 23, 25
meters, household / people, 282–283
Miller v. California, 318
Milton, John, 334
Moussaoui, Zacarias, 315
MSN, 320
Murrow, Edward R., 57, 341
MusicNet, 323
must-carry rules, 304–305, 319–320

names, style for treating, 27, 30
Napster ruling, 323
narration
   script, 192–193
   track, 192 (Figure 9.4), 194 (Figures 9.5, 9.6)
   voice over, 187, 188, 189, 190
narrowcasting, 291
National Association of Broadcasters, 320
National Public Radio URL, 55
natural sound / nats, 53, 133, 134, 186, 187, 188, 193, 206
NBC
   Dateline staging, 308
   and indecent programming, 318
negligence, proof of, 310, 313
Netcom, 322
Netscape, 320
network feeds, 222–223, 224
New York Times online, 55
news, 2, 171, 244, 342. See also features; media convergence; story
   audience desires for, 107, 295
   breaking, 89, 135, 234
   content guidelines, 110, 111
   content preferences, 294
   crime, 314, 341–342, 343
   elements of, 85, 87
   as entertainment, 107, 334–335
   ethic, 337
   formula approaches to, 292
   hard versus soft, 108–110
   instant, 341

judgment, 105–107, 110
line-up, 109, 185, 188, 225, 228, 233, 236
live coverage of, 204, 205, 237, 337–338, 339, 340
local, 109, 111
negative, 232
network, 204
as perishable commodity, 294
policy, 341
selection, 105–106
spot, 110–111
staged, 308
news department / organization, 1, 2, 5, 6, 9, 54, 241, 245, 341
control room, 230, 237
converged, 241–243, 244
cross-ownership of, 242–244
Internet, 4 (Figure 1.2), 7, 237, 241
local, 171
radio, 222–223, 224
small, 185
traditional organizational chart, 3 (Figure 1.1), 7
news director, 2, 7–8, 58, 107, 203, 206
in media convergence, 242
radio, 222, 223, 224
news hole, 227 (Figure 11.3), 230, 236
news magazines, 241
news package, editing, 187–193, 194 (Figures 9.6, 9.7)
news policy, sample guidelines, 312
news (or newscast) producer, 8, 11, 185, 186, 188, 222
TV, 227–228, 230, 232–234, 236
news production
Internet, 221, 222, 237–241
radio, 222–225
television, 222, 225–237
news resourcer, 242
news rundown format sheet, 228, 229 (Figure 11.4), 231 (Figure 11.5), 235 (Figure 11.6)
news script format for radio, 223, 224 (Figure 11.1)
news services, 7, 108, 172, 223
news story, 281
breaking, 2
format, 186–187
organization, 90, 134, 223
soft, 132. See also features
straight, 129–130
television, 54
news writer job, 10–11
newscast(s), 2, 8, 9, 11, 22, 24, 107, 108, 110, 151, 188, 221–222, 281. See also leads; radio; scripts; television
blocking, 109, 228
content of, 54, 110, 111
format sheet (TV), 229 (Figure 11.4), 231 (Figure 11.5), 235 (Figure 11.6)
producing, 185, 187, 227
radio, 222, 223 (Table 11.1), 223–224, 225
rehearsing, 237
timing, 233–234
newscaster, 8–9, 57, 94, 171, 172, 186, 224, 233, 236, 287, 291. See also anchors
newsflow manager job, 242
newsgathering, 2, 7, 242, 245, 312. See also electronic news gathering (ENG)

newspaper(s), 241, 342. See also print media
attribution in, 26
copy, 173
formatting, 239
libel suits against, 309
reporters, 339
story structure, 90
verb use in, 31
Web sites, 240
writing for, 21, 22
newsroom, converged, 242–245
Nielsen Media Research, 281, 282, 283, 286 (Figure 12.1), 289, 293. See also ratings
numbers, style for, 23

objectivity in reporting, 333
obscenity and obscenity cases, 317–318, 320, 321–322
Ogden, Roger, 341
on-camera reader format, 60, 63, 66
on-camera reader with graphic format, 60, 62, 64, 66
online
databases, 284
music piracy, 323
service providers, 320, 322
operations department, 5
organizations, media. See also news organization
differences between small and large, 6
news department, 2, 3 (Figure 1.1), 4
Internet news, 4 (Figure 1.2)
outcue, 58, 60, 156, 160
overlaps, sound, 189–190
overwriting, 134

pad
anchor, 234
radio, 224
TV / video, 60, 194, 236
Paley, William, 291
parroting, 156
Patriot Act, 316
people meters, 282–283, 289
personal conduct, 303
personalized journalism, 209, 232, 241
photographer, 10, 188. See also television news; videographer
pictures, writing to, 56–57, 134. See also visual
piracy on the 'net, 322
playback, 190, 191, 192, 193, 195, 196
Playboy TV case, 319
policies, media organization, 342–343
political candidates
and access, 307
and equal opportunity, 306
reporting on, 336, 340–341
pornography, regulating, 321
Powell, FCC Chairman Michael, 319
press conferences, 157, 174
Prime Time Live, Food Lion report, 308
print media, 86, 207, 339. See also newspapers
bites or quotes in, 152
government regulation of, 303
and Internet production, 238, 239

and libel, 320
writing for, 21, 22, 54, 55
privacy, 335–336
appropriation and, 311
and false light, 311
legal aspects of, 303, 311–313, 316, 320
and publication, 311
privilege, as libel defense, 310, 315
producer. See news producer; television newscast
production. See news production
professional
behavior, 343
codes, policies, and standards, 342, 343
program log, 8, 232
prominence (news element), 85, 87
promotion, news, 288–289
distortion, 313
graphics in, 290
image versus product, 289–290
product, 289
proof-of-performance, 290
topical, 290
weather as, 290, 294
pronunciation, phonetic, 32, 111
proximity (news element), 85, 87
psychographics, 292
public relations practitioners, 173–174, 175, 341
public right to know, 314, 333, 336
Public Telecommunications Act, 319
purpose, writing, 23
pyramid news structure, 90 (Figure 4.2), 91

"qualified privilege," 310
questions and questioning
as lead, 89
leading, 154
tough, in interviews, 153
quotes and quoting, style for, 27

radio, 86, 240, 241, 334
actualities, 57
attribution in, 26
audio / sound, 5, 53, 87
content guidelines, 111
delivery, 225
format, 224 (Figure 11.1), 239
lead-ins and tags, 156
newscasts, 222, 223 (Table 11,1), 223–224, 225
public relations, 174
scripts, 54, 57–58
time references in, 32–33
verb tense used in, 31
writing for, 223
Radio Act of 1912, 303
Radio Act of 1927, 304
rape victims, publishing names of, 311, 336
Rather, Dan, 336–337
ratings, market, 281–285, 286 (Figure 12.1), 293, 308
television news, 334, 338
reader formats (TV), 60–67
Reagan, Ronald, 306, 307
Recording Industry Association of America (RIAA), 322–323
Red Lion case, 305
reference materials, for broadcast writer, 111–112

referencing, in formatting the script, 56, 57
relatedness, 92–93
remote control, 109–110
reporters, 2, 9–10, 11, 108, 111, 130, 152, 157, 171, 203, 206, 333. See also journalists
audience recognition of, 287
ethics of, 336, 337
field, 233
Internet, 239
live, 205, 206–207, 338, 341
in media convergence, 242–243
narration, 192, 193
package, 186–187
role in production, 185–186, 188, 196
special assignment, 10
standup, 186, 187, 192, 193
story ownership by, 242–243
what to wear, 208
Reporter's Committee for Freedom of the Press, 316
reporting, 1
cultural differences and, 333
feature, 132
formula, 132, 133
on government, 342
print, 152
skills, 206, 245
research. See also market research
in-house, 284
sampling, 282
tracking, 284
rewriting, 111, 151, 172
lead-ins, 156–157
wire copy, 173
Ridge, Steve, 291
rights, first serial and one-time, 317
Rosengard, Dana, 208–209
RTNDA Code of Broadcast News Ethics, 342, 369 (Appendix D)
rundown format sheet, TV, 229 (Figure 11.4), 230, 231 (Figure 11.5), 234, 235 (Figure 11.6), 236

Salant, Richard, 337
satellite media tours, 174–175
satellite news gathering (SNG), 204
satellite programming, 319–320
scarcity doctrine, 304
Scherman, Chad, 322
Schwarzenegger, Arnold, 307
script(s), 59, 158
computer, 234, 236
converting to the Web, 176
formatting and formats, 54–56, 57–59, 64, 94
narrative, 56
radio, 54, 57–58
samples, 59–67, 159
stacking, 234, 236
television, 225, 226 (Figure 11.2), 234, 236–237
timing, 234, 236
voice-over, 192
writers, 227, 228
Section 315. See Communications Act
separateness of broadcast journalists, 107–108
share, market, 284–285
Shearer, Jackie, 133
Sheppard, Sam, case, 314
shield laws, 315
"shock jocks," 318

Shosteck, Herschel, 287
shot sheet, reporter's, 196
sign-off, 224
significance (news element), 85, 86, 87
Simon, Douglas, 174
Sixth Amendment, 313–314
slideshows, 244
slug, 223
Society of Motion Picture Technicians and Engineers (SMPTE) Time Code, 196
Society of Professional Journalists Ethics Code, 342, 373 (Appendix E)
"soft money," 307
soft news, 108–109, 130, 132. See also features
　lead, 89–90
Sol Estes, Billy, 315
Sonny Bono Copyright Extension Act, 316
sound, 55, 134, 186, 193, 334. See also radio; television
sound on tape (SOT), 53, 58, 60, 64, 156, 157, 160, 225
sound overlaps, 189–190
sound track, 189
soundbites, 53, 58, 151–152, 155, 156–157, 186, 188, 206–207
　editing, 157, 193, 194
　writing, 151–152, 158, 160
source, quoting, 27
split-squeeze remote, 58, 64
staged news, 308
standup
　bridge, 187
　reporter, 186, 187, 192, 193, 205
stereotyping, racial, 341–342
Stern, Howard, 318–319
Stevens, Justice John Paul, 321
story / stories. See also News story
　assignment meeting, 2
　"crisis," 205
　feature 89, 129–130, 132, 133, 136
　focused, 295
　format, 186–187
　freshening, 91
　Internet, 239, 240
　leads, 223
　localizing, 92, 111
　order, deciding, 230
　ownership, 171
　personalizing, 209, 232
　production, 185, 187. See also Newscast
　samples (TV), 59–67
　straight news, 129–130
　structure, 90
　updating, 91
　visual, 56–57, 225
story builder, 242
story structure
　conversational (pyramid), 90 (Figure 4.2)
　inverted pyramid, 90 (Figure 4.1)

story time, 58, 60, 235 (Figure 11.6)
storytelling, 56, 132, 136, 191, 224, 239. See also features; reporters
StreamCast, court case involving, 323
streaming, Internet, 4–5, 8, 22, 24, 54, 188, 205, 221, 237, 238, 239, 244, 320
stringers, 7, 171
style
　guidelines, 28–29
　wire service, 172
　writing, 23, 25
Sunshine in Government Act, 316
supers, 194
"sweeps," 283, 289

Tagliabue, Paul, 318
tags, 58, 60, 64, 156, 157
talent, on-air, 290–291
talking head, 206–207
tape crease, 196
teases, 176, 230, 233, 236, 290
technicians, 7, 196
techtvnews, 4, 55
telecast. See television newscast production
Telecommunications Act, 304, 319, 321
telephone
　interviews and rundowns, 155
　market surveys, 284, 292–294
TelePrompTer, 234, 236
television, sets owned, 281
television news, 54, 56, 57, 86, 107, 132, 185, 222, 240, 241, 335
　attribution in, 26
　audience, 335, 339
　coverage, 204, 205, 237, 337–338, 339, 340
　crime on, 341–342
　as entertainment, 334
　features in, 132
　live, 206
　operations, 341
　public relations, 174
　ratings, 334
　script, 55, 59, 158, 234
　story samples, 59–60, 64
　verb tense used in, 31
　visuals, 107, 225
　Web conversion, 176
　writing for, 134
television newscast production, 185, 222, 227, 230
　blocking, 228
　commercial breaks in, 232
　copy assignments in, 233
　format sheet, 228, 229 (Figure 11.4), 231 (Figure 11.5), 235 (Figure 11.6)
　pacing, 230, 232
　proofreading, 236
　rehearsing, 237
　script format, 225, 226 (Figure 11.2)

stacking, 234, 236
　and story order, 230
　teases in, 233, 236, 237
　timing the script and newscast, 233–234, 236
　transitions in, 233
　visuals, determining and assembling, 232
Tello, Steve, 171
thematic blocking, 109, 232
Thomas, Robert Alan and Carleen, obscenity case, 322
Timberlake, Justin, 318
time codes, SMPTE, 196
time references, 32–33
time-base corrector (TBC), 195–196
timeliness (news element), 85, 87
titles, style for, 27, 30
toss, 176
tracking adjustments, 195
tracking market research, 284
transitions, 233
trespassing, in privacy law, 312, 313
Trollope, Anthony, 31
TRT (total running time), 58, 59, 60, 64, 160
trust, public, 337, 369
truth, 333, 369
　as libel defense, 310
Turner Broadcasting, 304

U.S. Criminal Code, and obscene language in broadcasts, 317
"use," as legal term, 307

V-chip, 319
verbs, using, 31–32, 134
Viacom, 318
video, 134
　attribution in, 31
　B-roll, 174
　digital, 190, 225
　news releases (VNRs), 174–175
　newscasts, 187–188
　packages, 186, 189
　pad, 60
　preview, 56
　scripts, 55, 56, 57
　streaming, 4–5, 8, 24, 188, 204, 205, 221, 237, 238, 239, 320
video editor and editing, 11, 188, 189, 190, 191, 194, 235
video time (TRT), 59
videocassettes, 194, 225
videographers, news, 2, 186, 208–209
videotape (VTR), 225, 361 (Figure B-3)
violence, regulation of, 319
visual
　aspects of electronic media, 87, 238
　impact, 107
　story writing, 56–57
visuals, 225, 227, 232, 236
VO (voice-over), 58, 60, 64, 186, 225
　narration, 187, 188, 189, 190

VO-SOT-VO format, 60, 63, 64, 65, 186, 188
VU meter, 189 (Figures 9.1, 9.2)

Wallace, Mike, 207
"War of the Worlds," 308
Warren, Samuel, 311
WBBM news staging case, 308
weathercasts, 222, 223, 227
Web log. See blogs
Web news producer, 8
Web pages / Web sites, 5, 21, 54, 55, 205, 239, 240, 241, 244, 245, 283, 334, 355 (Appendix A). See also Internet
　and copyright law, 317, 322
　design, 8
　layout knowledge for, 238
　and libel, 320
　links, 240, 283
　news production on, 237
　and obscenity, 321
　story production for, 58, 237
　writing for, 175
webmasters, 4, 283, 320
Wells, Orson, 308
Whiting, Susan, 283
Wickham, Dr. Kathleen, 172
wire services, 7, 111, 171, 222, 223, 224
　editing copy from, 172, 173
　localizing copy from, 173
　"rip and read," 222
wireless technology, 320
Wolzien, Thomas, 341
word usage, 33–35
World Wide Web, 8, 320, 334. See also Internet; Web pages
writers, news, 10–11
writing, 134, 244–245
　to an audience, 23–25
　conversational, 92, 93
　creative, 57, 93, 129
　feature, 136
　freshening, 91
　Internet, 175–176, 237
　leads and lead-ins, 88–89, 156
　localizing, 92
　news, 21, 22, 36
　to the picture, 55, 56–57
　for print, 54
　purpose, 23
　relatedness of, 92–93
　soundbites, writing, 151–152, 158, 160
　technically correct, 93–94
　for television, 134, 233, 234
　updating, 91

Yahoo, 320

ZDTV, 4